The History of British Women's Writing, 1750–1830

The History of British Women's Writing

General Editors: **Jennie Batchelor** and **Cora Kaplan**

Advisory Board: Isobel Armstrong, Rachel Bowlby, Carolyn Dinshaw, Margaret Ezell, Margaret Ferguson, Isobel Grundy, and Felicity Nussbaum

The History of British Women's Writing is an innovative and ambitious monograph series that seeks both to synthesize the work of several generations of feminist scholars, and to advance new directions for the study of women's writing. Volume editors and contributors are leading scholars whose work collectively reflects the global excellence in this expanding field of study. It is envisaged that this series will be a key resource for specialist and non-specialist scholars and students alike.

Titles include:

Caroline Bicks and Jennifer Summit (*editors*)
THE HISTORY OF BRITISH WOMEN'S WRITING, 1500–1610
Volume Two

Ros Ballaster (*editor*)
THE HISTORY OF BRITISH WOMEN'S WRITING, 1690–1750
Volume Four

Jacqueline M. Labbe (*editor*)
THE HISTORY OF BRITISH WOMEN'S WRITING, 1750–1830
Volume Five

Forthcoming titles:

Elizabeth Herbert McAvoy and Diane Watt (*editors*)
THE HISTORY OF BRITISH WOMEN'S WRITING, 700–1500
Volume One

Mihoko Suzuki (*editor*)
THE HISTORY OF BRITISH WOMEN'S WRITING, 1610–1690
Volume Three

History of British Women's Writing
Series Standing Order ISBN 978–0–230–20079–1 hardback
(*outside North America only*)

You can receive future titles in this series as they are published by placing a standing order. Please contact your bookseller or, in case of difficulty, write to us at the address below with your name and address, the title of the series and the ISBN quoted above.

Customer Services Department, Macmillan Distribution Ltd, Houndmills, Basingstoke, Hampshire RG21 6XS, England.

The History of British Women's Writing, 1750–1830

Volume Five

Edited by

Jacqueline M. Labbe

First published 2010 by
PALGRAVE MACMILLAN

Palgrave Macmillan in the UK is an imprint of Macmillan Publishers Limited,
registered in England, company number 785998, of Houndmills, Basingstoke,
Hampshire RG21 6XS.

Palgrave Macmillan in the US is a division of St Martin's Press LLC,
175 Fifth Avenue, New York, NY 10010.

Palgrave Macmillan is the global academic imprint of the above companies
and has companies and representatives throughout the world.

Palgrave® and Macmillan® are registered trademarks in the United States,
the United Kingdom, Europe and other countries.

ISBN 978–0–230–55071–1   hardback

This book is printed on paper suitable for recycling and made from fully
managed and sustained forest sources. Logging, pulping and manufacturing
processes are expected to conform to the environmental regulations of the
country of origin.

A catalogue record for this book is available from the British Library.

A catalog record for this book is available from the Library of Congress.

10   9   8   7   6   5   4   3   2   1
19   18   17   16   15   14   13   12   11   10

Transferred to Digital Printing in 2011

For Rod, Indie, and Nathan

Contents

List of Figures

Series Preface

One of the most significant developments in literary studies in the last quarter of a century has been the remarkable growth of scholarship on women's writing. This was inspired by, and in turn provided inspiration for, a post-war women's movement which saw women's cultural expression as key to their emancipation. The retrieval, republication, and reappraisal of women's writing, beginning in the mid-1960s, have radically affected the literary curriculum in schools and universities. A revised canon now includes many more women writers. Literature courses that focus on what women thought and wrote from antiquity onwards have become popular undergraduate and postgraduate options. These new initiatives have meant that gender – in language, authors, texts, audience and in the history of print culture more generally – is a central question for literary criticism and literary history. A mass of fascinating research and analysis extending over several decades now stands as testimony to a lively and diverse set of debates, in an area of work that is still expanding.

Indeed so rapid has this expansion been, that it has become increasingly difficult for students and academics to have a comprehensive view of the wider field of women's writing outside their own period or specialism. As the research on women has moved from the margins to the confident centre of literary studies it has become rich in essays and monographs dealing with smaller groups of authors, with particular genres and with defined periods of literary production, reflecting the divisions of intellectual labour and development of expertise that are typical of the discipline of literary studies. Collections of essays that provide overviews within particular periods and genres do exist, but no published series has taken on the mapping of the field, even within one language group or national culture.

A History of British Women's Writing is intended as just such a cartographic standard work. Its ambition is to provide, in ten volumes edited by leading experts in the field, and comprised of newly commissioned essays by specialist scholars, a clear and integrated picture of women's contribution to the world of letters within Great Britain from medieval times to the present. In taking on such a wide ranging project we were inspired by the founding, in 2003, of Chawton House Library, a UK registered charity with a unique collection of books focusing on women's writing in English from 1600 to 1830, set in the home and working estate of Jane Austen's brother.

JENNIE BATCHELOR
UNIVERSITY OF KENT

CORA KAPLAN
QUEEN MARY, UNIVERSITY OF LONDON

Preface

It is a daunting task to attempt to produce a history of British women's writing for a period in which British women became one of the driving forces in the production of poetry, prose, non-fiction, drama: in fact, writing of all kinds. As soon as such a history is assembled, one is immediately conscious of what has been left out. Fortunately, as editor of this volume I have felt the full benefits of working with a team of scholars for whom the importance, centrality, and fullness of women's writing in the period is paramount. Each contributor has embraced the opportunity to explore, not only a specific area of women's writing or specific authors, but also the idea of history itself, during a period in which notions of what constitutes a 'history' were the subject of active debate. For their intellectual engagement with their subjects, their breaking of new ground, their refertilizing of discussions and conversations, and their deep commitment to a project such as this, I am indebted to the contributors to this volume.

I would also like to thank the general editors of this ambitious series, Jennie Batchelor and Cora Kaplan, for the opportunity to immerse myself in British women's writing from 1750 to 1830, and in the process to learn so much. Thanks are also due to Paula Kennedy, Christabel Scaife, and Steven Hall at Palgrave Macmillan for their commitment to the project and for their help, especially in the final days of preparing the manuscript.

A volume like this would not be possible without the decades of work undertaken by scholars of women's writing. Their challenging of the easy assumptions about quality and quantity that characterized an earlier form of literary criticism transformed the landscape of writing and made this volume possible. The literature of the period 1750–1830 has been repeopled through their work.

Finally, my own work is constantly enabled and energized by Indie and Nathan, whose developing understanding of writing and reading is itself a history, and by Rod Jones, whose support, amazingly, does not flag.

JL
Coventry, 2009

Acknowledgements

Count Ugolino and His Children by Sir Joshua Reynolds is reproduced by kind permission of The National Trust: this painting was handed to the National Trust in 1996. The Count is shown with four children, with light coming in through a barred window (accepted in lieu of tax by H.M. Treasury and allocated to The National Trust in 1995). Knole, The Sackville Collection (The National Trust) ©NTPL/Brian Tremain.

References to the Jane Porter letters are courtesy of The Carl H. Pforzheimer Collection of Shelley and His Circle, The New York Public Library, Astor, Lenox and Tilden Foundations.

Notes on the Contributors

Jennie Batchelor is Senior Lecturer in English and American Literature at the University of Kent. She has published and edited various essays on gender and material culture, and is the author of *Dress, Distress and Desire* (2005). Her current book project is entitled, *Woman's Work: Labour, Gender and Authorship, 1750–1830*.

Stephen C. Behrendt is George Holmes Distinguished University Professor of English at the University of Nebraska. In addition to his many books and articles on interdisciplinary aspects of Romantic-era literature and culture (including *British Women Poets and the Romantic Writing Community*, 2008), he is also a widely published poet whose latest book is *History* (2005).

Betsy Bolton is a Professor of English Literature at Swarthmore College, and the author of *Women, Nationalism, and the Romantic Stage: Theatre and Politics in Britain, 1780–1800* (2001). Other publications include essays in *Studies in Romanticism*, *English Literary History*, and *The Eighteenth Century: Theory and Interpretation*. She is currently working on two projects: one addressing sentimental drama and politics, the other focused on women poets and formal innovation.

Deirdre Coleman is the Robert Wallace Chair of English at the University of Melbourne. She is the author of *Romantic Colonization and British Anti-Slavery* (2005), and editor of the Australia volume of *Women Writing Home, 1700–1920: Female Correspondence across the British Empire*, 6 vols (2006).

Stuart Curran is Vartan Gregorian Professor of English at the University of Pennsylvania. Most recently, he served as general editor for *The Works of Charlotte Smith* (2005–07, 14 volumes).

Kate Davies is Senior Lecturer in the School of English at Newcastle University. She is the author of a book about Catharine Macaulay and Mercy Otis Warren and has written several essays about the transatlantic contexts of eighteenth-century women's writing. She is now completing a book about women in revolutionary Philadelphia, and beginning work on a new interdiscipinary project exploring eighteenth-century literature, textiles, and material culture.

Notes on the Contributors xv

Harriet Guest is Professor in the Centre for Eighteenth Century Studies and the Department of English and Related Literature at the University of York. Recent publications include *Empire, Barbarism, and Civilisation: James Cook, William Hodges and the Return to the Pacific* (2007), *Small Change: Women, Learning, Patriotism, 1750–1810* (2000), and, with Kate Davies, an edition of Charlotte Smith's *Marchmont* (1796) for the *Works of Charlotte Smith* (2005–07).

Jacqueline Labbe is Professor of English and Comparative Literary Studies at the University of Warwick. She is the author, most recently, of *Charlotte Smith: Romanticism, Poetry and the Culture of Gender* (2003), the editor of Smith's *The Old Manor House* (2000) and *Poems* for the *Works of Charlotte Smith* (2005–07), and edited and contributed to *Charlotte Smith in British Romanticism* (2008).

Donna Landry is Professor of English and American Literature at the University of Kent, where she directs the Centre for Studies in the Long Eighteenth Century. Her books include *The Muses of Resistance: Laboring-Class Women's Poetry in Britain, 1739–1796* (1990; reprint 2005), *The Invention of the Countryside: Hunting, Walking, and Ecology in English Literature, 1671–1831* (2001), and *Noble Brutes: How Eastern Horses Transformed English Culture* (2008).

Michelle Levy is an Associate Professor in the Department of English at Simon Fraser University. She is the author of *Family Authorship and Romantic Print Culture* (Palgrave Macmillan 2008), and is currently working on a book on amateur literary culture of the Romantic period. She has written articles on many female authors, including Jane Austen, Anna Barbauld, Mary Shelley, and Dorothy Wordsworth, and is the co-editor of Lucy Aikin's *Epistles on Women and other Works*, forthcoming.

Harriet Kramer Linkin is Professor of English Literature at New Mexico State University. She is the editor of the first scholarly edition of *The Collected Poems and Journals of Mary Tighe* (2005) as well as co-editor of two collections on Romantic women poets: *Romanticism and Women Poets: Opening the Doors of Reception* (1999) and *Approaches to Teaching Women Poets of the British Romantic Period* (1997).

Devoney Looser is Professor of English at the University of Missouri. She is the author of *Women Writers and Old Age in Great Britain, 1750–1850* and *British Women Writers and the Writing of History 1670–1820*. She serves as co-editor of the *Journal for Early Modern Cultural Studies*.

Olivia Murphy is a DPhil candidate at Worcester College, Oxford University, having previously completed an MPhil at Sydney University on Austen's juvenilia. She has published on Austen in *Eighteenth Century Studies* and *Sydney Studies in English*, and is currently in the final stages of a doctoral thesis on the subject of Jane Austen's critical art of the novel. The research for the chapter in this volume was undertaken during her fellowship at Chawton House Library.

Sarah Prescott is Senior Lecturer in English in the Department of English and Creative Writing, Aberystwyth University. She is the author of *Women, Authorship and Literary Culture, 1680–1740* (Palgrave 2003) and has written a number of articles and chapters on seventeenth and eighteenth-century women writers. She has also co-edited (with David E. Shuttleton) a collection of essays on *Women and Poetry, 1660–1750* (Palgrave, 2003).

Diego Saglia is Associate Professor of English Literature at the University of Parma, Italy. He is the author of *Poetic Castles in Spain: British Romanticism and Figurations of Iberia* (2000), and co-editor of *Il teatro della paura: scenari gotici del romanticismo europeo* (with Giovanna Silvani, 2005), *Re-Drawing Austen: Picturesque Travels in Austenland* (with Beatrice Battaglia, 2005), and *British Romanticism and Italian Literature: Translating, Reviewing, Rewriting* (with Laura Bandiera, 2005).

Betty A. Schellenberg is Professor of English at Simon Fraser University and has published *The Professionalization of Women Writers in Eighteenth-Century Britain* (2005), *Reconsidering the Bluestockings* (co-edited with Nicole Pohl, 2003), *Part Two: Reflections on the Sequel* (co-edited with Paul Budra, 1998), and *The Conversational Circle: Rereading the English Novel, 1740–1775* (1996).

Katherine Turner is Associate Professor of English at Mary Baldwin College. She is the author of *British Travel Writers in Europe 1750–1800: Authorship, Gender and National Identity* (2001), and co-editor (with Francis O'Gorman) of *The Victorians and the Eighteenth Century: Reassessing the Tradition* (2004). She has recently edited Laurence Sterne's *A Sentimental Journey* (2010) and several volumes of *Women's Court and Society Memoirs* (2010).

Chronology

Year	Events	Works
1750	Population of Britain reaches 5.7 million	Sarah Scott, *The History of Cornelia*
1751		Eliza Haywood, *The History of Miss Betsy Thoughtless*; Charlotte Lennox, *The Life of Harriot Stuart*
1752	Gregorian Calendar adopted	Charlotte Lennox, *The Female Quixote*
1753	Passing of the Marriage Act; founding of British Museum	Jane Collier, *An Essay on the Art of Ingeniously Tormenting*; Sarah Fielding, *The Adventures of David Simple. Volume the Last*; Eliza Haywood, *The History of Jemmy and Jenny Jessamy*; Charlotte Lennox, *Shakespear Illustrated* (1753–54)
1754	Anglo-French War in America begins; Royal Society of Arts founded	Sarah Fielding and Jane Collier, *The Cry*; Eliza Haywood, *The Invisible Spy*; Sarah Scott, *Agreeable Ugliness* and *A Journey Through Every Stage of Life*
1755	Lisbon earthquake	Frances Brooke, *The Old Maid* (1755–56); Charlotte Charke, *A Narrative of the Life of Mrs Charlotte Charke*; Eliza Haywood, *The Wife*
1756	Outbreak of the Seven Years' War; *Critical Review* begins publication	Frances Brooke, *Virginia*; Eliza Haywood, *The Husband*
1757	Victory in Battle of Plassey consolidated British power in Indian subcontinent via East India Company	Sarah Fielding, *The Lives of Cleopatra and Octavia*; Charlotte Lennox, *Memoirs for the History of Madame de Maintenon*
1758	Opening of the Magdalen House for the Reception of Penitent Prostitutes	Elizabeth Carter, *All the Works of Epictetus*; Charlotte Lennox, *Henrietta*
1759	Opening of British Museum; Siege of Quebec	Sarah Fielding, *The History of the Countess of Dellwyn*

(Continued)

Year	Events	Works
1760	Death of George II; accession of George III	[Sarah Fielding or Sarah Scott?], *The History of Some of the Penitents in the Magdalen-House*; Sarah Fielding, *The History of Ophelia*; Charlotte Lennox, *The Lady's Museum* (1760–61)
1761	Pitt the Elder resigns over war with Spain	Sarah Scott, *The History of Gustavus Ericson*; Frances Sheridan, *The Memoirs of Miss Sidney Biddulph*
1762	The Earl of Bute (a Tory) becomes Prime Minister	Elizabeth Carter, *Poems on Several Occasions*; Sarah Fielding, *Xenophon's Memoirs of Socrates*; Charlotte Lennox, *Sophia*; Sarah Scott, *A Description of Millenium Hall* and *The History of Mecklenburgh*
1763	Treaty of Paris ends the Seven Years' War	Frances Brooke, *The History of Lady Julia Mandeville*; Catharine Macaulay, *The History of England* (1763–83); Lady Mary Wortley Montagu, *Embassy Letters* (written 1716–18); Frances Sheridan, *The Discovery*
1764	James Hargreaves invents the Spinning Jenny	Phebe Gibbes, *The Life and Adventures of Mr Francis Clive*
1765	Stamp Act; acquisition of Bengal by Britain	
1766	Stamp Act repealed; Declaratory Act	Sarah Scott, *The History of Sir George Ellison*
1767		
1768	Cook's first voyage; Royal Academy of Arts founded; Octennial Act: Parliamentary reform in Ireland; first edition of *Encyclopaedia Britannica* begun	
1769	Wilkes expelled from Parliament	Frances Brooke, *The History of Emily Montague*; Elizabeth Griffith, *The Delicate Distress*; Charlotte Lennox, *The Sister*; Elizabeth Montagu, *Essay on the Writings and Genius of Shakespeare*

Year	Events	Works
1770	Horatio Nelson enters the Navy; Boston Massacre; Botany Bay discovered by Cook	*Lady's Magazine* begins publication (1770–1820)
1771	First edition of *Encyclopaedia Britannica* completed	Elizabeth Griffith, *The History of Lady Barton*
1772	The Somersett case made slavery in England, but not in the British empire, illegal; Cook's second voyage; Royal Marriages Act	Sarah Scott, *The Test of Filial Duty* and *The Life of Theodore Agrippa D'Aubigné*
1773	Boston Tea Party; Warren Hastings becomes first governor general in India; Regulation Act	Anna Laetitia Aikin [Barbauld], *Poems*; Hester Chapone, *Letters on the Improvement of the Mind*; Phillis Wheatley, *Poems on Various Subjects*
1774	Joseph Priestley discovers oxygen; accession of Louise XVI of France; the case of Donaldson versus Beckett puts an end to perpetual copyright; Quebec Act; Intolerable Acts	Mary Scott, *The Female Advocate*
1775	American Revolution begins with the Battle of Lexington	Anna Laetitia Barbauld, *Devotional Pieces*; Hester Chapone, *Miscellanies in Verse and* Prose; Hannah More, *The Inflexible Captive*; Mary Robinson, *Poems by Mrs Robinson*
1776	Declaration of Independence signed; Cook's third voyage	Hannah Cowley, *The Runaway*
1777	British defeated at Saratoga; Battle of Brandywine (Canada vs. North America)	Frances Brooke, *The Excursion*; Hannah More, *Percy*; Clara Reeve, *The Champion of Virtue* (published in 1778 as *The Old English Baron*)
1778	France declares war on Britain over America	Anna Laetitia Barbauld, *Lessons for Children*; Frances Burney, *Evelina* and *The Witlings* (1778–80); Mary Hamilton, *Munster Village*
1779	Spain declares war on Britain over America	Hannah Cowley, *Albina* and *Who's the Dupe?*; Hannah More, *The Fatal Falsehood*

(Continued)

Year	Events	Works
1780	Gordon Riots; taxes imposed on all adult male servants; 'Dunning's Motion': influence of the Crown should be lessened; inheritance tax introduced; Cornwallis led expedition to southern colonies of North America; Society for Constitutional Information founded; League of Armed Neutrality established; Battle of Charleston	Hannah Cowley, *The Belle's Stratagem*; Sophia Lee, *The Chapter of Accidents*
1781	Surrender at Yorktown; Battle of Guildford Courthouse; William Herschel discovers planet Uranus	Anna Laetitia Barbauld, *Hymns in Prose for Children*
1782	The Foreign Office established in Britain; James Watt invented rotary movement of the steam engine; Gilbert's Act: modifications to the existing Poor Law; American colonists achieve independence from British	Frances Burney, *Cecilia*; Hannah More, *Sacred Dramas*
1783	American Revolution ends with Treaty of Versailles; Pitt becomes Prime Minister; Montgolfier brothers' balloon flight; Newgate prison replaces Tyburn as the place for public executions	Hannah Cowley, *A Bold Stroke for a Husband*
1784	Britain introduces India Act	Elizabeth Inchbald, *The Mogul Tale*; Anna Seward, *Louisa*; Charlotte Smith, *Elegiac Sonnets* (new edns through 1814)
1785	Edward Cartwright patents the power loom	Anna Maria Bennett, *Anna; or Memoirs of a Welch Heiress*; Elizabeth Inchbald, *I'll Tell you What*; Sophia Lee, *The Recess*; Clara Reeve, *The Progress of Romance*; Charlotte Smith, *Manon Lescaut*; Ann Yearsley, *Poems on Several Occasions*

Year	Events	Works
1786		Helen Cowley, *School for Greybeards*; Elizabeth Inchbald, *The Widow's Vow*; Harriet Lee, *The Errors of Innocence*; Hester Thrale Piozzi, *Anecdotes of the Late Samuel Johnson*; Sarah Trimmer, *Fabulous Histories*; Hannah Maria Williams, *Poems*
1787	Signing of the American Constitution; impeachment of Warren Hastings; founding of the Society for Effecting the Abolition of the Slave Trade	Elizabeth Helme, *Louisa; or, the Cottage on the Moor*; Elizabeth Inchbald, *Such Things Are*; Charlotte Smith, *The Romance of Real Life*; Sarah Trimmer, *The Oeconomy of Charity*; Mary Wollstonecraft, *Thoughts on the Education of Daughters*
1788	Founding of Botany Bay penal colony; *Analytical Review* and *The Times* first published; death of Bonnie Prince Charlie in France	Elizabeth Inchbald, *The Child of Nature*; Hannah More, *Slavery, a Poem*; Charlotte Smith, *Emmeline*; Mary Wollstonecraft, *Mary, a Fiction* and *Original Stories*; Ann Yearsley, *A Poem on the Inhumanity of the Slave-Trade*
1789	Storming of the Bastille; outbreak of French Revolution; King George's first bout of madness; the mutiny on the Bounty; Declaration of Rights of Man	Charlotte Brooke, *Reliques of Irish Poetry*; Phebe Gibbes, *Hartley House, Calcutta*; Ann Radcliffe, *Castles of Athlin and Dunbayne*; Charlotte Smith, *Ethelinde*
1790	The founding of the Literary Fund (later the Royal Literary Fund)	Charlotte Lennox, *Euphemia*; Catharine Macaulay, *Letters on Education*; Amelia Opie, *The Dangers of Coquetry*; Ann Radcliffe, *A Sicilian Romance*; Mary Robinson, *Ainsi va le Monde*; Helen Maria Williams, *Letters from France* (1790–96) and *Julia*; Mary Wollstonecraft, *A Vindication of the Rights of Men*

(Continued)

Year	Events	Works
1791	Parliament rejects bill to abolish the slave trade; Birmingham Riots; foundation of United Irishmen	Anna Laetitia Barbauld, *Epistle to William Wilberforce*; Elizabeth Inchbald, *A Simple Story*; Ann Radcliffe, *The Romance of the Forest*; Mary Robinson, *Poems*; Charlotte Smith, *Celestina*
1792	Sugar boycott commences; founding of London Corresponding Society; the September Massacres (France); Seditious Libel Act	Anna Laetitia Barbauld, *Evenings at Home* (1792–96); Janet Little, *The Poetical Works of Janet Little, the Scotch Milkmaid*; Hannah More, *Village Politics*; Clara Reeve, *Plans of Education*; Mary Robinson, *Vancenza*; Charlotte Smith, *Desmond*; Mary Wollstonecraft, *A Vindication of the Rights of Woman*
1793	Louis XVI and Marie Antoinette executed; the Reign of Terror begins in France; Britain declares war on France	Anna Laetitia Barbauld, *Sins of Government*; Mary Hays, *Letters and Essays, Moral and Miscellaneous*; Elizabeth Inchbald, *Every One has His Fault*; Charlotte Smith, *The Emigrants* and *The Old Manor House*
1794	Execution of Robespierre (France); habeas corpus suspended; Treason Trials	Ann Radcliffe, *Mysteries of Udolpho*; Mary Robinson, *The Widow*; Charlotte Smith, *The Banished Man* and *The Wanderings of Warwick*; Priscilla Wakefield, *Mental Improvement* (1794–97); Mary Wollstonecraft, *An Historical and Moral View of ... The French Revolution*
1795	Treasonable Practises and Seditious Meetings Acts passed; Prussia and Spain make peace with France; Speenhamland Poor Relief introduced in Southern England	Maria Edgeworth, *Letters for Literary Ladies*; Eliza Fenwick, *Secresy*; Mary Meeke, *Count St. Blanchard*; Hannah More, *Cheap Repository Tracts* (1795–98); Charlotte Smith, *Montalbert* and *Rural Walks*; Ann Yearsley, *The Royal Captives*

Year	Events	Works
1796	Edward Jenner develops smallpox vaccination; Napoleon defends Paris	Frances Burney, *Camilla*; Sarah Harriet Burney, *Clarentine*; Maria Edgeworth, *The Parent's Assistant*; Elizabeth Hamilton, *Letters of a Hindoo Rajah*; Mary Hays, *Memoirs of Emma Courtney*; Elizabeth Inchbald, *Nature and Art*; Mary Robinson, *Angelina, Hubert de Sevrac* and *Sappho and Phaon*; Regina Maria Roche, *Children of the Abbey*; Anna Seward, *Llangollen Vale*; Charlotte Smith, *Marchmont* and *Rambles Farther*; Priscilla Wakefield, *Introduction to Botany*; Mary Wollstonecraft, *Letters Written During a Short Residence in Sweden, Norway and Denmark*
1797	Napoleon takes command of the French Army of Italy; *Anti-Jacobin* first published; monetary crisis: cash payments suspended at the Bank of England; The Bank Restriction Act; Nove Naval Mutiny; Spithead Naval Mutiny; legislation passed regarding 'Administering oaths by Unlawful Societies' (penal offence in Britain); Treaty of Campo Formio: France defeats Austria	Harriet Lee [and Sophia Lee], *Canterbury Tales* (1797–1805); Ann Radcliffe, *The Italian*; Mary Robinson, *Walsingham*
1798	Irish Rebellion; habeas corpus suspended; Battle of the Nile; coalition between Britain, Austria, Portugal, Naples, and Turkey formed against France; Invasion Crisis	Joanna Baillie, *Plays on the Passions* (vol. I); Maria and R.L. Edgeworth, *Practical Education*; Mary Hays, *An Appeal to the Men of Great Britain in Behalf of Women*; Elizabeth Inchbald, *Lovers' Vows*; Charlotte Smith, *The Young Philosopher*; Priscilla Wakefield, *Reflections on the Present Condition of the Female Sex*; Mary Wollstonecraft, *The Wrongs of Woman; or Maria*

(Continued)

Year	Events	Works
1799	London Corresponding Society declared illegal; Napoleon becomes First Consul of France; Royal Institution founded; introduction of income tax for the wealthy	Mary Hays, *The Victim of Prejudice*; Hannah More, *Strictures on the Modern System of Female Education*; Mary Ann Radcliffe, *The Female Advocate*; Mary Robinson, *The False Friend*, *The Natural Daughter* and *A Letter to the Women of England*; Anna Seward, *Original Sonnets*; Jane West, *Letters to a Lady*
1800	Act of Union with Ireland; Trevithick invents non-condensing, high pressure engine; Census Act (Britain)	Anne Bannerman, *Poems*; Maria Edgeworth, *Castle Rackrent* and *Ennui*; Elizabeth Hamilton, *Memoirs of Modern Philosophers*; Mary Robinson, *Lyrical Tales*; Charlotte Smith, *Letters of a Solitary Wanderer*
1801	First British census; act to reduce costs of illegal enclosure of land	Maria Edgeworth, *Belinda*, *Early Lessons* and *Moral Tales for Young People*; Elizabeth Hamilton, *Letters on ... Education*; Amelia Opie, *Father and Daughter*; Sydney Owenson (Lady Morgan), *Poems*; Mary Robinson, *The Memoirs of Mrs Robinson*; Priscilla Wakefield, *The Juvenile Travellers*
1802	*Edinburgh Review* begins publication; Peace of Amiens ended war with France; first Factory Act, limiting hours and establishing working conditions	Joanna Baillie, *Plays on the Passions* (vol. II); Amelia Opie, *Poems*; Jane West, *The Infidel Father*
1803	Resumption of war with France	Mary Hays, *Female Biography*; Sydney Owenson, *St. Clair*; Jane Porter, *Thaddeus of Warsaw*
1804	Napoleon becomes Emperor of the French	Mary Matilda Betham, *A Biographical Dictionary of the Celebrated Women of Every Age and Country*; Maria Edgeworth, *Popular Tales*; Mary Hays, *Harry Clinton*; Anna Seward, *Memoirs of the Life of Dr Darwin*; Charlotte Smith, *Conversations Introducing Poetry*; Priscilla Wakefield, *A Family Tour through the British Empire*

Year	Events	Works
1805	Battle of Trafalgar	Charlotte Dacre, *Hours of Solitude* and *Confessions of the Nun of St Omer*; Maria Edgeworth, *The Modern Griselda*; Elizabeth Inchbald, *To Marry, or Not to Marry*; Hannah More, *Hints for Forming the Character of a Young Princess*; Amelia Opie, *Adeline Mowbray*; Sydney Owenson, *Hibernian Melodies* and *The Novice of Saint Domnick*; Mary Tighe, *Psyche*
1806	Deaths of William Pitt and Charles Fox	Charlotte Dacre, *Zofloya*; Maria Edgeworth, *Leonora*; Jane Marcet, *Conversations on Chemistry*; Sydney Owenson, *The Wild Irish Girl*; Charlotte Smith, *The History of England*; Ann and Jane Taylor, *Rhymes for the Nursery*
1807	British Parliament abolishes the slave trade; founding of the Female Penitentiary	Harriet Corp, *An Antidote to the Miseries of Human Life*; Sydney Owenson, *Patriotic Sketches of Ireland* and *Hibernian Melodies*; Charles and Mary Lamb, *Tales from Shakespeare*; Anna Maria Porter, *The Hungarian Brothers*; Charlotte Smith, *The Natural History of Birds* and *Beachy Head, Fables and Other Poems*
1808	Napoleon invades Spain: start of the Peninsular War	Anne Grant, *Memoirs of an American Lady*; Elizabeth Hamilton, *The Cottagers of Glenburnie*; Felicia Hemans, *Poems* and *England and Spain*; Amelia Opie, *The Warrior's Return and Other Poems*
1809	Drury Lane Theatre destroyed by fire; opening of the new Covent Garden Theatre	Maria Edgeworth, *Ennui* and *Tales of Fashionable Life*; Hannah More, *Coelebs in Search of a Wife*; Sydney Owenson, *Woman; or, Ida of Athens*; Anna Maria Porter, *Don Sebastian*

(Continued)

Year	Events	Works
1810	Burdett riots, London	Lucy Aikin, *Epistles on Women*; Joanna Baillie, *The Family Legend*; Mary Russell Mitford, *Poems*; Anne Plumptre, *Narrative of a Three Years' Residence in France*; Jane Porter, *The Scottish Chiefs*; Ann and Jane Taylor, *Hymns for Infant Minds*
1811	Prince of Wales becomes Prince Regent; Luddite riots in the Midlands and the north of Britain (last through 1816)	Jane Austen, *Sense and Sensibility*; Mary Brunton, *Self-Control*; Charlotte Dacre, *The Passions*; Alicia LeFanu, *Strathallan*; Mary Leadbetter, *Cottage Dialogues among the Irish Peasantry*; Sydney Owenson, *The Missionary: an Indian Tale*; Mary Russell Mitford, *Christina*; Hannah More, *Practical Piety*
1812	Assassination of British Prime Minister Spencer Perceval; War of 1812 between Britain and America begins; Napoleon's invasion of Russia	Joanna Baillie, *Plays on the Passions* (vol. III); Anna Laetitia Barbauld, *Eighteen Hundred and Eleven*; Elizabeth Benger, *Marian, The Absentee*; Felicia Hemans, *The Domestic Affections and Other Poems*; Mary Russell Mitford, *Watlington Hill*; Hannah More, *Christian Morals*; Amelia Opie, *Temper; or, Domestic Scenes*; Jane West, *The Loyalists: An Historical Novel*
1813		Jane Austen, *Pride and Prejudice*; Mary Russell Mitford, *Narrative Poems on the Female Character*; Amelia Opie, *Tales of Real Life*
1814	Treaty of Ghent ends war between America and Britain; anti-Napoleon coalition invade France; Napoleon exiled to Elba; end of Peninsular War	Jane Austen, *Mansfield Park*; Mary Brunton, *Discipline*; Frances Burney, *The Wanderer*; Maria Edgeworth, *Patronage*; Sydney Owenson, *O'Donel*; Anna Maria Porter, *The Recluse of Norway*

Year	Events	Works
1815	Battle of Waterloo; Napoleon escapes Elba and later exiled to St Helena; passing of the Corn Laws; Restoration of Louis XVIII; Davy Lamp invented: deep mining now possible	Mary Hays, *The Brothers*
1816	Spa Fields Riot, London; Coinage Act: Britain adopts the Gold Standard; income tax abolished in Britain; Bread or Blood Riots in response to inflation and high unemployment	Jane Austen, *Emma*; Lady Caroline Lamb, *Glenarvon*; Felicia Hemans, *The Restoration of the Works of Art to Italy*; Hannah More, *Poems*
1817	Habeas corpus suspended	Maria Edgeworth, *Ormond* and *Harrington*; Mary Hays, *Family Annals*; Felicia Hemans, *Modern Greece. A Poem*; Sydney Owenson, *France*; Anna Maria Porter, *The Knight of St John*; Jane Porter, *The Pastor's Fireside*
1818	Habeas corpus restored	Jane Austen, *Northanger Abbey* and *Persuasion*; Susan Ferrier, *Marriage*; Sydney Owenson, *Florence Macarthy*; Mary Shelley, *Frankenstein*
1819	Peterloo Massacre; first steam powered crossing of Atlantic; London riots; Cato Street Conspiracy; Six Acts: stamp duty on publications; Second Factory Act	Felicia Hemans, *Tales and Historic Scenes*; Jane Marcet, *Conversations on Natural Philosophy*; Hannah More, *Moral Sketches of Prevailing Opinions and Manners*
1820	Death of George III; accession of George IV; revolution in Spain	Caroline Bowles, *Ellen Fitzarthur*; Felicia Hemans, *The Sceptic, A Poem*; Amelia Opie, *Tales of the Heart*
1821	Death of Napoleon; cash payments resumed by Bank of England	Joanna Baillie, *Metrical Legends of Exalted Characters*; Mary Hays, *Memoirs of Queens, Illustrious and Celebrated*; Felicia Hemans, *Dartmoor*; Laetitia Landon, *The Fate of Adelaide*; Sydney Owenson, *Italy*
1822	The New Marriage Act; Corn Law Amendment Act; Irish Constabulary founded	Caroline Bowles, *The Widow's Tale*; Amelia Opie, *Madeline*

(Continued)

Year	Events	Works
1823	Society for the Mitigation and Gradual Abolition of Slavery founded	Felicia Hemans, *The Siege of Valencia* and *The Vespers of Palermo*; Harriet Martineau, *Devotional Exercises*; Mary Shelley, *Valperga*
1824	Opening of the National Gallery; *Westminster Review* begins publication; Combination Acts repealed; RSPCA founded	Susan Ferrier, *The Inheritance*; Laetitia Landon, *The Improvisatrice*; Mary Russell Mitford, *Our Village*; Sydney Owenson, *The Life and Times of Salvator Rosa*
1825	Economic depression in Britain; act to reinstate the Combination Laws in Britain; Law Society established; first steam-powered locomotive travels between Stockton and Darlington	Felicia Hemans, *The Forest Sanctuary*; Maria Jane Jewsbury, *Phantasmagoria*; Letitia Landon, *The Troubadour*; Amelia Opie, *Illustrations of Lying in all its Branches*
1826	Founding of the Society for the Diffusion of Useful Knowledge and the University of London; Britain favours state-aided emigration; first railway crisis in Britain (finances)	Caroline Bowles, *Solitary Hours*; Harriet Martineau, *Addresses, with Prayers and Original Hymns*; Ann Radcliffe, *Gaston de Blondeville*; Mary Shelley, *The Last Man*
1827	Treaty of London: to protect the nation from foreign threats	Felicia Hemans, *Hymns on the Works of Nature*; Sydney Owenson, *The O'Briens and the O'Flahertys*; Charlotte Tonna, *The System*; Jane Webb, *The Mummy*
1828	Duke of Wellington becomes Prime Minister; repeal of the Test and Corporation Acts	Felicia Hemans, *Records of Women with Other Poems*; Maria Jane Jewsbury, *Letters to the Young*; Amelia Opie, *Detraction Displayed*; Mary Russell Mitford, *Rienzi*
1829	Catholic Emancipation Act; founding of the Metropolitan Police by Robert Peel	Maria Jane Jewsbury, *Lays of Leisure Hours*; Letitia Landon, *The Venetian Bracelet ... and Other Poems*; Harriet Martineau, *Traditions of Palestine*; Sydney Owenson, *The Book of the Boudoir*

Year	Events	Works
1830	George IV dies; accession of William IV	Catherine Gore, *Women as they Are*; Maria Jane Jewsbury, *The Three Histories*; Felicia Hemans, *Songs of the Affections*; Sydney Owenson, *France in 1829–30*; Mary Shelley, *The Fortunes of Perkin Warbeck*

(With thanks to Jennie Batchelor and Adrian Wallbank, whose help in composing this chronology was invaluable)

Introduction: Defining 'Women's Writing'; or, Writing 'The History'

Jacqueline M. Labbe

Although scholars of literature are usually quick to claim for their own periods key originating moments, it is nonetheless safe to assert that the years 1750–1830 witnessed the first full flowering of women's writing in Britain. Building on the success and popularity of earlier poets, novelists, playwrights, and philosophers, British women consolidated their significance as writers in the late eighteenth century; they created and supported movements (Bluestocking intellectualism, the call for abolition, new understandings of class, religion, and identity), initiated literary styles (the novel of sensibility, the historical novel, the elegiac sonnet, the hybrid ballad), and signalled transitions (from the Enlightenment to Romanticism, from Romanticism to early Victorianism). The last twenty-five years of scholarship and textual recovery have overturned the convention that women wrote unambitiously, mostly anonymously, and concentrated on 'feminine' concerns like the family and the home. Instead, an understanding of the period which sees Mary Wollstonecraft, Dorothy Wordsworth, and Jane Austen as only the more familiar of a host of writers has become standard. And as these previously marginalized writers have been brought back into notice, everything has changed: our understandings of literary history, and who did what when; our understandings of culture and the manifold relationships between writers and their societies; our understandings of not merely the limitations but the distortions of a canon that reads the development – the 'rise' – of the novel and poetry solely through a small cadre of male writers; even our understandings of Wollstonecraft, Wordsworth, and Austen. As the chapters below make clear, the moment that women's writing receives the same serious and thoughtful attention and critical evaluation that has always been accorded to men's, the easy assumptions that allowed even a pioneering

1

critic such as J.M.S. Tompkins to begin her study of 'the popular novel in England' by 'justif[ying]' her 'display of tenth-rate fiction'[1] lose whatever validity they might once have had. Although this volume, like the series of which it forms a part, is devoted to writing by women, as many of the chapters show, women and men wrote not in separate spheres but as part of a culture highly interested in questions of family, politics, history, science, war, art, selfhood: the big questions that perennially occupy humanity. For those writing in the period 1750–1830, these questions assumed the utmost importance and women worked out their reactions to them, and advances on them, through their writing, while literary culture enjoyed the advantages inherent in the growing utilization of female intelligence and imagination.

Why we read what we read now

Few readers now would accept the thesis of Ian Watt's important, if limited, study *The Rise of the Novel* that the modern form of the novel is the result of developments by Defoe, Richardson, and Fielding that culminated in the work of Austen, with the slightest of nods to Burney.[2] But as late as 1996, *The Cambridge Companion to the Eighteenth-Century Novel* devoted six chapters to named male writers (Defoe, Swift, Richardson, Fielding, Sterne, and Smollett), and only one to a named female: Burney, with a separate essay on 'Women Writers and the Eighteenth-Century Novel'.[3] Similarly, the much more recent *Cambridge Companion to English Literature, 1740–1830* contains chapters on Johnson and Boswell; Sterne; Blake; Wordsworth and Coleridge; Keats, Shelley, Byron, and the Hunt circle; and John Clare. A chapter on Richardson and Henry Fielding also names Sarah Fielding; there is one on Barbauld, Robinson, and Smith; and one on Jane Austen.[4] As texts aimed at the advanced student, they perpetuate an imbalance that seems to require detailed study of familiar figures while corralling whole groups on the basis of gender. As Judith Pascoe asks in her astute fashion, 'why do we assume that these three women writers [Barbauld, Robinson and Smith] share a common poetic aesthetic? Largely because the three of them floated across our field of vision at the same time...'[5] Readers of these Companions, and of other similar studies, are nonetheless presented with the implications of a homogeneous group, 'women writers', whose approach to text and composition overrides individuality in the way that Smollett's, Richardson's, William Wordsworth's do not.

And yet, given the way in which Watt sets aside women's 'quantitative dominance' in the field of novel-writing, that women as a group are capable of writing texts that should be read is only now being generally accepted. As the past decades of feminist literary criticism suggest, before the writer who is a woman can be usefully studied, we need to investigate the existence as well as the achievements of a group who, despite its numerical dominance, was yet defined as obscure or minor. It was in the 1980s that studies of women writers in the late eighteenth and early nineteenth centuries really took off, but before that two major studies explored the meaning of the writing woman: Ellen Moers's *Literary Women: The Great Writers* (1977) and Sandra Gilbert and Susan Gubar's *The Madwoman in the Attic: The Woman Writer and the Nineteenth-Century Literary Imagination* (1979).[6] As Moers observes, by the mid-1970s not even Austen 'is mentioned (no less included) in the standard anthologies which today are the staple introductions to English ... literature for students' (p. xv). Moers characterizes as a 'narrow view' the idea that 'separating major writers from the general course of literary history on the basis of their sex was futile', but she takes this further than Watt's reliance on 'feminine sensibilities'; for her, 'women's issues and women's traditions ... have been shaping forces in *all* modern literature' (p. xv, emphasis added). For Moers, although it is useless to deny women's distinctive experiences, nonetheless those experiences have *generally* informed the development of modern culture and modern writing, by which she means the period starting in the late eighteenth century. Although the earliest writer she concentrates on is Austen, Moers's index and notes namecheck many of the most significant female writers of the mid- to late eighteenth century: Mary Brunton, Ann Radcliffe, Charlotte Smith, Sarah Fielding, Maria Edgeworth, Fanny Burney, Elizabeth Montagu, Mary Hays, Mary Wollstonecraft. And she makes the essential point that a writer like Austen read the 'major English writers' and 'the best poetry of her day', which implicitly includes 'the female fiction that Austen's letters inform us was her daily sustenance in the years that she became one of the greatest writers in the language' (p. 66). Moers does not make the point overtly; she offers this 'mass of women's novels, excellent, fair and wretched, for [Austen] to study and improve upon' as something rhetorically separate from the 'major English writers' of her previous paragraph (p. 67). But nonetheless her study enrols the women she discusses, and their influences and forebears, in this pantheon, since it is through study and imitation as well as innovation that someone such as Austen 'became' great. Thus, while Moers's study begins in earnest with the early nineteenth century, its inevitable chronology populates the earlier period as well, holding Richardson and his brothers to one side. Moers makes 'literary *women*' – the group, engaged in a common discipline – visible.

Gilbert and Gubar similarly concentrate on a modern period that begins with Austen and includes Mary Shelley, and like Moers they approach 'woman' as a category with its own distinct parameters: 'we were surprised by the coherence of theme and imagery that we encountered in the works of writers who were often geographically, historically, and psychologically distant from each other .... [W]e found what began to seem a distinctively female literary tradition...' (p. xi). Gilbert and Gubar's woman writer is defined by traps, enclosures, constrictions, and restrictions; where Moers builds an edifice of female writing that acts as a kind of town meeting hall for culture, Gilbert and Gubar present the woman writer as 'enclosed in the architecture of an overwhelmingly male-dominated society' and her main 'female impulse' as a struggle for freedom (p. xi). They present their writers, and themselves, as operating outside of and against 'male-defined literary history', exploring 'dialogue' and 'consensus', rejecting the 'pen/penis' and the 'prison of the male text' (pp. 3, 44). The woman's world, and her texts, are resolutely separate from and different to those of a man; the only relationship that can be textualized is one of struggle and escape. Where Moers seems to see the possibility of influence and change, Gilbert and Gubar see essential difference. Moers's repopulated history provides context for the genius of the individual; Gilbert and Gubar's contributes to the critical mass needed for escape velocity. But, crucially, for these critics the existence of the group 'women writers' itself needed no justification; in other words, Watt's 'quantitative dominance' has become a virtue rather than an embarrassment.

Almost immediately, the new decade of the 1980s develops the insights of Moers and Gilbert and Gubar while also exploring in more detail and with more textual attention the works that informed both Austen and the productions of her contemporaries.[7] Margaret Homans's *Women Writers and Poetic Identity: Dorothy Wordsworth, Emily Brontë, and Emily Dickinson* (1980) counters what she calls the 'masculine tradition' with close studies of three women writers who were defined in many ways by their self-imposed isolation and sense of domestic refuge. 'Where the major literary tradition normatively identifies the figure of the poet as masculine, and voice as a masculine property, women writers cannot see their minds as androgynous, or as sexless, but must take part in a self-definition by contraries' (p. 3). All women, not just the writing kind, felt the pressure to conform to ideal patterns, 'none of which included the possibility of a poet's vocation' (p. 5). This is the key theme of Mary Poovey's highly influential study, *The Proper Lady and the Woman Writer: Ideology as Style in the Works of*

Mary Wollstonecraft, Mary Shelley, and Jane Austen (1984): 'how could real women express themselves at all, since self-expression ... requires at least the assumption of autonomy and the power to participate in culture as an initiating subject?' (p. iv). Those women who 'became professional authors despite the strictures of propriety' (p. x) both embody and battle the 'feminine sensibilities' that Watt felt made Austen, for instance, the suitable inheritor of the eighteenth-century novel tradition. To write at all required struggle, but against oneself as well as the social constraints identified by Gilbert and Gubar. Both Homans and Poovey follow the template that opposes women's culture and their writings to men's, offering as a necessary corrective to assumptions of female intellectual inferiority a reading of the female imagination as always engaged with, although in opposition to, a masculine culture that has arranged society to suit masculine needs and follow masculine structures. Women such as Wordsworth or Shelley or Austen write *despite* social constraints; they create a separate aesthetic that hews to their separate experience and reflects their separate social milieus.

This sense of separation and difference persists in the title of Mary Anne Schofield and Cecilia Macheski's groundbreaking collection, *Fetter'd or Free? British Woman Novelists, 1670–1815* (1986).[8] But the sheer breathtaking variety of the contents overrides any sense of constraint indicated by the title. While it was possible to find the odd essay on Burney, or Smith, or Radcliffe, or Frances Sheridan, or Hannah More, for the first time a volume of essays explored women's writing in a way that both normalized the category and backed it up with detail. And the editors ask the question that followed from the earlier emphasis on women's social and imaginative imprisonments, given their 'extreme social subordination':

> [i]n the guise of their sentimental heroines, their aggressive female manipulators, and the like, these novelists explore the perimeters of their being and that of the female self in general ... are they fettered by literary conventions, social mores, and economic limitations, or are they free to invent a female rhetoric, to express a selfhood, and to develop economic independence?
>
> (p. 1)

This necessary step in the scholarship of women's writing moves beyond a kind of victim politics to explore what it means to be a rational and intelligent person living the life of a woman in the eighteenth century. It also begins the difficult work of textual recovery of those writers who had been obscured in the way that Austen, Wordsworth, Wollstonecraft, or Shelley never had been. Moers asks, in the voice of 'scholarship', 'Who wants to associate the great Jane Austen ... with someone called Mary Brunton? Who wants to read or indeed can find a copy of *Self-Control...*' (p. 66). *Fetter'd or Free* provides an insightful essay on Brunton in the same section that offers readings of Austen and Burney, suggesting that by 1986 'scholarship' not only wanted to read Brunton, 'it' wanted to study her.[9] And the collection advances the thesis put forward by Gilbert and Gubar (that there is a 'female tradition in literature' defined by the trope of imprisonment) by recasting this as a series of dichotomies: 'gender and genre ... freedom and enslavement ... not only are the questions thus raised worth asking, but ... asking the question is itself part of the answer' (p. 5). In the same year, Jane Spencer's *The Rise of the Woman Novelist: From Aphra Behn to Jane Austen* (1986; repr. 1987) made plain the scholarly limitations of Watt's version of the rise of the novel, as she laid out with great élan the development of 'women's writing' in the seventeenth and eighteenth centuries.[10] As she notes, 'the rise of the novel cannot be understood fully without considering how its conventions were shaped by the contributions of a large number of women, their writing deeply marked by the "femininity" insistently demanded of them by the culture to which they belonged' (p. viii). Spencer's book shows incontrovertibly that not only were female novelists 'quantitatively dominant' in the period, they were also qualitatively unmissable.

What is astonishing is the speed with which evaluations and understandings of women's writing in the period develop. Of course, scholars read and react to one another, and statements of meaning are commonly followed by refinements of those statements. But in a short ten years, and without easy access to texts, scholars succeeded in making the field of women's writing fertile and lush. Indeed, in *The New Eighteenth Century: Theory, Politics, English Literature* (1987), the editors Felicity Nussbaum and Laura Brown not only included four essays dealing specifically with a variety of writing women (Aphra Behn, Mary Collier, writers of scandalous memoirs, Ann Radcliffe), they also made plain that the volume as a whole was concerned with '"women, popular culture, [and] sexuality"' (p. 3), a conjunction that, I would argue, only became possible once the study of women's writing as serious and valued literature had begun. Their volume's easy inclusion of essays dealing with writing by women as well as writing about women is in stark contrast to the conservative nature of such approaches in the Cambridge Companions cited above. Nancy Armstrong's influential

Desire and Domestic Fiction: A Political History of the Novel (1987) complements Nussbaum and Brown's emphasis on the sexual politics of writing, reading the novel, especially as written by women, as 'the bearer of modernity', and the female writer herself as neither ethically heroic nor bravely victimized, but instead as fully human.[11] And Anne Mellor's essential collection *Romanticism and Feminism* (1988) furthers the comparative and inclusive methodology, discussing male and female writers from a feminist standpoint and developing completely new insights into standard authors such as Byron, Scott, and Keats. Crucially, this collection also repopulates the Romantic corpus with Stuart Curran's 'The I Altered' (pp. 185–207), possibly the most important essay on Romantic women's writing to be published.[12] Curran's essay rethinks that most Romantic of tropes, the construction of subjective selfhood, reading it through a stylistics that privileges the quotidian rather than the visionary and the ethereal. Where earlier critics read the writing woman as restricted by her social oppression, Curran reverses this, positing a female poetics that celebrates its association with the world of house and home. Curran's essay inaugurates what becomes, in the 1990s, the dominant reading of late eighteenth-century women's writing: a separate but equal, at times even superior, mode of writing.

This is the point where Romantic criticism begins not only to investigate the existence of writers other than the Big Six of Wordsworth, Coleridge, Blake, Byron, Shelley, and Keats, but also to postulate that women wrote out of their experience of being women, and men wrote out of their experience of being men. By extension, Romanticism itself, if defined through the writing of the Big Six (as tended to be the case), was in a sense not available to female writers who were thus forced to formulate their own version (the quotidian, for instance). Marlon Ross's magisterial *The Contours of Masculine Desire: Romanticism and the Rise of Women's Poetry* (1989) seeks to situate Romanticism 'within history' and as driven by 'desire', broadly defined as 'the engine of pure process': human life, in essence, as recorded through and by art such as poetry (p. 7). Ross contends that 'masculine poetry precedes feminine poetry' (p. 11), that different and competing concerns underlie and inform the male and the female in their poetic production. Ross's emphasis on a historically-informed approach finds play as well in Janet Todd's *The Sign of Angellica: Women, Writing and Fiction, 1660–1800* (1989).[13] Where Ross finds in women's poetry the most focalized expressions of literary femininity, Todd locates this in women's fiction 'as the genre with which women were pre-eminently associated and which most influenced female consciousness' (p. 5). Todd also engages with the tricky question of 'aesthetic principles', the value judgements that underlay critical discussion, noting that 'our critical assumptions have been fashioned through a particular body of male literature and literary criticism' (pp. 5, 6). Todd articulates the challenge that most defines the recovery of women's writing through the 1980s: it is not merely about listing titles and authors, developing alternative imaginative methodologies, or denouncing oppression politics; it is also about understanding conscious and unconscious critical complicity: about accepting one's inability to approach literature outside ideological frames. At the same time, these major studies of the 1980s begin to shift those frames, creating new expectations and assumptions for those just beginning their studies as well as encouraging the evolution of terms of reference within the academy. The sweeping nature of *The Madwoman in the Attic*, in other words, belongs to its historical moment, which itself has passed only a decade later. In its place stands a more complex understanding of women's writing as a conglomeration of differences, albeit linked by the shared experience of being female in a male-oriented world.

Throughout the 1980s, then, 'women's writing' is refined and complicated in ways that open new avenues of study. Vivien Jones's anthology *Women in the Eighteenth Century: Constructions of Femininity* (1990) reflects this; even in its title the anthology signals its awareness of the 'impossib[ility] for "women" to operate as a fixed and knowable category'.[14] As Jones goes on to note, 'though it is strategically important to focus on women in the period, it is equally important not to repeat the asymmetry which defines men in terms of variety and difference and women as a unified object of knowledge' (p. 9). By offering a variety of writings by women in the eighteenth century, Jones's anthology makes it impossible to continue to see 'women's writing' as itself unified; in particular, the sections on 'self-images' and 'public images' clarify the multitudinous approaches to 'women' by suggesting both the attractions of public pictures of compliant femininity and the various ways in which women overturned or rejected such pictures. Jones's multiple perspectives are complemented by Donna Landry's landmark book *The Muses of Resistance: Laboring-Class Women's Poetry in Britain, 1739–1796* (1990). If a corollary to gender criticism is class criticism, then Landry's book brings the two together in a salutary reinforcement of Jones's point about the contested nature of the category 'women'. Even as 'women's writing' was undergoing increased scrutiny, the women who wrote it had, it seemed, remained more or less within the same social sphere: middle to upper class. But Landry is unequivocal about the limitations of such class blindness: 'No feminist literary history that seeks to trace a "female" tradition while remaining blind to the operations of class difference, conflict, and deliberate or unconscious repression will come close to giving a sufficiently nuanced account of women's literary production...' (p. 2). Landry's study reverses the oppression theories of the early 1980s; as she concludes, writing itself functions as 'a form of critical articulation and resistance to oppression ... [T]hese women were neither abject nor silent' (p. 280).

Dale Spender's collection *Living by the Pen: Early British Women Writers* (1992) weaves together essays on individual women with more general theoretical narratives that place women as active participants within their historical periods, rather than as observers or marginalized reactors.[15] Anne Mellor's *Romanticism and Gender* (1993) develops a fully-formed 'feminine Romanticism' based on rationality and domestic politics, carrying on the approach signposted by Curran in 'The I Altered'. Mellor's separated Romanticisms have been controversial, but at the same time she enabled a discussion of women's writing that attempted to move beyond reactive writings; Mellor posits 'feminine Romanticism' as a collection of 'alternative poetic genres' exhibiting 'cultural power', and situates 'masculine' and 'feminine' Romanticism not as 'binary opposites but rather the endpoints on a continuum that ranges not only through the entire range of literary Romanticism but also through the corpus of individual writers' (p. 11). *Re-Visioning Romanticism: British Women Writers 1776–1837* (1994), edited by Carol Shiner Wilson and Joel Haefner, acknowledges the slippery nature of a term like 'Romanticism', and seeks to enlarge its parameters perhaps more fluidly; the editors describe a 'dynamic vision of Romanticism, one that is shaped by the recovery of long-neglected women writers' made ever easier by the publication in the early 1990s of a variety of anthologies (they cite Breen, Rogers and McCarthy, Uphaus and Foster, Lonsdale, Mahl and Koon, and Feldman) (pp. 1, 14). Their implicit goal of 'institutionalizing a new paradigm for Romantic studies' (p. 9) points to some of the effects of their re-visioning: a Romanticism that expands to accommodate the new, rather than one that is static and entrenched, and an approach that does not need to segregate women's writing or create an alternative canon, but that, instead, recognizes the integrated and embedded nature of culture where there is, arguably, no single 'female' or 'male' experience. The complementary collection *Romantic Women Writers: Voices and Countervoices* (1995) 'bring[s] together ... a critical mass of commentary, not only to demonstrate the range and complexity of women's writing during the Romantic period but to aid in establishing a set of critical terms and directions with which to continue investigating this important body of writing' (p. 1). The editors, Paula R. Feldman and Theresa M. Kelley, make a virtue of 'differences between commentators', and note that the 'history of the exclusion of women's voices from the ever-changing Romantic canon says more, in some ways, about our own century than about theirs, for contrary to conventional wisdom, the writing of many women Romantics survived through the nineteenth century and into the twentieth' (p. 2). By now, it is precisely difference and variety that legitimizes women's writing, a point also evident in *Women's Poetry in the Enlightenment: The Making of a Canon, 1730–1820* (1999): 'cherished "hegemonic" notions concerning the public and private spheres allocated to men and women, on which so much discussion of gender and writing has been founded, have to be questioned .... The [volume's contents] testify to the prolific creativity of women's poetry in the eighteenth and early nineteenth centuries, and to their engagement with major issues of their culture', say the editors, Isobel Armstrong and Virginia Blain (pp. vii, xi). The contents pages alone of these significant essay collections make all the more striking the virtual re-erasure – or, at best, re-homogenizing – of women's writing in Richetti's 1996 *Cambridge Companion to the Eighteenth-Century Novel*.

Scholars in the early twenty-first century thus inherit more than thirty years of serious reconsiderations of women's writing in the long eighteenth century. Early emphases on imprisonment, whether by culture or nature, the Other or the Self, gave way to investigations of freedom and exploration, which in turn led to definitions of styles of writing derived from gender identity and, conversely, styles based on understandings of the constructedness of such identities. Thematics moved from the domestic and the quotidian to the worldly and the political; women gradually gained the ability to be as different from one another as their writing showed them to be. In the 2000s, scholarship has reached a stage where women's writing begins to reflect women's prominence not merely in the private sphere (and it is important to acknowledge, as do the editors of *Women, Writing and the Public Sphere, 1700–1830* (2001), that the notion of 'separate spheres' is itself 'problematic and inaccurate if approached through the contemporary writings of women'[16]) but also in the world of letters, history, and politics. Harriet Guest's *Small Change: Women, Learning, Patriotism, 1750–1810* (2000) presents the last half of the eighteenth century as a period of 'important change in the way middle-class women think of themselves' (p. 14) and, hence, how they write about 'learning, patriotic politics, and work' (p. 15). *Women, Writing and the Public Sphere* focuses on 'women in the

public eye' such as artists, consumers, and 'cosmopolitan intellectuals' (Table of Contents). Devoney Looser and Anne Mellor figure the
writing woman as public historian and 'cultural authority' in *British
Women Writers and the Writing of History, 1670–1820* (2000) and *Mothers
of the Nation: Women's Political Writing in England, 1780–1830* (2002).[17]
Betty Schellenberg presents the Bluestocking writers as 'professionalized
subjects, as agents in the public sphere of letters' and in the 'literary
marketplace', overturning the standard picture of them as salon-bound
(read: domestic) or as thoroughly embedded in their gender identity.[18]
In *The Professionalization of Women Writers in Eighteenth-Century Britain*
(2005), Schellenberg concludes on a note that would have been inaudi-
ble to Gilbert and Gubar:

> It is only when we are prepared to let go of gender as our funda-
> mental interpretive category, it is only when we self-consciously
> rethink the frameworks through which we currently see and do not
> see mid-eighteenth-century women writers, it is only as we begin to
> consider women writers and their texts as the participants in literary
> and publishing networks that they were, that we will be freed of the
> constraining picture of their working in the shadow of the dominant
> male writers of their day...
>
> (p. 182)

It is worth adding that as scholarship builds on its own advances, we
may also come to question the familiar picture of 'the dominant male
writers of their day'; given what we now know about the numbers of
women who wrote, read, and reviewed, perhaps this picture of dominance is as much a part of our own cultural expectations as the conviction that women struggled to free themselves from cultural femininity
once was.

And so Paula Backscheider can open *Eighteenth-Century Women Poets
and their Poetry: Inventing Agency, Inventing Genre* (2005) not by asserting an overarching sameness but with an emphasis on her 'exploration of the forms in which women poets wrote' (p. xiii), and end
it by stating that, '[t]o a considerable extent ... the reassessment of
Restoration and eighteenth-century poetry remains to be done' (p. 402).
It is easy to overlook the small rhetorical change: Backscheider refers
not to 'women's' poetry, but simply to 'poetry'. Embedded in that
shift of phrasing is a suggestion that we are now entering a new phase
in scholarship: that any new understanding of 'women's poetry' or
'women's writing' in general advances our knowledge of literature *in*

toto, by women and men. It does not just provide a corrective or allow us to recover lost works or assert that yes, indeed, women wrote in all genres in the long eighteenth century, or even supply ammunition to replace Watts's generalized and faceless 'quantitative dominance' with names and titles. The writing woman has, perhaps, gained enfranchisement; she expects to be read and counted as a part of literary culture, not counter-culture. As Susan Staves observes in her essential *A Literary History of Women's Writing in Britain, 1660–1789* (2006), literary merit needs to enter the conversation: 'it cannot be a sin against feminism to find that some women wrote well and others badly ... [W]omen writers [like men] must be judged by what they accomplished in their work' (p. 439). From what we now know about the women who wrote in the long eighteenth century, learned from the studies discussed here and the many others that have appeared, judgement on merit was their usual expectation in their own time, despite the discomfort that accrued from the sneers of *some* (not all) commentators. The woman writer was a proper lady, after all.

Women's writing, 1750–1830

Although this volume, and the series of which it is a part, make use of the term 'women's writing', it is the intention that the essays contained herein interrogate the contours of the term as well as develop readings of writing by women that will contribute to the fleshing out of its history. Conventional literary history – that is, a history based on writings by men – follows an Enlightenment to Romanticism to Victorianism trajectory and reads something like this: the mid-eighteenth-century novelists (Richardson, Fielding, Smollett, Sterne) give way to the poets of Revolution, subsequent quiescence, and youthful backlash (Blake, Wordsworth, Coleridge, Byron, Keats, Shelley). The Enlightenment 'lasts' until the reverberations of the French Revolution and the utter novelty of the *Lyrical Ballads*. The novel does not become readable until the age of Scott and Austen. Austen herself is the exception that proves the rule that women did not write, or did not write major texts (otherwise surely we would know of them). Then, after the deaths of Keats, Byron, and Shelley, nothing really happens until Tennyson and Dickens begin to publish: the 'lost decade' of the mid-1820s to the mid-1830s. As a counter to this system, the essays in this volume are grouped, within its parameters of 1750–1830, around the turn of the century: 1800, the year of Mary Robinson's death and of the publication of her *Lyrical Tales*, is a significant date in the history of women's writing. But this remains an arbitrary division; as the chapters below suggest, the history of writing contains few 'everything changes' moments; the idea that the *Lyrical Ballads* of 1798, for instance, transformed British poetry becomes untenable as soon as Charlotte Smith's poetry re-enters the field, given that several of her non-sonnet poems, from the fifth edition of the *Elegiac Sonnets* (1789) onwards, contain recognizable 'lyrical ballads', even if the label had not yet been formulated.[19] And although Robinson's collected *Lyrical Tales* appear after the anonymous first edition of *Lyrical Ballads*, she had begun publishing its poems in the periodicals in 1796.[20] 1798 is certainly a significant year in the life of William Wordsworth, but it is only in a schema that disenfranchises writing by women that it becomes pivotal in the history of literature.

Or take, briefly, the Graveyard School of poetry, whose representatives, for instance Robert Blair and Edward Young, created an introspective subjectivity and an intense connection with the natural world that has commonly been seen as the precursor to Romanticism as well as to the Gothic (as a style it runs parallel to, but separate from, Enlightenment intellectualism). In order to uphold this leap of poetics from the 1740s–1750s to the 1790s, we must continue to ignore Anna Seward, Anna Laetitia Barbauld, Elizabeth Carter, Anne Yearsley, Smith, and Robinson. And yet once we factor these authors in, a standard genealogy becomes increasingly unstable: to take only one example, Barbauld's 'Washing Day', published in 1797 and hence a poem of the Romantic period, at the same time bears striking witness both to its author's longevity and her modernity:

> The Muses are turned gossips; they have lost
> The buskin'd step, and clear high-sounding phrase,
> Language of gods. Come, then, domestic Muse,
> In slip-shod measure loosely prattling on
> Of farm or orchard, pleasant curds and cream,
> Or drowning flies, or shoe lost in the mire
> By little whimpering boy, with rueful face;
> Come, Muse, and sing the dreaded *Washing-Day*.

The poem opens in pure Enlightenment style that merges with the language of daily life: the 'real language' of, here, women:

> Ye who beneath the yoke of wedlock bend,
> With bowed soul, full well ye ken the day
> Which week, smooth sliding after week, brings on
> Too soon; for to that day nor peace belongs

> Nor comfort;...
> ...never yet did housewife notable
> Greet with a smile a rainy washing-day.

And the entry of the speaker, with her invocation of memory and the implication of the formative nature of past events on present selfhood, is pure Romantic:

> I well remember, when a child, the awe
> This day struck into me; for then the maids,
> I scarce knew why, looked cross, and drove me from them;
> .... so I went
> And shelter'd me beside the parlour fire:
> There my dear grandmother, eldest of forms,
> Tended the little ones, and watched from harm,
> Anxiously fond...

The movement of the poem from its Miltonic opening to its domestic middle shows a writer at ease with both traditions, but this is not in and of itself an aspect of women's writing; although it is true, as the survey of scholarship above pointed out, that many critics would read the turn to the domestic as uniquely female, such an emphasis is also found in many of Coleridge's conversation poems, for instance. The poem's combined points of view, however, demonstrate that for Barbauld, there is no necessary break between the 'Enlightenment' and the 'Romantic';[21] she is comfortable with an Enlightened Romanticism, one that also points towards a postmodern deconstruction of all literary terms and conditions:

> Earth, air, and sky, and ocean, hath its bubbles,
> And verse is one of them – this most of all.

Playful rather than lacking in confidence, these last two lines on one level undercut the staying-power of poetry that is implicit in the invocation of the Muse with which the poem opens. And yet the 'bubble' that inspires the final image is not an evanescent reminder of 'women's work', but a reference to scientific advances and humanity's potential for knowledge: Montgolfier's hot-air balloon, first afloat in 1783. Or rather, it is both: and hence the poem, instead of popping like a soap-bubble, persists as an example of human ingenuity like Montgolfier's balloon, a symbol of futurity. Barbauld, who has been in the public eye since the 1770s, does not write as an Enlightenment holdover; by the 1790s she is writing 'modern' poetry, just as she did in the 1770s.[22]

As the contributions to this volume show, it would be a distortion to insist that texts from 1750 and from 1830 do not bear the marks of their decades. But equally, these essays make manifest the continuities that exist as we move from decade to decade. And as we are now at the point, in criticism, where we are interrogating the validity of the separate spheres argument put forward by Jürgen Habermas, so too essays tracing the history of British *women's* writing open up new avenues for questioning the received wisdom about British *men's* writing. Neither sex wrote without an awareness of the other in this period, and after a good thirty years of recovering women writers and building the structure of a women's writing tradition, we are now at the point of departure for a radical reassessment of literary culture and history, a reintegration of the male and female tradition, and a new understanding of a repopulated period that does not underplay the legal, cultural, and social constraints that affected women, but that also recognizes how successful women were, in the period 1750–1830, at negotiating these boundaries, and at making their names, theories of poetry and fiction, and literary works part of mainstream culture.[23] Writings by men, then, need to be re-evaluated as part of a two-sex model; the essays in this volume, by tracing the nuances of women's contributions to the writing culture of the period, will enable this enterprise. As the chronology on pages xvii–xxix shows, women wrote constantly and fluently throughout the period, so in constructing this History there has been no attempt to provide surveys of women's writing in specific genres within specific dates; rather, the writers have focused on key themes and authors while also creating lines of argument with implications beyond the limits of their individual chapters.

In the period under review, the novel achieved its modern form and poetry underwent several metamorphoses, Britain moved in and out of conflicts with a variety of enemies, class and gender identities and affiliations became less fixed and immovable, the identity of the nation shifted from agrarian and inward-looking to industrial and imperial, and its domestic territories gained in familiarity what they lost in autonomy. As the essays in this volume show, women's writing responded to and reflected these key cultural developments. For example, Jennie Batchelor and Stuart Curran in Part II and Devoney Looser and Olivia Murphy in Part III trace the manifold ways in which women affected the nature of the novel. In Chapter 4, Batchelor draws some intriguing links between women's understanding of the fictive and their representations of the so-called real, investigating 'such self-reflexively fictitious novels' as Jane Collier and Sarah Fielding's *The Cry* and the unattributed *The Histories of Some of the Penitents in the Magdalen-House*. Batchelor calls into question the privileging, following Watt, of formal realism, arguing that women writers contest a hostile reality through their rendering of plainly fictitious plots. Thus, in decades in which the morality of the novel's truth-function underwent close scrutiny, women invited their readers 'to confront the limitations of fiction as a representational mode'; in writing plain fiction, women were calling reality into question. Curran follows this in Chapter 9 with a reappraisal of the textual relationship between Charlotte Smith and Mary Wollstonecraft. Pointing out the unexamined 'quiet doubling of titles' between Smith's *The Romance of Real Life* and Wollstonecraft's *Original Stories from Real Life*, Curran shows that by the decades of the French Revolution, the real and the fictive had converged in the representation of women in the novel. Smith 'forces the novel to a new level of realism' and 'continually tests her readers to accommodate unsettling truths and distasteful circumstances', while Wollstonecraft, in her 'most powerful rendering of the real', writes Jemima in *Maria* as an 'existential proletariat' who would be more at home in the nineteenth-century novel. This forward-looking characteristic is shared by the subjects of Looser's Chapter 11, Anna and Jane Porter, whose self-belief as novelistic trailblazers – their 'historical fiction broke new ground' – resonates particularly strongly in decades in which Scott assumed his eminence. The Porters engaged with battle scenes and created heroic and sympathetic soldiers based on historical figures, but within a fictitious context, and thus showed how romance and reality could fuse, but they continually felt overlooked, their professionalism underestimated. Looser identifies what she calls the 'self-assurance topos', 'ripe to appear during an era in which the professional woman novelist experienced a great rise in popularity and status, followed by an equally great and precipitous fall' – the fall into the expectation of domestic confinement so aptly imaged by Austen's two inches of ivory. In Chapter 14, Murphy takes up the challenge of situating Jane Austen within her novelistic context, and finds that even as Austen records within her writing her interest in and indebtedness to her female contemporaries and forebears, she also published just at the point where 'the revisionist attempts of the newly professionalised, male-dominated critical industry to erase the earlier efforts of women writers and commentators on the novel' was under way. As Murphy notes, this 'industry ... seemed entrenched by the beginning of the Victorian period'. As these four chapters show, women novelists, even as they advanced ideas of the real and the imaginary, also recorded their anxieties about loss.

Loss is also a theme that links the chapters by Kate Davies and Harriet Guest, though to different effects, and complemented by a tentative move towards gain, as discussed by Betsy Bolton. In Chapter 6, Davies concentrates on Helen Maria Williams's *Ode on the Peace* as almost uniquely, in the period, a 'poem *of* the peace .... [It is] a text whose principal concern is the response *to* the war, rather than the war itself' (first emphasis added), and it figures that response 'in the emotive and pleasurable spectacle' of grieving women whose emotion can be translated into a 'nationalist sensibility that prompts everyone to suffer everyone else's suffering'. Women's response to war can only ever be emotional if it is to be endorsed, but that very display of emotion enables a new national response; hence, Williams's *Ode* becomes as central a text to the post-war period as any parliamentary Act, and here and in her other poetry Williams 'is producing a nationalist poetry' that centralizes, rather than sidelines, feminized responses to state-sanctioned violence and its aftermath. Only ten years later, as Guest shows in Chapter 10, the national impulse has changed, and the poems that Charlotte Smith and Mary Robinson published in 1793 reflect what has become 'the difficult politics of sensibility'. Unlike Williams, who seemed able to appeal to, or create, a cohesively emotional readership, neither Smith nor Robinson can count on or appeal to a seamless response. Not only is emotion suspect (and the poets' concentration on Marie Antoinette as a symbol enhances this, given her association with emotional excess both positive and negative), so too are emotional displays in a decade wherein restraint, fortitude, and self-control were the safest routes. Thus the political and politicized poetry of Smith and Robinson reflects the changing social understanding of feeling, and laments it; where Williams's *Ode* filled hungry hearts, their poems mirror an increasing national emptiness. Joanna Baillie's *Plays on the Passions* focalize this emphasis on feeling and its performative affect, and as Bolton shows in Chapter 12, this coalesces around the topoi of emblem and allegory as filtered through comedy. Baillie's 'comedy' is not farce, but rather an intellectual stance, a mode drawing on themes of history and personal and cultural re-evaluation. Baillie, as 'the most respected female dramatist of the early nineteenth century', straddled the line between the closet and the stage; as Bolton argues, her theatricalization of the passions as filtered through history and genre are themselves emblematic of women's drama: 'at the turn of the century, theatrical form held out important possibilities for female power and influence'.

Davies, Guest, and Bolton thus explore the interface between writing and displaying feeling, about conflict in a public and named way. Betty Schellenberg (Chapter 3) considers an aspect of writing that is often held to function on a separate plane: women's manuscript writings in the form of letters, journals, and manuscript poetry. As a coterie, the Bluestockings participated in a mode Schellenberg calls 'scribal practice', using the private circulation of texts to forward their intellectual and literary projects. But Schellenberg offers the intriguing suggestion that 'many mid-century forms of print publication are embedded in, and shaped by, conversation and manuscript circulation' and that 'Bluestocking women might be recognized as a significant force *through*, not *despite*, their use of ostensibly private modes.' The public/private model thus is further called into question, as is a generic binary that distinguishes the published from the unpublished. As Batchelor also shows in her investigation of the fictitiousness of reality, such binaries are increasingly unworkable once women's writing is fully a part of literary history. But these contributions, spanning as they do the mid-eighteenth to the early nineteenth century, also chart the changing cultural function of such modes and binaries. By the early nineteenth century, as Harriet Kramer Linkin shows in Chapter 15, the private world of the coterie has become more guarded and more familial, and sociability itself, whether worldly or textual, is presented more as a temptation than an accepted aspect of a woman's life. We might see in Mary Tighe's preference for coterie circulation evidence of a shift from a public style of authorship to a proto-Victorian emphasis on domesticized femininity, but we can also see the conflict this engenders; in *Psyche*, the protagonist is made to choose, frequently, between the attractions of the coterie's sociability and its potential for her to participate as a poet, and her quest to regain domestic security. Linkin's essay implies that what was possible for the Bluestockings – a public privacy – is no longer an option by the early 1800s: as she expresses it, 'coterie authorship enabled Tighe to circumvent the anxieties of publication but ultimately frustrated her desire for fame'.

Tighe, as Linkin shows, writes partly as an Irish woman, her coterie Dublin-based. In Chapter 8, Deirdre Coleman, too, demonstrates a connection between regional identities and a sense of writing as a project. In her study of abolition poems published between 1788 and 1792, she notes a move from the urban, English poetics of Hannah More, Ann Yearsley, and Helen Maria Williams to the regionalized voice of Mary Birkett, writing from Ireland. Place allies with politics: although written from different points of view, united only by their opposition to the trade and practice of slavery, such poems would make no sense if their authors and their readers viewed women as thoroughly divided from the public sphere; moreover, the writers themselves could not hope to have much of an impact if they wrote from a sheltered, anonymous position. Their 'powerful intervention[s]' emanated from an activist desire 'to make their mark in the extra-parliamentary arena', and was predicated on an understanding of the British character as intrinsically enlightened and therefore 'shamed' by slavery. Abolition poems thus argue 'for the public and central role of women's economic [and literary] power', presenting women as able to effect change and as seeing themselves in the role of social and cultural arbiters. The idea that national identity can be reflected in, even inflected by, writing is key to Sarah Prescott's essay exploring the emerging field of Anglophone Welsh writing. Prescott's essay shows new ways in which women's writing can emanate from a sense of geography and locatedness. Although this has long been a major component of Romantic studies, especially focusing on associations such as those represented by the Lake School and the Cockney School, Prescott reveals how a poetic identification with place pre-dates the traditionally masculine parameters of Romanticism; further, her study of Jane Cave and Anne Penny suggests ways in which the 'predominantly Anglo-centred' approach to 'British' women's writing might enlarge its boundaries. Whether through a language of religion, or through the recovery of a Celtic past 'fuelled by the antiquarian work of Welsh scholars and the patriotic London-Welsh societies', Cave and Penny bring the politics of identity into their poetry, along the way claiming the positions of lay preacher and informed antiquarian. Thus, as with abolition and coterie poetry, a sense of national as well as personal identity is formulated and communicated to these poets' readers.

The domestic focus of the earlier decades expands in the post-Napoleonic wars period, when Europe re-enters public consciousness as a viable destination, although, as Diego Saglia shows in Chapter 13, there is a discernible internationalism in the poetry of writers like Smith, Robinson, and Williams to counter what Peter Mortensen has characterized as the Europhobia of the late eighteenth century.[24] Saglia describes women writers as 'active contributors of domestic, local, and regional kinds of literature that ultimately feed into, expand, and enhance the store of national culture', which nicely sums up the impact of Linkin's, Coleman's, and Prescott's essays. But he sees the early nineteenth century as a period in which women writers 'explore foreign traditions, past and present, and enmesh their own production, and British literature at large, in an increasingly complex web of intercultural exchanges'.

Although many of these writers did not physically travel in the ways that Byron and Percy Shelley did, nonetheless their writing displays a Europhilia expressed through the modes of translation, adaptation, and a kind of textual ventriloquism. As Katherine Turner (Chapter 2) makes plain, however, a good many women did travel, to a variety of European and global destinations, and saw their voyages as not only culturally acceptable but also as educational, undertaken for personal enrichment but also to set examples for other female potential travellers. Turner shows that from the middle of the eighteenth century onwards, women travelled frequently and widely, and publishing their travel writings 'conferred upon them, if only for one print run and a couple of reviews, the status of authoritative cultural commentator'. This search for author/itative status belies the still-common assumption that women did not seek publicity; Turner's essay establishes the fact that, as it 'opens up amazing vistas into newly discovered worlds [while also] expos[ing readers] to the sheer tedium of travelling', women's travel writing fully enrols female travellers as serious cultural commentators.

The explorations of identities and cultures evident in these four chapters once again challenge the stereotype that women wrote domestically and subjectively. Current cultural concerns are as much a focus of their work as it is of their male counterparts, balancing the explorations of genre and form they also undertook. And as Saglia's range of writers shows – from Williams to Rose Lawrence in the 1830s – the neatness of this volume's date divisions are indeed no more than tidying devices, as is further demonstrated by the remaining essays. Two take on the idea of transition: in Chapter 7, Donna Landry explores how representations of benevolence take us from Sarah Fielding to Romantic Pantisocracy, while in Chapter 16, Stephen Behrendt charts how poetic memorials spanning generations as often seek to establish the writer's presence as they do to perpetuate the memory of the lost forebear. Landry, like Batchelor, sees Fielding as key to an understanding of generic development in the mid-eighteenth century; she shows how Fielding and her contemporaries wrote 'materially grounded' narratives in which sentimental charity was figured through 'actual material and monetary giving'. This kind of textual generosity allows women to at least achieve a kind of financial independence in the imaginary realm, which, although it has little impact in the real world, shows their intellectual engagement with ideas of need and accountability. Looking forward to the late eighteenth century, and backward to 'the radical religious enlightenment of the seventeenth century', Landry's essay is predicated on the basis that 'women's writing sometimes suggests alternative periodizations to traditional literary historical ones', and that it enrols women in a process of social engineering that valued the redistribution of wealth, and that showed, for instance, Wordsworth's 'poetry of emotion' as directly deriving from the novelistic benevolence of Fielding, Mary Collyer, Elizabeth Justice, and others. So Enlightenment becomes Romantic; or, rather, decades resolve, sometimes dissolve, into their successors. Behrendt's treatment of the transition from the Romantic to the Victorian makes this plain. Tracing the way in which the ungendered term 'poet' became the highly gendered, and insubstantial, term 'poetess', he also, like Linkin, follows a movement of changing legitimacies: 'the poet*ess* may lament the loss of the woman *as domestic female*, [but] the *poet* necessarily memorializes the woman *as public figure*, as activist in the arena of public affairs'. Smith is remembered as a poet, Tighe as a poetess. As Behrendt shows, women were aware of the underlying dichotomy and the perils of such labelling, and he plots moments of self-presentation and representation from the 1790s to the 1830s. By the 1830s, something has happened; the ease with publicity and the mutually-effecting 'spheres' of the public and the private have hardened into a new separation: incipient Victorianism with its socially-mandated rigidities, a mode so familiar that its affects resonate backwards. From there we receive the first studies of 'women writers' as a separate, anxious, and oppressed crew, instead of the population of diverse, committed, socially- and politically-aware women, artistically up-to-date as well as innovative, for whom the years 1750–1830 represented textual expansion and prominence on an entirely new scale. This is made clear in Michelle Levy's richly-detailed essay, with which this collection opens and which maps a print culture marked by women's participation as authors, readers, publishers, and distributors, what she calls 'women's thorough enmeshment in the material history of print'. Watts's 'quantitative dominance' comes alive in Levy's tracing of women's literary and commercial activities, increasingly available through print and online databases and bibliographies.

In practice, a volume of this type could never hope to be comprehensive; there are simply too many women writing, in all genres and across all class lines, for a study of the period 1750–1830 to be anything other than selective. In the space available, the essays herein have opened many new avenues of study and reiterated the centrality of women to the development of modern literary culture. There could have been more done with the sheer volume of poetry written by women in the last half of the eighteenth century, exploring their innovations as well as their combinations of styles as hinted at only briefly in my discussion of 'Washing Day' above. Women's writings about empire and imperialism, their invention of a literature specifically aimed at children, and their innovative participation in the fields of science, history-writing, philosophy, and translation studies all deserve attention.[25] In other words, much has been left out, but in being omitted, and not by choice, these gaps verify the complete presence and meaningfulness of women writing between 1750 and 1830. No matter the literary movement, style, development, or innovation, we see women writing, and cannot deny the conviction that without them, the history of British writing would be rather less exciting than these essays show it to be.

Notes

1. See J.M.S. Tompkins, *The Popular Novel in England 1770–1800* (London: Methuen and Co Ltd, 1932), p. v. Although Tompkins does not limit her study to women writers, they form the bulk of her examples.
2. See Ian Watt, *The Rise of the Novel: Studies in Defoe, Richardson and Fielding* (1957; London: Hogarth Press, 1987). Watt notes towards the end of his book that 'the majority of eighteenth-century novels were actually written by women, but this had long remained a purely quantitative assertion of dominance; it was Jane Austen who completed the work that Fanny Burney had begun, and challenged masculine prerogative in a much more important manner' (p. 298). Watt's language is instructive; he situates the history of writing as another form of the battle of the sexes, with masculine dominance of the form as a right – a 'prerogative' – and Austen's and Burney's triumphs as due to their 'feminine sensibility'. Meanwhile, the 'quantitative' dominance of women writers is easily dismissed.
3. See *The Cambridge Companion to the Eighteenth-Century Novel*, ed. John Richetti (Cambridge: Cambridge University Press, 1996). 'Women Writers and the Eighteenth-Century Novel', by Jane Spencer, is found on pp. 212–36.
4. See *The Cambridge Companion to English Literature, 1740–1830*, ed. Thomas Keymer and Jon Mee (Cambridge: Cambridge University Press, 2004), esp. chapters 8–16.
5. '"Unsex'd females": Barbauld, Robinson and Smith', in *The Cambridge Companion to English Literature, 1740–1830*, p. 215.
6. Ellen Moers, *Literary Women: The Great Writers* (Garden City, NY: Anchor Books, 1977) and Sandra Gilbert and Susan Gubar, *The Madwoman in the Attic: The Woman Writer and the Nineteenth-Century Imagination* (1979; New Haven: Yale University Press, 1984). See also, of course, Elaine Showalter, *A Literature of their Own: British Women Novelists from Brontë to Lessing* (Princeton: Princeton University Press, 1977), and Patricia Meyer Spacks, *The Female Imagination* (London: George Allen and Unwin, 1975). Showalter and Spacks, like Moers and Gilbert and Gubar, focus on the nineteenth and twentieth centuries, although Spacks devotes some space to Burney in addition to Austen.

7. In the discussion that follows I describe what I see as touchstone texts of the 1980s, 1990s, and 2000s. There will inevitably be omissions, which are due only to space constraints and the parameters of my prose rather than any value judgements. As the work to enlarge the canon and properly represent women's literary achievements is an ongoing process, any attempt to capture an overview of that process is dogged by what gets left out.

8. Mary Anne Schofield and Cecilia Macheski, eds, *Fetter'd or Free? British Women Novelists, 1670–1815* (1986; Athens, OH: Ohio University Press, 1987). It's necessary to at least mention Cora Kaplan's *Sea Changes: Essays on Culture and Feminism* (London: Verso, 1986), which follows a nuanced psychological methodology in its approach to texts from the late eighteenth century on. Kaplan, like the others discussed so far, works within Moers's 'modern' period. In addition, Moira Ferguson publishes, in 1985, her anthology *First Feminists: British Women Writers 1578–1799* (Bloomington: Indiana University Press, 1985), which repopulates with the detail missing in earlier publications the two centuries preceding this 'modern' era.

9. See Sarah W.R. Smith, 'Men, Women, and Money: The Case of Mary Brunton', in Schofield and Macheski, *Fetter'd or Free?* pp. 40–58. *Fetter'd or Free* was reprinted in paperback in 1987: a significant achievement for an academic study.

10. Jane Spencer, *The Rise of the Woman Novelist: From Aphra Behn to Jane Austen* (1986; Oxford: Basil Blackwell, 1987). Dale Spender's *Mothers of the Novel* (London: Pandora, 1986) appeared in the same year and, although more polemical in tone, made an equally compelling case for the intricate connections between the novel's development and women's writing. In addition, her series *Mothers of the Novel*, published by Pandora Press throughout the 1980s, made many of these novels available for the first time in centuries in affordable paperback editions.

11. I am grateful to Cora Kaplan and Jennie Batchelor both for the phrase 'the bearer of modernity' and for the insights on Armstrong's text.

12. Stuart Curran's two contributions to his own (as editor) *The Cambridge Companion to British Romanticism* (Cambridge: Cambridge University Press, 1993) run a close joint second: 'Women Readers, Women Writers' and 'Romantic Poetry: Why and Wherefore?' sharply observe not merely the presence but the formative influence of women writers in the Romantic period, concluding that 'our own reimagining of them will have a profound effect on our conception of the Romantic age' ('Women Readers, Women Writers', p. 195) – as indeed they have had.

13. Janet Todd, *The Sign of Angellica: Women, Writing and Fiction, 1660–1800* (London: Virago, 1989). Todd notes that she has 'not tried to weave history into literature' but instead has 'juxtaposed' fiction 'to the more historical chapters' (p. 3).

14. Roger Lonsdale's *Eighteenth-Century Women Poets* (1989; Oxford University Press, 1990) is of course another essential anthology; its more than 500 pages of poetry considerably revised readers' expectations of who wrote what in the period, as well as how many were writing.

15. Dale Spender, ed., *Living by the Pen: Early British Women Writers* (New York: Teachers College Press, 1992). An indication of the increasing mainstreaming of

'women writers' is Jane Stevenson's *Women Writers in English Literature* (Harlow: Longman, 1992), which spans the Anglo-Saxon era to the modern period.

16. Elizabeth Eger, Charlotte Grant, Clíona Ó Gallchoir, and Penny Warburton, eds, *Women, Writing and the Public Sphere, 1700–1830* (Cambridge: Cambridge University Press, 2001), p. 3.

17. Devoney Looser, *British Women Writers and the Writing of History, 1670–1820* (Baltimore: Johns Hopkins University Press, 2000). The phrase 'cultural authority' is Mellor's; see Chapter 4 of Anne K. Mellor, *Mothers of the Nation: Women's Political Writing in England, 1780–1830* (2000; Bloomington: Indiana University Press, 2002), pp. 85–102.

18. Betty A. Schellenberg, *The Professionalization of Women Writers in Eighteenth-Century Britain* (Cambridge: Cambridge University Press, 2005). Norma Clarke, in *The Rise and Fall of the Woman of Letters* (London: Pimlico, 2004), reads the 'woman of letters' as a central 'public figure' in the eighteenth century, 'intensely and inescapably political' (p. 2), although she loses her hold in the wake of Godwin's misconceived *Memoirs of the Author of the Vindication of the Rights of Woman*.

19. 'Elegy', 'The Peasant of the Alps' (*Celestina*, 1791; *Elegiac Sonnets*, 1792), 'The Female Exile' and 'The Forest Boy' (1792) all function clearly as lyrical ballads in style, tone, and structure, and raise interesting and essential questions of influence given Wordsworth's deep reading and appreciation of Smith's writing.

20. It should, however, be noted that most of the poems appeared in the early months of 1800 in the *Morning Post*; see Judith Pascoe, ed., *Mary Robinson; Selected Poems* (Peterborough, ON: Broadview Press, 2000), pp. 394–429 *passim*.

21. Because the 'Romantic novel' is still a relatively new category, there has been less periodizing associated with fiction, especially after 1778 when Burney published *Evelina*. As the preface to this novel suggests, the issue with prose is less about period than it is about gender, a proposition that is confirmed by Jennie Batchelor's chapter below. However, one might consider how the trope of sensibility and its attendant genre of romance develops from the 1750s onwards. By the time Austen publishes, each has undergone a number of permutations, yet Austen can reference both the quixotic devotion to romance of Lennox's *The Female Quixote* (1752) and the developments in the portrayal of sensibility from Burney, through Smith and Edgeworth, all in one text: I speak, of course, of *Northanger Abbey*.

22. An analogous example in male writing might be William Wordsworth, whose post-'Romantic' writing is routinely ignored by scholars for whom 'Wordsworthian' is synonymous with 'Romanticism'. Up until the last few years, most of Wordsworth's later writings have distressed critics, for whom it is neither really Romantic nor Victorian. That he, and other writers whose oeuvre spans more than one literary era such as the women discussed in this volume, might stand as a salutary lesson in the relative uselessness of such distinctions is seldom discussed.

23. Here, the work of Clarke, *Rise and Fall*, and Susan Staves, *A Literary History of Women's Writing in Britain, 1660–1789* (Cambridge: Cambridge University Press, 2006) is especially resonant.

24. See Mortensen, *British Romanticism and Continental Influences: Writing in an Age of Europhobia* (Basingstoke: Palgrave Macmillan, 2004).

25. See, for instance, Margaret Alic, *Hypatia's Heritage: A History of Women in Science from Late Antiquity to the Late Nineteenth Century* (London: The Women's Press, 1986); Ann B. Shteir, *Cultivating Women, Cultivating Science: Flora's Daughters and Botany in England, 1760 to 1860* (Baltimore: Johns Hopkins University Press, 1999); Patricia Fara, *Pandora's Breeches: Women, Science, and Power in the Enlightenment* (London: Pimlico, 2004); Looser, *British Women Writers*; Karen O'Brien, *Women and Enlightenment in Eighteenth-Century Britain* (Cambridge: Cambridge University Press, 2009); Barbara Taylor, *Mary Wollstonecraft and the Feminist Imagination* (Cambridge: Cambridge University Press, 2003); Susan Bassnett, *Translation Studies* (London: Routledge, 2002).

Further Reading

Armstrong, Isobel and Virginia Blain (eds), *Women's Poetry in the Enlightenment: The Making of a Canon, 1730–1820* (Basingstoke: Macmillan, 1999).

Armstrong, Nancy, *Desire and Domestic Fiction: A Political History of the Novel* (New York: Oxford University Press, 1990).

Backscheider, Paula. *Eighteenth-Century Women Poets and Their Poetry: Inventing Agency, Inventing Genre* (Baltimore: Johns Hopkins University Press, 2005).

Breen, Jennifer, *Women Romantic Poets, 1785–1832* (London: Dent Everyman, 1992).

Feldman, Paula R., ed., *British Women Poets of the Romantic Era: An Anthology* (Baltimore: Johns Hopkins University Press, 1997).

Feldman, Paula R. and Theresa M. Kelley, eds, *Romantic Women Writers: Voices and Countervoices* (Hanover, NH: University Press of New England, 1995).

Guest, Harriet, *Small Change: Women, Learning, Patriotism, 1750–1810* (Chicago: University of Chicago Press, 2000).

Homans, Margaret, *Women Writers and Poetic Identity: Dorothy Wordsworth, Emily Brontë, and Emily Dickinson* (Princeton: Princeton University Press, 1980).

Labbe, Jacqueline M., ed., *Charlotte Smith in British Romanticism* (London: Pickering and Chatto, 2008).

Landry, Donna. *Muses of Resistance: Laboring-Class Women's Poetry in Britain, 1739–1796* (Cambridge: Cambridge University Press, 1990).

Mahl, Mary R. and Helene Koon, eds, *The Female Spectator: English Women Writers Before 1800* (Bloomington: Indiana University Press, 1977).

Mellor, Anne K., ed., *Romanticism and Feminism* (Bloomington: Indiana University Press, 1988).

Mellor, Anne K., *Romanticism and Gender* (New York: Routledge, 1993).

Nussbaum, Felicity and Laura Brown, eds, *The New Eighteenth Century: Theory, Politics, English Literature* (New York: Methuen, 1987).

Rogers, Katherine M. and William McCarthy, eds, *The Meridian Anthology of Early Women Writers: British Literary Women from Aphra Behn to Maria Edgeworth, 1660–1800* (New York: New American Library, 1987).

Poovey, Mary, *The Proper Lady and the Woman Writer: Ideology as Style in the Works of Mary Wollstonecraft, Mary Shelley, and Jane Austen* (Chicago: University of Chicago Press, 1984).

Ross, Marlon, *The Contours of Masculine Desire: Romanticism and the Rise of Women's Poetry* (New York: Oxford University Press, 1989).

Uphaus, Robert W. and Gretchen M. Foster, eds, *The 'Other' Eighteenth Century: English Women of Letters, 1660–1800* (East Lansing, MI: Colleagues Press, 1991).

Wilson, Carol Shiner and Joel Haefner, eds, *Re-Visioning Romanticism: British Women Writers, 1776–1837* (Philadelphia: University of Pennsylvania Press, 1994).

Part I
1750–1830: Overviews

1
Women and Print Culture, 1750–1830

Michelle Levy

When asked to give a lecture on 'women and fiction' in 1928, Virginia Woolf admitted to being confounded at the possibilities: 'Women and fiction might mean ... women and what they are like; or it might mean women and the fiction that they write; or it might mean women and the fiction that is written about them; or it might mean that somehow all three are inextricably mixed together.'[1] Any attempt to examine the ostensibly broader category of women and print, even if confined to the period 1750–1830, suffers from the same problem of inexhaustibility.

To date, most of the scholarly effort devoted to women and print has focused on recovering acts of female authorship – with the result that the work of a handful of later eighteenth and early nineteenth-century women writers is now reasonably well known, and is taught in specialized, field-based courses at college level. Yet even the dozen or so writers who appear with some regularity in anthologies represent only the tip of the iceberg: thousands of women participated directly in print culture as authors, editors, and translators, though much of their work is entirely forgotten, and indeed may not survive in even a single copy.[2] While online databases and anthologies are improving access to existing materials, and other resources now provide critical information about the lives of many women writers, female authorship is only the best documented area of women's involvement with print; very little is known about the much larger class of women (and girls) who participated in other ways in the print world.[3] For women not only wrote books but sold them and other forms of print on street corners and in shops; they set type and ran circulating libraries; they coloured illustrations and engraved frontispieces; and they wrote anonymous reviews and sent contributions (usually anonymous or pseudonymous) in vast quantities to periodicals and newspapers. In short, they were authors, publishers, printers, distributors, sellers, and critics of the vast quantities of printed material that appeared during these eight decades, and they read or were otherwise exposed to all forms of print.[4] Indeed, as Vivien Jones observes, the widespread practices of reciting ballads and broadsides, and adapting popular print texts for the stage and other dramatic forms, meant that 'print culture profoundly affected the lives of many who could not actually read'.[5] Given that female literacy generally lagged behind that of men, their exposure to print through oral culture was perhaps even more significant than it was for men.[6]

The recovery of forgotten women writers has necessarily preceded attention to the broader and arguably more elusive topic of women and print culture. Yet the time seems ripe for further study in this wider field, particularly since many of the most pervasive myths about female authorship – that women didn't begin to write until some specified historical moment; that if they wrote, it was not for print; that if women wrote for print, they did so anonymously, and without commercial or critical success – have all, one after the other, been debunked.[7] Now that we know women wrote vast quantities of print, that in large numbers they attached their name to their writing, and that they earned both material reward and fame, we might move beyond the study of individual (or small groups of) women to begin to consider the full range of women's involvement in print during the period.

Of course, women's engagement with print was in many respects indistinguishable from men's: their books were sold beside one another in the same shops and reviewed in the same journals, and many women worked alongside men, as authors and in printing houses and bookshops. Just as there were no 'separate spheres' that divided men and women's literary productions, there were no separate print cultures for men and women. And yet most book historians tend to assume that the participants of print culture are genderless; Robert Darnton's famous conception of the communications circuit and his accompanying diagram, depicting a circuit from author to reader, is silent on the question of gender.[8] It is undeniable, however, that gender impacted women's involvement with print, in large part because Woolf's central insight in *A Room of One's Own* about the effects of women's dependent economic position holds true throughout the period 1750–1830. Women faced challenges and opportunities unique to their sex, and these special circumstances inevitably bear upon their interactions with print culture. For example, it was women, by and large, who were attacked for their authorship and consumption of novels; it was women who, as authors, initiated genres that related directly to women's experience and needs;

indeed, everything from what they wrote to where they wrote, from how they presented themselves and their texts to the public to how they were received, was inflected by their gender.[9] Women also appear to have been beneficiaries of the late eighteenth-century print boom, insofar as their participation in particular fields of culture increased at higher rates than did their male counterparts. In the following chapter, I attempt to offer a gendered account of the communications circuit, emphasizing those aspects of women's involvement in the print world that were appreciably different to men's. Much of the discussion will focus on female authorship, as the area most thoroughly researched. Nevertheless, I do hope to suggest lines of inquiry into the much larger role women played in British print culture during the period 1750–1830.

Women and literary production

The late eighteenth century occupies an important place in print history, for it was in the closing decades that Britons experienced a 'print avalanche', an expansion in printed materials unequalled since the invention of the press.[10] Between 1750 and 1775 the total number of print titles available in Britain rose from 2000 to 3000; over the next twenty-five years they rose even more sharply, from 3000 to 8000.[11] Research conducted over the past few decades has made it possible to quantify women's contribution to the overall growth in print production, particularly for the novel, which has been the subject of comprehensive bibliographical survey. During the period 1770–1830, the overall number of new novels published each decade rose from 315 in the 1770s and 405 in the 1780s to 700 new titles in the 1790s, and then fluctuated above and below this number for the next 30 years with 770 titles in the 1800s, 662 in the 1810s, and 824 in the 1820s.[12] Figure 1.1 charts the relative contributions of men and women to this overall growth (based on known attributions), from 1750 through 1830. Male contributions outstrip female production only at the start and end of the period, with the latter reversal possibly a result of Sir Walter Scott having effectively cleared the way for other male novelists.

We also know that 'individual women were more prolific than their more numerous male counterparts'.[13] Several of the period's women were fantastically productive, from Charlotte Smith, who wrote ten novels, to Anna Maria Mackenzie Johnson, who wrote 15, to Mary Meeke, who wrote a stunning 26, rivalling the indefatigable Sir Walter Scott.[14] This pattern continues through 1830: 13 of the 18 most prolific

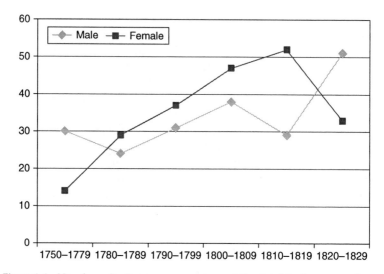

Figure 1.1   Novel production as a percentage of the total by known male and female authors, by decade, 1750–1830

Source: Data from Raven, 'Historical Introduction', I, 41–2 and Garside, 'The English Novel', II, 65–76. Both in *The English Novel 1770–1829*, 2 vols, ed. Peter Garside, James Raven, and Rainer Schowerling (Oxford and New York: Oxford University Press, 2000).

novelists (those who published 10 or more novels) working between 1800–29 were women.[15]

A similar pattern holds with respect to books of poetry. The period saw several prolific female poets: Felicia Hemans wrote 24 books of verse between 1808 and 1835; Hannah More wrote 30 between 1774 and 1833. J.R. de J. Jackson has traced the steady climb of women's volumes of poetry, starting from a low of four new editions in 1770 and steadily rising to 45 new editions in 1835.[16] Approximately 900 women wrote a total of 1402 new books of poetry during these decades, a number nearly identical to the 1375 novels that are known to have been written by women over the same sixty years.

The print boom also extended to children's literature, a genre in which women writers were particularly successful. Sarah Trimmer spoke with some disdain about the 'rage for new publications [that] is excited in the nation', such 'that even *children* are taught to expect a *daily supply of literature*, and a daily supply is industriously provided for their gratification'.[17] Yet it was women like Trimmer who dominated the field, penning books of all kinds for young persons as well as those aimed at parents on education, childrearing, cookery, and household management. Some women who had begun writing in other genres turned to children's books as a means of supplementing their incomes: children's books usually took less time to write, and required little or no research beyond what most women acquired by virtue of their domestic lives. Jane and Ann Taylor's *Original Poems* went through a staggering 31 editions between 1804 and 1832,[18] and a dozen of Priscilla Wakefield's books went into no less than 60 editions, not including piracies, in twenty years.[19] These books also often had very strong transatlantic sales (though these rarely benefited the authors, given the lack of international copyright agreements), and works by Anna Laetitia Barbauld, Maria Edgeworth, the Taylors, and Wakefield were continuously in print for decades.[20]

Women figured significantly in other genres as well: in drama (Joanna Baillie, Elizabeth Inchbald, Hannah Cowley); in literary criticism, as editors and reviewers (Barbauld, Mary Hays, Elizabeth Inchbald, Clara Reeve, Mary Wollstonecraft);[21] and they inaugurated or reinvented several subgenres, from Ann Radcliffe's powerful reimagining of the Gothic in the 1790s, to Joanna Baillie's psychological dramas and the feminist histories of Mary Matilda Betham, Lucy Aikin, and Mary Hays. Women's observations about life outside England also inaugurated new generic developments: Helen Maria Williams wrote an eight-volume eyewitness account of the French Revolution in *Letters from France* (1790–96), which reminded one reviewer of 'women's superiority to men in informal epistolarity, [or] "chatting on paper"'[22]; and Mary Prince's *The History of Mary Prince, a West Indian Slave* (1831) recounted her enslavement in the West Indies and attempts to secure her freedom in England, the first known narrative by a slave woman and one that records the unique suffering of female slaves. Women also penned countless memoirs, and it was not unknown for their letters and even their anecdotes to be published during their lifetimes or after their deaths. And they contributed to the boom in newspapers and periodicals as well as in other forms of popular print and ephemera, though their involvement has not yet been subject to independent study.[23]

While many female writers were chided as mere scribblers and 'Bluestockings', women themselves offered a more sympathetic explanation for their prodigious literary output. Writing was something that originated in their domesticity: they were expected to write letters, and it was customary in many families for women to keep journals of their home life and journeys, and to compose lessons, verse, and stories for the instruction and enjoyment of their domestic circle. Women's exclusion from the formal education received by men could also work to their advantage: in 'On Female Studies', Anna Barbauld points out that the professional skills men must acquire demand 'a great deal of severe study and technical knowledge; much of which is nowise valuable in itself'.[24] And in *Letters for Literary Ladies*, Maria Edgeworth went even further, arguing that because women were spared a classical education, they became better writers than men:

> The genius of living and of dead languages differs so much, that the pains which are taken to write elegant Latin frequently spoil the English style. – Girls usually write much better than boys; they think and express their thoughts clearly at an age when young men can scarcely write an easy letter upon any common occasion.[25]

Women and publication

Many women who wrote during the period from 1750 to 1830 did so with the clear aim of printing their work. More often than is acknowledged, however, women's intentions respecting their writing were more ambiguous. Indeed, a great proportion of the period's writing by both men and women arose within manuscript culture; specifically, it took the material form of what Donald Reiman has termed 'confidential' manuscripts, writing that was neither fully private nor public, but was intended for a circumscribed readership either known or presumed friendly to the author.[26] The confidential, sociable, occasional, and local aspects of this intermediary manuscript culture constitute a large quantity of late eighteenth and early nineteenth-century writing, as it had for previous generations. But what Margaret Ezell has termed 'social authorship' had undergone considerable changes at the end of the eighteenth century as a result of improved access to the press, such that many works that began in more private or sociable contexts rapidly migrated to more social and public media.[27]

The ease of this movement may in fact provide one of the reasons for women's prominence in later eighteenth and early nineteenth-century literary culture. Writing of all kinds was a part of their daily lives, through which they not only developed their abilities but became accustomed to having their work received and critiqued by others. Many authors were encouraged to print their confidential manuscripts only after their worth had been proven amongst a smaller circle of readers, as was the case with the poems that Anna Barbauld collected and printed in 1773 at her brother's urging. A similar trajectory is described for Barbauld and Aikin's shared six-volume miscellany for children, *Evenings at Home*, and in the advertisement to Barbauld's three-volume *Lessons for Children*: 'This little publication was made for a particular child, but the public is welcome to the use of it.'[28] More private forms of writing, such as the letters Mary and Percy Shelley wrote for friends and family during their two continental visits, were also, with slight revisions, printed (in their *History of a Six Weeks' Tour*); and indeed it seems that even when composing these letters to friends in England the Shelleys had an eye towards print publication.

The decision about whether to print one's writing, and if so under what conditions, was a complex one. Many women of the upper classes, including Susanna Blamire and Catherine Maria Fanshawe, shied away from print altogether, allowing their writing to circulate only in manuscript during their lifetimes. Mary Tighe elected a marginal print form for her *Psyche; or, the Legend of Love* in 1805, privately printing only 50 copies, which she distributed to friends and family. Other female authors had more difficulty in transforming their family writing for print. This was the case with Austen, who struggled to craft fiction that would be accepted by publishers: it was nearly two decades between the completion of the fair copy of her juvenile writing, in 1793, and the appearance in print of her first published novel, *Sense and Sensibility*, in 1811.[29] Other women encountered disapproval from family members and friends: Burney did not reveal to her father that she had written and published *Evelina, or, A Young Lady's Entrance into the World* (1778); Maria Edgeworth wrote her first book for print, *Letters for Literary Ladies* (1795), to rebut the strong views held by family friend Thomas Day against women publishing; and Ann Taylor would always recall the 'remark made by my father..., – "I do not want my girls to be authors."'[30]

For most women, however, economic need overcame any objections that there might have been to print. While some women, like Jane Austen and Dorothy Wordsworth, sought to become print authors to supplement otherwise modest incomes, others were motivated by more desperate circumstances: Charlotte Smith wrote from debtors' prison to secure the release of her bankrupt husband and to support her nine living children; and Felicia Hemans wrote to support her mother and five sons after her husband abandoned them. It was the rare woman who did not concern herself with money, and who published without hope of reward. Thus, even though both men and women could take advantage of the improved access to print at the end of the eighteenth century, the extremely limited career choices available to middle-class women made print authorship highly desirable. While Ann Taylor would speak of her father's decision to apprentice her and her sister as engravers as 'nearly the [only] respectable, remunerative, appropriate employment of young women', insisting that, 'we were never ashamed of it', both sisters abandoned engraving at the earliest opportunity for the more refined and, for them, more lucrative profession of authorship.[31] Women from the labouring classes had an even greater impetus to become published authors: whether as dairy maids (Ann Yearsley and Janet Little), servants (Elizabeth Hands and Charlotte Richardson), or washerwomen (Mary Collier), working women were subject to relentless, physically demanding labour for extremely low wages (Richardson was paid £4 per annum as a cook-maid). Even a single publication could earn sums it could take a lifetime (or several lifetimes) for a working woman to earn: Janet Little reportedly earned £50 for a collection of poems printed in 1792, and Ann Yearsley earned a staggering £600 profit for *Poems, on Several Occasions* in 1785.[32]

Women who wished to print their writing had to come to an agreement with a publisher. For new authors, these negotiations were often conducted by a male family member or patron, whereas more established female authors tended to deal directly with publishers themselves. As Jan Fergus has shown in her discussion of Austen's career, women generally had four choices available to them: sale of copyright, commission, profit sharing, and subscription.[33] By far the most common was the sale of the copyright, by which an author would receive a set fee regardless of sales. While sale of the copyright guaranteed a certain sum, the fees paid could be very low; for novels, they were 'usually pitiful', with one well-established publisher advertising the 'ominous starting price of 5 guineas'.[34] Female authors early in their careers had no choice but to accept these arrangements, though even the sale of the copyright did not ensure that the book would in fact be published: Austen sold the copyright for *Susan* (later *Northanger Abbey*) for £10, though the publisher declined (for reasons unknown) to print it. She sold her second printed novel, *Pride and Prejudice*, to another publisher for £110 – a disappointing sum (she had hoped for £150), and, ultimately, a poor arrangement for her, since it proved to be her most popular work, earning for the publisher at least £450 on the first two editions alone.[35] Similarly, the Taylor sisters, though initially happy with the earnings of £10 for the first volume and £15 for the second volume of *Original Poems*, quickly realized what a small proportion of the volumes' actual profits this represented; they had to wait until the copyright term expired in 1814 to negotiate a new fourteen-year term, which secured them about £600 a piece.[36]

After *Original Poems*, the Taylors quickly moved to publishing on commission, sometimes referred to as publishing 'on account of the author'; according to Ann, it was 'not until we began to publish for ourselves that we felt the solid advantage that literature might bring to us.'[37] In this arrangement, the author was responsible for all costs associated with printing and marketing the work, and the publisher retained 10 per cent commission from each copy sold. Their *Hymns for Infant Minds* (1810) earned the Taylors £150 over the first year – that is, nearly ten times what they received for all editions of *Original Poems* before 1814. It was a risky method for untried authors, for if sales were poor they could end up owing money to the publisher, but it was worthwhile for Charlotte Smith, who contracted with the well-known publishing houses of Dodsley and then Cadell for her *Elegiac Sonnets, and other Essays*, first published in 1784 and by 1800, in its ninth edition, filling two volumes.

Profit-sharing seems to have been favoured by some publishers; here, the publisher bore the expense of bringing the book to the market, and agreed to share profits (if there were any) equally with the author.[38] Amelia Opie earned most of her estimated £4280 lifetime earnings by profit-sharing.[39] Publication by subscription, though becoming less common, remained viable; here the author (or her patron) solicited subscribers in advance of publication. It was a widely used method for female labouring-class poets; according to Tim Burke, 'women were ... far more likely than their male counterparts to have their work presented for sale as an opportunity for the prospective reader to participate in an act of charitable rescue'.[40] Very large numbers of subscribers were found for some publications – Hannah More gathered more than 1000 names for Ann Yearsley's *Poems, on Several Occasions* in 1785, and 1935 individuals subscribed to Elizabeth Bentley's *Genuine Poetical Compositions* in 1791. The large sums earned by Yearsley and Bentley enabled their upward mobility: Yearsley purchased a circulating library, whereas Bentley kept a small boarding-school.[41] Yet these patronage relationships could quickly sour: More and Yearsley famously quarrelled about whether Yearsley should receive the entire profits from her first book without encumbrance. Established authors also used subscription to their advantage: Charlotte Smith did so selectively, as did Fanny Burney, who earned £1000 from subscribers plus that amount again from the sale of copyright.[42]

Some women, like Burney, were highly strategic in their publication decisions, and thus earned significant sums through their writing: Ann

Radcliffe earned an astonishing £500 for *The Mysteries of Udolpho* in 1794 and £800 for *The Italian* in 1797; Maria Edgeworth was paid £1050 for the second series of *Tales of Fashionable Life* in 1812 and £2100 for the less successful *Patronage* in 1814, and her lifetime earnings were just over £11,000. Charlotte Smith had earned £4190 by the end of her life.[43] Elizabeth Inchbald (a former actress) earned high fees for her nineteen plays – as much as £900 for *Such Things Are* in 1787 and £700 for *Every One has his Fault* in 1793 – both of which were performed and printed.[44]

But Inchbald, who was both financially successful and highly prolific, was the exception rather than the rule; most women earned very little from their writing, and most wrote no more than one title that appeared in print. Even women writers with considerable celebrity struggled to earn meaningful sums from their writing: during a four-and-a-half year period in which Mary Robinson published three novels, a sonnet sequence, and a play, she earned less than £10 from her publishers.[45] And Jane Austen – nearly the only female author whose work has remained both popular and critically acclaimed throughout the two hundred years since her death – earned only small amounts from her writing: it is estimated that her total lifetime earnings were no more than £630.[46] The overall record in terms of women's earnings is therefore mixed; on the one hand, some women were adept at negotiations with publishers, securing generous payments and favourable terms, including advances when this was not a common practice for male authors;[47] on the other hand, many women made poor decisions, either because they miscalculated the market or failed to understand publishing practices. Ultimately, as Edward Copeland has shown, very few female authors of the period – even the most successful – could subsist on their writing, and the vast majority of women, whose involvement with authorship was fleeting, earned only trifling sums.[48]

Most of the female writers already discussed, however, became prolific and successful and hence may be characterized as professional authors. According to Clifford Siskin, Betty Schellenberg, and Linda Zionkowski, authorship became increasingly professionalized during the eighteenth century, and many women participated fully in the literary marketplace as such.[49] Yet being a professional author did not mean subsisting on one's earnings. Furthermore, many women who earned little or nothing from their writing were highly professionalized – as measured by their commitment to their writing and their literary associations. Categorizing women as amateurs or professionals is a fraught exercise: how might we classify Dorothy Wordsworth, for example, who though she printed little laboured tirelessly on her writing? Women writers who appear to fit the amateur characterization more readily include the countless authors, most of whom are entirely unknown today (and indeed were hardly known in their own day), who published only a single work, printed in only a single edition, during their lifetimes. According to my calculations, of the 714 known poets in Jackson's bibliography *Romantic Poetry by Women*, 490 women, or 68 per cent of the cohort, published only a single volume of verse; a further 112 women, or 16 per cent, published two books of verse. According to Jackson's data, a full 84 per cent of all women poets in the Romantic period printed no more than two separate poetry titles. By contrast, only 43 women, or 6 per cent, wrote five or more titles, and only eight, or 1 per cent, wrote more than ten. Similarly, the novel was, according to James Raven, an 'ephemeral' production, with fewer than a quarter of the 3677 novels published between 1770 and 1829 being reprinted even once.[50] For the most part, the literary economy was driven by women (and men) without extraordinary expertise, talent, or ambition, most of whom made only a single, transitory appearance in print, creating in effect a 'long-tail' marketplace saturated with unpopular titles.[51]

The final decision that fell to female authors was whether they should put their names to their print publications or remain anonymous, the latter being a practice that was widely followed throughout the period. Women had a variety of options in this regard: many (and even a few men we know of) signed their works 'by a lady' (in the late 1780s, this signature accompanied 30 per cent of all novels); they signed works with the soubriquet 'by the author of', thereby indicating a body of work as a whole; they included identifying features in anonymous publications, such as dedications and place of publication, from which their names could be deciphered; and, though more uncommon, they used pseudonyms. Scholarship by Paula Feldman and Lee Erikson on the use of anonymity in women's poetry has demonstrated that care must be taken not to overstate women's dependency on this authorial device, and to distinguish between genres in which very disparate practices prevailed. In poetry, for example, anonymity was not the rule. According to Feldman,

[t]he evidence shows ... that during the period 1770–1835, women rarely published books of verse anonymously. With surprisingly few exceptions, women who published poetry books proudly placed their real names on the title page from the very outset of their careers. ... When a woman did bring out a book of poetry anonymously, it was

often her first book, and her name appeared quickly on the title pages of subsequent editions and later volumes.[52]

Feldman speculates that 'gender may not have been as much of an issue in anonymity as is sometimes supposed', and this is borne out by Lee Erikson's calculation that women were 'only slightly more inclined to publish anonymously at some time'.[53] Feldman notes that for most authors anonymity was 'often either a temporary state or a transparent pose', and Erikson similarly points out that few poets who met with any success remained anonymous.[54]

The difficulty that scholars face in evaluating the gendered use of anonymity is readily apparent when we turn to the novel. In the 1770s and 1780s anonymity was particularly common, with over 80 per cent of all novels published anonymously; this number drops to 60 per cent in the 1790s, and falls precipitously in the coming decades, to between 10 and 30 per cent from 1800 to 1830.[55] Feldman's conjecture that anonymity was less gendered than previously believed seems borne out in relation to the novel as well – though the data remain ambiguous in that many authors are still unidentified. Figure 1.2, which tracks

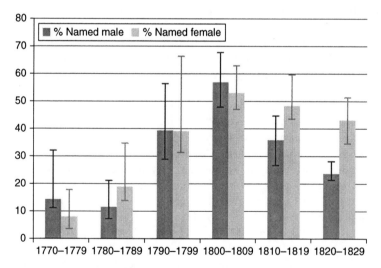

Figure 1.2 Named authorship of novels by men and women as a percentage of the total by gender, 1770–1830

Source: Data from Raven, 'Historical Introduction', I, 41–2 and Garside, 'The English Novel', II, 65–76. Both in *The English Novel 1770–1829*, 2 vols, ed. Peter Garside, James Raven, and Rainer Schowerling (Oxford and New York: Oxford University Press, 2000).

named authorship by men and women through the Romantic period as percentages of the total number of novels written by each gender, takes into account the uncertainty resulting from the high number of unidentified anonymous authors. Each error bar represents the range of possible percentages for each gender, with the upper end assigning all of the unattributed titles to the gender in question and the lower end assigning none; the solid bars show what would result if the unknown titles were assigned by gender in the same proportion as the known titles. What this figure reveals is that prior to 1790, few women or men named themselves as authors; that from 1790 through to 1810, men and women were equally likely to name themselves; and that from 1810 onward, women were more likely than men to name themselves. Thus it appears that, for most of the period, men were at least as likely as women (if not more so) to withhold their name from novel publication.

Women as publishers, printers, distributors, sellers, and readers

From at least the late seventeenth century, many women were directly involved in the business of print. According to William St Clair, widows but also unmarried daughters were active as owners and managers in large part 'to preserve the pre-emption rights in a guild system'; that is, women's involvement was necessary to ensure that the bookselling cartels that dominated the trade would remain closed to outsiders.[56] Most of our knowledge of women's activities as publishers and printers in Britain derives from the late seventeenth and early eighteenth centuries, largely through the work of Paula McDowell in *The Women of Grub Street*.[57] It may be, as both she and St Clair suggest, that women's work in the print trade declined between 1700 and 1800 as a result of the waning power of the bookselling cartels, particularly in the wake of the House of Lord's decision in 1774 ending perpetual copyright, but also as a result of the ascendant ideology of women's separation from work.[58] Even though the printing trade remained family-based and women undoubtedly continued to labour in these family businesses, as I argue elsewhere, 'middle-class respectability in the Romantic period was increasingly defined by an idealized separation *between* work and home, which demanded that women and children not be seen to engage in any form of productive labor.'[59]

Scholarship has uncovered only a few scattered examples of women's involvement in the printing business during the period under consideration. Mary Bryan took over her husband's printing business after his death, operating as 'Mary Bryan and Co.' in Bristol from 1815 to 1823; however, the business was so heavily indebted that Bryan, as an impoverished and widowed mother of six very young children, also attempted to support her family through authorship, (self-)publishing her *Sonnets and Metrical Tales* in 1815.[60] The female family members of radical publisher Richard Carlisle were also invested in the business; after he was imprisoned for publishing a work found to be blasphemous, his wife took over the business; and after she was imprisoned for continuing to sell the book, her sister took over from her.[61] Even less is known about the many working-class women and girls employed as engravers, illustrators, binders, and hand-colourists, and those who distributed and sold print. We also know very little about the large class of women writers who distributed more ephemeral forms of print, from newspapers to journals to pamphlets, broadsides, posters, and handbills. And the study of female readership is in its infancy.[62] Women's involvement in all aspects of print production, distribution, and reception is a field of social, economic, and literary history that bears much fuller investigation. It has taken feminist scholars thirty years to repopulate the literary landscape with forgotten female authors; in the decades to come, we should seek to develop an even broader understanding of women's thorough enmeshment in the material history of print.

Notes

1. Virginia Woolf, *A Room of One's Own and Three Guineas* (Oxford: Oxford University Press, 1992), p. 3.
2. James Raven, 'Historical Introduction: The Novel Comes of Age', in *The English Novel 1770–1829*, ed. by Peter Garside, James Raven, and Rainer Schowerling, 2 vols (Oxford and New York: Oxford University Press, 2000), I, 15–121 (pp. 18–19).
3. Important online databases of primary material include: British Women Playwrights around 1800 <http://www.etang.umontreal.ca/bwp1800/>; British Women Romantic Poets Project, 1789–1832 <http://digital.lib.ucdavis.edu/projects/bwrp/>; Brown University Women Writers Project <http://www.wwp.brown.edu/>; A Celebration of Women Writers <http://digital.library.upenn.edu/women/>; and Eighteenth-Century Collections Online <http://www.bestpoetry.com/DigitalCollections/products/ecco/>.
4. Paula McDowell makes a similar point in speaking of the late seventeenth and earlier eighteenth centuries: 'There was a vast network of women printers and publishers in Britain (especially London), and women participated in the new print culture not only as authors and readers but also as printers, booksellers, hawkers, ballad-singers and others.' 'Women and the Business

of Print', in *Women and Literature in Britain*, ed. by Vivien Jones (Cambridge: Cambridge University Press, 2000), p. 135.

5. 'Introduction', *Women and Literature in Britain*, ed. by Jones, p. 3.
6. It has been estimated that in the late eighteenth century, male literacy was around 60 per cent, female literacy about 40 per cent. See J. Paul Hunter, *Before Novels: The Cultural Contexts of Eighteenth-Century Fiction* (New York: Norton, 1990), p. 72.
7. Woolf argued that 1800 was the turning point: 'towards the end of the eighteenth century a change came about which, if I were rewriting history, I should describe more fully and think of greater importance than the Crusades or the Wars of the Roses. The middle-class woman began to write' (*A Room of One's Own*, p. 84).
8. See Robert Darnton, 'What is the History of Books', in *The Kiss of Lamourette: Reflections on Cultural History* (London: Faber and Faber, 1991), pp. 107–36.
9. Peter Garside, 'The English Novel in the Romantic Era: Consolidation and Dispersal', in *The English Novel 1770–1829*, ed. by Peter Garside, James Raven, and Rainer Schowerling, 2 vols (Oxford and New York: Oxford University Press, 2000), II, 15–103 (p. 17), and see *Women and Literature in Britain*, ed. by Jones, p. 4: 'it is women's writing that is repeatedly singled out for comment, a disproportionate reaction which raises questions not just about literacy levels, but about what literacy, and literariness, meant'.
10. James Raven, 'The Book Trades', in *Books and their Readers in Eighteenth-Century England: New Essays*, ed. by Isabel Rivers (London and New York: Leicester University Press, 2001), pp. 2–3.
11. James Raven, *The Business of Books: Booksellers and the English Book Trade 1450–1850* (New Haven: Yale University Press, 2007), p. 8.
12. Raven, 'Historical Introduction', I, 46–7; Garside, 'The English Novel', II, 73.
13. Raven, 'Historical Introduction', I, 48.
14. Raven, 'Historical Introduction', I, 39.
15. Garside, 'The English Novel', II, 64.
16. See J.R. de J. Jackson, *Romantic Poetry by Women, A Bibliography, 1770–1835* (Oxford: Oxford University Press, 2003), pp. 393–4.
17. Sarah Trimmer, *Guardian of Education*, 5 vols (London: Hatchard, 1802–07), I, 15–16.
18. Jackson, *Romantic Poetry*, pp. 324–6.
19. F.J. Harvey Darton, 'Children's Books', in *The Cambridge History of English and American Literature*, ed. by Ward and Trent et al. (New York: G.P. Putnam's Sons, 1907–21; New York: Bartleby.com, 2000) <http://www.bartleby.com/221/1611.html> [accessed 15 July 2009].
20. For a detailed account of the rise in children's book publications, see Michelle Levy, *Family Authorship and Romantic Print Culture* (Basingstoke: Palgrave Macmillan, 2008), pp. 71–81.
21. An examination of women's work in the reception of literary works is beyond the scope of this chapter; for scholarship on women's literary criticism generally see Anne Mellor, 'A Criticism of their Own: Romantic Women Literary Critics', in *Questioning Romanticism*, ed. by John Beer (Baltimore: Johns Hopkins University Press, 1995), pp. 29–48; Claudia Johnson, '"Let Me Make the Novels of a Country": Barbauld's "The British Novelists"',

NOVEL: A Forum on Fiction, 34(2) (2001), 163–79; and Mary A. Waters, *British Women Writers and the Profession of Literary Criticism, 1789–1832* (New York: Palgrave Macmillan, 2004).

22. Susan Brown, Patricia Clements, and Isobel Grundy, eds, Helen Maria Williams entry: Writing screen within Orlando: *Women's Writing in the British Isles from the Beginnings to the Present* (Cambridge: Cambridge University Press Online, 2006) <http://orlando.cambridge.org.proxy.lib.sfu.ca/> [accessed 9 June 2009].

23. For general studies of newspapers during the period, see Hannah Barker and Simon Burrows, eds, *Press, Politics and the Public Sphere in Europe and North America 1760–1820* (Cambridge: Cambridge University Press, 2002), pp. 5–6, and on magazines, see Mark Parker, *Literary Magazines and British Romanticism* (Cambridge: Cambridge University Press, 2000), and David Higgins, *Romantic Genius and the Literary Magazine: Biography, Celebrity and Politics* (London: Routledge, 2005); none of these studies, however, offers a gendered analysis of these print media.

24. *Selected Poetry and Prose of Anna Barbauld*, ed. by William McCarthy and Elizabeth Kraft (Peterborough, ON: Broadview Press, 2002), pp. 475–6.

25. Maria Edgeworth, *Letters for literary ladies. To which is added, an essay on the noble science of self-justification. The second edition* (London: J. Johnson, 1799), pp. 78–9.

26. Donald Reiman, *The Study of Modern Manuscripts: Public, Confidential, and Private* (Baltimore: Johns Hopkins University Press, 1993).

27. Margaret J.M. Ezell, *Social Authorship and the Advent of Print* (Baltimore: Johns Hopkins University Press, 1999), pp. 39–40.

28. *Lessons for Children from Two to Three Years Old* (London: J. Johnson, 1778), n. p.

29. See my forthcoming article, 'Austen's Manuscripts and the Publicity of Print' in *ELH*.

30. See Ann Taylor Gilbert, *Autobiography and other Memorials of Mrs Gilbert (formerly Ann Taylor)*, ed. by Josiah Gilbert (London: Henry S. King & Co., 1874), pp. 165, 102.

31. For more on the Taylors, see my discussion in *Family Authorship*, pp. 88–107.

32. Pam Perkins, 'Little, Janet (1759–1813)', *Oxford Dictionary of National Biography*, Oxford University Press, September 2004 <http://www.oxforddnb.com/view/article/40635> [accessed 2 June 2009]; Mary Waldron, 'Yearsley, Ann (bap. 1753, d. 1806)', *Oxford Dictionary of National Biography*, Oxford University Press, 2004 <http://www.oxforddnb.com/view/article/30206> [accessed 2 June 2009].

33. Jan Fergus, 'The Professional Woman Writer', in *The Cambridge Companion to Jane Austen*, ed. by Edward Copeland and Juliet McMaster (Cambridge: Cambridge University Press, 1997), pp. 12–31.

34. Raven, 'Historical Introduction', I, 50, 54.

35. Fergus, 'The Professional Woman Writer', p. 21.

36. See Ann Taylor Gilbert, *Autobiography and other Memorials of Mrs Gilbert (formerly Ann Taylor)*, p.169; and Linda David, *Children's Books Published by William Darton and his Sons: A Catalogue of an Exhibition at the Lilly Library, Indiana University, April–June, 1992* (Bloomington: Indiana University Press, 1992), p. 42.

37. Ann Taylor Gilbert, *Autobiography*, p. 190.
38. See Jan Fergus and Janice Farrar Thaddeus, 'Women, Publishers, and Money, 1790–1820', *Studies in Eighteenth-Century Culture*, 17 (1987), 191–207 (pp. 193–4).
39. Fergus and Thaddeus, 'Women, Publishers, and Money', p. 198.
40. *Eighteenth-Century English Labouring-Class Poets 1700–1800*, 3 vols, Volume III: 1780–1800, ed. by Tim Burke (London: Pickering and Chatto, 2003), p. xx.
41. See Mary Waldron, 'Yearsley' (note 32 above) and Donna Landry, 'Bentley, Elizabeth (bap. 1767, d. 1839)', *Oxford Dictionary of National Biography*, Oxford University Press, 2004 <http://www.oxforddnb.com/view/article/62688> [accessed 4 June 2009].
42. Jan Fergus has argued that this was highly unusual, a reflection of Burney's pre-eminence as a novelist ('The Professional Woman Writer', p. 16). For a detailed account of Burney's use of subscription, see Emma Pink, 'Frances Burney's Camilla: "To Print My Grand Work ... by Subscription"', *Eighteenth-Century Studies*, 40(1) (2006), 51–68.
43. See Raven, 'Historical Introduction', I, 52; Garside, 'The English Novel', II, 45; Fergus, 'The Professional Woman Writer', p. 28. For a comprehensive account of Smith's revenues and expenses, as well as the circumstances of her inheritance, see Judith Phillips Stanton, 'Charlotte Smith's "Literary Business": Income, Patronage, and Indigence', in *The Age of Johnson: A Scholarly Annual*, vol. 1, ed. by Paul Korshin (New York: AMS Press, 1987), pp. 375–401.
44. See Jane Spencer, 'Inchbald , Elizabeth (1753–1821)', *Oxford Dictionary of National Biography*, Oxford University Press, 2004 <http://www.oxforddnb. com/view/article/14374> [accessed 2 June 2009].
45. Fergus and Thaddeus, 'Women, Publishers, and Money', p. 196.
46. Fergus, 'The Professional Woman Writer', p. 28.
47. Fergus and Thaddeus, 'Women, Publishers, and Money', p. 199.
48. Edward Copeland, *Women Writing about Money: Women's Fiction in England, 1790–1820* (Cambridge: Cambridge University Press, 1995), pp. 191–212.
49. See Clifford Siskin, *The Work of Writing: Literature and Social Change in Britain, 1700–1830* (Baltimore: Johns Hopkins University Press, 1998); Betty A. Schellenberg, *The Professionalization of Women Writers in Eighteenth-Century Britain* (Cambridge: Cambridge University Press, 2005); and Linda Zionkowski, *Men's Work: Gender, Class, and the Professionalization of Poetry, 1660–1784* (New York: Palgrave Macmillan, 2001).
50. Raven, 'Historical Introduction', I, 35, 63; Garside, 'The English Novel', 97.
51. See Chris Anderson, *The Long Tail: Why the Future of Business is Selling Less of More* (New York: Hyperion, 2006).
52. Paula Feldman, 'Women Poets and Anonymity in the Romantic Era', *New Literary History* 33(2) (Spring 2002), 279–89 (p. 279).
53. Feldman, 'Women Poets', p. 281; Lee Erikson, '"Unboastful Bard": Originally Anonymous English Romantic Poetry Book Publication, 1770–1835', *New Literary History*, 33(2) (Spring 2002), 247–78 (p. 251).
54. Feldman, 'Women Poets', p. 281; Erikson, 'Unboastful Bard', p. 249.
55. Raven, 'Historical Introduction', I, 41–2; Garside, 'The English Novel', II, 74.
56. William St Clair, *The Reading Nation in the Romantic Period* (Cambridge: Cambridge University Press, 2005), p. 96.

57. See Paula McDowell, *The Women of Grub Street: Press, Politics, and Gender in the London Literary Marketplace 1678–1730* (Oxford: Oxford University Press, 1998), especially pp. 25–62. There is also comparatively more data on women's involvement in the printing trade in colonial America: see Marjorie Dana Barlow, *Notes on Woman Printers in Colonial America and the United States 1639–1975* (New York: University Press of Virginia, 1976), and Leona M. Hudak, *Early American Women Printers and Publishers 1639–1820* (New Jersey and London: Scarecrow Press, 1978).

58. See St Clair, *The Reading Nation*, p. 96, and McDowell, 'Women and the Business of Print', p. 149.

59. See Levy, *Family Authorship*, p. 72.

60. For more information on Bryan's writing career – she published a novel in 1829 – as well as her correspondence with Walter Scott, see Sharon Ragaz, 'Writing to Sir Walter: The Letters of Mary Bryan Bedingfield', *Cardiff Corvey: Reading the Romantic Text*, 7 (Dec 2001) <http://www.cf.ac.uk/ encap/corvey/ articles/cc07_n02.html> [accessed 3 June 2009].

61. St Clair, *The Reading Nation*, p. 313.

62. Jan Fergus has written one of the few empirical analyses of women's reading habits in the period: see 'Women Readers: A Case Study', in *Women and Literature in Britain*, ed. by Jones, pp. 155–75 and *Provincial Readers in Eighteenth-Century England* (Oxford: Oxford University Press, 2006).

2
Women's Travel Writing, 1750–1830

Katherine Turner

During the last twenty years, women's travel writing has moved defini-
tively into the foreground of the Romantic literary landscape, and
critical work has opened up global vistas onto women's experience
during this period. Although still under-represented in modern editions in comparison to their Victorian counterparts, the primary texts
are becoming more widely available, in traditional book format and
through electronic resources like *Eighteenth-Century Collections Online*
and Google Books. It is now feasible to research and write on the
material – even teach it to undergraduates – in a way that was simply
not possible two decades ago.[1]

Despite the increasing accessibility of the primary material, however, academic coverage remains patchy. Jane Robinson's 1990 bibliographical and biographical listing, *Wayward Women: A Guide to Women
Travellers*, with entries on some 400 British women writers including
about thirty from the period 1750–1830, remains the most comprehensive reference guide, despite its eccentric organization.[2] There are
some excellent studies of particular writers, geographical areas, or
themes, but as yet no authoritative study of women writers during
the 'long Romantic' period. This chapter cannot realistically hope to
plug that gap, but will offer a delineation of the genre's development
followed by an outline of key critical work and suggestions for future
approaches. I am concerned here with the world of published narratives, and am thereby highly conscious of a deficiency, since numerous
manuscript accounts of travels from our period survive, many of them
following the generic conventions of printed texts.[3] So, the field of
potential scholarship is even larger than my outline here can hope to
suggest.

Not unusual productions

Before 1770, only two travel narratives by British women were published: Elizabeth Justice's *A Voyage to Russia* in 1739, and Mary Wortley Montagu's so-called *Embassy Letters* in 1763.[4] Relative peace in Europe after 1763 (at least until the French Revolution), coupled with improved roads and transportation, encouraged a rise in middle-class tourism, which in turn generated an increasing number of travel narratives. By 1777 the *Critical Review* could observe that the 'Letters of female travellers are now become not unusual productions.'[5] By 1800, around twenty women had published travel books. (Bear in mind, however, that several hundred travelogues by men were published during the eighteenth century.) Between 1800 and 1830, 25 to 30 more women entered the field: some, like Maria Graham and Sydney Owenson (Lady Morgan), published several substantial works, so that the number of published travel narratives by women between 1800 and 1830 is probably over 50. Travel was curtailed during the French Revolution and Napoleonic wars (although there were compensatory opportunities for travelogue-as-reportage), at which point travel within Britain became more fashionable (and indeed patriotic) – especially for women.[6]

After 1815, the geographical scope of British travel widened enormously, whilst the expressive possibilities of European tourism were enlarged by the eminently quotable works of Romantic poets, especially Byron, which appealed both to middle-class tourists delineating sublime landscapes, and to aristocrats describing the hectic whirl of social life in great cities.[7] The growing interest during the Regency in the pursuits of the upper classes (which we see also in the fashion for courtesans' memoirs and scandalous prints) gave a new lease of life to Grand Tour narratives, so that a text as trivial as Lady Blessington's *Journal of a Tour through the Netherlands in 1821* receives four pages of excerpts in the *Monthly Review*: although they 'do not indicate profundity of thought or research', the reviewer concedes, they demonstrate her lively 'style' and her passion for 'strewing ... lea[ves] of laurel over the tomb of Napoleon'.[8] (Whether as hero or villain, and often filtered through *Childe Harold*, Napoleon had become a popular theme in travel writing by the 1820s.) Recreational travel became increasingly acceptable even for single women: Elizabeth Strutt's *A Spinster's Tour in France, the States of Genoa, &c* (1827) encourages other 'Spinster Ladies' to 'obtain substantial pleasure ... from the contemplation of nature's most beautiful scenes, and the conviction that kindliness and hospitality are bounded neither by sea nor mountain' (p. iv). The *Monthly Review* praises the 'agreeable' style and 'descriptive rapture' of 'our fair spinster' – such enthusiasm would have been unthinkable in the insular and anxious 1790s. After 1815, more exotic destinations, such as Russia, Egypt, and India were both safer and fashionable, and increasingly accessible to the wives of those merchants, diplomats, and military men who were sowing the seeds of empire overseas. In 1829, 'Mrs Charles Lushington' (Sarah) published her *Narrative of a Journey from Calcutta to Europe, by Way of Egypt, in the Years 1827 and 1828* – an overland itinerary far more adventurous than the usual sea voyage – specifically so that other women might 'judge of the practicability of the undertaking, especially by ladies' ('Preface', p. [ix]).

The best-known eighteenth-century travelogue by a woman is perhaps the most uncharacteristic. Lady Mary Wortley Montagu's celebrated *Embassy Letters* (published posthumously in 1763) are now firmly canonical, and have generated an extensive bibliography, rivalled only by Wollstonecraft's Scandinavian *Letters* of 1796.[9] Montagu's book appeared in a strangely belated fashion: the letters were written more than forty years prior to their publication. So, the romanticized visions of Turkey which Montagu describes were already a little outdated by 1763, but perhaps all the more appealing – they were greeted with widespread acclaim – in the wake of a war which had seen Enlightened ideals compromised by nationalistic greed.

Just four years later, in 1767, however, a spurious fourth volume of the *Letters* appeared, offering strikingly up-to-date opinions on Turkey: 'what can you expect from such a country as this, from which the muses have fled, from which letters seem eternally banished, and in which you see, in private scenes, nothing pursued as happiness but the refinements of an indolent voluptuousness, and where those who act upon the public theatre live in uncertainty, suspicion, and terror'.[10] By 1789, Elizabeth Lady Craven could claim with impunity that Montagu's letters were inauthentic – 'she never wrote a word of them' – not least because of their non-imperial sensibility. (Craven's own travelogue envisages 'a colony of honest English families ... waking the indolent Turk from his gilded slumbers'.[11]) Paradoxically, then, while Montagu's book opened the field for a growing number of published travel narratives by women, its overt admiration for foreign practices (arguably its most distinctive feature) was not to be widely emulated: most of her successors (especially those of the middling sort) were careful to craft an authorial persona grounded in domestic virtue and patriotism, for all their daring to travel abroad and publish.

Just as Montagu's forty-year-old recollections enjoyed a celebratory moment on first publication, followed by a complex afterlife, Eliza Fay's

Original Letters from India (Calcutta, 1817) were published some thirty-five years after the events they describe, and have enjoyed periodic revivals of interest. Belatedness is about all Montagu and Fay have in common, however – Eliza Fay, an unsuccessful milliner, is a consciously middle-brow writer (E.M. Forster in 1925 calls her 'underbred'[12]), whose pertness and self-importance make her narrative at times quite hilarious. Nevertheless, Fay's explanation of her delayed publication is revealing:

> When, after residing two years in India, the author … returned to her native country, she was repeatedly urged by several of her friends to publish some account of the events that had befallen her, being connected with important circumstances in the lives of well known and respectable individuals. … But, at this period a woman who was not conscious of possessing decided genius or superior knowledge could not easily be induced to leave 'the harmless tenor of her way', and render herself amenable to the 'pains and penalties' then, generally, inflicted on female authorships; unless inspired by that enthusiasm that tramples on difficulties, or goaded by misfortune which admits not of alternative. …
>
> Since then, a considerable change has gradually taken place in public sentiments, and its developement, we have now not only as in former days a number of women who do honour to their sex as literary characters, but many unpretending females, who fearless of the critical perils that once attended the voyage, venture to launch their little barks on the vast ocean through which amusement or instruction is conveyed to a reading public. … A female author is no longer regarded as an object of derision, nor is she wounded by unkind reproof from the *literary Lords of Creation*.[13]

This is a significant retrospective survey of the field. The later eighteenth century had indeed seen publications by women of 'decided genius' or 'superior knowledge', amongst whom Fay presumably would have ranked Anna Miller, whose *Letters from Italy* (1776) comment extensively upon the fine arts and were found by the *Monthly Review* to 'discover a solid understanding, liberal sentiments, and a cultivated taste';[14] Ann Radcliffe, whose patriotic *Journey made in the Summer of 1794, through Holland and the Western Frontier of Germany* (1795) was likewise well received (although it carefully eschews the colourful description for which her novels had made her famous); and perhaps also Mariana Starke, who integrates art appreciation, valetudinarianism and anti-Catholic patriotism into her *Travels in Italy, between the Years*

1792 and 1798 (1800), and who casts herself as a travelling nurse to emphasize her domestic femininity.[15] Fay's reference to 'that enthusiasm that tramples on difficulties' seems directed at writers like Mary Wollstonecraft and Helen Maria Williams, who had met with celebrity and opprobrium in equal measure for their accounts of revolutionary France. Williams's *Tour in Switzerland* (1798) had attracted disapproval even from the radical *Analytical Review* (for which Wollstonecraft herself had reviewed), less for its politics than for displaying 'That common disease of female minds, of perpetually longing for something beyond or out of themselves, without appreciating the object, and of placing happiness on any other spot than where they are.'[16] Although Wollstonecraft's Scandinavian *Letters* had initially been greeted with more critical acclaim (the *Monthly Review* praising the '*masculine* ... mind of this female philosopher', and *The British Critic* admiring her for 'joining to a *masculine* understanding, the finer sensibilities of a female'), her own posthumous reputation deteriorated rapidly after Godwin's frank *Memoir* in 1798.[17] By the time Fay writes her 'Preface', Wollstonecraft is a cautionary example, not an inspiring foremother.

The third of Fay's categories of women who dared to publish – those 'goaded by misfortune which admits not of alternative' – doubtless refers to the practice of publishing (often by subscription) to raise funds for the distressed or widowed writer. Jemima Kindersley's *Letters from the Island of Teneriffe, Brazil, the Cape of Good Hope and the East Indies* appeared in 1777, eight years after her husband had died at Calcutta, and the reviews chivalrously praised both her 'ease and simplicity' and her attention to feminine detail.[18] The 'distressed widow' trope persisted well into the nineteenth century, mobilized most often (not surprisingly) by women whose travels took themselves and their usually less robust husbands to distant and difficult locations. Keturah Jeffreys published *The Widowed Missionary's Journal; containing Some Account of Madagascar, and also, A Narrative of the Missionary Career of the Rev. J. Jeffreys; who died on a passage from Madagascar to the Isle of France, July 4ᵗʰ 1825, aged 31 Years* (1827) 'not only to record the excellencies of her departed husband, but to assist her in providing for the future support of four orphan children' (p. x), while Lady Alfred Bartram published (anonymously) *Recollections of Seven Years Residence at the Mauritius or Isle of France. By a Lady* (1830), 'appealing to the kind feelings of British hearts' (p. vii) to offset the feeble pension on which she was to support herself and her daughters, after her husband – a sickly and underpaid diplomat – had died in Mauritius.

As even this brief survey suggests, travel writing as a genre was very varied: even more so once the full range of male-authored texts is taken into account. If weighty exploration narratives sponsored by the Royal Society represent the most intimidating (and masculine) end of the spectrum, a host of humbler travels and tours cluster at the other end. For non-professional writers, the publication of a travel narrative – perhaps the only foray into print they were to make in their life – conferred upon them, if only for one print run and a couple of reviews, the status of authoritative cultural commentator. The occasional nature of much travel writing, as well as its generic conventions, require us to read it in particular ways, and not necessarily to judge it within conventional aesthetic categories. Susan Staves has recently called for a reinstatement of aesthetic value judgements in feminist literary criticism: 'women writers must be judged by what they accomplished in their work, not merely sympathized with because they suffered from patriarchy or from misogynistic critics'.[19] There is certainly a need to move beyond sexual politics as our main critical criterion: however, by Staves's own aesthetic criteria (she berates scandalous memoirists like Charke who '[failed] to develop a successful literary career' once the occasion for their publications had passed [p. 283]), few women travel writers would pass muster – and few of them, indeed, feature significantly in Staves's study.

Eighteenth-century readers and critics, by contrast, placed a high value on such occasional publications, especially within the prestigious genre of travel writing. Not surprisingly, travel literature played an important role in discussions of British national identity, of which gender was a central component. Hence, women's travel accounts were generally welcomed, despite the pervasive anti-travel discourse which also exerted its pressures upon women. Writing a travelogue gave women the freedom (relatively speaking) to enter into discourses otherwise unavailable to them, because of the genre's remarkable permeability to other kinds of writing. So, for example, a travelogue might well mobilize (whether consciously or not) the discourses of agriculture and trade; anti-Catholicism; British liberty; imperialism; aesthetics and the sublime; 'manners and customs' (which we would now describe as ethnography and anthropology); valetudinarianism; war reportage; natural history and Linnaean classification; humanitarianism; and the over-arching discourse of sensibility, which certainly contributed to the growing cultural interest in travelling women and their observations. In 1799, the novelist Jane West complains that 'the title of a work no longer announces its intention: books of travels are converted into vehicles of politics and systems of legislation. Female letter-writers teach us the arcana of government, and obliquely vindicate ... manners and actions at which female delicacy should blush'.[20] The generic permeability of travel writing – for West, a sign of its indecorum and subversion – was, for writers and reader alike, a major source of the genre's appeal.[21]

Critical horizons

Perhaps surprisingly, the discursive heterogeneity of the primary material is not fully reflected in the scholarship it has generated, although impressive work has been done during the past twenty years. In particular, the feminist Foucauldian model provided by Sara Mills in *Discourses of Difference* (1991) has encouraged us to examine the different (often conflicting) discourses and subject positions available to women.[22] In 1992, Mary Louise Pratt's *Imperial Eyes* offered a ground-breaking account of how the colonial 'fringe' helped produce European metropolitan culture after 1750.[23] Concerned primarily with Africa and South America, Pratt's coverage of women travel writers is not extensive, but she offers deft readings of Anna Maria Falconbridge, Maria Graham, and Flora Tristan, and highlights women's ambivalent position within early imperialism. Elizabeth Bohls's study of *Women Travel Writers and the Language of Aesthetics* (1995) showed how women interrogated the prevailingly masculine discourse of aesthetic response, not only to expose the harsh ideological functions of that discourse (which objectified ruined landscapes, picturesque poor people, and distressed females), but also to offer alternative modes of aesthetic perception and social relationship.[24] The essay collection *Romantic Geographies: Discourses of Travel 1775–1844* appeared in 2000,[25] devoting seven of its thirteen essays to women writers. An important materialist intervention in ongoing debates about Romanticism, *Romantic Geographies* affirmed the centrality of women (as well as geography) to the complicated processes of national self-definition. My own study of *British Travel Writers in Europe 1750–1800* appeared in 2001, with a substantial chapter on 'The Rise of the Woman Travel Writer'.[26]

Generally, these studies are more subtle than much of the postcolonial criticism on eighteenth and especially nineteenth-century literature, which tends to mine texts either for racist and imperialist statements, or for moments at which women writers seem to subvert such prevailing ideologies, at which point they are congratulated for being simultaneously feminist and anti-imperialist.[27] (For instance, Eliza Fay's fantastically gossipy, comically pert account of India, notable for its cast of disreputable ex-pats and its almost palpable evocation of dirt and exhaustion, is represented time and again as – simultaneously – a racist and feminist text, on the strength of one oft-cited paragraph pronouncing Hindu widows who commit suttee to be less heroic than British women who have to endure marriage to a tyrannical fool.[28]) Nevertheless, there is still a tendency to privilege political readings and to overemphasize the shaping force of a rather narrow range of discourses. Recognizing that writing about texts is absolutely no substitute for reading them, I conclude this chapter with a few brief examples of what might be gained by a broader set of reading practices, based on the contention that women's travel writing is more nimble and multifaceted than we have previously acknowledged.

Maria Graham, one of the first professional women travel writers, has generated some excellent scholarly discussion. Mary Louise Pratt has characterized her as a 'social exploratress' whose 'reinvention of America coincides with a reinvention of self', while Nigel Leask has delineated the rational and reformist agenda of her *Journal of a Residence in India* (1812).[29] Such models certainly help to structure a reader's critical appreciation of Graham's work, but the experience of reading, for example, Graham's *Journal of a Residence in Chile* (1824) is, inevitably, quite different from reading any critic's account of the text. The *Journal* is almost overwhelming in its exhaustive descriptions of Chilean daily life and politics, and its interweaving of personal emotion with empirical observation. Pratt claims that Graham rejects 'sentimentality and romanticism' (p. 159), but this rather downplays the text's insistence upon sensitive response to the people Graham encounters, and to the landscape she admires. Graham's text is peppered with quotations from Romantic poets, especially Byron, through which she claims the status of the solitary wanderer, not generally (in the 1820s) seen as a congenially feminine posture (although, of course, Wollstonecraft's own *Letters* had in fact pioneered that trope). The landscape, indeed, becomes directly threatening at times, particularly in an extended description of a succession of earthquakes, which come at a time when she is taking care of her consumptive soldier cousin who has rather inconveniently fetched up in Chile. Here, Graham's text is particularly compelling. She conjures physical terror and dramatizes herself as torn between different roles and responses:

> Never shall I forget the horrible sensation of that night. In all other convulsions of nature we feel or fancy that some exertion may be made to avert or mitigate danger; but from an earthquake there is neither shelter nor escape: the 'mad disquietude'[30] that agitates

every heart, and looks out in every eye, seems to me as awful as the last judgment can be; and I regret that my anxiety for my patient overcoming other feelings, I had not my due portion of that sublime terror: but I looked round and I saw it. Amid the noise of the destruction before and around us, I heard the lowings of the cattle all the night through; and I heard too the screaming of the sea-fowl, which ceased not till morning.[31]

This is a veritable cocktail of discourses – sublime, apocalyptic, poetic, domestic – which (for all our critical itemization) only goes to prove the complex and irreducible nature of the experiences described.

It is worth recalling here that Graham wrote this book while recently widowed: rather than returning to England on the death of her sea captain husband off Cape Horn, she took up residence in Chile, apparently with a view to producing a travelogue. The pathos of her situation breaks through only occasionally, and the capacious energies of her writing override any tendency to self-pity. The same is true of other 'widow' narratives. Keturah Jeffreys's *The Widowed Missionary's Journal; containing Some Account of Madagascar* (1827) offers a powerful evocation of this remote island. She describes the sickening, hot and monotonous voyage out, followed by arduous hiking and canoe-travel into the swampy and disease-ridden interior of Madagascar. They pass the tombs of several of their predecessor missionaries, but are undeterred from their mission to establish Christian schools in remote villages. Not surprisingly, snatches of Evangelical hymns pepper the narrative, which also juxtaposes horrified accounts of savage dancing to the 'Tum-Tum' drums with cheerfully brave declarations that 'Our route still continues to be very delightful' (p. 50), and earnest appeals for the continued abolition of slavery in the French possessions. The busy plenitude of Jeffreys's observations gives the lie to the assumption that missionary texts are unimaginatively monologic.[32]

These widows' narratives, then, which one might expect to find dominated by pathos (if not downright self-pity), are surprisingly capacious and generous, displaying a variety of interests and attitudes – overlaid by a discernible engagement with the physical world – which would be remarkable in any text. Their energies are to some extent attributable to their need to please a reading public, who are, after all, purchasing a travel narrative, not a sob story (a nice instance of how the exigencies of print culture could improve the aesthetic quality of published writings).[33] It's noteworthy also that these women seem less like passive vehicles for specific discourses, and more like ironically self-aware *bricoleuses*, certainly capable of a broader range of 'subject positions' than Foucault would have thought possible.

Other women display a curious talent for self-censorship and significant silence, sidestepping certain discursive realms. In her *Narrative of a Ten Years' Residence at Tripoli in Africa* (published in 1816, though recounting events between 1783 and 1795), 'Miss Tully' offers an extraordinary account of life at the Bashaw's court, beset periodically by marauding Turks and Arabs, repeated attacks of the plague, and internecine violence within the royal family. Funerals abound, as do distressed women of many different races and classes, and by the end of the narrative we hear of royal children 'cut to pieces' by the Turks as the European diplomats take ship for Gibraltar. At several points, Tully draws a veil over events – 'the scenes here have been too shocking to relate, I therefore pass them over in silence' (p. 350) – and the opportunity to describe lesser, more tangible evils is frequently taken, with arresting results – as in this account of a plague of locusts (which in fact comes as light relief from the actual plague at Tripoli, and the more sinister Turkish 'invaders'):

> They fly in compact bodies through the air, darkening the atmosphere, and occupying a space of many miles in their passage. They make a noise in the act of nipping off the corn and herbage that cannot be mistaken, and which is distinctly heard at a great distance. While these invaders pass along, as if by enchantment, the green disappears and the parched naked ground presents itself. The locusts are salted down in great quantities at Cairo and Alexandria, and carried to different parts of Africa: many are brought to this place and eaten by the inhabitants.
>
> (pp. 109–10)

It's only by listening to the small sounds (the locusts nipping off the corn) as well as the louder ones (the wailing of the Muslim mourners, the cannons of the Turkish fleet) – and by noticing the silences – that we can do proper justice to the complexity of Tully's text and the experiences it describes.

Another writer who excels at fine sensuous detail is Maria Riddell. In her brief but eloquent *Voyages to the Madeira, and Leeward Caribbean Isles: with Sketches of the Natural History of these Islands* (1792) she draws on the systems of Linnaeus and Pennant, but strays creatively beyond the boundaries of scientific discourse in gorgeous accounts of exotic flora and fauna. Her account of 'two young dolphins' netted alongside the ship has a Coleridgean intensity: 'they ... wreathed themselves about in various shapes, and swelled their lucid scales, that instantly assumed the most brilliant colouring imaginable, displaying alternately the glossy tints of the sapphire, the emerald, the topaz, the amethyst, and the brightest violet colour ornamented with streaks of gold, silver, and azure' (p. 35). Once settled at Antigua, she tests the truth of the legend that ground lizards are hypnotized by music: 'I have frequently, when sitting in the garden, sung an air in a soft voice, which, in a few minutes, would draw the lizards from the shrubs and trees around ... they would remain with their little heads gently inclined, their eyes immovably rivetted to the place from whence the sound proceeded, and their glossy scales presenting a thousand different hues every moment' (p. 65). Elsewhere, her text offers the merest hint of more troubling political contexts – there are brief references to slave rebellions and to well-equipped army barracks – and she apologizes, in the 'Dedication', that her book is unfinished, thanks to 'my marriage', which 'by obtruding on me a number of domestic occupations, interrupted my course of study' (p. iv). Riddell was the daughter of one plantation owner, and married another. Her silence on the subject of slavery is hardly admirable, but nor is it surprising, and her investment in the natural world is an interesting (if evasive) strategy for generating meaning and purpose in an otherwise disempowering world.

Some observations on a few representative texts have been offered here, less as models of critical activity (I have had to resort to the practice of selective quotation, the dangers of which I am of course trying to point out) than as a reminder of the complex challenges and rewards which such re-readings can supply. While we are unlikely to alter our own political judgements of the material – after all, we inhabit a very different value system from the writers under consideration here – we are likely to gain a more nuanced apprehension of how their values were produced, given the relentlessly material conditions of these women's experiences. Margaret Anne Doody has written of women's poetry from the late eighteenth century that 'the women poets present us with a clearly sensuous world. The mind cannot divorce itself from the senses.' Their work forces us to see, smell, and feel.[34] This is certainly true of women's travel writing, which opens up amazing vistas into newly discovered worlds, but also exposes us to the sheer tedium of travelling, the filthy terrors of the voyage, and the steadily corrosive influence of bad company upon one's nerves and equanimity. Open-minded engagement with other cultures, it becomes clear, is a luxury dependent upon a certain level of physical and emotional comfort, which for many of these women was simply unavailable, if, for instance, they had spent five months 'in a ship crowded with passengers little known, or too well known, and distracted by the mirth or fractiousness of numerous children'.[35]

Notes

1. Mary Wortley Montagu and Mary Wollstonecraft remain the only women whose texts are readily available in paperback: see for Wollstonecraft the new Oxford World's Classics *Letters written during a Short Residence in Sweden, Norway, and Denmark*, ed. by T. Brekke and J. Mee (Oxford: Oxford University Press, 2009). Montagu's *Turkish Embassy Letters*, ed. by Anita Desai and Malcolm Jack (London: Virago, 1994) remains the most accessible version. Scholarly editions are available in *The Complete Letters of Lady Mary Wortley Montagu*, ed. by Robert Halsband, 3 vols (Oxford: Oxford University Press, 1965–67). Less canonical travel writers have recently benefited from a steady (and continuing) stream of scholarly editions. See Deidre Coleman's admirable *Maiden Voyages and Infant Colonies: Two Women's Travel Narratives of the 1790s* (London: Cassell, 1999), containing Anna Maria Falconbridge's *Two Voyages to Sierra Leone, During the Years 1791–2–3* (1794) and Mary Ann Parker's *A Voyage Round the World* (1795); see also Jennifer Hayward's edition of Maria Graham's *Journal of a Residence in Chile during the Year 1822, and A Voyage from Chile to Brazil in 1823* (Charlottesville: University of Virginia Press, 2003). Through Chawton House Library, publication is ongoing of a series of annotated facsimile texts (series editors S. Bending and S. Bygrave, published in London by Pickering & Chatto) of Romantic women's travel writings in France, Italy, Iberia, North Africa, and the Middle East. See www.pickeringchatto.com for a full list. Pre-Victorian women are sketchily represented in *An Anthology of Women's Travel Writing*, ed. by Shirley Foster and Sara Mills (Manchester: Manchester University Press, 2002) and Jane Robinson's *Unsuitable for Ladies: An Anthology of Women Travellers* (Oxford: Oxford University Press, 1994).
2. Jane Robinson, *Wayward Women: a Guide to Women Travellers* (1990; Oxford: Oxford University Press, 2001).
3. See Zoe Kinsley, *Women Writing the Home Tour, 1682–1812* (Aldershot: Ashgate, 2008).
4. The full title is *Letters of the Right Honourable Lady M—y W—y M—e: Written, during her Travels in Europe, Asia, and Africa, to Persons of Distinction, Men of Letters, &c. in different Parts of Europe*, 3 vols (1763).
5. *Critical Review*, 43 (1777), 439.
6. See Adriana Craciun, *British Women Writers and the French Revolution: Citizens of the World* (Basingstoke: Palgrave Macmillan, 2005) on Wollstonecraft, Williams, and others. Charlotte Eaton published a grisly account of *The Battle of Waterloo. By a Near Observer* in 1815. See also Kinsley, *Women Writing the Home Tour*.
7. See Nigel Leask, *Curiosity and the Aesthetics of Travel Writing, 1770–1840* (Oxford: Oxford University Press, 2002), pp. 219–20, on the impressionistic and allusive style of travel writing of the 1820s and 1830s.

8. *Monthly Review*, 100 (1823), 99–104.
9. For bibliography on Montagu, see Sukanya Banerjee, 'Lady Mary Montagu and the "Boundaries of Europe"', in *Gender, Genre and Identity in Women's Travel Writing*, ed. by Kristi Siegel (New York: Peter Lang, 2004), pp. 31–54. For Wollstonecraft, see Brekke and Mee's recent edition of the *Letters*.
10. *An Additional Volume to the Letters of the Right Honourable Lady M— W— M—e* (1767), pp. 27–8.
11. See Katherine Turner, 'From Classical to Imperial: Changing Visions of Turkey in the Eighteenth Century', in *Travel Writing and Empire: Postcolonial Theory in Transit*, ed. by Steve Clark (London: Zed Books, 1999), pp. 113–28.
12. Mrs Fay, *Original Letters from India; Containing a Narrative of a Journey through Egypt, and the Author's Imprisonment at Calicut by Hyder Ally* (Calcutta, 1817; repr. with jaunty introduction by M.M. Kaye and notes by E.M. Forster, London: The Hogarth Press, 1986), p. 11.
13. Fay, *Original Letters*, pp. 27–9.
14. *Monthly Review*, 55 (1776), 105.
15. On Starke, see Jeanne Moskal, 'Politics and the Occupation of a Nurse in Mariana Starke's *Letters from Italy*', in *Romantic Geographies: Discourses of Travel 1775–1844*, ed. by Amanda Gilroy (Manchester: Manchester University Press, 2000), pp. 150–64. In 1820, John Murray published Starke's *Travels on the Continent: written for the Use and Particular Information of Travellers* (London, 1820), upon which he modelled his long and influential line of Murray Handbooks.
16. *Analytical Review*, 27 (1798), 566.
17. *Monthly Review*, new ser. 20 (1796), 251; *British Critic*, 7 (1796), 607. William Godwin, *Memoirs of the Author of a Vindication of the Rights of Woman* (London: J. Johnson, 1798).
18. *Monthly Review*, 57 (1777), 243. See Felicity Nussbaum, 'British Women Writers Write the East after 1750: Revisiting a "Feminine" Orient', in *British Women's Writing in the Long Eighteenth Century: Authorship, Politics and History*, ed. by Jennie Batchelor and Cora Kaplan (Basingstoke: Palgrave Macmillan, 2005), pp. 121–39.
19. Susan Staves, *A Literary History of Women's Writing in Britain, 1660–1789* (Cambridge: Cambridge University Press, 2006), p. 439.
20. *A Tale of the Times* (1799); quoted in *Romantic Geographies*, ed. by Gilroy, p. 1.
21. Lady Morgan's political account of *France* (2 vols) in 1817 generated critical hostility, but her publisher, Henry Colburn (with John Murray, one of the key publishers of travel narratives during this period) commissioned her to produce a similarly trenchant account of *Italy* (3 vols) in 1823. See Jeanne Moskal, 'Gender, Nationality, and Textual Authority in Lady Morgan's Travel Books', in *Romantic Women Writers: Voices and Countervoices*, ed. by Paula R. Feldman and Theresa M. Kelley (Hanover: University Press of New England, 1995), pp. 171–93.
22. Sara Mills, *Discourses of Difference: An Analysis of Women's Travel Writing and Colonialism* (London: Routledge, 1991).
23. Mary Louise Pratt, *Imperial Eyes: Travel Writing and Transculturation* (London: Routledge, 1992).
24. Elizabeth Bohls, *Women Travel Writers and the Language of Aesthetics 1716–1818* (Cambridge: Cambridge University Press, 1995).

25. See note 15 above.
26. Katherine Turner, *British Travel Writers in Europe, 1750–1800: Authorship, Gender and National Identity* (Aldershot: Ashgate, 2001).
27. See, for instance, Nandini Bhattacharya, *Reading the Splendid Body: Gender and Consumerism in Eighteenth-Century British Writing on India* (London: Associated University Presses, 1998); Claire Midgley, *Gender and Imperialism* (Manchester: Manchester University Press, 1998).
28. Bhattacharya, in *Reading the Splendid Body*, pp. 142–3, 154–5, lambasts the 'discursive monoglossia' of such 'racist' passages, seemingly uninterested in the heteroglossic energies of Fay's work as a whole. See also Felicity Nussbaum, *Torrid Zones: Maternity, Sexuality, and Empire in Eighteenth-Century English Narratives* (Baltimore: Johns Hopkins University Press 1995), pp. 186–8, for a complementary reading of Fay. Nussbaum's later essay, 'British Women Write the East after 1750', follows a post-colonial methodology, but also acknowledges a wider context, 'a crowded conglomeration of views, chaotically and intoxicatingly rich with meanings' (p. 124).
29. Pratt, *Imperial Eyes*, p. 169; Leask, *Curiosity*, p. 207.
30. Byron, 'Darkness', line 29 (the poem describes a visionary dream of apocalypse).
31. Graham, *Journal of a Residence in Chile*, ed. by Hayward, pp. 150–1.
32. See, for instance, *An Anthology of Women's Travel Writing*, ed. by Foster and Mills, p. 93.
33. Another impressive widow's narrative, Mary Ann Parker's *A Voyage Round the World* (1795), was dedicated to the Princess of Wales, and prefaced by a long 'List of Subscribers' (413) including high-ranking naval and military personnel, as well as Joseph Banks, Hannah More, and Richard Twiss (an eminent travel writer).
34. Margaret Anne Doody, 'Sensuousness in the Poetry of Eighteenth-Century Women Poets', in *Women's Poetry in the Enlightenment: The Making of a Canon, 1730–1820*, ed. by Isobel Armstrong and Virginia Blain (Basingstoke: Macmillan, 1999), pp. 3–32 (p. 4).
35. Mrs Charles Lushington, *Narrative of a Journey from Calcutta to Europe*, p. 2: this scenario is precisely what Sarah Lushington hoped to avoid by travelling overland with a cavalcade of servants.

Part II
1750–1800: Revolutions in Female Writing

3
Bluestocking Women and the Negotiation of Oral, Manuscript, and Print Cultures

Betty A. Schellenberg

As the editor of this volume has noted, one of the tasks facing twenty-first-century historians of women's writing is that of demonstrating 'how and in what ways, rather than whether, women's writing is key to literary history'.[1] For the eighteenth century, this issue is overlaid by the persistence of non-print modes of production at a time when the world of letters was undergoing rapid transformation into a print-based culture. Thus the gender divide has often been mapped onto a divide between non-print and print media; between a feminized, private use of oral and manuscript forms on the one hand, and a masculine, public use of print on the other. Margaret J.M. Ezell's influential 1993 work on *Writing Women's Literary History*, for example, argued powerfully that a modern identification of authorship with print publication had led, anachronistically, to the neglect of much pre-eighteenth-century writing by women.[2] And many writers have insisted that the lingering stigma of print as commercialized and vulgar was felt in a particularly acute way by women writers.[3] Proper women, it could be inferred, predominantly conversed, wrote letters, kept journals, and exchanged manuscript poetry, while men dominated the production of periodicals and pamphlets and published the vast majority of religious, scientific, critical, and literary works.

One obvious and well-represented corrective to this generalization has been to problematize the gender component of the dichotomy: to look for women's active participation in print as the sign of their success in exploiting this increasingly universal medium.[4] A more recent critical trend has attended to the persistence of forms of manuscript culture into the eighteenth century, noting, as Ezell has in her 1999 study of 'social authorship', that 'the older notion of the text as a dynamic and collaborative process coexisted [with a proprietary view of authorship based in print technology] well into the mid-eighteenth century'; furthermore, '[b]y denying the significance of script authorship, manuscript circles, and social texts, we have in the name of democracy [associated with print] apparently disenfranchised the participation of the majority of the literate population of the period'.[5] An important recent project bringing together questions of women's authorship and ongoing scribal practice in the eighteenth century is George L. Justice and Nathan Tinker's edited collection *Women's Writing and the Circulation of Ideas: Manuscript Publication in England, 1550–1800*, which presents case studies of women's manuscript writing through to Frances Burney's suppressed play *The Witlings*. While the common thread which holds these essays together is a recognition that women who 'used manuscript rather than print for the circulation of their various works' did so as the result of 'a set of choices, made in positive terms for the most part',[6] only one essay, Kathryn R. King's study of 'Elizabeth Singer Rowe's Tactical Use of Print and Manuscript', focuses on a productive interplay of scribal and print forms over an author's writing career.

This is the direction that this chapter will pursue for a group of women often seen as influenced by Rowe's authorial model.[7] Specifically, I wish to blur the boundary between 'public' print on the one hand and 'private' manuscript and orality on the other, looking at how women's ongoing use of non-print forms – conversation and letter-writing most particularly – played a part in the development of the period's print-based literary culture, whether directly by fuelling the popularity of revived and emergent forms such as the dialogue and novelistic conversation, or indirectly through patronage and the management of reception. This approach is grounded on a model of mid-eighteenth-century media coexistence as a fluid continuum rather than a sharp divide, and on the now-general recognition that for the period the public and the private were always relative, and were moderated by the numerous social spaces through which they were mutually defined. Ultimately, my argument suggests that many mid-century forms of print publication are embedded in, and shaped by, conversation and manuscript exchange, whether in the eventual appearance in print of work long known through manuscript circulation, in formal strategies adapted from these non-print media, or in reflections of patronage and criticism practised in these media.

My focus will be on the Bluestocking women who flourished as public figures and writers in mid-eighteenth-century England. I will interpret 'Bluestocking' broadly to refer to mid-century women whose public personae were built around intellectual accomplishment (as reflected in textual production), female friendship, an Anglican-centred piety, and social responsibility. I include relatively professionalized writers such as Sarah Fielding at the one extreme and the publication-shy Catherine Talbot at the other, with Sarah Scott, Elizabeth Carter, Hester Chapone, and Elizabeth Montagu somewhere between. Of course others in the mid-eighteenth century actively advocated and practised conversational and manuscript modes of production – David Hume's essays popularizing his philosophical views, Thomas Gray's circulation of his poems and travel writings in manuscript, and William Shenstone's exchanges of poetry and landscape description among a circle of men and women centred in the Birmingham area are cases in point. In addition, the women we think of as Bluestockings were themselves integrated into broader literary exchange networks. My claim, therefore, is not that these women were single-handedly responsible for forming the print-based literary culture that went forward in the 1780s into the age of the literary anecdote, the extract, and the niche-marketed educational work. However, in the case of the Bluestockings, their extensive use of non-print modes has often been seen as impeding an argument for their cultural and literary significance. Even Gary Kelly, whose claims for 'the extent, complexity, and influence of Bluestocking feminism' are significant in his general introduction to the six-volume *Bluestocking Feminism* collection, notes somewhat apologetically that, in light of this ideological influence, 'it may seem that [the Bluestockings] themselves published relatively little'; his four-page account of 'Bluestocking Writing' includes only one reference to manuscript circulation, the 'extensive private correspondence amongst themselves', noting that it was 'selected, "edited," and published by certain male descendants' in the early nineteenth century.[8]

Kelly's claims in fact invite us to question this disjunction between private writing and public silence, and its extrapolation to a presumed incommensurability between public production and public influence. Was there indeed a fissure between manuscript and print in mid-eighteenth-century literary culture, and if not, what mechanisms operated in the manuscript-print interface? Is the manuscript circulation of the Bluestockings accurately described as private? How might their conversational and manuscript production have been publicized? Harriet Guest has suggested, with respect to Bluestocking political importance, that the space inhabited by learned women in the second half of the century might be described more as a sociable than as a private one, or as a private sphere whose boundary with the public had become permeable, creating a space of feminized civility that took on national symbolic significance.[9] In a similar argument for media 'space', this chapter will focus specifically on how Bluestocking women might be recognized as a significant force *through*, not *despite*, their use of ostensibly private modes.

Bluestocking fame

John Duncombe's 1754 poem *The Feminiad* illustrates how the apparent boundary between manuscript and print media can in fact be reconfigured as a continuum, an opportunity for the expansion of an already-existent sociable publicity. Duncombe's printed celebration of the accomplishments of recent and contemporary British women writers is introduced with an Advertisement that begins to dismantle even as it gestures toward the boundary:

> The following Poem, however favourably it may have been receiv'd among a Circle of private Friends, appears to Disadvantage in Public, as some of the LADIES here mention'd are unknown, their Performances being yet in Manuscript. Should the public Curiosity be hereby rais'd, and could the Diffidence of the fair Authors be so far remov'd as to gratify it, *one* great End of the present Publication would be answer'd.

Thus print publication is both instigated by active manuscript circulation and serves to extend the reach of that circulation. Duncombe's 'unknown ladies' include Hester Mulso (later Chapone), whom he notes as having written odes to Peace, Health, and the Robin Red-breast, and as having been 'celebrated in a sonnet by Mr. [Thomas] Edwards, Author of the Canons of Criticism'. The 'Ode to Peace. Written during the Late Rebellion. 1745' and the 'Ode to Health', addressed to Elizabeth Carter in 1751, had clearly been circulating long and widely enough by 1754 to establish Chapone's reputation in various active manuscript-exchange networks, including the Richardson and Bluestocking circles, and to make the veil of pseudonymity (Chapone is referred to as 'Delia' in the poem) easy to penetrate by an even wider public. Through Duncombe's poem, Chapone (and with her, several other young women) is at once being represented as part of, and being placed into, a community of literary accomplishment that includes published writers such as Elizabeth Carter ('Eliza'), described as the joy of Plato and admiration of Newton, 'equal'd', according to Duncombe's note, 'by few of either sex for strength of imagination, soundness of judgment, and extensive knowledge'.[10]

Other works naming the Bluestockings similarly attest to a public awareness and an impact which are being furthered and celebrated, yet not initiated, by print. Mary Scott's 1774 *The Female Advocate*, for example, sets out to add to Duncombe's list of 'Female Geniuses'. Scott in part advocates for those who have 'obliged the world with their literary productions' since 1754, putting well-published writers such as Fielding and Charlotte Lennox together with Anna Williams and Mary Whateley Darwall, both poets who had published single volumes by subscriptions influentially supported by the Bluestockings and other coterie circles (the latter is referred to as the 'daughter of Shenstone'). But she also celebrates Elizabeth Montagu, who is not only the author of criticism on Shakespeare, but also, having a mind 'expanded' by 'sweet Philanthropy', 'Feels for the welfare of all human-kind', and Catherine Talbot, who before her posthumous publications, is praised for personal qualities: 'Genius and Wit were but thy second praise / Thou knew'st to win by still sublimer ways; / Thy Angel-goodness, all who knew approv'd, / Honour'd, admir'd, applauded too, and lov'd! / Fair shall thy fame to latest ages bloom'.[11] While such coupling of personal and personally known virtues with authorship has often rankled with critics trained in the protocols of print publication, who prefer to think of a work as distinct from its author's identity, it can be understood as well to demonstrate, in Guest's terms, 'how much it was the lives and characters of these women, as well as or even rather than their publications, that were important to their reputations, their perceived cultural significance'.[12] Moreover, as Scott's poem demonstrates, these social qualities accompanied an author's identity and reception into the medium of print.

In such a climate, it is not surprising that what Ezell has called 'social authorship', the production and circulation of works through individual exchanges of manuscripts, which retains a physical link, through the acts of reading aloud, copying, and handing about, to the embodied author, could be as efficacious as extensive print publication.[13] Writing to her sister Sarah Robinson Scott about the latter's recently published history *The Life of Theodore Agrippa D'Aubigné* (1772), Elizabeth Robinson Montagu lists 'Lady Frances Coningeslye & Mrs. Trever', 'many of their acquaintance', 'a Dr Jeb a Clergyman of remarkable learning', and 'Mr. Garrick & Mr Cumberland' who are all 'high in the praise of the work'; as a result, Montagu is 'convinced that great honour will accrue to you from it'. In concluding her letter, Montagu refers to this as her sister's 'Fame', which she hopes Sarah will live long to enjoy.[14] What makes this 'great honour' and this 'Fame' remarkable is that *D'Aubigné* was published anonymously; its only possible fame, then, had to accrue from conversational and epistolary knowledge of its authorship. While I have elsewhere discussed limitations to Scott's fame,[15] Montagu's assertion, and its basis in non-print forms of publicity, remains true for these women as a whole, whose descriptions and names, as the Duncombe and Scott examples illustrate, appear in poems, paintings, and theatrical pieces throughout the period I am looking at.

Bluestocking correspondence

The first step in bridging the gap between Bluestocking conversation, which of course was not recorded either for us or for their contemporaries, and their preferred print forms is an attentiveness to the Bluestockings' letters, in which they cultivated what Nicole Pohl has described, referring to Madame de Sévigné, as 'an artless and dialogic writing style that was associative and spontaneous', differing in this respect from the formality of received letter conventions.[16] The letters of Elizabeth Montagu, for example, are remarkable for the range of subject matter, tone, and degree of informality she displays according to her correspondent. When cultivating the friendship of Elizabeth Carter, for example, Montagu deploys a witty yet self-deprecating persona, emphasizing her inferiority to the solid learning that Carter can bring to the relationship in a delicate manoeuvre around the socially inferior Carter's diffidence, all couched in a tone of intimacy and selective confidence:

> I can perfectly understand why you were afraid of me last year, and I will tell you, for you won't tell me; perhaps, you have not told yourself; you had heard I set up for a wit, and people of real merit and sense hate to converse with witlings; as rich merchant-ships dread to engage with privateers: they may receive damage and can get nothing but dry blows. I am happy you have found out I am not to be feared; I am afraid I must improve myself much before you will find I am to be loved.

With her elder cousin the Reverend William Freind, on the other hand, Montagu is sententious, soberly lamenting, at the ripe old age of twenty-three, the frivolity of young girls' reading ('I believe it is of great consequence to young people to read none but the very best authors, which will not be the case of the women while French trumpery is so much the fashion among them'). With the octogenarian Lord Bath she is the flirtatious mistress ('As I do not expect a billet-doux every morning, I was unluckily asleep (observe that I do not say dreaming of my Lord Bath) when your letter arrived. [...] As I have yet got but half way towards the ardours of fourscore, your Lordship will not expect I should immediately comply with your proposal; but if you will be content with a sentimental love till I arrive at the tender age of eighty, a person and a passion so ripened by time must be very yielding'), while to Lord Lyttelton's son she is the voice of maternal wisdom ('The morning of life, like the morning of the day, should be dedicated to business. On the proper use of that "sweet hour of prime", will depend the glory of your noon of life, and serenity of its evening. Give it, therefore, my dear Mr. Lyttelton, to the strenuous exertion and labour of the mind, before the indolence of the meridian hour, or the abated fervour of the exhausted day renders you unfit for severe application').[17] While these statements move far from the unshaped rhythms of everyday speech, they nonetheless retain the dialogic flavour of the period's conversational ideals.

Given the virtuoso quality of many of these letters, it is not surprising to learn from casual references throughout the Bluestocking correspondence that these letters were read aloud in domestic circles as a regular practice; no doubt they were written with an awareness of potential audiences other than the individual recipient. On the purely familial level, Montagu complains to her sister Sarah, 'I should write oftener to my Dear Sall but there is no comfort in writing a publick letter: it is quite ye same to me in a manner whether I write to you or my Mother while she has an equal property in both letters.'[18] Often, however, these letters contain set pieces of description or critical analysis that take on a life of their own. When Montagu describes to her friend Gilbert West the charitable, orderly, and pious 'life of reason', like that of a 'convent, for by its regularity it resembles one', lived by her sister, now Sarah Scott, and her companion Lady Barbara Montagu, West replies that 'I and indeed all one Company, to whom I communicated your Letter very much applaud and even commend your Friends at Bath-Easton. A Life spent in doing good to our Fellow Creatures is most certainly a Life of Reason, & as such ought most certainly to be esteemed a happy Life, and the proper Life of Man.'[19] In Guest's terms, 'Letters circulated in selected extracts and through gossip are the basis for reputation, and whet public culture's taste for learned women. They grant wide but oblique access to lives whose modesty they also serve to confirm.'[20] In the case of the description of Scott's Batheaston establishment, this exchange demonstrates the mechanism by which the Bluestocking

'Life of Reason' was made public; when Scott's fictional female utopia *A Description of Millenium Hall* appeared in print seven years later, the published work, with its frame narrative of two gentlemen visitors who learn about the society through conversations with its founders and then go forth to do likewise, at once narrates and offers to the general reader a replica version of this experience of social authorship.

Conversation and dialogue: the case of Sarah Fielding

As largely self-educated and privately mentored women, the Bluestockings admired the classical literary models, but simultaneously felt self-conscious about a distance from them that was imposed, first by their sex, and more practically, by their need in many cases to read them in translation. This effect was counterbalanced to some extent by an increasing tendency in the eighteenth century to view women as the practitioners, inspirers, and arbiters of refined conversation. This is indicated not only by the reputations of French *salonnières* such as Madame de Sévigné, but also by writings like David Hume's essay 'Of Essay-Writing', in which he assigns to women dominion over 'the conversable world', as those who have formed a league with philosophers from the alternative 'learned world'.[21] This role arguably encouraged women to practise and promote one classical mode of composition in particular: the dialogue form.

Nicole Pohl has observed that 'the essence of [French] salon sociability was the dialogue', in the sense of 'a conversation that sought reciprocal engagement'.[22] In an early letter to her older friend Anne Donnellan, Montagu shows her awareness of a connection between conversational practice and the dialogue genre. Although her tone is playful, one glimpses how the rational conversation of a select society might be viewed as a truer, more original version of the written form:

I have been dumb with a sore throat, and the shock of so unusual a distemper took away all power of writing; [...] One would not part with one's darling folly for the finest accomplishment, or best qualification in the world; and truly, till my tongue could fidget, and my voice pronounce ten thousand words in five minutes, I was quite low spirited. I read dialogues, studied well penned narrations, read whole books of question and answer, and in short meddled with no work that was not entitled a discourse upon something or other. But these were but the shadows of the felicity of prating. However, I am at last restored to the substantial bliss of talking all day long; and now in good health and high spirits enjoy the agreeable society here [...]

Printed dialogues may be for Montagu a poor cousin to actual speech, but they are a relation nevertheless of the 'pacific tête-a-tête' she tells Donnellan she is learning to cultivate.[23] About twenty years later, she expresses a similarly self-conscious sense of the generic relation, while again asserting the superiority of embodied conversation:

> If it was in my power to be of real use, and exist more substantially to my poor neighbours, I should not think this kind of life [that is, of solitude] much amiss; though I should still feel very sensibly the absence of my dear Mrs. Carter and some others, and not the best Oration of Demosthenes, could I read him in his native Greek, would make amends to me for the loss of my Lord Bath's company, or Lucian's Dialogues stand in the place of Monsey's stories [...] .[24]

This generic self-consciousness and confidence arguably manifests itself in mid-century intellectual women's persistent practice of the dialogue genre. From Elizabeth Carter's translations of Algarotti as *Sir Isaac Newton's Philosophy Explain'd for the Use of the Ladies, in Six Dialogues on Light and Colours* (1739) and of *All the Works of Epictetus* in dialogue form (1758), to Elizabeth Montagu's publication of three dialogues in George Lyttelton's 1760 *Dialogues of the Dead*, to Clara Reeve's use of the dialogue form for her theoretical and historical overview of the romance (or novel) in *The Progress of Romance through Times, Countries, and Manners* (1785), women used the form to invoke at once classical authority, Enlightenment rationality, and female conversational refinement. In so doing, they asserted in print the authority established in private and coterie spheres. Further, they contributed through writing and publishing dialogues to the development of forms such as realist fiction, criticism of English-language literature, and specialized teaching materials, all increasingly important to print publication in the latter half of the century. If this Bluestocking literary activity is not visible to us as a significant pattern, it may be more because of our own insensitivity to the dialogue as genre in the period, than because of its invisibility at the time.[25]

One case study for these claims about print manifestations of intellectual women's conversational practice is Sarah Fielding's career, at its height during the 1750s and 1760s. Fielding's first full-length publication, *The Adventures of David Simple* (1744), and its 1753 sequel, *Volume the Last*, are remarkable for their ironic narrative tone and extensive use of conversational scenes. Both of these works include chapters with titles such as 'Which contains a Conversation, in which is proved, how high Taste may be carried by People who have fixed Resolutions of being Criticks', or 'In which is a very uncommon Dialogue'; in these two cases, the conversation itself is presented in dramatic dialogue format, complete with stage directions.[26] Fielding's published output was clearly nurtured by her social connections, especially with the three sisters with whom she shared a home until their deaths in 1750–51; with her co-author Jane Collier; with her brother Henry, Arthur Collier, and James Harris of her childhood Salisbury acquaintance, all strongly classicist in their literary leanings; and with Samuel Richardson, who in later years printed some of her works, but in her early career seems primarily to have provided a literary circle within which his novels and her writing projects were discussed. Her brother provided the preface for Fielding's topically conceived *Familiar Letters between the Principal Characters in David Simple* (1747), in which he praises his sister's letters for their knowledge of human nature, which he asserts can be acquired more effectively by someone 'who, to use the common Phrase, hath *seen* [...] *little of the World*', but who possesses 'True Genius, with the help of a little Conversation', than by 'those who are placed in the Crouds, either of Business or Pleasure'.[27] Harris in turn contributed two comic dialogues to the book, which Sarah acknowledges as 'a kind present to the Author by a Friend'.[28]

In the next year, Richardson's *Clarissa* inspired Fielding's critical pamphlet *Remarks upon Clarissa, Addressed to the Author*, published in 1749 within a month of the novel's final instalment and taking the form of a series of conversational debates, while *The Governess, or Little Female Academy*, published in the same week, used a series of conversations between young girls at a boarding school to create what has often been called the first novel written specifically for children. The 1750s saw Fielding produce, in addition to *Volume the Last*, *The Cry: A New Dramatic Fable*, a sort of court case featuring several speakers and a chorus of fashionable gossips, and *The Lives of Cleopatra and Octavia*, presented as two dramatic monologues from the dead. By this time, Elizabeth Montagu, Sarah Scott, and their various contacts were personal friends of Fielding and were very actively engaged in promoting *The Lives* as a subscription publication, an effort which they continued for her translation from the Greek of Xenophon's *Memoirs of Socrates* in dialogue form. The subscription for this work elicited, as Sarah Scott put it, 'the genteelest Letters accompanied with more substantial services from most of the scientificks & beaux Esprits of our Kingdom, those especially who are highest in reputation'.[29] Thus the latter, the culminating work of Fielding's publishing career, brought together Harris's books and expertise for consultations about the Greek, the Bluestockings' proven success at raising subscriptions for projects they believed in, and Richardson's printing house. In this way it epitomizes the interdependence of coterie connections and print-trade networks in mediating Fielding's representations of the conversational ideal. And Fielding's well-received work itself can be viewed as consistently bringing to public attention the moral and aesthetic refinement practised and developed within coterie conversational circles featuring strong female speakers who convince through graceful and rational argument.[30]

Although space does not permit an elaboration of the mid-eighteenth-century print trade's reliance on dialogue and conversation as forms,[31] it is noteworthy how often novel writers drew on them for some of their most memorable effects, including Henry Fielding's stagecoach dialogues, Charlotte Lennox's culminating 'conversion' dialogue between Arabella and the Doctor in *The Female Quixote*, even *Tristram Shandy*'s elaborately associative conversations (Lawrence Sterne was a cousin and for some time a social associate of Montagu and her sister, who exchanged letters comparing his conversation and his writing). While criticism has often focused on the epistolary form of much mid-century fiction, novelistic conversation is also one of the innovations of this period.[32] At least some of this was intended to at once reflect and model rational and morally improving conversation like that advocated by the Bluestockings: there is extensive evidence in Richardson's correspondence from the early 1750s of his efforts to refine the speech of his *Sir Charles Grandison* characters according to the style of friends such as Catherine Talbot and her circle.[33] Conversationally-structured printed works seem also to have lent themselves well to a reverse media shift in the form of communal reading of favourite excerpts; thus Catherine Talbot writes in 1753 of returning to Fielding's *Familiar Letters* with a group of friends during a coach ride: 'I scarce know a greater pleasure than reading over a book one is fond of with persons of taste and candour, to whom it is entirely new.'[34]

Published letters

Just as dialogues and conversational novels affirmed the link between women and refined conversation, publications in the form of letters also exploited the association of intellectual women with epistolary skill. Chief among such publications is Hester Mulso Chapone's *Letters on the Improvement of the Mind* (1773). Again, Chapone's reputation as a skilled letter-writer began to build long before this collection appeared in print: her prose writing first began to circulate in the form of an extensive exchange with Richardson on the subject of women as rational beings and the potential conflict ensuing between filial duty and rational choice. Hester's brother John's report to Gilbert White that 'Several great men as the Bp of London, the Speaker &c: have seen this Dispute & think Mr R — hard pressed, & Heck has gained great Honour' demonstrates the sort of reputation to be gained through such exchanges; this episode may have led as well to several letters by Hester appearing in Johnson's *Rambler* No. 10 in 1750.[35]

Chapone's very popular *Letters*, her brother later insists, carried into print their private origin as written advice to her eldest niece, resulting in an 'animation' that remained evident on the inanimate page: 'How was it with Mrs. Chapone? it was the genuine Affetuoso, the con amore of her Book that gave it it's Run: Had She wrote to an imaginary Niece the most animated Traits would have escap'd her Pen.'[36] Chapone cultivated this impression in the presentation of her work, locating the text in a purely private communication with one beloved individual: 'I never entertained a thought of appearing in public, when the desire of being useful to one dear child, in whom I take the tenderest interest, induced me to write the following Letters.' Significantly, it is the sociable forms of conversation and manuscript exchange that mediate the rendering of this private relation into a public form of which many children can partake. Thus Chapone's statement of privacy is located in her dedication of the work to Montagu as both patron ('perhaps it was the partiality of friendship, which so far biassed your judgment as to make you think them capable of being more extensively useful, and warmly to recommend the publication of them') and adviser ('some strokes of your elegant pen have corrected these letters') who has enabled its publication. The letters themselves begin with an expression of intimacy and the power of truth as these operate through the physical gestures of writing and reading a letter:

My dearest niece, Though you are so happy as to have parents, who are both capable and desirous of giving you all proper instruction, yet I, who love you so tenderly, cannot help fondly wishing to contribute something, if possible, to your improvement and welfare:— And, as I am so far separated from you, that it is only by pen and ink I can offer you my sentiments, I will hope that your attention may be engaged, by seeing on paper, from the hand of one of your warmest friends, Truths of the highest importance, which, though you may not find new, can never be too deeply engraven on your mind.[37]

Chapone here draws on the ancient, concrete image of the word carved on a tablet to assert that the experience of reading both the handwritten letter and its printed re-mediation will be one of transparent graphic immediacy.

And of course the published correspondence of Montagu, Carter, Talbot, and Chapone further reified the Bluestocking letters as central to their legacy. Introducing his 1809–13 edition of Montagu's correspondence, her nephew Matthew Montagu justifies his inclusion of her youthful letters to the Duchess of Portland, despite their tendency to satire, as 'written with the freedom of intimate conversation, and [...] principally dictated by the desire of amusing her friend', and therefore also useful in 'exhibit[ing] the progress of her mind'.[38] In discussing his editorial policy, Carter's nephew Montagu Pennington is even more explicit about preserving the flavour of conversational and manuscript intimacy in print as a means of offering the reader a part in that intimacy:

> in publishing letters, the epistolary form and manner must be preserved; [...] in a long and affectionate friendship, such notices of the health of the writer [as have been retained] are expected of course; and [...] if every thing were to be expunged from letters, but disquisitions upon moral and religious subjects, the politics of the day, and opinions upon books, they would lose their chief interest: because that interest principally arises from the incidental mention of such topics, as they happen to come into the writer's mind, from the casual circumstances which had been before the subject of conversation, or from the varying chances of public or private events. The work would then be a collection of aphorisms, or opinions, [...] which, having no connection with each other, would be reduced to the dryness of abstract truths. Instead of sentiments flowing immediately from the heart, uttered extemporaneously as the immediate occasion gave rise to them, they would appear to have been the fruit of study, and written on purpose for the press. They would lose what may be called that local and personal charm, which arises from their being identified with the two friends, in whom, it is hoped, the reader will take an interest. [...][39]

Thus the letters become the physical trace of lost conversation, of a form of communication not 'written on purpose for the press', yet they in turn are made accessible beyond the boundaries of manuscript circulation and decay through print. Even this transition, however, represents a continuity; for Elizabeth Montagu, it is clear from her manuscript letters, was having them copied and returned to her as early as 1763, whether her intent was to facilitate their expanded manuscript circulation or to provide for publication after her death; her editor-nephew avows that

> the publication is here termed a duty, because it was frequently enjoined by Mrs. Montagu herself in consequence of the reiterated request of many of her correspondents, upon whose taste and judgment she had every reason to rely. Lord Lyttelton and Lord Bath in particular, her favourite friends, will be found in the course of the correspondence strongly and repeatedly urging their future publication.[40]

Whatever their concerns about the use of print during their lifetimes, the Bluestockings do not appear to have believed that there was an inherent quality in the medium itself that would hinder the representation of their epistolary achievements.

Mediating publicity

As Elizabeth Carter's publication of Catherine Talbot's works after the latter's death illustrates, Bluestocking friendship could also be significant in the bringing of work to print publication. In addition to the Chapone dedication quoted above, the various correspondences between Montagu, Carter, Talbot, and Scott suggest that many of these women's works, including Montagu's 1769 *Essay on the Writings and Genius of Shakespeare*, Carter's *Epictetus*, and Scott's histories, would not have reached print without the topic suggestions, loans of books, critical feedback, encouragement to proceed, and networking in which they engaged on each others' behalf. Thus, paradoxically, one of the principal influences of Bluestocking manuscript culture might be seen to be the appearance of Bluestocking works in print. As Montagu puts it to Carter in a witty and persuasive letter of 1760:

> I am sorry for your tremors and trepidations, but they are mere nervous disorders, and the manuscript must be printed; so, my dear Urania, away with your lamentations, sit down, revise, correct, augment, print, and publish. I am sure you will have a pleasure in communicating the pious, virtuous sentiments that breathe in all your verses. My inferior soul will feel a joy in your producing such proofs of genius

to the world; let it see that all your advantages are not derived from study. The envious may say you brought your wisdom from Athens, your wit is your own [...] every thing you can say in plain prose, I shall be unmoved as a rock. Rocks themselves have been moved by the strains of Orpheus, send me therefore a copy of verses to dissuade me from the point in question, and I will – send you them back again to be printed in the collection. The very best of your poetical productions have never been published, they may indeed have been seen by a few in manuscript, but the finest things in sheets are soon lost; foliis tantum ne carmina manda; Ne turbata volent rapidis ludibria ventis; print them and bind them fast, I beg you.[41]

Such evidence suggests, again, that it is erroneous to imagine coterie and print cultures as distinct; rather, as King has argued for Rowe's late and very successful publication of *Friendship in Death* (1728), it is useful to understand these women as 'seeking to [enter] the marketplace of print from within the protected precincts of [...] feminine manuscript networks'.[42]

In particular, the liaison work which these women did with booksellers when they were in London appears frequently to have furthered negotiations on behalf of someone like Scott, writing in the provinces and publishing anonymously or pseudonymously. Thus Carter is described by Montagu to Scott in 1761 as having 'just gone home with yr manuscript [likely of *The History of Gustavus Augustus*] sticking like a gizzard under her wing', and several years later as having been told by 'Mr Rivington' that 'he did not care to purchase the copy of Mrs Macs work as he did not think it of general use. Mrs Carter will speak to any other bookseller you recommend, she is not personally acquainted with any of the business, but will follow any directions in the affair'; this manuscript again seems to be one of Scott's own (likely of *Sir George Ellison*), since two weeks later Montagu is writing, 'I am afraid you don't intend printing the manuscript this year. Mrs Carter & I think it very well written & that it would be very useful.' Three years later it is Montagu herself who says, 'I have the pleasure to tell you that in an hour or two after I had yours last night I got into quiet possession of yr manuscripts [...] I will do the needful with Mr Cadell as the Bankers write. I should have sent it this morning and had got the card written, but to say the truth I like the reading of the manuscript and could not get it finished.' And in 1772, she appears to have shared the services of her own secretary to produce a fair copy of Scott's *D'Aubigné*: 'I like DAubigné still better in Print than I did in manuscript, which our great

Amanuensis Henry Bliss Esq[?] might take amiss if he knew it, for I dare say he thinks your History and my Essay never made so good a figure as in [...] his Write.'[43]

If intellectual women of the mid-eighteenth century encouraged and abetted one another's publications, they were perhaps even more crucial in enabling the appearance of the work of the many less-privileged authors whose subscriptions they promoted. Their subscription efforts on behalf of Sarah Fielding, who was very insecure financially, the blind poet Anna Williams, and Mary Darwall have already been mentioned; others they supported included James Woodhouse, whom Montagu calls 'my poetical shoemaker', and Ann Yearsley, the 'Bristol Milkwoman'. Their correspondence expresses the power they saw themselves wielding to this effect. In the case of Samuel Johnson's 1750–52 *Rambler* papers, for example, Carter and Talbot record their attempts to further what they saw as a very worthy project. In their view, its demise after a two-year run was not a failure of their zealous patronage, but rather a consequence of the stubborn refusal of its author to accommodate readers' tastes; thus Talbot writes:

> I assure you I grieved for [the death of that excellent person the Rambler] most sincerely, and could have dropt a tear over his two concluding papers, if he had not in one or two places of the last commended himself too much; for I knew there were people whose very unjust prejudices against him would be strengthened by them. Indeed 'tis a sad thing that such a paper should have met with discouragement from wise, and learned, and good people too – Many are the disputes it has cost me, and not once did I come off triumphant.[44]

The frequent acknowledgments of both Scott and Sarah Fielding to Montagu for her subscription-raising efforts on behalf of the latter's translation of Xenophon record an instance of more effective support.[45] And most paradoxically, Hannah More's anger at Ann Yearsley's ultimate ingratitude toward her leads in late 1785 to a dark prediction ('It is amazing how notorious she has contrived to make her own business. I have had near a hundred letters on the subject, and the Booksellers assure me that her behaviour had quite spoilt the sale of the book, which wou'd have been very great') whose accuracy, in terms of Yearsley's long-term reception, was nevertheless temporarily forestalled by the prior success of More and her Bluestocking connections in raising a subscription of over one thousand names for the volume.[46]

* * *

What, then, did intellectual women writers of the mid-eighteenth century who actively cultivated conversational, epistolary, and manuscript exchange contribute to the shaping of the print sphere as it emerged from this period? For one thing, they insisted on a link between authorial and textual bodies, a link fundamental to manuscript culture, which may well have confirmed the direction of English printing away from anonymity and towards a cult of the author. In her comparison of Demosthenes with Lord Bath and of Lucian with Dr Monsey, quoted above, Montagu continues:

> there are some living geniuses of my acquaintance whom I read, and some dead authors whom I love. There is requisite a certain degree of goodness and benevolence in a character however great or ingenious, to make us feel a kind of interest without which every thing appears faint and languid: where affection is united with admiration, and esteem with delight, there the heart and head are pleased and contented, and one feels a joy books cannot communicate.[47]

Nor is this insistence one-dimensionally moralistic; it expresses a value for techniques that preserve the intimacy of conversational and epistolary sociability in print, like those of the dialogue or letter forms as practised by Sarah Fielding and Hester Chapone. Thus the Bluestockings may also be seen to have influenced the readerly tastes which ultimately gravitated to the popular collections of literary anecdotes and letters of the late eighteenth and early nineteenth centuries, of which Boswell's *Life of Johnson* has been the most enduring example, but which also includes works such as Hester Thrale Piozzi's 1786 *Anecdotes of the Late Samuel Johnson, L.L.D.* and the published collections of the Bluestockings' own letters.

With respect to women's writing, their practice of making suggestions for projects, mutual encouragement, critiques of each other's ideas and manuscripts, and mediation on each other's behalf with booksellers undoubtedly led to the composition, thorough revision, print publication, and wide distribution of the kind of work that might not otherwise have emerged from the pressured conditions of the economically-driven print trade of the day: Greek translations, critical essays, and histories of Protestant heroes produced by women.[48] In this they did not so much create forms or styles as broaden the expected range of women's literary activity. However, although it has become customary to speak of a second generation of Bluestockings, the uneasy relations of Montagu in particular with the likes of Frances Burney, Hester Thrale Piozzi (even before her second marriage), and Anna Letitia Barbauld may in fact mark their greatest failure: the failure to nurture, and ultimately free from the threat of their censure, a generation of successors. To be sure, some of this tension arose from the critical perspectives of those successors; no doubt the model of Montagu reigning as, in Burney's rather cutting description, 'the lady of the castle' presiding over a 'semi-circle that [...] retained during the whole evening its unbroken form, with a precision that made it seem described by a Brobdingnagian compass',[49] or writing flattering epistles to her highly placed male friends, or hosting dinners for 500 chimney sweeps, had come by the late 1780s to represent an earlier, less socially fluid and responsive time.

Nevertheless, in their heyday the Bluestockings can be seen as creating what Ezell has attributed rather to George Ballard's *Memoirs of Several Ladies of Great Britain* (1752) and to Richardson's heroine Clarissa: the model of 'feminine accomplishment' demonstrated by 'witty conversation supported by the reading of the finest authors' and by the pursuit of 'authorship and education [as] upper- and middle-class activities, designed for the benefit of the writer and her immediate circle, not for a popular or commercial audience'.[50] While Ezell rightly disparages this model for the limitations that it reveals in retrospect, in the mid-eighteenth century it effectively harnessed the persistence and prestige of conversational and manuscript culture to further a recognition of women's intellectual capacities, social talents, and artistic skill. By exploiting the social spaces within which an expanding print culture was embedded, these women achieved maximum publicity while remaining at arms' length from the print trade – an achievement that continues to challenge the categories of media and literary histories today.

Notes

1. Jacqueline Labbe, private correspondence.
2. Margaret J.M. Ezell, *Writing Women's Literary History* (Baltimore: Johns Hopkins University Press, 1993).
3. Early examples of this include Jacqueline Pearson's *The Prostituted Muse: Images of Women and Women Dramatists, 1642–1737* (New York: Harvester, 1988), Janet Todd's *The Sign of Angellica: Women, Writing and Fiction, 1660–1800* (New York: Columbia University Press, 1989), and Mary Poovey's *The Proper Lady and the Woman Writer: Ideology as Style in the Works of Mary Wollstonecraft, Mary Shelley, and Jane Austen* (Chicago: University of Chicago Press, 1984).
4. This is the ultimate implication of Catherine Gallagher's *Nobody's Story: The Vanishing Acts of Women Writers in the Marketplace, 1670–1830* (Berkeley and

Los Angeles: University of California Press, 1994); see also Paula McDowell's *The Women of Grub Street: Press, Politics and Gender in the London Literary Marketplace 1678–1730* (Oxford: Clarendon Press, 1998) and, more recently, Betty A. Schellenberg, *The Professionalization of Women Writers in Eighteenth-Century Britain* (Cambridge: Cambridge University Press, 2005).

5. Margaret J.M. Ezell, *Social Authorship and the Advent of Print* (Baltimore: Johns Hopkins University Press, 1999), pp. 141, 102. For Ezell, the definitive shift to print predominance occurred with the emergence of marketed literary series such as Bell's *British Poets*, 1777–89, and the London-based *The English Poets* with Johnson's prefaces, 1779–81. However, she does not discuss any cases of social authorship beyond the 1730s.

6. George L. Justice and Nathan Tinker, eds, *Women's Writing and the Circulation of Ideas: Manuscript Publication in England, 1550–1800* (Cambridge: Cambridge University Press, 2002), p. 5.

7. Several critics, beginning with Sylvia Harcstarck Myers, *The Bluestocking Circle: Women, Friendship, and the Life of the Mind in Eighteenth-Century England* (Oxford: Clarendon Press, 1990), pp. 48–9, 59, have noted that Elizabeth Singer Rowe's successful deployment of the image of virtuous provincial retirement was likely a model for Elizabeth Carter. Harriet Guest has examined in detail how Carter's stance of modest retirement took on public significance (*Small Change: Women, Learning, Patriotism, 1750–1810* (Chicago: University of Chicago Press, 2000), ch. 5).

8. Gary Kelly, General Introduction to *Bluestocking Feminism: Writings of the Bluestocking Circle, 1738–1785*, 6 vols (London: Pickering and Chatto, 1999), I, xlvii–li.

9. Guest, *Small Change*, p. 69.

10. John Duncombe, *The Feminiad; or, Female Genius, A Poem* (London, 1754), pp. 4, 26, 22.

11. Mary Scott, *The Female Advocate; A Poem* (London, 1774), p. v; ll. 371–82; ll. 401–5.

12. Guest, *Small Change*, p. 100.

13. Although Ezell does not provide a formal definition of the term in *Social Authorship and the Advent of Print*, it is clear that she is invoking the embodied context within which authors wrote.

14. Elizabeth Montagu to Sarah Scott [May 1773], The Huntington Library, Montagu Collection mo5941. All manuscript letters are from this collection, and are reproduced by permission of *The Huntington Library, San Marino, California*.

15. See Schellenberg, *Professionalization of Women Writers*, pp. 91–3.

16. Nicole Pohl, 'Salon Culture and Epistolary Conversations', *Women's Writing*, 13 (2006), 139–59, p. 145. In describing this style as dialogic, Pohl repeatedly draws a connection between it and the Enlightenment adoption of the dialogue genre (see, for example, p. 146), but she does not offer contemporary evidence of self-consciousness about this media-crossing link. See my discussion of this issue below.

17. Matthew Montagu, ed., *The Letters of Mrs. E. Montagu, with Some Letters of her Correspondence*, 4 vols (London, 1809–13), IV, 75–6; II, 39; IV, 333 (parenthetical insertion in original); IV, 86–7.

18. Montagu to Scott, [June] 10 [1744], mo 5680.
19. Montagu to Gilbert West, 16 October 1755, mo6731; West to Montagu, 20 October 1755, mo6679; see also Myers, *The Bluestocking Circle*, pp. 180, 185 for several other examples.
20. Guest, *Small Change*, p. 109.
21. David Hume, 'Of Essay Writing', *Essays Moral, Political and Literary* (London: Oxford University Press, 1963), p. 568.
22. Pohl, 'Salon Culture', p. 140.
23. Montagu, ed., *Letters*, II, 31–5.
24. Montagu, ed., *Letters*, IV, 348–9.
25. One exception to an apparent lack of interest in the dialogue as form is *Compendious Conversations: The Method of Dialogue in the Early Enlightenment*, ed. by Kevin L. Cope (Frankfurt am Main: Peter Lang, 1992); see especially Jennifer Georgia's essay on 'The Joys of Social Intercourse: Men, Women, and Conversation in the Eighteenth Century', pp. 249–56.
26. Sarah Fielding, *The Adventures of David Simple and Volume the Last*, ed. by Peter Sabor (Lexington: University Press of Kentucky, 1998), Book II, chapter II; Book VI, chapter VII.
27. Henry Fielding, 'Preface: Written by a Friend of the Author', to Sarah Fielding, *Familiar Letters between the Principal Characters in David Simple* (London, 1747), pp. vi, x–xi, xiv–xv.
28. Fielding, *Familiar Letters*, II, 276n.
29. Scott to Montagu, [20? June 1760], mo5281.
30. These strong female speakers include Cynthia in *David Simple*, who is explicitly described as the intellectual leader of the circle of two couples; Miss Gibson in the *Remarks*; Mrs Teachum and Miss Jenny Peace in *The Governess*; Portia in *The Cry*; and Octavia.
31. In a 2008 search, the database 'Eighteenth-Century Collections Online' listed more than 370 distinct publications with the words 'dialogue' or 'dialogues' in their titles; although many of these were comic poems or pastoral dialogues, a significant proportion were educational works covering all subjects from philosophy and theology to optics and medicine.
32. Although Lennard J. Davis has emphasized how late eighteenth-century novel dialogue became distinct from conversation for ideological reasons ('Conversation and Dialogue', *The Age of Johnson* 1, ed. by Paul J. Korshin (New York: AMS, 1987), pp. 347–73), I have argued elsewhere that much mid-century fiction reveals the influence rather of the ideals of conversational sociability; see my *The Conversational Circle: Rereading the English Novel, 1740–1775* (Lexington: University Press of Kentucky, 1996), especially ch. 1, 'Consensus, the Conversational Circle, and Mid-Eighteenth-Century Fiction'.
33. Talbot appears to have been the most committed of the mid-century Bluestockings to a manuscript model of literary production, producing her work for particular occasions and recipients while very reluctant to go to print (see Myers, *The Bluestocking Circle*, pp. 207–11). Yet by 1741 her reputation by word-of-mouth was such that Elizabeth Carter sought to be introduced to her, and in the early 1750s it is clear that her conversational and epistolary advice about the character and manners of a 'good man' influenced Samuel Richardson in his creation of the hero of *Sir Charles*

Grandison. See T.C. Duncan Eaves and Ben D. Kimpel, *Samuel Richardson: A Biography* (Oxford: Oxford University Press, 1971), pp. 357–63 for an overview of Talbot's role in the preparation of this novel.

34. Montagu Pennington, ed., *A Series of Letters between Mrs. Elizabeth Carter and Miss Catherine Talbot*, 4 vols (London, 1809), II, 131.
35. John Mulso, quoted in Myers, *The Bluestocking Circle*, p. 146.
36. Ibid., p. 231.
37. Hester Chapone, *Letters on the Improvement of the Mind, Addressed to a Young Lady*, 2 vols (London, 1773), I, iii–iv, 1–2.
38. Montagu, *Letters*, I, 8–9.
39. Montagu Pennington, Dedication to *Letters from Mrs. Elizabeth Carter to Mrs. Montagu between the Years 1755 and 1800*, ed. Montagu Pennington, 3 vols (London, 1817), I, xi–xiii.
40. See Scott to Montagu [1763?], mo5308; also Montagu to Scott [25 September 1765], mo5825, and Montagu to Scott [21 October 1765], mo5827. This despite her nephew's assertion that 'on no occasion did she write foul copies, or keep copies of them, and very seldom did she recollect to affix a date' (Montagu, *Letters*, II, 312).
41. Montagu, *Letters*, IV, 350. The Latin, from Virgil's *Aeneid*, in Dryden's translation reads 'commit not thy prophetic mind / To flitting leaves, the sport of ev'ry wind' (John Dryden, trans., *Virgil's Aeneid*, ed. by Charles W. Eliot (New York: Collier, 1909), 6.116–17).
42. Kathryn R. King, 'Elizabeth Singer Rowe's Tactical Use of Print and Manuscript', in *Women's Writing and the Circulation of Ideas*, ed. by Justice and Tinker, pp. 158–81, 169.
43. Montagu to Scott [c. 1761], mo5786; 13 April 1765, mo5821; 20 April 1765, mo5822; [27 December 1768], mo5914; 4 June [1772], mo5927.
44. Pennington, ed., *Letters between Carter and Talbot*, II, 73–4.
45. Scott to Montagu [20? June 1760], mo5281; [June? 1760], mo5283; [6 May 1762?], mo5292.
46. Hannah More to Elizabeth Montagu, 20 October [1785], mo3993; see also the *Oxford Dictionary of National Biography*'s account of Yearsley. As I have argued elsewhere, using the case of Charlotte Lennox, Bluestocking disfavour could indeed be effective in diminishing an author's reputation; see Schellenberg, *Professionalization of Women Writers*, pp. 166–70.
47. Montagu, ed., *Letters*, IV, 349.
48. A negative point of comparison would be the poverty which brought to an abrupt end Elizabeth Elstob's promising scholarship on the Anglo-Saxon language.
49. Frances Burney, *Memoirs of Doctor Burney, Arranged from his own Manuscripts, from Family Papers, and from Personal Collections*, 3 vols (London, 1832), II, 270.
50. Ezell, *Writing Women's Literary History*, p. 87.

4

'[T]o strike a little out of a road already so much beaten': Gender, Genre, and the Mid-Century Novel

Jennie Batchelor

When Frances Burney published *Evelina* (1778), she famously situated her foray into the 'republic of letters' in relation to the careers of an impressive list of male literary forebears.[1] '[E]nlightened' by Samuel Johnson's 'knowledge', 'charmed' by Jean-Jacques Rousseau, 'softened' by Samuel Richardson, and 'exhilarated' by Henry Fielding's 'wit' and Tobias Smollett's 'humour', Burney declared that she 'presume[d] not to attempt pursuing the same ground' that these eminent figures had 'tracked', for 'imitation' in 'books' could not 'be shunned too sedulously' (pp. 9, 8). Her decision partially to depart from the example of her august predecessors was not so much motivated by a lack of confidence in her abilities, however, as it was urged by her concern for the novel's past and its future. In their efforts to establish the genre as a legitimate literary form, Burney argued, the novel's most eloquent practitioners had unwittingly orchestrated its demise. By the late 1770s, fiction was no longer novel and rarely displayed the hallmarks of innovation that had once characterized its appeal. In developing alternative modes of story-telling and characterization to those deployed in older prose forms such as romance, novelists including Fielding, Johnson, and Richardson had closed off others. Thus, although these writers had 'cleared' prose fiction of the 'weeds' that had formerly inhibited its growth, they had 'also culled the flowers' that had made it so alluring. The novel's path may have been 'plain' by 1778, according to Burney, but it was also 'barren' (p. 9).

Burney's commonly overlooked assessment of the novel's rise and imminent demise, recalling as it does the phrase from Jane Collier and Sarah Fielding's *The Cry* (1754) quoted in the chapter title above, raises some pressing questions about the construction and gendering of literary genealogies, and about the role that mid- to late eighteenth-century women writers played as practitioners and theorists of the novel.[2] Should we, for example, read Burney's attempt to align herself with an illustrious list of male authors, as Betty Schellenberg has done, as evidence that she was complicit with 'the Great Forgetting' of female novelists that gathered momentum in the eighteenth-century's latter decades and culminated in Ian Watt's homocentric rise of the novel thesis?[3] Or, might we understand her writing out of literary history those figures such as Frances Brooke, Sarah Fielding, and Charlotte Lennox, all of whom undeniably influenced her fiction, as disingenuous?

Even if we assume that Burney's allusion to Collier and Fielding's experimental novel was accidental rather than deliberate, there is ample evidence to corroborate the second of these claims. For although the preface to *Evelina* openly acknowledges its author's debt to male writers only, it characterizes that debt as a problematic one. *Evelina*, like *The Cry* before it, paid respect to the literary heritage from which it emerged, but promised to cultivate a more fertile ground for fiction, one that would propagate new growth and encourage the return of the 'flowers' its author's predecessors had destroyed in the name of progress. It is in this acknowledgement of its author's indebtedness to prominent male figures, coupled with her claims for the necessity of textual innovation, that the preface to *Evelina* most forcefully reminds us of the female-authored texts it otherwise seems to obscure. For in taking this stance, Burney looks back to the work of a number of writers, including Brooke, Collier, Sarah Fielding, and Lennox, as well as Eliza Haywood, Sarah Scott, and Frances Sheridan, many of whom benefited from close connections with Fielding, Johnson, and Richardson, but who also contested the intimately related models of genre and gender their male interlocutors constructed. It is with women writers' qualifications and rejections of these paradigms, their participation in contemporary debates on the novel, and the implications of these interventions for the reception of their works and careers, that this chapter is concerned.

The mid-eighteenth century, once a virtual blind spot in literary studies, has recently become the focus of a small, but significant, body of scholarship, which has demonstrated how different the novel's rise appears if we view the publication of *Pamela* (1740) and *Tom Jones* (1749) not as definitive events, but as two key moments in a long and disputed history. Novelists of the 1750s and 1760s, keen to pay homage to, to exploit, or to challenge the narrative models espoused by their predecessors, produced some of the most innovative experiments in novelistic form of the eighteenth, or perhaps of any, century. Despite the emergence, and increasingly normative prescriptions of, the two prominent literary reviews (the *Monthly* and the *Critical*), this was, in Paul Francis Burditt's words, a period of 'uncertain generic potentiality', in which the 'thoroughly modern novel' was born.[4] Laurence Sterne's *The Life and Opinions of Tristram Shandy* (1759–67) is only the best-known example of the mid-century determination to re-imagine the novel's formal, thematic, and discursive possibilities, as Thomas Keymer has argued.[5] Burditt's and Keymer's studies rewardingly re-map eighteenth-century literary history, not least by demonstrating that the legacies of Richardson and Fielding were as complex as their achievements were considerable. Nonetheless, such accounts have done little to illuminate the vital role that women writers played in the novel's development during these formative years. Even those scholars who have explored the careers of women writers of this period in some detail have tended to confirm Frank Donoghue's claim that such figures were compromised by their sex, and forced, for fear of transgressing the bounds of feminine propriety, to produce fictions that comprised, in Janet Todd's words, '[t]issues of clichés and influences', and 'purveyed a common fantasy' of 'passive femininity'.[6] Yet as Felicity Nussbaum has argued, women writers of this period were, of necessity and by inclination, much more innovative and experimental than literary historians have often assumed them to be. Occupying 'decidedly different positions within economic and social structures' to men, women writers 'could not simply imitate male patterns of authorship and narration', and thus 'experimented with ways to master the craft and their own subjectivities through the invention of new plots, the manipulation of genres and the inclusion of innovative subject matter'.[7] The novels discussed below more than bear out Nussbaum's claims. None subscribes to the ideologies of domesticity and female passivity alluded to by Donoghue and Todd; indeed, all are linked by their authors' ambitious endeavours to exploit the novel's supposed primacy as a vehicle for conveying truth in order to expose fantasies and clichés of gender. In order to distinguish between the moral truths that were deemed to be the novel's proper preserve and the social and gendered fictions the novel spuriously passed off as 'truths', these writers had recourse to a series of innovative textual strategies that many conventional histories of the novel have been unable to accommodate. In the process, they attempted to establish new possibilities for women in the private sphere of the home and the public sphere of print.

That genre as much as gender is implicated in these writers' historical occlusion from genealogies of the novel's rise is a central claim of this chapter. For as Schellenberg has suggested, close attention to the careers of mid-century women writers suggests that 'gender, while one determinant of a woman writer's career, was far from the only, and perhaps not always the most significant determinant of that career's trajectory'.[8] The novelists examined below produced oriental tales, historical novels, dramatic fables, children's books, and proto-Gothic narratives. A number of their works pushed the novel's geographical boundaries to embrace the colonies and beyond: America in the case of Lennox's *Harriot Stuart* (1751), Canada in Brooke's *Emily Montague* (1769), and Persia in Sheridan's *The History of Nourjahad* (1767). Those writers who worked more commonly within British or European contexts nonetheless often borrowed from non-European narrative traditions, as Scott and Haywood did in their deft and often ironic use of the frame narrative, popularized by the publication of *Les Mille et Une Nuits* (1704). As the novel's geographical scope and structural frames widened, so conceptions of the genre's status and function were re-imagined in ways that had far-reaching implications for the form. One of the most insistent features of women's fiction of this period is its self-conscious fictionality, a fictionality manifest not only in the novels' prefaces and re-workings of well-known plot structures, but in digressions in which narrators speak directly to readers, and in chapter summaries that anticipate and foreclose various kinds of readings. 'The novel' is, thus, not only the form that these fictions take, but, to a greater or lesser extent, these fictions' subject and overriding preoccupation.

Conventional histories of the novel, particularly those that emphasize the emergence of 'formal realism', have found it difficult to accommodate such self-reflexively fictitious novels, in which the relationship between the real and the fictive is deliberately and vigorously contested.[9] Nor is it coincidental that many of these writers' claims for their works fail to chime with traditional conceptions of the novel. Indeed, a number of the fictions produced by women during this period were characterized by their first reviewers as bad novels, either because they were deemed imperfect examples of the form, or because they were not, in fact, recognizable as novels. In order fully to grasp the significance of these writers' contributions to the novel's development, it is essential to recognize that they wrote in a period in which the genre was viewed as an unstable form, the path of which was not yet as 'barren' as Burney would find it in the 1770s. The following sections of this chapter examine the ways in which women exploited this instability to contest emergent notions of the novel and the 'truths' fiction was supposed to tell in order to imagine new ways of perceiving and inhabiting the world.

The 'excellence of falshood':[10] theorizing the novel at mid-century

Johnson's *Rambler* 4 is perhaps the most famous theorization of the novel not to use the word in any of its pages. (Johnson's formulation is 'the comedy of romance'.)[11] The essay, which built upon the work of Richardson and Henry Fielding, among others, formed a point of dialogue for a number of women writers, particularly for Collier, Fielding, and Scott, each of whom was as committed as their male contemporaries to analysing the novel's function and responsibilities, its relationship to history and romance, and, most particularly, its claims to moral and ethical truth. Of particular concern for mid-century women writers was the novel's new-found preoccupation with 'familiar histories', which, in Johnson's words, were more likely than the other-worldly and 'wild strain[s]' of romance to encourage readers to view characters' strengths and weaknesses as mirrors of their own, and thus to 'regulate their [...] practices' (p. 21). The novel's superiority to romance lay in its mimetic reproduction of 'human manners', which unlike the fantastic inventions of romance and the dry axioms of 'History', provided 'lectures of conduct, and introductions into life' for those readers whose minds were 'susceptible of impressions' (pp. 20–1). In making this argument, *Rambler* 4 affirmed a mid-century commonplace: that, as Patricia Meyer Spacks observes, 'fiction justifie[d] itself by the truth' it told. For Johnson, as for the writers discussed below, 'truth' signalled 'moral or ethical' verisimilitude – truth about the workings of the human mind and character in various, and sometimes implausibly dramatic, circumstances – rather than what we might anachronistically term 'realism'.[12] As such, and as the Doctor attempts to persuade Arabella in Lennox's *The Female Quixote* (1752), 'Truth' was not always injured by 'Fiction' (p. 377). Rather, fiction gave access to truths that otherwise lay beyond their readers' power to grasp, by offering vicarious experiences designed to provoke readerly identification and reflection, safely contained by the fictionality of the medium itself. Not all of the so-called 'truths' told by novels were objectively determined, however, and, as Spacks argues, could be presented so as to construe the 'vicissitudes of phallic power' as fact; that is, to pass off culture as nature.[13] Mid-century women writers were no less keenly aware than Spacks that the novel and the supposed 'truths' it imparted were inextricably implicated in cultural constructions of gender; yet their fiction proves them to be far more determined to expose this fact than her study allows.[14] Female authors active in this period were just as convinced as many of their male contemporaries by the novel's ability to convey moral and ethical truths incommunicable in other prose forms, but were vociferous in their condemnation of the novel's fabrication of certain social 'truths' designed to legitimize the wrongs of woman. It was precisely the novel's role as a vehicle for truth, these writers contended, that uniquely fitted it to deconstruct fictions of gender.

Many of the most compelling contributions made by women writers to this debate are made outside the plots proper of their works, in their carefully crafted prefaces. Prefaces to female-authored texts of this period have too often been given short shrift by critics, quick to label them as formulaic articulations of female authors' awareness of the indelicacy of their profession. Closer attention demonstrates that the preface was a far more complex space, in which, as Cheryl L. Nixon comments, writers 'adopted a range of 'formal strategies [...] to construct the character of the woman author in the text'.[15] In addition to holding up the female author to scrutiny, the preface was often a space in which the novel itself was held to account. Among the most theoretically sophisticated prefaces of this kind are those found in the works of Fielding and her collaborator Collier. In a series of texts spanning over ten years, both writers teased out the gendered implications of their contemporaries' claims for the novel's relationship to romance, history, and truth. In her preface to Fielding's *The Adventures of David Simple, Volume the Last* (1753), for example, Collier decried the genre's 'earnest Thirst after Novelty' for novelty's sake and pointed to the ridiculousness of those who would dismiss the sequel to the highly successful *The Adventures of David Simple* (1744) on the grounds that its author should have 'rais[ed] up a new set of Company of the same Turn of Mind' rather than attempt a continuation of the earlier work.[16] Rehearsing the common metaphor of reading-as-eating, Collier argued that readers who sought 'such Food only' deserved not to have their appetites satisfied by so ingenious a confectioner as Fielding (pp. iv–v). Enthusiastically mixing her metaphors, Collier went on to suggest that the act of writing was akin to musical composition. Just as the composer was limited to prescribed scales, so the novelist should confine herself to 'known and remarkable Characters': 'The beautiful Novelty of a musical Passage', she argued, 'arises not from the new simple Sounds, which it is impossible to make, but from a melodious Variation on the same notes' (pp. vi–vii). It was not that the novel should abandon its aspirations to novelty altogether – there were clear advantages to placing familiar characters in unfamiliar 'Situations', as this powerful sequel to *David Simple* amply demonstrated (p. vi). However, the pursuit of novelty was not to be allowed to compromise the genre's function as a vehicle for conveying the indisputable moral and ethical truths that were supposed to form its subject. After all, often rehearsed sentimental tales of the corruptibility of man and the vulnerability of virtue were neither less truthful, nor less efficacious as vehicles for the readers' self-improvement, for their familiarity.[17]

Yet, as Fielding made clear in the preface to *The History of the Countess of Dellwyn* (1758) maintaining fidelity to truth was no mere simple exercise for writers. In order to achieve this end, the author was bound, on the one hand, to create probable characters and events which could 'unravel the intricate Labyrinths of the human Mind'; on the other, she had to ensure that her readers were in no doubt that the 'familiar histories' she related were, in fact, nothing more than fictions.[18] The purveyor of 'truth', Fielding claimed, had to be practised in the art of deception; crucially, though, she had to be open about her deceitfulness. For if romance imperilled the reader by encouraging her to take 'absurd' and fanciful 'Fictions' as 'Histories', as Lennox's Arabella had done (*The Female Quixote*, p. 374), then the novel, in the hands of the credulous, was an even more dangerous art form. The apparent plausibility of the novel – its familiarity – made those readers who 'delight[ed] in making Applications' still more likely than romance enthusiasts to arrive at 'far-fetched Deductions' about the relationship of its contents to real life events (I, p. v). To prevent such misapplications, and thus to preserve the 'Air of real Truth' that was fiction's greatest achievement, Fielding enjoined that the novel should be self-conscious about its fictionality (I, p. xi). At stake, here, is not simply a question of authorial honesty; the deception authors practised upon readers when they asked them to believe in the veracity of their fiction's contents were of little consequence, she argued, when set against the greater fraud writers committed when they failed to recognize the novel's obligation to 'profit' its readers by applying itself to their 'Service and Emolument'.[19] Drawing attention to a novel's fictionality generated such returns, Fielding indicated, by dissipating the effects of the potential 'violence' that Johnson feared might take possession of vulnerable readers' minds through a careful policing of their identification with a novel's characters (*Rambler*, 4, p. 22). The reader who was in no doubt of the fictitiousness of a David Simple or a Countess of Dellwyn would not fall into the trap of attempting to identify these 'Chimeras' as persons 'whom [she] kn[e]w' in real life (I, p. iv). Reading fiction as fiction, rather than biography, such a reader would not be distracted from the novel's principal aim, which was to conjure 'Images' of mankind whose virtues and faults reflected aspects of her own personality, rather than disguised portraits of identifiable individuals. Only when a novel's characters were recognized as such – as fictional embodiments of common human virtues and frailties – could they function as morally edifying examples and, thus, could truth be served.[20]

Neither Collier nor Fielding makes in these prefaces an explicit distinction between the novel's effects upon male and female readers. Yet women writers' contributions to the debate on the genre's status and function were often unambiguously linked to debates on gender, as the preface to *The Histories of Some of the Penitents in the Magdalen-House* (1760) reveals.[21] Like so many of the novels discussed, here, *Histories*, sometimes although probably spuriously attributed to Fielding, eschews the Richardsonian pretence of narrative realism by insisting upon the novel's fictiveness and the necessity that readers engage with it only upon such terms. This self-conscious fictionality is all the more intriguing in the case of this particular novel, which was inspired by the real-life Magdalen House for the Reception of Penitent Prostitutes, an institution that relied upon its inmates' testimonies to generate subscriptions. It is further remarkable given that the majority of prostitution narratives from this period subscribed to what Mary Peace terms a '"realist" [narrative] epistemology' characterized by 'the act of revealing the self entirely through the presentation of exhaustive evidence'.[22] Fully aware that the novel flouted its readers' expectations, the preface, written at Richardson's behest, opens with the author's acknowledgement that 'Some apology may be judged necessary for a work which assumes real characters, tho' in the title-page it acknowledges itself to be a fiction' (p. 3). The *Monthly Review* determined this apology well placed. The writer's failure to present the Magdalens' narratives as '*real* histories' was not only a sign of 'consciencious [*sic*] ingenuity', but of naivety. Fiction was entertaining because it satisfied the reader's 'wish to be deceived', and thus any effort to disabuse the public of this fact made, 'though perhaps unaccountably', a novel 'less interesting', and ensured that it would be less 'universally read'.[23] Yet, the reviewer failed to realize that the author's strategy was essential to her decidedly non-apologetic theorization of the novel. Adopting Johnson's notion of 'familiar histories' as a structural device, the author of *Histories* pitted the novel against 'works of imagination [...] fit only for the entertainment of an idle hour'. Her primary target, however, was not romance but 'History', which, she argued, was as dangerous as romance in the hands of readers whose minds 'reach no farther than the facts': 'To such a reader, Livy and Tacitus can give no greater improvement than the

Seven champions of Christendom, or the wonderful adventures of Guy Earl of Warwick' (p. 8). The novel was a much more effective prose form than history, *Histories* suggested, for although 'the facts' the former presented were 'imaginary', 'the consequences' that might be 'drawn from them' were 'real'. Fiction engaged the reader in such a way that her 'observing mind' was encouraged to move from particulars, or 'first principles', to generalizable moral conclusions grounded in 'reason', but informed by 'imagination'. If the mind of the complacent history-reader was little more than an 'index', then that of the reflective novel-reader resembled a compendium, according to which she could more accurately interpret the world (p. 8).

Such arguments for the edifying qualities of probabilistic narrative would not be out of place in any number of mid-century valorizations of the novel; yet, *Histories* goes further in its understanding of the relationship between truth and fiction, and its implications for both genre and gender. The novel's power rested not, its author contended, in its ability to render truths about the workings of society and the human character as convincingly as possible in fictional form, largely because these 'truths' were often little more than fabrications conveniently passed off as fact in order to naturalize various kinds of injustice and inequality. Rather, by drawing attention to the fictionality of its rendering – by emphasizing the constructed nature of narrative itself – it could importantly lead the reader to question these supposed realities. In short, fiction's duty was not simply to 'imitate nature'; its primary responsibility was to use artifice to fight artifice and to reveal how nature had been supplanted by culture speciously passed off as 'truth' (p. 8). Thus, *Histories*' project was to educate readers in the art of discriminating between these fictions and genuine displays of 'truth, faith, and humanity'. Such, for example, is the motive behind the text's vehement condemnation of those women who condemned prostitutes as whores while casting the men who reduced them to 'penury, disease, and infamy' as figures of 'gallantry', and who maintained their own reputation only by 'cruel[ly]' casting 'odium' upon their fallen counterparts (pp. 4–6). Through the relation of 'a series of probable events' – the penitents' narratives of their respective falls into prostitution – the author hoped to break such cycles of injustice, to incline the genteel reader to see through entrenched discourses of femininity and sexuality she had internalized and 'to [so] pity the frailty of one of her own sex, as to forgive the past, and enable the offender to efface her guilt by sincere repentance and a blameless life' (p. 4). With these words, a preface that begins with an ambivalent note of 'apology' develops into an unequivocal vindication of the power of self-consciously fictive writing to enable the reader to deconstruct texts and the culturally constructed fictions of rank, gender, and sex that this novel, like a number of mid-century fictions, set out to challenge.[24]

'[T]o unfold the labyrinths of the human mind, [...] 'tis necessary to assume a certain freedom in writing'[25]

Drawing attention to the novel's fictionality was not a uniquely feminine strategy, of course. What is distinctive about the women writers discussed here, however, is the way in which each makes this move to demystify fictions of gender. The devices through which female authors forced readers to confront the fictiveness of narrative and gender were numerous and by no means confined to their prefaces. Eliza Haywood's *The History of Jemmy and Jenny Jessamy* (1753), for example, contained a number of Fieldingesque direct addresses to readers in the form of chapter titles and extended 'digressions' from the main narrative. There is much more to be said about the narrator's laconic style – evident in such chapter titles as 'In a digression of no consequence to the history, and may therefore be read or omitted at discretion', or 'Affords some very useful and exemplary hints to young persons of both sexes; which if they are not the better and wiser for, it is wholly owing to themselves, and not the fault of the author' – than can be dealt with here.[26] For the present purposes, it is perhaps sufficient to point out that such interventions crucially determine how this novel – notable, in John Richetti's words, for its 'unsentimental realism' – is read. The narrator's comments bristle with an irony that, as Richetti continues, signals 'an objective moralism' that counters the conventionally sentimentalized rhetoric in which marriage and courtship was often represented in the mid-century novel.[27]

Others deployed more elaborate textual ruses that surely entitle them to be considered among the earliest practitioners of metafiction. Some advertised their novel's textuality by overlaying their narratives upon known plots. Sheridan's *Nourjahad*, for example, partly models itself upon Johnson's vanity-of-human-wishes tale, *The History of Rasselas* (1759), but in a conclusion in which everything is concluded, provides a feminist revisioning of the original moral tale. With the revelation that Mandana, beloved yet believed to be dead by Nourjahad, is not only living but has been the principal agent in the sultan's extravagant scheme to trick him out of his 'insatiable desire of pleasure' and 'wealth', the reader, as Nussbaum comments, 'retroactively reconstitutes' the novel's plot and realizes her central role both in authoring the events the novel describes and in leading its male protagonist to truth through the construction of an elaborate, yet morally justifiable, fiction.[28] Unlike *Rasselas*, which finally envisions its eponymous hero imagining himself governing a 'dominion', the 'limits' of which he is ominously reluctant to 'fix',[29] Sheridan's work concludes with 'a woman's vision of male power and authority, employed for good ends, through a woman's agency'.[30]

Scott similarly turned to the structure, if not the substance, of the oriental tale to analyse both genre and gender in her third novel, *A Journey Through Every Stage of Life* (1754), which both borrowed from, and inverted, the *Arabian Nights* paradigm by having a servant, Sabrina, relate a series of eight tales in order to save the soul of her narcissistic mistress, Carinthia. Throughout the first of these tales, 'The History of Leonora and Louisa', metaphors of artistry recur in order to emphasize the constructed nature of fiction and the truths it sanctioned. The servant's extended commentary upon her narrative practice – upon the 'innocent Art[s]' she deploys to arouse her superior's 'Curiosity', and the care she takes to make the 'Moral' of the tales palatable to her unresponsive auditor – draws attention to narrative artifice and the central role that artfulness plays in the construction of morally truthful fiction.[31] It is, therefore, no coincidence that the servant's first, and favourite, heroine masquerades for a period as a male painter, during which time she accepts a commission from a rake to paint the portrait of a woman he intends to seduce. Rightly perceiving the commission as a pretext to gain proximity to the object of his affections, Leonora seizes an opportunity to reform the libertine by revealing the excellence of the woman upon whom he has designs. However, the heroine's attempts 'to rectify *Dorinton's* Principles' during Lucy's sittings for the portrait carry an aesthetic price, distracting the painter to such an extent that she 'distort[s] the Features on which she was at Work':

> When her Thoughts were too much engaged in trying to purify the Mind, [...] the unregarded Hand, by mixing some wrong Colour on the Pallet, would darken the Complexion, and turn a *Venus* into a Negroe, or change a Skin of Roses and Lillies into a Jaundice Hue.
>
> (p. 55)

Given that *A Journey* explicitly links Leonora's labours with the narrative work of the outspoken Sabrina through metaphors of artistry, it is tempting to read this passage as thinly metafictional commentary.[32]

Scott's bold juxtaposition of the artistic and the moral, coupled with her revelation that the fulfilment of these (potentially contrary) impulses might disfigure an artwork, is striking in an age in which the novel commonly claimed to be uniquely able to blend amusement and edification. At stake, here, is also a thorny authorial dilemma: how can a writer manipulate the conventional aesthetics of novel writing in order to serve her own artistic and moral agendas without alienating an audience that was inhospitable to anything that fell short of its often conservative expectations? The answer lies in the metaphors of artistry in which the question is couched: the novelist must adhere to fictional conventions to secure a readership, but by drawing her readers' attention to the arbitrariness of these constraints, she need not sacrifice her 'Principles'. This is precisely the effect of Sabrina's declaration of 'Disgust' when she reveals that, after successfully providing for herself and two female dependants by masquerading as a man, such an 'uncommon' heroine as Leonora should follow the example of many a heroine before her and do so 'so common a Thing as marrying' in her narrative's conclusion (p. 68). Scott's novel conforms to readers' expectations that narrative closure be achieved through the fulfilment of a romantic plot-line, but does so grudgingly, revealing the artistic compromises such a resolution forces. By staging her dissatisfaction with the arbitrariness of the narrative's conclusion, the novelist underscores her argument that, as Haywood and the author of *Histories* would no doubt have agreed, it is 'Custom, not Nature, [that] inflicts that Dependence in which [women] live, obliged to the industry of Man for our Support, as well as to his Courage for our Defence' (p. 7).

Arguably a more sophisticated mid-century attempt to deconstruct fictions of gender through a deconstruction of genre occurs in Collier and Fielding's *The Cry*. With its direct addresses to readers, its reworking of sentimental conventions and its experimental, dramatic structure (three-volumes, five parts, with an introduction, prologues and epilogue), *The Cry* mobilizes all of the textual strategies highlighted above, and develops innovations of its own, to produce an original work, in which 'familiar histories' are of interest only to the extent that they serve the text's primary aims 'to paint' 'human nature' in its true colours (I, p. 15) and 'to strip, as much as possible, *Duessa* or Falshood [sic], of all her shifts and evasions' (I, p. 13). To describe the novel's plot is largely to miss Collier and Fielding's point, which is to 'unfold the labyrinths of the human mind' (I, p. 14) and to praise disinterested benevolence above the petty 'spiteful and malicious' motives that characterize those 'enemies' to 'Truth', and to whose slanders the virtuous fall prey

(I, p. 13). Nonetheless, a brief account of *The Cry*'s contents is useful for those unfamiliar with its extraordinary contours. The text opens with the learned and self-assured Portia being brought before the eponymous Cry – a hostile assembly united only in their 'common clamour against Truth and her adherents' (I, p. 20) – accompanied by a lone ally, an allegorical embodiment of Simplicity, Una. The members of the Cry, who are '[a]s strongly different [from Portia and Una] as light from darkness (or indeed as truth from error)', taunt the heroine as she relates her life-story, her love for Ferdinand, and the deceptions practised upon her and her lover by Ferdinand's scheming brother (I, p. 22). At every turn, Portia's words are misconstrued and her motives questioned as the Cry determine to expose her patently evident virtue as fraudulent.

Volume two introduces the story of Cylinda, a former mistress of Ferdinand's father, whose quixotism serves further to emphasize Portia's constancy. Like Portia, Cylinda has received a classical education – she has been educated in such masculine subjects as Latin and Greek – but unlike her more virtuous counterpart, she has developed a fatally uncritical enthusiasm for moral sense philosophy, and particularly for Shaftesbury's conviction that 'RIDICULE', rather than the reason and experience espoused by Portia, be made a 'TEST of TRUTH' (II, p. 276). Moving quixotically from Shaftesburian, to Platonic, Epicurean, and Lucretian philosophy, Cylinda remains constant only in her puzzlement with Christianity and belief that, in the absence of religious faith – without which, as Linda Bree explains, 'the logic and philosophy of the classical writers is shown to be worthless' – she must look to herself as 'the sovereign judge of all things' (II, p. 276).[33] Needless to say that Cylinda is received more hospitably by the Cry than Portia, at least until she repents of her past, and earns Una's approval and Portia's friendship. Having been unable to discredit Portia, or to enlist Cylinda as one of their own, the Cry begin to 'wrangle, contend, and abuse each other in such a manner that it was impossible for them to remain in one collective body' (III, p. 294). The company disbands, although they remain individually committed to 'support[ing] affectation and fallacy, and to oppos[ing] simplicity and truth' (III, p. 294).

Portia's and Cylinda's narratives pay more than lip service to the preoccupations of sentimental fiction. Courtship rituals, female education, affective bonds, sibling rivalry, filial duty, and parental responsibility are as central to the women's autobiographical narratives as they are to *Clarissa* (1747–48). What differentiates their tales from other sentimental narratives is the significance given to their telling and the author's refusal to allow the reader to suspend disbelief and forget that this is a work of imagination. Centring on the monologues of two women, who have been removed from the domestic sphere and relocated in an allegorical courtroom in which their tales are subject to intense scrutiny and widespread misunderstanding, *The Cry* privileges narrative construction and interpretation above content. This unfamiliar rendering of the heroines' 'familiar histories' invites the reader to confront the limitations of fiction as a representational mode and the failure of conventional interpretive frameworks (whether drawn from romance or philosophy or from courtship and marriage rituals) to accommodate women's emotional and intellectual needs. It is, therefore, unsurprising that genre and language – the form and substance of these oppressive structures – are, as several critics have noted, subjected to sustained scrutiny throughout the novel. As Collier and Fielding declare in the introduction, *The Cry* will not see its heroine imperilled by the giants' castles and 'gloomy forests' of romance; rather, 'the puzzling mazes' into which Portia is thrown 'are the perverse interpretations made upon her words; the lions, tigers, and giants, from which [the authors] endeavour to rescue her, are the spiteful and malicious tongues of her enemies' (I, p. 13). The Cry's 'twist[ing] and wrest[ing of] *Portia*'s words into a thousand different meanings, which she never so much as thought of' (I, p. 59), coupled with its futile determination to find her a hypocrite, metonymically represents society's efforts to force women to disguise their true selves in the name of virtue. In fiction, as in life, however, the truth will out. Portia vows not to live in such a 'continual state of war', and refuses to allow her 'adversaries' to prevent her from acknowledging freely the 'affections of [the] heart' (I, pp. 40–1).

Mary Anne Schofield links *The Cry*'s interest in exposing the complicity of genre and language with female subjugation to questions of gender: 'unmasking the romance genre', she argues, entails an investigation of 'the use of language seen through the disguise of male words and idioms' forced upon women.[34] Mika Suzuki, who assumes Fielding's sole authorship of the novel, has recently contested Schofield's claims, arguing that 'Fielding's awareness of the precariousness of language' is not so much tied to questions of gender as yoked 'to her perception of authorship' and anxieties about readers 'who represent (always distorting) autonomous constructions of the meaning beyond the author's control'.[35] Schofield's and Suzuki's accounts need not be antagonistic, however. Indeed, as I have implied throughout this chapter, such tendencies to read women writers' contributions to debates on gender in isolation from their contributions to debates on genre, and vice versa, are in danger of producing their own distortions. In Collier and

Fielding's view, and as indicated in the quotation cited in the heading of this section, literary and psychic freedom were inextricably linked. To convey truth through an 'unfold[ing of] the labyrinths of the human mind', it was 'necessary to assume a certain freedom in writing' because existing prose forms had, in their attempts to pass off socially fabricated fictions as facts of life, been instrumental in misrepresenting the 'realities' they claimed as their subject. For Fielding and Collier, as for many mid-century women writers, new forms of fiction were the best antidotes to the old.

Some readers were apparently immune to such prescriptions, however. In a review of *The Cry* which appeared in the *Monthly Review* in 1754, for example, an anonymous critic, while lavish in his praise for a work that 'contain[ed] more literature and good sense, than, a few only excepted, all our modern novels put together', noted that its style was 'too much abstracted from the present taste, to procure [it] as many readers as it deserves'.[36] The relative paucity of modern scholarly accounts of the novel when compared with the volume of work devoted to Fielding's no less interesting, but less obviously experimental, *David Simple* suggests that the reviewer's comments were prophetic as well as pertinent. With the exception of Lennox's *Female Quixote*, none of the novels cited here is as well known (or as widely regarded) as *Evelina*. Yet, for all her attempts to avoid acknowledging their achievements, it is hard to imagine that Burney's astute observations on the politics of female identity in the plot of her first novel, and her canny assessments of the contemporary literary marketplace in its paratexts, would have been possible without the work of a previous generation of women writers who were as committed to finding new and fertile ground for fiction as she was.

Given these authors' significance – a significance that Burney intimates even though she does not openly acknowledge it – how are we to account for the still marginal presence of these writers' works in genealogies of the novel? My contention is that it is not their writers' sex per se that has been at issue, here, although the privileging of sex has undoubtedly obscured certain aspects of their work which have determined their self-presentation and reception. Rather, it is the inassimilable qualities of their fiction that render it so challenging both to eighteenth-century readers and to more recent genealogies of the novel: novels that take the novel as their subject have all too often seemed to represent an interesting sub-category of the genre proper, as opposed to an integral part of its history. In falling foul of such prejudices, women writers have suffered a similar fate to those male writers who produced experimental narratives, Sterne being the exception that proves the rule of readers' unwillingness to grapple with the challenges posed by such self-reflective and challenging fiction. But while this chapter does not claim that women were the only producers of innovative and metafictional narrative in the mid-eighteenth century, there is nonetheless, I want to suggest, something distinctive about the explicitness and persistence with which women writers yoked their experiments with form and interventions into debates on the novel's role and responsibilities to socially-authored constructs of marriage, sexuality, and morality. By turning our attention to these innovations and to the interdependence of questions of gender and genre in mid-century fiction we can, perhaps, begin to grasp the relationship between fictional forms and fictions of gender, and in the process, find the truth of women's contribution to the novel's rise.

Notes

I would like to thank Markman Ellis, Elaine McGirr, and Chloe Wigston Smith for their thoughtful responses to earlier drafts of this essay.

1. Frances Burney, *Evelina, or the History of a Young Lady's Entrance into the World*, ed. by Edward A. Bloom and Lillian Bloom (Oxford: Oxford University Press, 1998), p. 7. Subsequent references will appear in the text.
2. [Jane Collier and] Sarah Fielding, *The Cry*, ed. by Mary Anne Schofield, 3 vols (Delmar, NY: Scholars' Facsimiles and Reprints, 1986), I, 8. Subsequent references will appear in the text.
3. Betty A. Schellenberg, *The Professionalization of Women Writers in Eighteenth-Century Britain* (Cambridge: Cambridge University Press, 2005), pp. 141–61. The 'Great Forgetting' is Clifford Siskin's coinage in *The Work of Writing: Literature and Social Change in Britain, 1700–1830* (Baltimore: Johns Hopkins University Press, 1998).
4. Paul Francis Burditt, 'The Novels of the 1750s: A Literary Investigation', unpublished PhD dissertation, University of Oxford (2005), pp. 34, 3. On the reviews see Frank Donoghue, *The Fame Machine: Book Reviewing and Eighteenth-Century Literary Careers* (Stanford, CA: Stanford University Press, 1996).
5. Thomas Keymer, *Sterne, the Moderns, and the Novel* (Oxford: Oxford University Press, 2002).
6. Frank Donoghue, *The Fame Machine*, pp. 159–74; Janet Todd, *The Sign of Angellica: Women, Writing and Fiction, 1660–1800* (London: Virago, 1989), p. 177. More recently still, Susan Staves, in her magisterial literary history of women's writing from the Restoration to the 1780s, has presented the mid-century novel as a 'claustrophobic' form. While acknowledging a number of ways in which female authors manipulated the constraints of the genre, she argues that most women writers working between the 1750s to the 1780s 'embrace[d] the obligation to inculcate virtue in their readers and accept[ed] the rule that respectable women novelists should confine themselves to

matters domestic'. *A Literary History of Women's Writing in Britain, 1660–1789* (Cambridge: Cambridge University Press, 2006), pp. 289, 339.

7. Felicity A. Nussbaum, 'Women Novelists 1740s–1780s', in *The Cambridge History of English Literature, 1660–1780*, ed. by John J. Richetti (Cambridge: Cambridge University Press, 2005), p. 759.

8. Schellenberg, *The Professionalization of Women Writers*, pp. 95–6.

9. On the long shadow such accounts have cast see J. Paul Hunter, 'Novels and History and Northrop Frye', *Eighteenth-Century Studies*, 24.2 (1990–91), 225–41.

10. Charlotte Lennox, *The Female Quixote*, ed. by Margaret Dalziel, with an introduction by Margaret Anne Doody (Oxford: Oxford University Press, 1998), p. 378. Subsequent references will appear in the text.

11. Samuel Johnson, *Rambler* 4 (31 March 1750), reprinted in *The Yale Edition of the Works of Samuel Johnson*, ed. by W.J. Bate and Albrecht B. Strauss, 16 vols (New Haven and London: Yale University Press, 1969), III, 19. Subsequent references will appear in the text.

12. Patricia Meyer Spacks, *Desire and Truth: Functions of Plot in Eighteenth-Century English Novels* (Chicago and London: University of Chicago Press, 1990), p. 2.

13. Spacks, *Desire and Truth*, pp. 5–6.

14. Spacks claims that until the late 1760s, when 'plot structure [...] weaken[ed]' in a post-Shandean age and 'new ideological possibilities emerge[d]', the 'distinction between "male" and "female" plots' (or truths) 'has little relevance' (*Desire and Truth*, pp. 6–7).

15. Cheryl L. Nixon, '"Stop a Moment at the Preface": The Gendered Paratexts of Fielding, Barker, and Haywood', *JNT: Journal of Narrative Theory*, 32.2 (2002), 123–4.

16. Jane Collier's Preface to Sarah Fielding's *The Adventures of David Simple, Volume the Last* (London: A. Millar, 1753), p. vi. Subsequent references will appear in the text.

17. This phrase, taken from Beattie's *Dissertations Moral and Critical* (1783), is analysed by Spacks, who contends that Beattie uses it in two conflicting senses: first, by claiming that fictional narratives are acceptable only insofar as they do not claim to be truthful; second, by asserting that such narratives are justifiable only as 'vehicles for truth' (*Desire and Truth*, p. 44). In fact, as I suggest in my discussion of the anonymous *Histories of Some of the Penitents in the Magdalen-House* (1760), these claims are interdependent rather than irreconcilable. Its author, like a number of those discussed here, claimed that fiction which acknowledged its fictionality was uniquely able to wrestle with and deconstruct falsehood in the world at large.

18. Sarah Fielding, *The History of the Countess of Dellwyn*, 2 vols (London: A. Millar, 1758), I, xv. Subsequent references will appear in the text.

19. Sarah Fielding, *The Lives of Cleopatra and Octavia*, ed. by R. Brimsley Johnson (London: Scholartis Press, 1928), p. xliii.

20. Fielding, *Cleopatra and Octavio*, p. xliii. As Mika Suzuki has suggested, Fielding's prefaces demarcate two principal functions of reading: 'reading as a stimulus to contemplation and an inducement to self-analysis'; and reading as a guide 'to express sentiments'. 'Sarah Fielding and Reading', *Eighteenth-Century Novel*, 2 (2002), 104–5.

21. Contemporary correspondence between Lady Barbara Montagu and Samuel Richardson indicates that the author of the novel was a female friend of Montagu's. Anon., *The Histories of Some of the Penitents in the Magdalen-House*, ed. by Jennie Batchelor and Megan Hiatt (London: Pickering and Chatto, 2007). On the attribution question see pp. xx–xxiii. Subsequent references will appear in the text.

22. Mary Peace, 'The Figure of the Prostitute in Eighteenth-Century Sentimental Discourse', unpublished PhD thesis, University of York (1996), p. 139.

23. *Monthly Review*, 21 (1759), 450. The novel was published in 1759 but dated 1760.

24. For further discussion of these issues, see Jennie Batchelor and Megan Hiatt's introduction to the novel, pp. 3–8.

25. [Jane Collier and] Sarah Fielding, *The Cry*, I, 14.

26. Eliza Haywood, *The History of Jemmy and Jenny Jessamy*, ed. by John J. Richetti (Lexington: University Press of Kentucky, 2005), pp. 179, 107.

27. See Richetti's Introduction to the Kentucky edition of the novel, pp. xxxii–xxxiii.

28. Felicity A. Nussbaum, *Torrid Zones: Maternity, Sexuality and Empire in Eighteenth-Century English Narratives* (Baltimore: Johns Hopkins University Press, 1995), p. 132.

29. Samuel Johnson, *The History of Rasselas, Prince of Abissinia*, ed. by D.J. Enright (Harmondsworth: Penguin, 1985), p. 150.

30. Nussbaum, *Torrid Zones*, p. 133.

31. Sarah Scott, *A Journey Through Every Stage of Life*, ed. by Gary Kelly, in *Bluestocking Feminism: Writings of the Bluestocking Circle, 1738–1785*, general editor Gary Kelly, 6 vols (London: Pickering and Chatto, 1999), V, 105. Subsequent references will appear in the text.

32. On the metafictional qualities of Scott's fiction, see my 'Woman's Work: Labour, Gender and Authorship in the novels of Sarah Scott', in *British Women's Writing in the Long Eighteenth Century: Authorship, History, Politics*, ed. by Jennie Batchelor and Cora Kaplan (Basingstoke: Palgrave Macmillan, 2005), pp. 19–33.

33. Linda Bree, *Sarah Fielding* (New York: Twayne Publishers; London: Prentice Hall, 1996), p. 99.

34. Mary Anne Schofield, *Masking and Unmasking the Female Mind: Disguising Romances in Feminine Fiction, 1713–1799* (Newark: University of Delaware Press; London and Toronto: Associated University Presses, 1990), p. 113.

35. Suzuki, 'Sarah Fielding and Reading', pp. 91–2.

36. *The Monthly Review*, 10 (1754), 282.

5
Anglophone Welsh Women's Poetry 1750–84: Jane Cave and Anne Penny

Sarah Prescott

Feminist literary history has now reached that stage of maturity which includes the capacity not only to reflect, but also to move forward. Since the first outpouring of scholarship on eighteenth-century women's writing in the 1980s, which focused on the recovery of women writers and their work, there has been an ongoing debate about the terms upon which women's literary history is practised and the critical frameworks within which women's writing is discussed.[1] Despite the study of 'British' women's writing 'coming of age' as a discipline, it is still the case that the histories and frameworks that we construct are predominantly Anglo-centred, especially in relation to eighteenth-century texts. Although 'archipelagic' literary studies have gained considerable ground in the last decade, the idea that we should be inclusively British in our approach to literary history is taking longer to establish itself as a key component to the study of women's writing. More specifically, the fact that Wales is often hardly registered as one of the archipelagic nations in supposedly inclusive studies of British literature means that Welsh women writers suffer a double marginalization in terms of both gender and nation. If Anglophone writing by eighteenth-century Welsh men has been comparatively neglected, then the fate of their female counterparts has been doubly dire.[2]

In the context of early modern women's writing, Kate Chedgzoy has recently argued that

> When we study early modern English women's writing, we need to pay more attention to texts in the English language produced in Wales, Scotland, Ireland, British North America and the Caribbean as well as England. And we need to do so in the context of new geographies of that changing world that enable us to grasp the full

complexity of the locations the writing comes from, and how and why that locatedness matters.

Furthermore, as Chedgzoy suggests, it is also necessary to make 'an effort to learn more about the ways in which women perceived themselves as Irish, Scots, Welsh, English and/or British'.[3] In the present chapter I explore how eighteenth-century women's poetry from Wales might offer new perspectives in terms of rethinking and expanding the methodologies used for reading and understanding women's writing in the period as a whole. In order to do so, it is imperative to understand Welsh writing as 'national' rather than 'regional'. Harriet Kramer Linkin's chapter on Mary Tighe in this volume demonstrates that women's non-metropolitan literary culture in the eighteenth century was vibrant and productive. Furthermore, this culture often relied on channels of communication and networks of support which, as Linkin shows, could be mapped onto a nexus such as Dublin-London-Llangollen rather than exclusively clustered in and around the English metropolis.[4] However, in what follows I am interested less in the geographical scope of particular coteries and more in the way in which women writers express – self-consciously or not – a sense of national identity that can be described as Welsh in orientation and expression. Such an emphasis does not necessarily mean that the women writers I study clearly define a national*ist* consciousness, but that we should read their work – and not just their biographies – as shaped by their relations to Wales as a nation distinct from England, Ireland, and Scotland. What I attempt to do in this chapter is to suggest how a study of Wales's women writers can develop understanding of how Welsh identities could be poetically expressed in the period and to demonstrate some ways in which poetry by women could be read as adumbrating distinctly Welsh national voices.

How, then, do we define a specifically Welsh imaginative consciousness for eighteenth-century women? Indeed, in relation to the sixteenth and seventeenth centuries, Chedzgoy notes a general 'avoidance of the national' in most women's texts, and emphasizes instead the 'multiple modes of belonging from which national imaginings would have to be fashioned'.[5] In contrast to these earlier periods, however, eighteenth-century women did become more openly national and the topic of women and patriotism has been a subject of lively discussion. Linda Colley's chapter on 'Womanpower' in *Britons*, for example, draws attention to the way in which prominent women such as Georgiana, Duchess of Devonshire, became increasingly involved in overtly political patriotism.[6] In her study *Small Change*, Harriet Guest has explored the 'feminisation of patriotism' in the last quarter of the century which built on the identification of a link between civic virtue and the family rather than an older, more masculine, model of land ownership as the foundation of a patriotic political voice.[7] Both Colley and Guest raise some fascinating questions about women and patriotism, but both studies are primarily interested in English women and/or the construction of an Anglo-British identity for women.[8]

While recognizing this important work on women and patriotism, it is with Chedgzoy's more fluid conception of earlier 'national imaginings', as opposed to openly patriotic sentiment, that I explore the poetry of two Welsh women poets. The literary expressions of national belonging in the work of Jane Cave and Anne Penny are articulated in more complex and unexpected ways than overt loyalty to a clearly defined national body. Their poetry does not reflect clearly defined nationalist allegiance, nor does it constitute a unified Welsh identity where both women invest in Wales in a similar fashion. In fact, those aspects of their writing which might be defined as Welsh are very different from each other and it is crucial to emphasize the plurality of forms that national allegiance can take. Jane Cave's Welsh identity is defined by her poetic expressions of Calvinist Methodism, a religious movement which was particularly strong in eighteenth-century Wales. By contrast, Anne Penny expresses her national allegiance through her poetic engagement with the ancient bardic poetry of Welsh tradition and therefore eighteenth-century Welsh antiquarianism in general, a movement predominantly associated with the Anglican clergy in Wales. However, albeit in different ways and from what might be seen as opposing perspectives, both women can be said to create distinctive subject positions for authorizing their poetry which are directly enabled and shaped by their Welsh inflections.

'A heart inflam'd with JESU's love': Jane Cave and Calvinist Methodism

Eighteenth-century women's involvement in Methodism was, of course, not confined to Wales. However, within Wales, Calvinist Methodism was not only a dominant religious movement, but was to become (along with nonconformity more generally) a defining factor in the nation's identity. As Jane Aaron has argued:

> Ostensibly, the energies of the chapel-goers were dedicated to the building and maintaining of a religion, not a nation; [...] Nevertheless, what later came to be accepted by late nineteenth-century national- ists as defining features of Welsh national identity were based on the

distinctive way of life developed by the Dissenting communities, so much so that it is difficult fully to appreciate the aims and ambitions of the *fin-de-siècle* nation-builders without an understanding of the values and lifestyles of Welsh Nonconformity.[9]

Calvinist Methodism also provided a rich seedbed for the work of Welsh-language poets and hymn writers in the eighteenth century, such as Ann Griffiths and William Williams, Pantycelyn. What is especially interesting about Jane Cave, however, is that she wrote in English. As Aaron notes, 'Unexpectedly, perhaps, English was the language of the first woman to make a name for herself through poeticizing aspects of the Calvinist Methodist experience.'[10] Roland Mathias has explained Cave's use of English by suggesting that her poetry is not Calvinist but demonstrative of Wesleyan Methodism, the beliefs and influence of which were more prevalent in an English context. Mathias suggests that because she chose the Wesleys over Daniel Rowland and George Whitefield's Calvinist Welsh followers, it was 'inevitable that [she] should write in English', adding that she 'certainly could not have written in any other language'.[11]

In contrast, I will argue that Cave's poetry clearly aligns her with the Calvinist Methodism which flourished in, and was associated with, Wales. Furthermore, even given her particular brand of Calvinist Methodism, was it so exceptional that Cave wrote in English? Indeed, as has often been noted, the sometime leader of the Welsh Methodists, Howel Harris, conducted most of his business in English and his extensive diaries are also exclusively written in English. Furthermore, some historians suggest that 'the eighteenth-century Welsh Methodist revivalists and their successors [were] "blatant Britishers all"', who only preached and wrote hymns in Welsh 'because the common people were monoglot'.[12] Therefore, although the influence of Welsh Methodism was to become fundamental to a later sense of Welsh identity and was to prove enabling for the Welsh language, it has been argued that national solidarity was not an important issue for the eighteenth-century Methodists such as Harris, who 'preferred to celebrate their connections with other evangelical movements across the world'.[13] However, as E. Wyn James observes, other historians have argued that this international frame did not necessarily cancel out a Welsh identity, indeed that 'whatever their contacts with the wider Methodist and evangelical world [...] Welsh Methodist leaders were very consciously Welsh'.[14] In relation to Jane Cave, I will suggest that although her poetry does occasionally dramatize international evangelist successes, appropriately with reference to Whitefield's activities in North America, it is also possible to argue for the specific

Welsh angle to her writing, particularly through her connections with Howel Harris. Moreover, as John Davies explains, Calvinist Methodism did have a more specifically Welsh focus stemming from the beliefs of its leading proponents, particularly the Calvinist doctrine of predestination: 'It was its Calvinism (and its language – Wesley became restless on hearing Welsh) which gave the Methodism of Wales its separate identity.' Moreover, it was the fundamental split between the 'Arminianism of the Wesley brothers and the Calvinism of George Whitefield' that paved the way for the different development of Methodism in Wales.[15]

Jane Cave was born in about 1754 and was brought up in her birthplace in Brecon, South Wales where her English father was an Excise officer who had converted to Calvinist Methodism and was a supporter of Howel Harris.[16] It was most likely through her father's connections that Cave became involved in Calvinist Methodism and this may also partly explain her use of English as a medium for her poetry: there is no evidence that she knew Welsh but this doesn't rule out a working knowledge of the language or a basic aural comprehension. Eighteenth-century Brecknockshire was a stronghold of Calvinist Methodism in Wales so its culture would have been a strong influence on Cave as she was growing up, whether she knew the Welsh language or not. Cave did not spend the majority of her adult life in Wales, however. From the evidence of various editions of her poetry, it is clear that by 1783 she lived in Winchester and by 1786 in Bristol, where she married Thomas Winscom, an Excise officer like her father. However, she was resident in her native land when she died at Newport in Monmouthshire in 1813 at the age of 58. Cave's poetry is interesting on a number of fronts. Her *Poems on Various Subjects* (1783) went through several editions and eventually attracted approximately 2000 subscribers.[17] Her treatment of 'personal' topics, such as childbirth, family relations, and social networks, sit alongside her more abstract verse on religion and death. Elegies are a staple of her poetic oeuvre and cover the deaths of family members as well as the deaths of public figures such as Whitefield and Harris. The 1786 Bristol edition of Cave's poetry, published after she had moved to the city and begun married life, includes extra poems which deal specifically with her experience of marriage, childbirth, and motherhood.

On a broader level, then, Cave is an interesting example of the lower-class yet educated, provincial woman writer who became prominent in the later eighteenth century and as such warrants further study. However, the area of her work that I focus on here is her religious poetry, much of which explicitly expresses Calvinist Methodist beliefs and sympathy as well as knowledge of its key figures and communities. Jane Aaron has noted that despite her natal identity and poetic engagement with 'the religion of Wales [...] it is perfectly possible that Jane Cave did not conceive of herself as Welsh. Wales does not even feature as a region of "Western England" in her writing'.[18] Nevertheless, Aaron does draw attention to the 'democratic strain' which could be said to underlie Welsh nonconformity and which informs many of Cave's secular poems, especially those questioning conventional class hierarchies.[19] And, while not explicitly 'Welsh' in subject matter or theme, Cave's poems can nevertheless be said to engage in a more fluid and complex sense of national belonging through a poetic commitment to the religion which came to be a staple of Welsh identity: Calvinist Methodism. Furthermore, and in a similar manner to older Puritan traditions, Calvinist Methodism could provide a context for self-expression through emphasizing the physical experience of conversion rather than the processes of reasoned intellect. For women, conversion thus imagined could also provide a subject position from which to shape their creative writing. As Jane Aaron has noted, in the emphasis on 'feeling, the body, passivity and a more permeable ego' the conversion experience appeared to 'requir[e] and valu[e] stereotypically feminine modes of response. Christ is the bridegroom and the convert the bride, whatever the sex of the sinner'.[20] The poetry of dissent and later of Methodism does indeed provide examples of women being enabled by a dissenting 'poetic': the hymns of Ann Griffiths, for example, the most famous of the female Welsh-language hymn writers of the Romantic period, rely heavily on the eroticized tropes of conversion found in the Song of Songs as a route for female expression.[21] As well as developing a form of hymnody appropriate for a feminine subject position, Methodism as a movement also encouraged the practical participation of women in its activities much more than did traditional Anglicanism.[22]

In what ways, then, do Cave's poems express Calvinist Methodist sentiment and with what effect? In order to answer this question I will explore several poems from the 1783 edition which specifically engage with Methodism, focusing on 'On the Much Lamented DEATH of the Rev. Mr. WHITFIELD, who died in NEW ENGLAND, Sept. 30, 1770', 'On the Death of the Rev. Mr. HOWEL HARRIS, who died JULY 21, 1781',[23] and 'An HYMN for CONSECRATION, sung at the Opening of the Countess of *Huntingdon's* Chapels in *Brecon, Worcester*, &c.'[24] It is significant that two of these poems are elegies. As Brynley F. Roberts has explained, although the early Methodists were 'neither a denomination nor a church', there was a sense of 'corporate fellowship' which was promoted further by the prevalence of 'elegies to the leaders'. Such elegies, in which category Cave's contributions can be counted, 'became a means of preserving and transmitting the common memory'.[25] 'On the Much Lamented DEATH of the Rev. Mr. WHITFIELD' commemorates the life and works of George Whitefield, the most charismatic Methodist preacher of the eighteenth century. Whitefield was a divisive man: some worshipped him, some detested his approach and beliefs. Although Whitefield was the object of many a satirical attack in the eighteenth century, Cave's version of his career is of the hagiographical kind, as the opening lines illustrate:

> WHY doth all Nature wear an awful
>   gloom?
> And why, alas! exults yon distant tomb?
> Why doth a sable cloud the sky o'er-spread?
> WHITFIELD alas! seraphic WHITFIELD's
>   dead,
> The Friend, the Christian, the approv'd
>   Divine,
> The Saint in whom the life of GOD did shine,
> The man whom Heav'n ordain'd to preach
>   for all,
> And thousand by his ministry to call. (p. 77)[26]

In keeping with Whitefield's fame as a charismatic preacher, Cave emphasizes the eloquence of his evangelistic zeal and its effect on his audience which, as Cave notes, often ran into thousands of people when he performed in the open air:

> His tongue was touch'd with evangelic fire,
> And heav'nly raptures did his soul inspire.
> Then forth into the World this Herald came,
> Resolv'd to propagate IMMANUEL's name;
> To set his glory forth from pole to pole,
> Were the capacious breathings of his soul.
> He loudly did the Gospel trumpet sound,
> Whilst thousands trembl'd as they stood
>   around,
> Proclaim'd the suff'rings of a dying GOD,
> Invited sinners to his pard'ning blood. (p. 78)

Cave's tribute is successful in capturing both the style of Methodist Revival in general and of Whitefield's individual preaching in particular, both through her focus on the physical reaction of the crowd to the 'evangelic fire' of his words and the loud 'trumpet sound' of his proclamations. However, although George Whitefield is often seen as the leader of the Welsh Methodists, the 'our nation' which Cave refers to in the next few lines as having benefited from Whitefield's ministration is clearly England. It is Whitefield's 'dear English friends' who will lament his passing most: 'But did this Champion for the living GOD, / Appear in England only, to do good?'(p. 79) she asks. This leads her into praise of Whitefield's activities in North America where he is figured as converting the 'Negroes souls' (p. 79) in particular. He is seen as successful in his mission 'To cleanse their spotted souls from deepest dye' through the eloquence of his 'pathetic accents' (p. 79). Throughout the poem, Whitefield's work in America is seen as key to his evangelizing mission which upholds the view of the transatlantic perspective of eighteenth-century Methodism. So far, despite the strength of religious feeling here, the overt emphasis is on Methodism's English and global success. However, although the direct subject of the poem might not immediately suggest a Welsh inflection, the style of the tribute is clearly demonstrative of a revivalist ethos associated primarily with Wales.[27] Eighteenth-century Methodist belief centred on the nature of Christ's sacrifice and the Last Judgement and Cave duly makes these topics central to her religious verse. The elegy to Whitefield ends with Cave imagining 'the last tremendous trump' (p. 83) where Whitefield is pictured with angels and saints singing 'the wonders of redeeming love, / With all the blood-bought company above' (p. 83). John Davies's description of 'the message of the revivalists' provides a powerful context for understanding Cave's verse and its blood-soaked aesthetic: 'eternal torment in hell would be the fate of those who did not have a personal awareness of Christ's sufferings and sacrifice'.[28]

Cave's elegy on the death of Howel Harris, often called 'the father of Welsh Methodism', is similarly enthusiastic about its subject's virtues and service to God.[29] Eight years after Harris's death, this elegy endorsed Cave's association with Calvinist Methodism, and the poem's status as a memorial, by its appearance as a preface for an English-language biographical account of Harris: *A Brief Account of the Life of Howel Harris* (1791).[30] However, the poem is written in a much more personal tone than the elegy to Whitefield, implying that, even if Harris was not an actual acquaintance, he was nevertheless a more familiar figure for the poet than the impressive yet remote figurehead of Whitefield. Although Cave declares that his death is commonly lamented – 'All ZION's sons will deeply feel the wound' of his passing (p. 83) – Harris's position is figured as that of a family relation or friend: 'A brother, friend, a father dear is gone! / HARRIS is dead; his crown of glory's won!' (p. 84). Harris is, of course, also explicitly associated with Wales and here the Welsh people in particular are seen as being saved by his divine mission:

> The man whom GOD first raised (in his
>   youth)
> In WALES, to propagate the Gospel truth,
> He set his brow as brass, no flesh he fear'd,
> Essential truth he faithfully declar'd.
> His grace, and knowledge, numbers to him
>   drew,
> They to his house, like doves to windows, flew,
> Thousands he caus'd, by the great pow'r of GOD,
> To part with sin, and fly to JESU's blood. (p. 86)

Significantly, given Cave's links with Brecon, the domestic imagery pertaining to Harris's presence in Wales centres on the Methodist community that he founded at Trefeca in Brecknockshire and whose influence, Cave claims, affects the heart of every Christian.[31] Cave imagines the converted as flying to Harris's house 'like doves to windows', a clear allusion to Isaiah 60:8 where the converts 'fly as a cloud, and as the doves to their windows'. To reiterate my earlier point about the possibility that Cave knew Welsh and how this might affect a reading of her poetry, it is worth noting that William Williams's elegy to Harris from 1773 (the year of Harris's death), where he describes his conversion after hearing Harris preach in Talgarth, contains very similar imagery to Cave's description of the saved above:

> Haeddiant IESU yw ei araeth,
>   Cysur enaid a'i iachâd,
> Ac euogrwydd dua pechod
>   Wedi ei ganu yn y gwaed.

[The merit of Jesus is in his words, which bring comfort and healing to the soul, and in that the blackest guilt of sin has been bleached in the blood.][32]

As in the poem to Whitefield, Cave's elegy to Harris ends with an invocation of Judgement Day when Harris triumphantly enters heaven to take his place with God:

> And when the great I AM shall burn the
>   skies,
> And bid unnumber'd Worlds to Judgement
>   rise,

Then HARRIS by his Lord shall be confest,
And soul, and body, enter into rest,
Return triumphant to his destin'd Throne,
And dwell with God, in extacies unknown. (p. 89)

Appropriately for the leader of Calvinist Methodism in Wales, Harris's final union with God is figured as a predestined return. The line 'Return triumphant to his destin'd Throne' clearly signals the Calvinist belief that Harris was a member of the elect, previously chosen by God although tested through grace, conversion, and salvation.

These two elegies are important as public expressions of Cave's admiration of the two key figures of Calvinist Methodism, but her poetic treatment of her religious belief continues beyond the poems on Whitefield and Harris. In the next elegy in the collection, 'On the Death of the Rev. Mr. Watkins, of Lanursk, in the County of BRECON', which continues the same blood-soaked aesthetic, the concluding lines give a sense of how glorious death could be longed, or 'panted', for in the Methodist imagination:

Children of God, who now the body wear,
Are not your hearts now panting to be there?
Are not your very inmost souls on fire,
Thus to be chanting with the heav'nly choir? (pp. 93–4)

Despite its emphasis on the desire to be free of the body, the imagery the poem employs is that of physicality. The body that the children of God wish to shed is vividly imagined, despite 'hearts now panting to be there'. However, despite the physicality expressed in her verse, Cave does not often write with the Song of Songs as a poetic model. Rather, she seems to assume the position of the evangelistic preacher in her strength of expression, a stance which is in keeping with later Welsh-language women poets who were similarly outspoken through their adoption of an evangelizing style.[33] As well as employing much of the staple imagery associated with the Methodist imagination, Cave also demonstrates knowledge of Methodist controversy, specifically the split between Calvinism and Arminianism. In 'Love, the ESSENCE of RELIGION', Cave dramatizes the speaker's awareness of a choice of 'sect', but argues that overall it is Christian 'love' that matters the most:

What if with Calvin I agree,
Or to Arminian doctrines flee,

> I still remain a child of sin,
> If love does not preside within. (p. 149)

Given that the majority of poetic expressions of Calvinist Methodism by near contemporary Welsh-language women writers took the form of hymns (Ann Griffiths, for example), it is significant that Cave presents her poem on the consecration of the Countess of Huntingdon's chapels as precisely that.[34] 'An HYMN for CONSECRATION, sung at the Opening of the Countess of *Huntingdon's* Chapels in *Brecon, Worcester,* &c.' thus situates Cave's work in the context of a tradition of hymn writing more generally associated with the Welsh language. The poem also publicly announces her support for the controversial endeavours of the countess who in 1783 had formed the 'rigidly Calvinistic' sect known as the Countess of Huntingdon's Connexion.[35] Cave presumably learned of the countess's activities through the latter's involvement with Whitefield and the assistance she gave to Harris in the opening of Trefeca College in Brecknockshire in 1768 (Cave's home county). The countess was associated with 'more than sixty chapels' at her death in 1791 and in her poem Cave focuses on those areas in Wales and the English borders familiar to her as a child: Brecon and Worcester.[36] Cave's central poetic point in the hymn is that buildings themselves are meaningless before being filled with the spirit of Jesus. Her hymn works as an alternative act of consecration for the chapels, a making sacred of a place which, in the eyes of the Anglican Church, would have had no official status as a religious space:

> In vain we are assembl'd here;
> If JESUS does not come:
> Appear, thou bleeding Lamb, appear,
> Let ev'ry heart make room! (p. 131).

The presence of the bleeding lamb will lead the way to grace for the sinners who enter and are then converted:

> Now, Saviour, now thy work begin,
> Thy potent arm display:
> Let some poor rebel dead in sin
> Be made alive to-day! (p. 132)

Cave's focus is on the capacity for evangelical religion to bring sinners back to life through the process of conversion and therefore salvation.

Given the strength of religious feeling and the extensive knowledge of the major figures and events in eighteenth-century Methodist circles shown in these poems, it seems extraordinary that Jane Cave's work has not, until recently, been seen in the context of her Methodism.[37] As I suggested at the start of this chapter, this is partly due to the lack of attention paid in mainstream feminist literary histories to women writing outside the English context as well as to the relative neglect of national identity as a critical category when discussing women's writing. It is also the case that, following the influential work of Carol Barash, scholarship on English women's poetry in the eighteenth century has tended to highlight the work of High Church Tory Royalists, such as Anne Finch, and to underplay the poetry of dissenting and Whiggish writers, such as Elizabeth Singer Rowe.[38] However, as is increasingly being recognized, both old dissenters (Presbyterians, Baptists, Quakers) and the newer sects, including Methodism, can be said to have offered increased opportunities for eighteenth-century women to articulate 'private' religious feeling in more public ways and therefore, albeit unconsciously in many respects, to have encouraged female poetic self-expression. Furthermore, Methodist works were often directed specifically at women and, as Eryn White has argued, the prominence of female characters in Methodist religious manuals may also have encouraged women to read and become literate.[39] More specifically, Jane Aaron has suggested that the Calvinist doctrine of 'pre-election of individual souls through grace' was especially influential in creating a space or subject position within which women could develop an authoritative and forceful poetic voice.[40] I have here suggested that Jane Cave's poetry can be read as an English-language intervention into a tradition of poetic expressions of Welsh Calvinist Methodism and that, like her Welsh-language counterparts, her distinctive poetry demands to be read through the interconnected spiritual and geographical contexts of her religious faith. Although Cave wrote in English, mainly for English readers, I argue that the hallmarks of her religious verse are Welsh. As such, the religious poetry contained within her miscellaneous collections brought the poetics, if not the language, of Calvinist Methodist Wales to the ears of a very different audience.

'O! Taliesin guide my Hand': Anne Hughes Penny

If Methodism is one significant way of defining Welsh identity in the eighteenth century, in terms of the literary and cultural development of a more clearly defined national consciousness the crucial influence was the so-called Celtic revival. The interest in Celticism in a Welsh context was fuelled by the antiquarian work of Welsh scholars and the patriotic London-Welsh societies, the Cymmrodorion (est. 1751) and the Gwyneddigion (est. 1770), which were dedicated to recovering and translating the glories of the ancient Welsh literary past. The key publication in this movement was the Revd Evan Evans's *Some Specimens of the Poetry of the Antient Welsh Bards* (1764). The *Specimens* contained a ground-breaking collection of ten examples of Welsh poetry, ranging from the work of the *Cynfeirdd* (the 'first or earliest' bards such as Aneirin and Taliesin) to the *Gogynfeirdd* (the 'not so early' bards).[41] Through his antiquarian researches, Evans was, along with other Welsh scholars such as Lewis Morris, participating in the pan-European 'search for origins which became a key aspect of the modern process of nation building and which involved the attempt to define a nation as an ancient, established, historically rooted "fact"'.[42] However, whereas Methodism encouraged, albeit obliquely, female creativity, the Welsh societies and the antiquarian movement more broadly were heavily dominated by men and tended to exclude female participation at least until the early nineteenth century.

Despite the masculine nature of the antiquarian movement in general, the various English translations of Welsh literature that were published from mid-century onwards could have provided women with access to a literary culture hitherto hidden from them in libraries and inaccessible manuscript collections. The translations of Virgil and Homer by John Dryden and Alexander Pope in the earlier period could be said to have performed a similar service, enabling eighteenth-century women to read classical literature not conventionally included in their education. However, in terms of poetic practice, it could be argued that the translations of Evan Evans and others provided liberation from that classical precedent, which was especially useful for women poets:

> The antiquarians' editions and translations of the early Welsh bards offered to an enthusiastic audience new models of poetic style, liberated, in their primitive directness, from the eighteenth-century orthodoxies of verse.[43]

Just as Calvinist Methodism could create a space for a specifically female subjectivity, the new enthusiasm for all things Celtic and 'primitive' might be said to have provided new poetic opportunities for the woman writer in particular. The poetry of Anne Hughes Penny (1729–84) is one example of the way in which, through the work of Evan Evans, the antiquarian recovery of the Welsh past directly influenced eighteenth-century Anglophone women's poetry.

Anne Penny's parents were from Bangor, North Wales where her father was a vicar from 1713 to 1723.[44] From evidence in her work it is probable that she knew Welsh and it may possibly have been her first language, although she was living in London when she began her publishing career. Like Jane Cave, her *Poems, with a Dramatic Entertainment* (1771) attracted a substantial list of subscribers, including, in Penny's case, Samuel Johnson. Two of the poems in Anne Penny's collection are poetic versions of English translations in Evans's *Specimens*: 'Taliesin's Poem to Prince Elphin' and 'An Elegy on Neest' are both noted in her *Poems* as 'from Mr. Evans's Specimens of the Welch Poetry'. Penny includes some background to the poems in the 'advertisements' which precede them which, in the case of the Taliesin poem, form a very condensed version of Evans's scholarly introduction in *Specimens*. Penny informs her reader that the sixth-century Taliesin was the 'Chief of the Cambrian Bards' and explains, following Evans, that Prince Elphin, son of Gwyddno Garanir, King of Cantre'r Gwaelod, was his patron. As the poem relates, Taliesin is said to have been found in a 'leathern bag' floating in a weir and went on to be a celebrated bard and prophet. Although Penny follows Evans's four stanzas she converts and expands his literal prose translations into rhyming couplets. In this she contributes to what might be termed a subgenre of eighteenth-century poetry which attempted to versify Evans's translations, criticized at the time for being un-poetic.[45] Despite her possible knowledge of Welsh, it is clear that her poem is indebted to Evans and not to the original Welsh. An example of the way in which she versifies Evans's prose translation is demonstrated below:

> ELPHIN with the lovely qualities, thy behaviour is unmanly, thou oughtest not to be over pensive. To trust in God is better than to forebode evil. Though I am but small and slender on the beach of the foaming main, I shall do thee more good in the day of distress than three hundred salmons. (*Specimens*, p. 49)

> Elphin! fair, with Virtue blest,
> Let not that Virtue idly rest;
> If rous'd 'twill yield thee sure relief,
> And banish far unmanly Grief:
> Think on that Pow'r whose Arm can save,
> Who e'en can snatch thee from the Grave;
> He bade my Harp for thee be strung,
> Prophetick Lays he taught my Tongue.
> Though like a slender Reed I grow,

> Tost by the Billows too and fro,
> Yet still, by him inspir'd, my Song
> The Weak can raise, confound the Strong:
> Am not I better, Elphin! Say,
> Than Thousands of thy scaly Prey? (pp. 6–7)[46]

What is fascinating about this poem is the evidence it provides both of a woman poet adopting the voice of the foremost Welsh bard and prophet and of one direct way in which Evans's scholarship enabled women's poetry in particular. The poem is written in the first person, allowing Penny to assume the authority of the bard in addition to displaying knowledge – through Evans – of the cultural history and poetic legacy of Wales. What was normally a masculine endeavour – antiquarian scholarship, bardic poetry, ancient history – is here appropriated by a woman poet as a suitable subject for the female imagination.[47] Indeed, despite the masculine exclusivity of antiquarianism itself, the figure of Taliesin is on one level a very appropriate model for a woman writer in that it offers a feminized subject position. Taliesin is small, slender, and tossed 'by the Billows too and fro', yet he also possesses lyrical strength. Through God, Taliesin speaks with a prophetic voice which authorizes his speech, a familiar authorizing strategy for women writers. Penny's assumption of the voice of Taliesin, then, adds a further dimension to our understanding of the ways in which women authorized their poetic utterances in the eighteenth century. As a woman she is, like Taliesin, seemingly insignificant yet she can also speak with poetic force.

Penny's second choice from Evans's *Specimens*, 'An Elegy on Neest', ostensibly addresses a subject more obviously suited to a female pen: the death of a lover. In this poem, Penny could also be said to interpret her carefully chosen examples of ancient poetry in terms of eighteenth-century sentimental standards of taste, as the opening stanza suggests:

> FAIR blooms the Spring, in vernal Honours gay,
> The thick'ning Groves their warbling Tenants shade,
> Where each, extatic, swells th' harmonious Lay,
> And kens with Rapt'rous Eye the verdant Glade. (p. 11)

Yet despite the recognizably late eighteenth-century language ('warbling Tenants'), it is the grieving male voice in the poem that Penny adopts as her own. As in the poem to Elphin, she succeeds as a woman poet in adopting the role of the bard, albeit mediated through eighteenth-century vocabulary and style:

> O! gen'rous Neest, in Earth's cold bosom laid,
> Safe in thy lone Retreat thy Ashes rest,
> Strong as Pryderi's was my Grief display'd,
> Fresh Sorrow's hoarding in my pensive Breast. (p. 16)

These renditions of Evans's *Specimens* illustrate the way in which a woman poet could use Welsh literary tradition to formulate a different approach to female poetic authority. However, Penny's direct responses to Evans's *Specimens* are not the only poems in which she addresses topics of Welsh interest. In a poem 'Addressed to Thomas Gray, Esq.', she continues the bardic themes of the previous two poems through her praise of Thomas Gray as the author of *The Bard* (1757), the poem that famously immortalized the suicide of the last Welsh bard in defiance of the incursions of Edward I into Wales. In this poem Penny is inspired by Gray and hopes to be able to 'strike the Lyre' to create 'Celestial Poësy with native Fire' (p. 133). Although the retirement trope of the equally influential *Elegy Written in a Country Churchyard* might seem a more appropriate model for a woman, instead she chooses to emulate Gray's vision of the last bard who sings of the destruction of Welsh independence and freedom:

> O! come, nor o'er my Soul refuse
> Thy choicest Raptures to diffuse;
> For I the Eagle Bard would celebrate,
> That sung of ruthless Edward's Fate:
> He sung – Old Cambria heard with awe,
> And, in the wond'rous Youth, her Bards immortal saw. (p. 133)

Penny's view of Edward I as 'ruthless' alludes to Gray's famous opening lines – 'Ruin seize thee, ruthless King!' Her representation of Edward is also in keeping with his reputation as the destroyer of Welsh independence and chimes with the myth of the king as perpetrator of bardicide: the (spurious) tradition that Edward had all the Welsh bards put to death to prevent them opposing his rule. For the Welsh, Edward I is a symbol of English cultural and military oppression as well as a figure of tyrannical monarchy. All these elements are present in Penny's description of the way in which the conquest obliterated the peace and freedom of Wales which had previously served to nurture poetry and song:

> 'Till grim Edward, haughty Lord,
> Cambria's peaceful Bosom gor'd;
> Seat of Freedom, Song divine,
> There each Grace was seen to shine,
> Tho' now no more explor'd [...] (pp. 134–5)

It could be argued as paradoxical that in her choice of Gray's *The Bard* as a model for her poetry, Penny is in fact drawn to an English poet as her inspiration. However, her use of Gray could also be said to place her writing even more firmly in a Welsh context. Gray's poem was hugely popular amongst the Welsh literati and was extremely influential for further literary representation of the Edwardian conquest and bardic massacre.[48] When read from a Welsh perspective it is clear that *The Bard* has patriotic potential and in a variety of works by patriotic eighteenth-century Welsh scholars, Gray's ode is discussed in glowing terms. In the course of denouncing Edward's 'inhuman massacre' of the bards in his *Specimens*, Evans himself remarks that this action 'gave occasion to a very fine Ode by Mr. Grey' (p. 45). Evans's sense of the original loss of the bards being partly compensated for by Gray's ode is compounded by Edward Jones in his *Musical Relicks of the Welsh Bards* (1794) where he remarks of the massacre that 'this lamentable event has given birth to one of the noblest Lyric compositions in the English language: a poem of such fire and beauty as to remove [...] our regret of the occasion, and to compensate for the loss'.[49] Penny also laments the loss of past glories for her native land in the context of Gray's poem. As a result of the Edwardian conquest, the harp is now 'mute' and the 'sweet strung Lyre' is 'silent'. Whereas Taliesin sang of the way in which the Welsh 'glorious liv'd of Old' (p. 134) and 'How Truth divine inspir'd each sweet prophetick Tongue', now this 'pure poetick Fire' is lost along with the 'Princes' and the 'Druids'. However, because of the poetry of Gray, Penny suggests in conclusion to the poem, these glories are even more immortal:

> Yet see! Still more immortal now they reign,
> For Briton's Genius smiles on favour'd Gray,
> Sublimest Bard amid the tuneful Train,
> Then bids him boldly tread their Starry-Way;
> And to record their Deeds, on purpose wrought,
> An adamantine Pen bestow'd, with Genius Fraught [...] (p. 135)

Penny is aware, however, of the temerity of emulating the famous Mr. Gray. To strengthen her position, she uses Taliesin for a second time as declared model and inspiration, depicted as a guide for her hand as she composes her verse:

> O! Taliesin guide my Hand,
> Attune the trembling Strings, inchant the Lay,
> That dares attempt to carol Gray,
> Thou long lost Homer of my native Land [...] (p. 134)

Furthermore, by figuring Taliesin as the 'long lost Homer' of Wales, Penny is able to establish her poetic authority as a Welshwoman writing, not in the neoclassical mode, but in the equally ancient and venerable tradition of her 'native Land'. As such, she can deflect any criticism that suggests she is over ambitious in her 'attempt to carol Gray'.

A further poem, 'Written on PARRY's playing upon the Welch Harp', continues the theme of the lost glories of Welsh poetic tradition as well as the references to Thomas Gray. John Parry (1710?–82) 'was harper to Sir Watkin Williams Wynn of Wynnstay' and played for Wynn's circle in London in the 1740s.[50] As is well known, Parry was thought to have been the inspiration behind Gray's completion of *The Bard* after he heard him play the triple harp in Cambridge in 1757: 'In a letter dated May 1757, Gray says that Parry "scratched out such a ravishing blind harmony, such tunes of a thousand years old", that he "put my Ode in motion again, and has brought it at last to a conclusion"'.[51] In Penny's poem, Parry functions in a similar way to his effect on Gray. Like Taliesin in the previous poem, Parry is imagined as the inspiration for a revival of Welsh literary and musical glory as he was himself, in turn, inspired by the spirits of the Cambrian Bards. Wales is described as the 'Seat once of flowing Verse, of magick Song' (p. 139) where the Bards once haunted 'Mona's Shadowy Isle' (p. 138). The untutored genius of Parry is helped by the ghostly bards of the past 'for that alone / Could Parry's artless Hand with Skill inspire' (p. 138). There is also hope for the present, Penny suggests, as the bards reassert their power through the beauty of Parry's harp playing. In fact, Penny addresses the whole poem to 'Ye Bards' who are called upon to guide a new generation and restring the silent harps of the Welsh into voice again. The poem thus goes beyond being just a lament of lost traditions to function as a clarion call to present-day Welsh bards to reanimate their native poetry:

> Still o'er your much lov'd Cambria, still preside;
> Seat once of flowing Verse, of magick Song;

> Your mighty Shades the feeblest Hand can guide,
> And bid their silent Harps again be strung.
>
> Your potent Aid can fan their dying Fire,
> Can call back Genius to each desart Grove;
> Your Sons will rouse when you their Bards inspire,
> Elate, their mighty Origin to prove. (p. 139)

In this sense, Penny's poetry goes further than the work of those patriotic scholars who saw the existence of Gray's ode as compensation for the loss of the original bards. The poem discussed above suggests that Penny viewed the ancient bardic past, brought to life by Parry's harp, as the spark that could ignite Wales's literary future.

In mainstream women's literary history, Anne Penny is best known for her patriotic British poem *An Invocation of the Genius of Britain* (1778).[52] The anthologized examples of Jane Cave's poetry are mostly her domestic poems and poems about marriage and children.[53] By focusing on those poems which invoke or are informed by a Welsh dimension, I hope to have shown in this chapter that for both women an awareness of their 'national belonging' can provide alternative ways of reading their poetry. Just as Cave's Calvinist Methodism shapes her store of poetic imagery, so too does the figure of the ancient bard Taliesin, and antiquarianism more generally, serve to authorize Penny's position as a woman poet. The key critical question we might ask of these two poets, then, is not only how far their poetry may have contributed to a broader process of nation-building, but also how more subtle identifications with Wales and Welsh culture shaped their work. In this chapter, I have been suggesting that Cave and Penny create distinctively Welsh versions of national belonging or imagining which unsettle the broader conclusions that have been drawn concerning women writers and national identities in this period. With the benefit of hindsight, however, it is significant that the two aspects of Welsh identity that inform the poetry of Cave and Penny – nonconformity and antiquarianism – were to come together to provide the keystone for a much more well-defined and overt sense of Welsh women's national identity in the century to follow, an identity which did indeed contribute to 'a new epoch of Welsh nation-building'.[54]

Notes

1. Margaret Ezell's invaluable *Writing Women's Literary History* (Baltimore: Johns Hopkins University Press, 1993) questions the narratives of women's literary

history dominant from the mid-1980s onwards. For a more recent meditation on the practice of writing the literary history of women, see Susan Staves's introduction to her *A Literary History of Women's Writing in Britain, 1660–1789* (Cambridge: Cambridge University Press, 2006).

2. By contrast, in recent years scholarship on nineteenth- and twentieth-century Welsh women's writing has been gathering pace. See, for example, Jane Aaron, *Nineteenth-Century Women's Writing in Wales: Nation, Gender and Identity* (Cardiff: University of Wales Press, 2007); Katie Gramich, *Twentieth-Century Women's Writing in Wales: Land, Gender, Belonging* (Cardiff: University of Wales Press, 2007); Catherine Brennan, *Angers, Fantasies and Ghostly Fears: Nineteenth-Century Women from Wales and English-language Poetry* (Cardiff: University of Wales Press, 2003). Brennan's study has a chapter on Jane Cave. See also her article: 'Irreconcilable Tensions: Gender, Class and the Welsh Question in the Poetry of Jane Cave', *Welsh Writing in English: A Yearbook of Critical Essays*, 2 (1996), 1–21.

3. Kate Chedgzoy, 'The Cultural Geographies of Early Modern Women's Writing: Journeys across Spaces and Times,' *Literature Compass* 3 (2006), pp. 3, 5. See also Chedgzoy's full-length study, *Women's Writing in the British Atlantic World: Memory, Place and History, 1550–1700* (Cambridge: Cambridge University Press, 2007).

4. For an extended discussion of English women writers' involvement in provincial literary culture in the earlier eighteenth century see Sarah Prescott, *Women, Authorship and Literary Culture, 1690–1740* (Basingstoke: Palgrave Macmillan, 2003).

5. Chedgzoy, 'The Cultural Geographies', p. 5.

6. Linda Colley, *Britons: Forging the Nation 1707–1837* (New Haven: Yale University Press, 1992).

7. Harriet Guest, *Small Change: Women, Learning, Patriotism, 1750–1810* (Chicago and London: University of Chicago Press, 2000).

8. Guest, *Small Change*, does discuss Anne Penny's poetry, but in terms of her construction of a national identity based on aristocratic and Whiggish Britishness. See especially pp. 90–2 and pp. 102–7.

9. Aaron, *Nineteenth-Century Women's Writing*, p. 12.

10. Ibid., p. 41.

11. Roland Mathias, 'Poets of Breconshire', *Brycheiniog*, XIX (1980–81), 27–49 (pp. 35–6).

12. E. Wyn James, '"The New Birth of a People": Welsh Language and Identity and the Welsh Methodists, c. 1740–1820', in *Religion and National Identity: Wales and Scotland c. 1700–2000*, ed. by Robert Pope (Cardiff: University of Wales Press, 2001), pp. 14–42 (pp. 18–19).

13. James, '"The New Birth of a People"', p. 19.

14. Ibid., p. 28.

15. John Davies, *A History of Wales* (Harmondsworth: Penguin, 1993), p. 310.

16. For Jane Cave's biographical details, see Catherine Brennan's chapter in *Angers, Fantasies and Ghostly Fears* and Isobel Grundy's entry in the *DNB*: 'Cave, Jane (*b.* 1754/5, *d.* in or before 1813)', *Oxford Dictionary of National Biography*, Oxford University Press, 2004 [http://www.oxforddnb.com/view/article/45838].

17. Brennan, *Angers, Fantasies and Ghostly Fears*, p. 23. For the purposes of this chapter, my focus is on the Winchester edition of 1783. A second edition was published at Bristol in 1786, an expanded edition at Shrewsbury in 1789, and there were further changes made for the fourth edition at Bristol in 1794.

18. Aaron, *Nineteenth-Century Women's Writing in Wales*, p. 42.

19. Such as her 'A Poem Occasioned by a Lady's doubting whether the Author Composed an Elegy, to which her Name is Affix'd'. Aaron, *Nineteenth-Century Women's Writing in Wales*, p. 41.

20. Aaron, *Nineteenth-Century Women's Writing in Wales*, pp. 15–16.

21. The religious verse of the dissenter Elizabeth Singer Rowe (1674–1737) also draws extensively on the imagery of the Song of Songs.

22. See Eryn M. White, 'Women, Religion and Education in Wales', in *Women and Gender in Early Modern Wales*, ed. by Michael Roberts and Simone Clarke (Cardiff: University of Wales Press, 2000), pp. 210–33.

23. The date of Harris's death is incorrect in the title. He died on 21 July 1773, not in 1781.

24. The poems to Whitefield and the Countess of Huntingdon's chapels appear in all editions of Cave's work. The elegy to Howel Harris only appeared in the first edition from 1783.

25. Brynley F. Roberts, 'The Literature of the "Great Awakening"', in *A Guide to Welsh Literature c. 1700–1800*, ed. by Branwen Jarvis (Cardiff: University of Wales Press, 2000), p. 298.

26. All page references to Cave's poems are from the 1783 edition.

27. See, again, Brynley Roberts, 'The Literature of the "Great Awakening"'.

28. Davies, *A History of Wales*, p. 308.

29. The phrase 'father of Welsh Methodism' is from Aaron, *Nineteenth-Century Women's Writing in Wales*, p. 41.

30. As noted by Aaron, *Nineteenth-Century Women's Writing in Wales*, p. 41. See 'An Elegaic Poem On the Death of Howel Harris, Esq', in *A Brief Account of the Life of Howel Harris, Esq,; extracted from papers written by himself* (Trevecka, 1791). The poem is presented anonymously but nevertheless demonstrates Cave's continuing connection with Wales and Calvinist Methodism into the 1790s.

31. For details of the way in which Harris transformed his home, Trefeca, into a Methodist community, see Derec Llwyd Morgan's entry in the *DNB*: 'Harris, Howel (1714–1773)', *Oxford Dictionary of National Biography*, Oxford University Press, 2004 [http://www.oxforddnb.com/view/article/12392].

32. Quoted in Kathryn Jenkins, 'Williams Pantycelyn', in Jarvis, *A Guide to Welsh Literature*, p. 257. The translation is by Jenkins.

33. The unpublished hymns of Margaret Thomas, for example. See Aaron, *Nineteenth-Century Women's Writing in Wales*, p. 21.

34. Cave's *Poems on Various Subjects* (1773) also contains numerous further examples of Cave's hymn writing, for example, 'An Hymn in the Time of Opposition' and 'A Hymn for a Child who has lost its Father and Mother'.

35. For further information on Selina Hastings, Countess of Huntingdon see Boyd Schlenther's entry in the *DNB*: 'Hastings, Selina, countess of Huntingdon (1707–1791)', *Oxford Dictionary of National Biography*,

Oxford University Press, Sept 2004; online edn, Jan 2008 [http://www.oxforddnb.com/view/article/12582]. See also Boyd S. Schlenther, *Queen of the Methodists: The Countess of Huntingdon and the Eighteenth-Century Crisis of Faith and Society* (Bishop Auckland: Durham Academic Press, 1997) and Edwin Welch, *Spiritual Pilgrim: a Reassessment of the Life of the Countess of Huntingdon* (Cardiff: University of Wales Press, 1995).

36. Schlenther, *Queen of the Methodists*, p. 6.
37. See Aaron, *Nineteenth-Century Women's Writing in Wales* and Brennan, *Angers, Fantasies and Ghostly Fears* and 'Irreconcilable Tensions'.
38. Carol Barash, *English Women's Poetry, 1649–1714: Politics, Community, and Linguistic Authority* (Oxford: Clarendon Press, 1996).
39. White, 'Women, Religion and Education in Wales', p. 229.
40. Aaron, *Nineteenth-Century Women's Writing in Wales*, p. 13.
41. For definitions of these terms and a good general discussion of early Welsh poetry see J.E. Caerwyn Williams, *The Poets of the Welsh Princes* (Cardiff: University of Wales Press, 1978).
42. M. Wynn Thomas and S. Rhian Reynolds, 'Introduction', *A Bibliography of Welsh Literature in English Translation* (Cardiff: University of Wales Press, 2005), p. xiii.
43. Aaron, *Nineteenth-Century Women's Writing in Wales*, p. 38.
44. For further biographical information, see Julia Gasper's entry in the *DNB*: 'Penny, Anne (*bap.* 1729, *d.* 1780/1784)', *Oxford Dictionary of National Biography*, Oxford University Press, 2004 [http://www.oxforddnb.com/view/article/74054].
45. For further discussion of Evans and eighteenth-century Welsh-English translation, see Sarah Prescott, *Eighteenth-Century Writing from Wales: Bards and Britons* (Cardiff: University of Wales Press, 2008).
46. All page references to Penny's poems are from the 1771 *Poems*.
47. There are of course some other examples of women engaging with antiquarianism. An earlier Anglophone Welsh example is Jane Brereton. See Sarah Prescott, 'The Cambrian Muse: Welsh Identity and Hanoverian Loyalty in the Poems of Jane Brereton (1681–1740)', *Eighteenth-Century Studies*, 38(4) (2005), 587–603.
48. See Prescott, *Eighteenth-Century Writing from Wales*, Chapter 3.
49. Edward Jones, *Musical Relicks of the Welsh Bards*, 2nd edn (London, 1800), pp. 20–1.
50. For further information about *Parry Ddall*/Blind Parry see Trevor Herbert's entry in the DNB: 'Parry, John (1710?–1782)', *Oxford Dictionary of National Biography*, Oxford University Press, 2004 [http://www.oxforddnb.com/view/article/21420].
51. Quoted in Herbert, 'Parry, John (1710?–1782)'.
52. For example, Guest's discussion in *Small Change*, see notes 7 and 8 above.
53. Roger Lonsdale includes Cave's 'A Poem for Children', 'Written by Desire of a Lady, on an Angry, Petulant, Kitchen-Maid', 'An Elegy on a Maiden Name', and 'Written a Few Hours before the Birth of a Child', *Eighteenth-Century Women Poets* (Oxford: Oxford University Press, 1990). In their co-edited *Welsh Women's Poetry 1460–2001: An Anthology* (Llandybïe: Honno Classics, 2003), Katie Gramich and Catherine Brennan include 'An Elegy

on a Maiden Name' and 'On Marriage', as well as the more Welsh-inflected 'A Poem occasioned by a Lady's doubting' and 'Thoughts, which occurred to the Author, at Llanwrtid, in Breconshire, in walking from Dol-y-Coed House to the Well', but none of Cave's religious verse.

54. Aaron, *Nineteenth-Century Women's Writing in Wales*, p. 73.

6
The Poem that Ate America: Helen Maria Williams's *Ode on the Peace* (1783)

Kate Davies

> While ALBION on her parent deep
> Shall rest, may glory gild her shore,
> And blossom on her rocky steep
> Till Time shall wing his course no more;
> Till angels wrap the spheres in fire,
> Till Earth and yon fair Orbs expire,
> While Chaos mounting in the rushing flame,
> Shall spread his cold deep shade o'er Nature's sinking
> frame.[1]

This is the final stanza of Helen Maria Williams's *Ode on the Peace*, a poem written after the settlement of the provisional treaty that ended the American War of Independence. It is an astonishing end to an extraordinary poem. What can Williams be saying about Britain's future? What is she suggesting about a peace that proved national defeat, confirmed imperial loss, and set the seal on the transatlantic discord and domestic disorder of a distressing civil war? Williams appears to conclude with the sublime vision of a perpetually triumphant Britain. But that apocalyptic end until which she hopes Albion will endure also appears to swallow up national glory. The end of time is written into Britain's new beginning as the sheer energy and terror of these lines engrosses the ostensibly commonplace patriotic sentiment they impart. Did Williams's *Ode* speak for and to the nation in 1783? Did Britain share the striking horror and elation of her closing lines? Was the national mood in response to the peace one of appalled consternation as much as hopeful applause?

In this chapter I'm going to show how Helen Maria Williams's *Ode* can be seen as typical of, but yet unique in, the political and literary

Britain of 1783. I begin by setting out the political context of the poem, continue by reading it in some close detail, and conclude by considering its cultural significance alongside Joshua Reynolds's *Ugolino*, a painting that plays a vital role in the *Ode*.

I

The concluding part of Williams's *Ode* received most contemporary attention. Several stanzas were reprinted in the *New Annual Register* alongside a positive review of the poem:

> The restoration of the peace was a proper subject for the muse, though being a political event, it was scarcely popular enough to excite much attention. Miss Williams's *Ode* upon it has not detracted from, but added to her reputation. The thoughts are well adapted to the occasion, the images truly poetical, the versification sweetly harmonious, and, towards the conclusion where the author describes the advancement of art and science, she rises to no small degree of sublimity.[2]

Deborah Kennedy interprets these remarks as 'acknowledg[ing] some surprise' that Williams chose to write on the 'political event' of the peace at all.[3] But what seems to me most intriguing about them is their sense that the *Ode* was unique in dealing with a subject whose lack of popularity meant that it had been largely ignored. Williams's poem was one of only a handful of publications to represent the peace as a cause for any sort of national celebration.[4]

By the time that the terms of Shelburne's treaty were announced in the spring of 1783, the nation was tired of the war and disgusted with itself. Though the involvement of Britain's old European enemies from 1778 had lent the conflict a new, more easily definable sense of international enmity, the national mood in the later years of the war was still less gung-ho patriotism than despondency. Burgoyne's spectacular defeat and the intense publicity of Keppel's court marshal meant that the war became a spotlight for military incompetence and naval disunity. As commerce suffered, the war fund was boosted by new taxation schemes and a ballooning national debt. In her 1778 *History of England*, Catharine Macaulay summed up national feeling in her account of a nation repeatedly 'beggared and fleeced' by ruinous civil warfare.[5] High prices, poor harvests and the effects of enclosure sparked fears of a famine among Britain's labouring ranks.[6] By the turn of the decade, the economic situation was regarded as so dire that a beggar's emaciated children might seem emblematic of the state of the nation (Figure 6.1). Then, in the summer of 1780, London witnessed violent riots and bungled repressions and saw in the flames rising from the burning houses of Holborn 'one of the most dreadful spectacles this country ever beheld'.[7] The internal political revolutions of both houses of parliament, meanwhile, were marked by a rancour whose strength, even by British standards, seemed really quite unprecedented. In the prints that depicted the ministerial conflicts of the early 1780s, America appeared less as a direct enemy or object of hostilities than as the defining backdrop of a more damaging internecine war (Figures 6.2 and 6.3).

By 1780, then, war perhaps seemed to be as much a matter of managing internal discord as dealing with the external problem of the colonies and their combined European allies. These internal hostilities and divisions did not just go away in 1783, but were in fact exacerbated by the peace and the heated political antipathies it spawned. If Britain had become increasingly troubled by the domestic outcomes of the war, it seemed perhaps equally anxious about the potential effects of a peace. Across the political spectrum during the spring of 1783, the state of national affairs seemed more suggestive of ruin or collapse than that

Figure 6.1   Mr Trade and family, or, the state of ye Nation (1779), Library of Congress

128

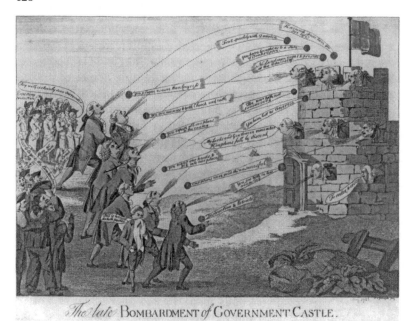

Figure 6.2   The Late Bombardment of Government Castle (1782), Library of Congress

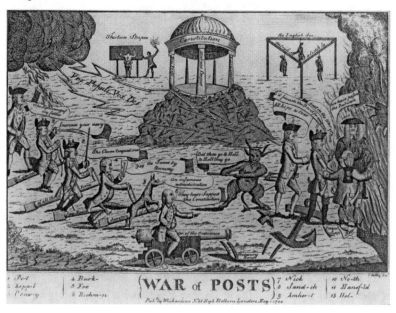

Figure 6.3   War of Posts (1782), Library of Congress

visionary national improvement *The New Annual Register* saw promised in the closing stanzas of Williams's *Ode.*

In the period's pamphlet literature and graphic satire, Shelburne's peace was regarded in terms of unqualified national humiliation. While a frustrated William Meredith examined the treaty's territorial losses and picked over 'the remains of our commerce', 'Portius' lamented Britain's 'melancholy prospect of departed greatness'.[8] John King's vision of the 'whole middle rank of people' who 'can no longer live here in decent mediocrity' emigrating and 'sacrific[ing] themselves and their families in ill-concerted schemes in America' was typical in regarding the treaty as a cause of additional patriotic betrayal.[9] Prints showed Britannia dismembered, John Bull hanging himself, and reached new levels of grisly severity on the subject of Shelburne's failure to secure the compensation or security of the exiled British loyalists (Figure 6.4).[10] A print mocking *The Blessings of Peace* neatly summed up the national mood (Figure 6.5). Across the Atlantic, Benjamin Franklin triumphantly crowns America's success, with Spain, France, and the Dutch Republic in happy attendance. In a desolate Britain, meanwhile, ministry and opposition lament

Figure 6.4 The Savages Let Loose, or The Cruel Fate of the Loyalists (1783), Library of Congress

Figure 6.5   The Blessings of Peace (1783), Library of Congress

and bicker ineffectually. Behind them, Lord Amherst attempts to quell the Gordon Riots with a raggedy band of veterans. A new dawn breaks in America as the sun sets on a nation torn from within by dissent and disorder. Above the dark clouds gathering on the horizon, a malevolent witch farts out 'P-E-A-C-E'.

The Blessings of Peace was accompanied by a line from the fourth act of *Macbeth*: 'Alas, poor country, almost afraid to know itself' (IV.iii). Ross's famous lament to the love of country captures precisely how Shelburne's peace fuelled a particular sense of confused identity and the loss of meaning. The dominating metaphors of the American conflict had always been private and domestic and in 1783, these metaphors of privacy drew more closely inward, intimate, and appalled (Figures 6.6 and 6.7).[11] The clashes of the imperial family had been replaced by the struggles of a divided personality, a nation 'afraid to know itself', and the war's close seemed a moment to be experienced with a sort of horror, a terror of self-recognition. What did the nation

Figure 6.6 Poor old England endeavoring to reclaim his Wicked American Children (1777), Library of Congress

Figure 6.7 Frontispiece, *Westminster Magazine*, vol. 6 (1778), Library of Congress

even *mean* anymore? What was this dismembered empire really *for*? Shelburne's peace made Britain hold a mirror up to itself, and it seemed decidedly shocked by what it saw.

Williams's *Ode* makes most sense, I think, if read in the context of the politics of Britain's post-war national gloom. I'll move on to read the *Ode* with this in mind.

II

As in much British literature about the American war, Williams's *Ode* conveys the horrors of civil conflict through scenes of domestic pathos. The youth of Britain were dying on America's eastern seaboard and in the deaths and grief of the nation's rising generation there was a pain that reached beyond the distressing to the agonized.[12] Williams's *Ode* follows this *topos*, but also represents intimate anguish as a disconcerting source of pleasure:

> The Object of her shiv'ring fear
> Lies bleeding, panting on the ground,
> She frantic pours her gushing tear
> That bathes the fatal gaping wound:
> The blood-stain'd hand she trembling grasps,
> Hangs on the quiv'ring lip, and clasps
> The fainting Form that slowly sinks in death,
> And meets the parting glance, and sucks the fleeting breath.

> (ll. 41–8)

As in some of her other poems, Williams is concerned with the problem of representing what is just too horrid to represent, and how, as writer and as reader, one is meant to react appropriately to that horror.[13] In the *Ode* she approaches this conundrum through layering scenes of painful – sometimes fantastical – excess. Affect is produced and reproduced again through spirals of consumption in which the reader repeatedly absorbs the feeling aroused by tableaux in which someone is absorbing someone else's feeling. And such consuming feelings are not, for Williams, passive at all, but dynamic, forceful or sometimes (as here) quite obviously libidinal. For the emblematic female figure in this scene, grief is more active engrossment than passive response and there is a disturbing pleasure to her (and our) visceral participation in her lover's death. She consumes his final moments in a sort of erotic glut of sensibility, and the agony of Eros and Thanatos, love consummated and disconnected, results in the terror of a divided self: 'she wept – and then in Horrors smil'd –' (l. 52). She 'sucks' in death itself in that last breath, and, in her madness and desperation, becomes a figure for all the unnatural bereavements of the war.

In later versions of her *Ode*, Williams changed that corporeal and active 'suck' to the rather less startling 'catch', but her initial choice of verb resonates with another popular contemporary text.[14] Samuel Jackson Pratt's sensational treatment of the transatlantic crisis, *Emma Corbett*, was prefaced with a frontispiece depicting the English heroine, 'sucking' the fatal wounds of her lover, injured while fighting in 'that cruel cause [...] the assassination of America'[15] (Figure 6.8). Dressed in the male attire with which she has disguised herself, a vigorous Emma clutches at the lifeless body, her mouth pressed to his chest. Because the image depicts two sets of men's legs entangled in their boots and breeches, on a first glance she appears to be straddling him in an attitude of erotic abandon. Sex and death are bound up with the depiction of a cruel and unnatural war whose very excess results in acts of desperate, and fatal, ingestion.[16] In much the same way as the bereaved woman in Williams's *Ode*, Emma Corbett's sensibility seems to have the power to incorporate, to *eat up*, the American war itself.

Perhaps the most striking contemporary image of a suffering, active sensibility that consumes the private horror of the American war occurs in Anna Seward's *Monody on the Death of Major Andrè* (a poem immensely important to the structural logic of Williams's *Ode*).[17] In the *Monody*, the only remnant of identity left to John Andrè during his captivity under the continental army is a portrait miniature of Honora Sneyd, a numinous relic of the doomed attachment which (for Seward) explained his decision to join a misguided conflict fuelled by 'haughty' Britain's 'inebriate rage'.[18] Andrè is only able to retain this treasured image of Honora by secreting it in his mouth. Faced with the disintegration of selfhood characteristic of prisoners of war, he confesses himself prepared to eat her: 'These lips shall resolute inclose / The precious soother of my ceaseless woes' (ll. 265–6). Andrè compares his situation to that of Portia swallowing burning coals. His act of self-individuation (and, implicitly, patriotism) can only be accomplished through ghastly incorporation (ll. 16–17). In the context of British attitudes to the war at the turn of the 1780s, it is as if the distinctive nihilism of figures such as Andrè provides a sort of private counterpoint to the predominant mood of exhaustion and disgust that the nation directed at itself. That is, all the internecine conflict that, in the wake of the crises of the early 1780s, was thought to be destroying Britain from the inside out, appears to be

134

She found the body yet warm;
extracted the arrow and suck'd the wound.

Angelica Kauffman in.   P.W.Tomkins Pupil of F.Bartolozzi Sculp.

London Publish'd April 23 1789 by T.Becket Pall Mall

Figure 6.8 Frontispiece, Samuel Jackson Pratt, *Emma Corbett, or, the Miseries of Civil War* (1789 edition) ©The British Library Board. Shelfmark 12614f8

internalized and embodied in his intimate agony. Like Emma Corbett he seems, in all their mourning and his madness, to swallow whole the grim trauma of civil discord – of a damaging war with oneself – and to eat up the sins of the nation with his destructive and consuming sensibilities.

It is as such a figure of consuming sensibility, a casualty of the 'soft despair' of thwarted affection, that Andrè appeared again in Williams's *Ode*:

> And lo! O'er hapless ANDRÈ's tomb
> Mild victim of his soft despair!
> Whose soul in Life's exulting bloom
> Deem'd not that Life deserv'd a care,
> O'er the cold earth his relicks prest
> Lo! BRITAIN'S drooping Legions rest;
> For him the blades they sternly grasp, appear
> Dim'd with a rising sigh, and sullied with a tear.
>
> While SEWARD sweeps her plaintive strings,
> While pensive round his sable shrine
> A radiant zone she graceful flings,
> Where full emblaz'd his virtues shine,
> The mournful Loves that tremble nigh
> Shall catch her warm melodious sigh,
> And drink the precious thrilling drops that flow
> From Pity's hov'ring soul, that pants dissolv'd in woe.
>
> (ll. 57–72)

Andrè seems of much less importance here than the *response* his fate has generated. While he is, of course, the ultimate focus of the layers upon layers of mourning that Williams piles up in these stanzas, it is really Seward that takes sensibility's first prize. The point is, again, that the reader's feeling for the subject (Andrè) is mediated and determined by the spectacle of someone else's feeling (Seward). We grieve because we see her grieving, because we see *just how* she grieves. The poignancy and pain of the war folds inward and upon itself like a set of emotive Russian dolls: we start with Andrè's doomed private affections, which are remembered in the tears of his fellow soldiers, which are contained in Seward's grief, which is depicted in her *Monody*, which is enclosed by reactions to the *Monody*, which are portrayed in Williams's *Ode*, which we are now reading. By the close of the second stanza where the 'mournful loves' are drinking Pity's tears, we are really at the stage where sensibility has begun to eat itself.[19]

In these stanzas, I think, we start to see how far Williams's *Ode*, unlike Seward's *Monody*, is a poem of the peace. That is, it is a text whose principal concern is the *response* to the war, rather than the war itself. In terms of that sense of disintegrating nationhood that characterized the Britain of 1783, this distinction is particularly important. The *Ode* implicitly acknowledges the ills of the nation and puts a question to it: how are we supposed to feel now? And then it shows Britain, in the emotive and pleasurable spectacle of a grieving Anna Seward, a particular way forward. The private feeling expressed in her *Monody* for an honourable soldier who has suffered *because* of his private feeling is something with which everyone in Britain, whatever their perspective on the war and its peace, might acceptably identify. Equally, the model of liberal nationhood Seward embodies as the steadfastly patriotic, but regretfully critical, female poet, is something everyone can admire. For Williams, the figure of Seward, with her *Monody* and her melancholy, suggests how the horrors of a divisive imperial war might be sublimated into pleasurable, and cohesive, national feeling. And perhaps a nationalist sensibility that prompts everyone to suffer everyone else's suffering shows how Britain could incorporate, could, as it were, eat up, its own estrangement from itself through acts of privatized, but shared, identification.[20]

Williams's *Ode* is one such act. Her poetics suggest that sensibility has an agency capable of consuming away in collective feeling the national discord the war generated. We can particularly see this at work in her account of the response of Charles Asgill's female relatives to his fate. Sentenced to death by Washington because of Clinton's refusal to deliver up a British officer held responsible for the hanging of Captain Huddy, in 1781 Asgill had threatened to become another Andrè: a blameless youth fatally punished for national faults for which he was not liable. Horrified by Washington's decree, Asgill's mother wrote a heartfelt letter to the Comte de Vergennes, asking him to intervene on behalf of her son. Vergennes's address to Washington as a 'man of sensibility' making 'earnest solicitations in favour of a mother and family in tears' moved the American Congress to Asgill's release. Across the transatlantic world, Asgill's mother and sister rapidly became sensibility's celebrities: women whose private feeling had the capacity to redirect international policy and change the fortunes of war.[21]

In the *Ode*, Asgill's sister calls upon the transatlantic gales to 'drink her soul-expressive tear' as she 'views the murder'd form – the quiv'ring

breath – / The rising virtues chill'd in the cold shade of death –'
(ll. 87–8). The reader can 'drink' up this grim fantasy in the knowledge that it is just that: we know Asgill survives, but it is crucial to the
sensational logic of the *Ode* that we suffer his imaginary death before
sensibility can, once again, resurrect him:

> Cease, cease, ye throbs of frantic woe!
> He lives parental love to bless,
> To wake the pure extatic glow
> The thrill of transport's sweet excess –
> Again his smile shall life endear,
> And pleasure pour her brightest tear!
> The private pang shall ALBION trembling share,
> And breathe with fervid zeal, a warm accepted prayer.
>
> (ll. 89–96)

The pleasurable excess of Asgill's reprieve is Albion's too. It is as if,
through experiencing the distressing familial fantasy of his death
followed by the private ecstasy of his release, the nation has finally,
fervidly, absolved itself of the American war.

III

Asgill's restitution provides the axis of feeling on which the *Ode*'s
structure turns: 'lo a lucid stream of light / Descends o'er Horror's
sable cloud'. While Peace is the agent of this nationalist illumination,
'horror' is associated for Williams with both war and empire: a term
she uses to describe the climatic extremes of the 'frozen' and 'torrid'
territories Britain's imperial flag has claimed, as well as in reference to
the madness of the young woman bereaved by war (ll. 52, 98, 153–60).
The *Ode* has confronted the imperial nightmare of the American war
and offered Britain a kind of patriotic reparation. But Williams's poetics
have also accomplished something more. As I have suggested, there is
a disturbing elation to the bereaved woman's divided identity, a certain
something to be gained from Asgill's sister's fantasy of fraternal loss. For
imperial horror to be sublimated into private, nationalist happiness, the
reader has to 'suck' a dying man's last breath and 'drink' in the alarming
vision of Asgill's corpse. Sensibility has carried us to the margins of the
bearable, and there we have been allowed to revel enjoyably, and perhaps
(like Emma Corbett) transgressively. There is an eerie gratification to

the *Ode*'s circuits of painful response, a greediness to its replication of Asgill's reprieve and Andrè's tragedy through so many tableaux of suffering. Yet it is by participating in these emotional excesses, through experiencing the spectacular and disquieting effects of the war, that the nation is finally taught how to feel about the peace. A lover bereaved, a sister forced to imagine the worst, a female poet grieving over her elegiac lyre – all these distressing (and pleasurable) examples of female sensibility show Britain how liberal nationhood might develop an agency capable of consuming away its own imperial horror.

Such acts of consumption are implicitly politicized, and it is in terms of their politics that Williams's 'sublime' closing stanzas should be understood. As I've said, the poem is not merely critical of Britain's imperial ambition, but intimates empire itself as a powerful source of horror. In tackling that horror, the poem also faces up to a nation 'afraid to know itself', and shows it how sympathetic response might offer an escape route out of the narrative of imperial decline and fall. Williams clearly regards peace as an opportunity for Britain to rebuild a radical 'new edifice' from the wreck and relics of an empire built on dominance and disproportion: 'Lo! rushing o'er the western main, / She spreads fair Concord's golden chain' (ll.165–6). Her emphasis on the reforming and restorative power of Anglo-American friendship and 'golden' commerce might usefully be read alongside Paine's *Thoughts on the Peace*, in which he described America as if 'she' were a virtuous woman of feeling, happily reinstated in 'the scenes of domestic life', erasing war's 'spectacle of woe' with the 'the finer sensations which [...] appear so amiable', thereby establishing 'a chastely just [...] fair reputation' through transatlantic commercial amity.[22] Of course, the feminization of peace and commerce was as much a commonplace of the language of radical dissent as other nationalist vocabularies, but there is something very distinctive about the way that gender is attached to the discourse of reform and revival that underlies the visionary closing sequence of Williams's *Ode*.[23] While Paine uses femininity to add emphasis to his arguments for social concord and a transatlantic sense of purpose, for Williams these ends are accomplished through the example of particular female figures.

For Williams, the function of spectacular women like Seward and the Asgills is to provide edifying paradigms for a disintegrating empire and a public sphere that had become distressingly estranged from itself. The mutual feeling they embody stands in marked contrast to the majority of responses to Shelburne's provisional treaty, in which peace was clearly regarded as the divisive property of faction. It is a sign of the

Ode's success that the potential radicalism of the national edifice envisioned in its closing lines is so subsumed in liberal feeling, that what Kennedy calls Williams's 'patriotic rhetoric' appears to cover up her politics.[24] In the final stanzas, the role of liberal femininity as a focus of national cohesion is played by Elizabeth Montagu:[25]

> Ah! still diffuse thy mental ray,
> Fair Science! on my ALBION'S plain,
> While oft thy step delights to stray
> Where MONTAGU has rear'd her Fane
> Where Eloquence shall still entwine
> Rich attic flowers around the shrine,
> View hallow'd Learning ope his treasured store,
> And with her signet stamp the mass of classic ore.

> (ll. 233–40)

Suggestive of the joint opportunities of peace-time commercial *and* cultural prosperity, Montagu here is a one-woman national mint, refining masculine 'ore' into feminized cultural coinage. Williams clearly sees national resurgence as the work of women of sensibility in a way that connects her poetics to that of her more conservative Bluestocking contemporaries.[26]

In its final stanzas, the *Ode* insists that the very rationale for peace-time art and culture is the representation of the war: to provide a focus for collective acts of remembering. Culture must *keep on* giving us occasion to respond to events that are difficult, distressing, and unspeakable, and art is there to provide opportunities for sensibility: a medium through which horror might be sublimated into aesthetic pleasure and thereby resolved. Williams gives several examples of particular works that have this effect on their audience, but the most striking is an image that had impressed itself upon the British imagination for the whole of the previous decade:

> Bright Painting's living forms shall rise,
> And still for UGOLINO's woe
> Shall REYNOLDS wake unbidden sighs

> (ll. 185–7)

In a startling way, the *Ugolino* captures those aesthetics of response that Williams's *Ode* attempts to resolve.

IV

Joshua Reynolds's *Ugolino* depicts the fate of the Guelph nobleman immortalized in Dante's *Inferno*, whose disloyalty to Pisa cost him his life and familial inheritance (Figure 6.9). With his male heirs, Ugolino was imprisoned in a tower and abandoned to starve to death. In the *Inferno*, Ugolino appears in that circle of hell reserved for traitors of their country, and for Dante, treachery against one's homeland, one's family, and oneself, is literalized as a species of anthropophagy. Ugolino is condemned to gnaw the skull of his enemy in perpetuity, and his re-telling of the story of his incarceration leaves the desperate lengths through which he attempted to stave off famine open to question.[27]

On a number of occasions between 1773 and 1783 Reynolds's *Ugolino* was discussed alongside the narrative of the American crisis. For example, in Giuseppe Baretti's *Dialogues* (1775), a dog and a cat visit the Royal Academy, where the latter, 'a cat of taste', is impressed by *Ugolino*.[28] The dog suggests that the cat is taken with Reynolds's painting because 'you love liberty, and so do the Americans'. The cat agrees that repressed freedom is powerfully suggested in the imprisonment of Ugolino by the tyrannical Ruggieri, but is more inclined to read the painting as a lesson about the damaging effects of faction: 'they were all gone mad with party rage'. 'Guelph and Ghibeline' are synonyms for 'Whig and Tory' and, in contemporary London as in Ugolino's Pisa,

Figure 6.9 Joshua Reynolds, *Count Ugolino and His Children* (1773), Knole, The Sackville Collection, The National Trust ©NTPL/Brian Tremain

public good has been lost in a grubby scramble for power and reward: 'every dog that can bark out the word Liberty, though quite ignorant of its true meaning, is to have statues and inscriptions, together with other privileges and honours, were he the worst Basset that ever barked at the moon'.[29]

The dialogue suggests that one contemporary response to the painting was as a critique of the effects of national discord and confusion on the eve of the war. But by 1780 – a year of violent riots and predicted famine and no end to the war in sight – Ugolino's story was interpreted rather differently. For example, in *The Calamities of England*, the desperate and suicidal 'genius' of the nation compares his fate to that of Ugolino, the 'gaunt Pisanian' who is depicted dividing the sky with groans of grief and regret.[30] Ugolino's anguish is certainly matched in the poem by that of England. The animated statues of British kings shield their faces in horror from the Gordon Riots, and, in some ghastly lines, America becomes a cannibal continent, where the flesh of England's dead is greedily consumed and rivers run red into the Atlantic. The misery of Ugolino is associated here with the agency of a monstrous and self-devouring empire.

One of the most intriguing things about contemporary responses to *Ugolino* was that the Count's aghast expression was regarded as a specific reaction to anthropophagy.[31] Over the decade that separated the exhibition of Reynolds's painting and the publication of Williams's *Ode*, anthropophagy had haunted the British imagination. In prints and poems, in pamphlets and in sermons, commentators found in the figure of the cannibal a fitting metaphor for what empire had become. I have discussed elsewhere how the idea of a mother consuming her own off-spring became, in the late 1770s, a grim metaphor of Britain's imperial self-estrangement.[32] Yet the figure of the *paternal* cannibal was also prev-alent and certainly equally shocking. Perhaps the most famous image is *The Allies* (1780) in which Lord North is depicted enjoying a cannibal feast of the bodies of dismembered children (Figure 6.10). The print was a specific reaction to increasingly shocking reports of the 'savage' conduct of Britain's Native American mercenaries, but is also powerfully suggestive of that disgust that characterized responses to transatlantic conflict at the turn of the 1780s: monstrous imperial Britain eats up America and itself.

The response of late eighteenth-century audiences to Reynolds's *Ugolino* should certainly be seen in the context of this association of anthropophagy with appalled reactions to the American war. But there is also an important distinction between the consuming patriarchs of

Figure 6.10   The Allies (1780), published by the radical printer, John Almon, Library of Congress

The Allies and *Ugolino*. Reynolds's gaunt and grief-stricken father may well call up the grisly spectre of anthropophagy, but he is also a figure of tremendous domestic pathos. He forcefully suggests horror, but he is supposed to invoke sympathy too. And his spectators found intense pleasure in that sympathy. 'The celebrated Ugolino family is almost too horrible to be looked at', Frances Burney confided to her journal, 'yet I was glad to see it again.'[33] Burney's gladness is intriguing. Is she pleased because seeing the painting anew prompts happy recollection of earlier moments of encounter? Is she glad because her ability to react appropriately to the painting confirms her sense of her own superlative sympathetic reactions? Or perhaps she is simply remarking on the intense power of the painting to produce enjoyment as well as horror? Indeed, Ugolino's capacity to induce both responses simultaneously was one of the reasons it was so celebrated,: 'Thy *Ugolino* gives the heart to thrill / With Pity's tender throbs and Horror's icy chill', enthused William Hayley.[34] For eighteenth-century audiences, then, Reynolds's *Ugolino* seemed to be there to address itself to, and, as it were, to endorse the restorative power of the sensibility of a spectator like Frances Burney. She is a spectator that might understand and celebrate her own modernity in terms of her capacity to sublimate terror into pleasurable response, a spectator whose tears shed for a father's remorse might absolve the desperate atrocity of patriotic and paternal betrayal. She is someone who might 'gladly' consume the horror of the American war, transform it into sympathetic feeling, and then leave the exhibition.

V

To conclude, then: I began by suggesting that Williams's *Ode* should be understood against the particular horror of Britain during the last years of the American war and the disaffection that accompanied the peace. In 1783, Britain looked at itself and saw an empire that appeared to be disintegrating, fragmentary, on the brink of collapse. A sense of national self-estrangement is central to the representation of America in the *Ode*, where figures of nihilistic sensibility embody the private pain and terror of a war against oneself. Yet the *Ode* also showed its readers, through the spectacular examples of Anna Seward and the Asgills, how national feeling might negotiate a way through the morass of suffering and conflict toward a culturally progressive peace.

My reading emphasized Williams's concern with the aesthetics of affect. I argued that she developed a poetry of response in which war's anguish was repeatedly reacted to, swallowed up, consumed. The reader comes to understand the horror of America by participating in poetic tableaux which replicate the suffering of the war through the eyes of those bereaved, those that mourned their bereavement, and those who wrote and read the poetry of mourning. I also suggested that there was a pleasurable excess to these escalating spirals of consumption. In her final stanzas, Williams offers a vision of a peace-time Britain in which works of art and culture operate as prompts to the collective sensibility that will effect national healing and reform. She illustrates this ameliorative process with Reynolds's *Ugolino* – a painting which, as I have shown, had been regarded in terms of the ways it reflected back to Britain the particular problems of the war. In the image of the father whose ambition led him to betray his country, starve (and potentially consume) his children, and suffer the hell of perpetual anthropophagy, Britain saw the violent and destructive energies of a self-consuming empire. But in Williams's poem, a culturally progressive future is suggested by the capacity to respond sympathetically to Ugolino's torments, his remorse and his despair. That is, in Britain's ability to consume the horror of the American war is found that very characteristic that promises both unanimity and national improvement. '*And still* for Ugolino's woe / Shall Reynolds wake unbidden sighs', she writes. By continuing to sublimate the agony of art like *Ugolino*, a pleasurable, instinctive, and consuming sensibility leads Britain into modernity along the 'soft path of Peace' (l.199)

*****

In describing Williams's *Ode* as 'the poem that ate America' I wanted to suggest not merely the particular way in which an active sensibility is proposed as a solution to the problems of the peace, but how Williams's poetics actually mirror, to a certain extent, those very consuming energies she saw as the cause of Britain's imperial woes and from which she enjoined the nation to absolve itself. This aesthetic conundrum – that the pleasurable solution sensibility offers actually seems to reproduce, and participate in, the horror of the problem itself – preoccupies many of Williams's poems, as well as the early volumes of her *Letters from France*. It operates to dizzying effect in her *Poem on the Bill* (1788), for example, in which both (corrupt) commerce and (restorative) sensibility, are associated with precisely the same language of consumption and desire.[35] In the *Ode*, the replication of problem with solution is even larger, particularly in the closing stanza that the *New Annual Register* described as 'sublime' and that is quoted at this chapter's start. In the prophetic vocabulary and energy of those lines, I think we can see just how clearly the *Ode* is the work of a radical dissenter whose attachment to Britain had not precluded her sympathy with the American cause. Like Tom Paine writing in a newly-independent Pennsylvania, Williams is producing a poetry that wants to take on the horror of the war and transform it into a futuristic, prophetic vigour. But the Albion that Williams says she loves is itself almost annihilated by her poetry: her patriotic attachment seems not a little disturbed by her vision of a Britain ruined in the end of time. The difficulty is, perhaps, that Williams, like Paine, Andrew Kippis, Priestley, Blake, and like many of their other dissenting contemporaries, was beginning to see America *itself* as the shorthand for modernity: the objective of a new *translatio studii* promising that liberty, equality, and *national* public culture from which British dissenters had been so long excluded. America is there, phoenix-like, in all the fire and chaos of Williams's final lines, ready to awaken in the dawn of a new empire.

One might read the contradictory – indeed, chaotic – logic of Williams's poetics as being resolved almost thirty years later in another, perhaps more familiar, and equally remarkable poem by a British woman writer. Yet in Barbauld's *Eighteen Hundred and Eleven*, the sensibility of those whom transatlantic conflict has bereaved has no power of national restoration, but merely serves as an indictment of a corrupt national culture which had, in the decades since the American war, created grotesque social inequalities: 'with grandeur's growth the mass of misery grows'.[36] While for Williams, sorrow heralds renewal, and national ruins prompt regeneration, for Barbauld grief is simply grief, and ashes are ashes. Britain's best hope has left with Priestley for the new United States; modernity is now situated on the other side of the Atlantic, and in the crumbling cultural wasteland that remains, Williams's Albion can only 'learn the lesson just / By Time's slow finger written in the dust'(ll. 213–14).

Williams's *Ode* is an intriguing poem. I've tried to explain what I find so interesting about it, in terms of the national(ist) context it occupied and the distinctive aesthetic choices its author made. I feel that it is crucial we now understand the language of sensibility – a language spoken by so many of the other important women writers in this volume – in terms of the moment and context in which it emerged during the American War of Independence. As Sarah Knott argues in her groundbreaking study, the emergence of a transatlantic language of sensibility in the 1770s and 1780s should be considered in specific relation to the cultural anxiety this war provoked. Williams's *Ode on the Peace* is one example of how clearly this is so. And the image of the agonized and grief-stricken parent who haunts the *Ode* with a terror that seems that of modernity itself was also to preoccupy the imagination of British women writers for many years to come. Becalmed without food on a Danish boat, Mary Wollstonecraft brought him to her mind: 'the child began to cry so bitterly for bread that fancy conjured up before me the wretched Ugolino, with his famished children; and I, literally speaking, enveloped myself in sympathetic horrors, augmented by every tear my babe shed; from which I could not escape'.[37] In his note to these remarks, Richard Holmes suggests that, in calling up this spectre of famine and anthropophagy, Wollstonecraft is 'indulging in black humour', but really, there is nothing amusing about it.[38] In the 'sympathetic horrors' Ugolino provokes, Wollstonecraft gathers up all the pain of physical separation from her child, the difficulty of envisioning a personal or political future in the wake of revolutionary terror and disappointed affection, and the consuming influences of a desperate and self-destructive sensibility. The complexity of this response, in which pity is bound up with physical necessity, and pleasurable anguish meets political despair, is crucial to understanding the direction and significance of women's writing as the nineteenth century turned. It first found articulation in Helen Maria Williams's *Ode on the Peace*.

Notes

I'd like to thank Harriet Guest, Mark Hallett, Sarah Knott, Meiko O'Halloran, and Jared Richman for stimulating debate and sharing ideas that have contributed to this essay.

1. Helen Maria Williams, *An Ode on the Peace by the Author of Edwin and Eltruda* (London: T. Cadell, 1783), ll. 249–56. All references are to the first edition. In subsequent references line numbers will be indicated in-text.
2. *The New Annual Register for the Year 1783* (London: Robinson, 1784), p. 275. The magazine was established by Williams's friend and patron, Andrew Kippis. See also *The Monthly Review*, 69 (1783), 167.
3. Deborah Kennedy, *Helen Maria Williams and the Age of Revolution* (Lewisburg: Bucknell University Press, 2002), p. 28.
4. *The New Annual Register for the Year 1783*, p. 275; see also *The Monthly Review*, 69 (1783), 167. Deborah Kennedy argues that it is probable that Kippis, a dissenting minister who moved in the circles of metropolitan Whigs and radicals who had opposed the war and supported American independence, had encouraged Williams to produce and publish the *Ode*. Kennedy, *Helen Maria Williams*, pp. 27–8.
5. Catharine Macaulay, *The History of England from the Revolution to the Present Time in a Series of Letters to a Friend* (Bath: R. Crutwell, 1778), p. 10.
6. See, for example, Andrew Kippis, *Considerations on the Provisional Treaty with America and the Preliminary Articles of Peace with France and Spain* (London: T. Cadell, 1783), p. 17: 'the poor are threatened with a scarcity which, it is to be feared, may amount to little less than a famine, before the return of Autumn. Perhaps nothing but the supply of grain which the peace may enable us to draw from America could effectually prevent so awful an event.'
7. *The Annual Register, or a View of the History, Politics and Literature for the Year 1780* (London: J. Dodsley, 1781), p. 261.
8. William Meredith, *A Letter on the Preliminaries of Peace* (London: n.pub., 1783), p. 26. Britain had ceded the islands of Tobago and St Lucia to France. [Unattrib.] 'Portius', *A Letter to the Earl of Shelburne on the Peace* (London: J. Debrett, 1783), p. 21.
9. John Barker King, *Thoughts on the Difficulties and Distresses in which the Peace of 1783 has involved the People of England* (London: J. Fielding, 1783), p. 7. For other representative arguments against the terms of Shelburne's peace see also [Unattrib.] 'Country Gentleman', *Candid and Impartial Considerations on the Preliminary Articles of Peace with France and Spain and the Provisional Treaty with the United States of America* (London: J. Robinson, 1783); [Unattrib.], *Consequences Not Before Adverted to that are Likely to Result from the Late Revolution in the British Empire* (London: G. Wilkie, 1783); Denis O Brien, *Remarks on the Report of a Peace* (Dublin: R. Marchbank, 1783); Richard Price, *The State of the Public Debts and Finances at Signing the Preliminary Articles of Peace* (London: T. Cadell, 1783); and Kippis, *Considerations*.
10. This print was published by William Humphrey in March 1783. On the complexity of responses to the peace, and particularly perceptions of the sacrifice of the loyalists to preserve British domestic order see Eliga Gould, *The Persistence of Empire: British Political Culture in the Age of the American Revolution* (Chapel Hill: University of North Carolina Press, 2000), Chapter 6.

11. On the familial metaphors of the British Empire see Jay Fliegelman, *Prodigals and Pilgrims: The American Revolution against Patriarchal Authority* (Cambridge: Cambridge University Press, 1982).

12. See, for example, Thomas Day, *The Desolation of America* (1777); Samuel Jackson Pratt, *Emma Corbett, or, the Miseries of Civil War*, 2 vols (1781; London: R Baldwin, 1783); and Anna Seward, *Monody on Major Andrè* (Litchfield: J. Jackson, 1781). See also Lynn Festa, *Sentimental Figures of Empire in Eighteenth-Century Britain and France* (Baltimore: Johns Hopkins University Press, 2006).

13. I am thinking particularly of Williams's 'Part of an Irregular Fragment Found in a Dark Passage of the Tower', in *Poems* (1786) and *A Poem on the Bill Lately Passed for Regulating the Slave Trade* (1788).

14. Helen Maria Williams, 'An Ode on the Peace' in *Poems*, 2 vols (London: T. Cadell, 1786), I, 39. The main change in this revised version is the tempering of the activity of some of Williams's verbs. The revised lines quoted read: 'In vain the dying hand she grasps, / Hangs on the quiv'ring lip, and clasps / The fainting form, that slowly sinks in death, / To catch the parting glance, the fleeting breath'.

15. Samuel Jackson Pratt, *Emma Corbett, or, the Miseries of Civil War*, p. 175. The frontispiece appeared from the fifth edition onward. I am grateful to Jared Richman for pointing out this image to me.

16. The poison Emma sucks from the wound is what ultimately kills her.

17. The definitive reading of Seward's *Monody* is Harriet Guest's: '"Britain Mourn'd": Anna Seward's Patriotic Elegies', in *Small Change: Women, Learning, Patriotism, 1750–1810* (Chicago: Chicago University Press, 2000), pp. 252–67.

18. Anna Seward, *Monody on Major Andrè*, p. 16. 'I have been taken prisoner by the Americans and stript of everything except the picture of Honora, which I concealed in my mouth. Preserving that, I think myself fortunat' (p. 16 [n]). In subsequent references line numbers will be indicated in-text.

19. Indeed, one might take this a step further and read Williams weeping over Seward weeping over Andrè into Wordsworth's first published poem, 'Sonnet On Seeing Miss Helen Maria Williams Weep at a Tale of Distress', *European Magazine*, 40 (1787), 202. See James Haverill, *Wordsworth and the Poetry of Human Suffering* (Ithaca: Cornell University Press, 1977), p. 32.

20. On the representation of suffering in the eighteenth century see William Wandless, 'Narrative Pain and the Moral Sense: Toward an Ethics of Suffering in the Long Eighteenth Century', *Literature and Medicine*, 24 (2005), 51–69. On the importance of ideas of liberal femininity to British nationalism in the 1780s see Kathleen Wilson, *The Island Race: Englishness, Empire and Gender in the Eighteenth Century* (London: Routledge, 2003), p. 19 and Guest, 'Britain Mourn'd'.

21. Vergennes's letter, and the appeal of Asgill's mother, were widely reprinted on both sides of the Atlantic. See, for example, *The Gentleman's Magazine*, 53 (1783), 177–8. My discussion of Asgill is indebted to Sarah Knott's important work, *Sensibility and the American Revolution* (Chapel Hill: University of North Carolina Press for the Omohundro Institute, 2009).

22. Thomas Paine, *Thoughts on the Peace and the Probable Advantages Thereof to the United States of America* (London: J Stockdale, 1783), p. 7.

23. On commerce and sensibility see Jacqueline LeBlanc, 'Politics and Commercial Sensibility in Helen Maria Williams' *Letters from France*',

Eighteenth Century Life, 21 (1997), 26–44; Kate Davies, 'A Moral Purchase: Femininity, Commerce, Abolition', in *Women, Writing and the Public Sphere 1700–1830*, ed. by Elizabeth Eger, Charlotte Grant, Clíona Ó Gallchoir, and Penny Warburton (Cambridge: Cambridge University Press, 2000), pp. 133–63; and Guest, *Small Change*.

24. Kennedy, *Helen Maria Williams*, p. 28.
25. On Montagu and national identity see Elizabeth Eger, 'Representing Culture: The Nine Living Muses of Great Britain', in *Women, Writing and the Public Sphere*, ed. by Eger et al., pp. 104–33. Williams had met Montagu in 1783, and was to dedicate her long poem *Peru* to her the following year. See Kennedy, *Helen Maria Williams*, pp. 27–9.
26. See the account of 'refinement' in Hannah More's *Bas Bleu*, a poem written the same year. See also Lucy Newlyn, *Reading, Writing and Romanticism: The Anxiety of Reception* (Oxford: Oxford University Press, 2000), pp. 237–41 and Emma Major, 'The Politics of Sociability: Public Dimensions of the Bluestocking Millenium', in *Reconsidering the Bluestockings*, ed. by Nicole Pohl and Betty Schellenberg (San Marino: Huntington Library, 2003), pp. 174–92.
27. The best reading of the Ugolino episode and its reception in eighteenth-century England is John Roe, 'Foreseeing and Foreknowing: Dante's "Ugolino" and the Eton College *Ode* of Thomas Gray', in *Dante's Modern Afterlife: Reception and Response from Blake to Heaney*, ed. by Nick Havely (Basingstoke: Macmillan, 1998). See also Martin Postle, 'Sir Joshua Reynolds, Edmund Burke, and the Grand Whiggery', in *Art and Culture in the Eighteenth Century: New Dimensions and Multiple Perspectives*, ed. by Elise Goodman (Newark: University of Delware Press, 2001), pp. 106–25; and *The Quarterly Review*, 56 (1823), p. 370.
28. Giuseppe Marco Antonio Baretti, *Dialogues for the Use of Young Ladies* (London: Cadell, 1775), p. 133. Baretti was employed by Hester Thrale as Italian tutor to her daughter, for whom these dialogues were originally written. The dog and cat agree that their understanding of the painting is far superior to that of their 'squeamish' contemporaries who object to the *Ugolino* on the grounds that it 'fills every beholder with horror', p. 136.
29. Baretti, *Dialogues*, pp. 136, 138, 140.
30. [Unattrib.], *A Poem Occasioned by the Late Calamities of England, in particular, Those on the 6th and 7th of June 1780* (London: T. Becket, 1780), p. 17.
31. The painting shows the moment when Ugolino realizes the fate he and his heirs will suffer. However, many spectators assumed the painting illustrated a point later in the 33rd Canto, when the children offer themselves to be eaten. See, for example, John Wesley, *An Extract of the Reverend John Wesley's Journal* (London: G. Whitfield, 1791), p. 203; Mary Robinson, *Monody to the Memory of Sir Joshua Reynolds Late President of the Royal Academy* (London: J. Bell, 1792), pp. 10–11; Frances Yates 'Transformations of Dante's Ugolino', *Journal of the Warburg and Courtauld Institute*, 1 (1951), pp. 92–117.
32. See Kate Davies, *Catharine Macaulay and Mercy Otis Warren: The Revolutionary Atlantic and the Politics of Gender* (Oxford: Oxford University Press, 2005), pp. 164–71.
33. Peter Sabor, ed., *The Journals and Letters of Fanny Burney* (Harmondsworth: Penguin, 2001), p. 132.

34. William Hayley, *An Essay on Painting in Two Epistles to Mr Romney* (London: J. Dodsley, 1781), p. 36.

35. There are a number of striking similarities between the *Poem on the Bill* and the *Ode on the Peace*. Compare, for example, *Ode on the Peace* l. 161 and *Poem on the Bill*, l. 209.

36. Anna Laetitia Barbauld, *Eighteen Hundred and Eleven: A Poem* (London: J. Johnson, 1812), l. 320.

37. Mary Wollstonecraft, *Letters Written During a Short Residence in Sweden, Norway and Denmark* (London: Joseph Johnson, 1796), p. 236.

38. Richard Holmes, ed., *A Short Residence in Sweden Norway and Denmark and Memoirs of the Author of the Vindication of the Rights of Woman* (Harmondsworth: Penguin, 1987), p. 293n.

7

Picturing Benevolence against the Commercial Cry, 1750–98: Or, Sarah Fielding and the Secret Causes of Romanticism

Donna Landry

> The last of the Flock is more gloomy than the rest. We are not told how the wretched hero of this piece became so poor. He had, indeed, ten children: but so have many cottagers; and ere the tenth child is born, the eldest begin to work, and help, at least, to maintain themselves. No oppression is pointed out; nor are any means suggested for his relief. If the author be a wealthy man, he ought not to have suffered this poor peasant to part with *the last of the flock*.
>
> Dr Charles Burney, *The Monthly Review* (1799)

> He [...] assured him, if his Fortune could any way conduce to his Happiness, whatever share of it was necessary for him, should be intirely at his Service.
>
> Sarah Fielding, *The Adventures of David Simple* (1744)

> [I]n our little Family of Love, each Day was employed in Endeavours to promote its common Welfare.
>
> Sarah Fielding, *The Adventures of David Simple: Volume the Last* (1753)

For most of the eighteenth century, the tenderest emotions were frequently accompanied by the clinking of purses. By the century's end, the connection between money and feeling had become more distant, more highly mediated and mystified. Benevolence no longer appeared in the pages of fiction figured so graphically in coins and banknotes, legacies or annuities, charitable endowments or gifts of money and parcels of land, freely given in a spirit of fellow feeling and sympathy. That fictional representations of benevolence and acts of charity came to hold a less fashionable place than they had once enjoyed testifies to a major ideological and aesthetic shift during this period. As capitalism developed during the long mercantilist moment that preceded the birth of industrial capitalism in the nineteenth century, political economic theorists replaced earlier religious views of charitable benevolence with a new religion of the market. Adam Smith's 'moral sentiments' were those that best served to constitute the self or subject most appropriate for the capitalist marketplace and commercial society, and were most easily reconcilable with producing the 'wealth of nations'.[1] These commercial tenets of social life displaced earlier debates about self-interest, the motivating force so crucial for Thomas Hobbes, John Locke, and Bernard Mandeville, in contention with the Earl of Shaftesbury and Francis Hutcheson's defence of the defining human attribute as benevolence, which manifested itself in a tendency towards universal sympathy with fellow creatures. A significant casualty of the war of political economic policy on the benevolent redistribution of wealth was charity towards the indigent poor in the direct form of almsgiving. Beginning in the 1770s and gathering force in the 1790s, political economy in theory and practice rendered risible or impracticable what had formerly seemed the noblest of human desires, or the most communal and politically progressive of Christian dictates.

Women writers played a particularly important role in perpetuating ideas of benevolence figured as actual material and monetary giving. The sentimental fiction penned by mid-century women writers such as Sarah Fielding, Jane Collier, Elizabeth Justice, Mary Collyer, Elizabeth Griffith, and Sarah Scott was popular and influential in its own day, although it has yet to make an equivalent impact on the emergent canon of eighteenth-century women's writing. When later in the century Frances Burney and Elizabeth Inchbald revived representations of sentimental benevolence, they appear to have been acknowledging this previous work by women. And when the backlash against picturing benevolence in novels and poetry came, female authors of sentimental fiction were implicitly targeted as the chief culprits to be criticized and superseded. Between the hard-nosed monetary calculation of Daniel Defoe, and the displacement of economic realities by the poetry of feeling in William Wordsworth, satirical attacks on charity were popularized by Laurence Sterne in *A Sentimental Journey* (1768) and Henry Mackenzie in *The Man of Feeling* (1771). Against the grain of Mandevillian cynicism, Smithian faith in market forces, Laurence Sterne's ironizing of the polite hypocrisies entailed by the English middling sort's reluctance to spend in almsgiving or selfless sympathy, and Henry Mackenzie's ambivalence towards *The Man of Feeling*'s generous sensibility, certain female-authored novels, and fleeting moments within novels, maintained a more materially grounded view of what constituted benevolence that not only Defoe but also many seventeenth- and early eighteenth-century writers on charity would have recognized.

In women writers' continued commitment to picturing benevolence as material as well as affective expenditure, against the later eighteenth-century tide of its suppression, we might detect the contradictory impulses produced by those twin narratives of eighteenth-century Enlightenment discourse, as Jean-François Lyotard once formulated them, the narrative of human emancipation and the narrative of the progress of knowledge.[2] By the end of the eighteenth century, progress could largely be translated into the progress of capitalism as it developed from mercantilism towards its fully-fledged industrial form, with an emphasis on productivity and technological innovation, while human emancipation, on the other hand, tugged either in the direction of idealist abstractions of universal brotherhood and the rights of man, or towards more materialist alternatives to laissez-faire ideology – proto-socialist and communist alternatives. Out of these contradictions would come Romanticism, itself a contradictory formation, divided between utopian socialist Pantisocratic impulses and the Wordsworthian programme of feeling as a sufficient good in itself. If women's writing sometimes suggests alternative periodizations to traditional literary historical ones, the case of mid-eighteenth-century Englishwomen's sentimental fiction, especially as exemplified in the works of Sarah Fielding, offers an as yet insufficiently appreciated or understood vision of continuity between the radical religious Enlightenment of the seventeenth century and the eighteenth-century novel.[3]

Charity begins at home: ideals of commonwealth and the family of love

Sarah Fielding was a paradoxical writer, at once almost unimaginably radical for her time and yet extremely popular. As James Raven's work on publication history has shown, for several decades, Sarah Fielding ranked just below her brother Henry and Laurence Sterne in popularity; indeed, as Peter Sabor has observed, she was 'among the most popular of all English novelists' and the third most popular female novelist of the century, behind Eliza Haywood and Marie Jeanne Riccobini, with sixteen editions to Riccobini's seventeen.[4] As Sabor notes, Sarah Fielding 'retained her popularity for some twenty years after her death'; her first novel *David Simple* (1744) was chosen in 1775 'by the publisher R. Snaggs as one of twelve best-selling novels to be issued in cheap abridgements as "little Books of Entertainment" – together with three by Henry Fielding, three by Samuel Richardson, two by [Tobias] Smollett, and *The Female Quixote*, by Charlotte Lennox – the only other woman writer on the list'.[5] Sarah Fielding pioneered a kind of fiction that was at once sentimental and utopian, backward-looking in its evocations of ideas of commonwealth and Christian charity, yet radically emancipatory if compared with later eighteenth-century writing.

For her female contemporaries and descendants, the novelists whose sentimentalism would be most directly parodied by Mackenzie's *Man of Feeling* in 1771, Sarah Fielding was a kind of 'guru'.[6] In Raymond Williams's terms, the 'structure of feeling' Sarah Fielding represented was an advocacy of benevolence and charity combined with an attack on self-interest and hypocrisy.[7] Elizabeth Justice's *Amelia; or, the Distress'd Wife* (1751) and Mary Collyer's *The History of Betty Barnes* (1753) perpetuate this view of charity in its glittering, clinking, most *materially* material form amongst the gentry, with its pretensions and insecurities, merchants, tradespeople, and skilled artisans and labourers perpetually teetering on the brink of poverty. Even Elizabeth Griffith's *The Delicate Distress* (1769), which is set in a much higher social circle – indeed, nearly every male character is a peer, and the married female characters all have titles – offers a striking vision of selfless charity amongst this usually avaricious elite. As Alessa Johns observes, Sarah Scott could be said to have inherited most directly from Fielding her utopian vision in *Millenium Hall* (1762).[8] So far as later generations of women writers are concerned, both Frances Burney and Elizabeth Inchbald appear indebted to Fielding. In 1780, two years after her triumphant debut with *Evelina* (1778), Burney visited Bath Abbey and studied the memorials there, including Sarah Fielding's; in her journal she asked herself, regarding Dr John Hoadly's epitaph: 'Will any future doctor do as much for me?'[9] Burney explicitly compared herself with Fielding, then, hoping not to be found wanting by men distinguished by the title of doctor, such as her father and Samuel Johnson. Burney shows in Evelina's parting with her purse to help the impoverished MacCartney a charitable spirit of the sort Fielding would have approved.[10] With its many echoes of Fielding's characteristic tropes, Inchbald's *Nature and Art* (published 1796, revised 1797) evinces how during the 1790s women's writing could represent a struggle against dominant aesthetic developments, harking back to female-authored fiction of the 1750s and 1760s.

The English Enlightenment's revolutionary origins remain legible in Sarah Fielding's work. Through the language of benevolence, she perpetuates the vision of economic redistribution associated with the most radical voices raised during the Civil War and Interregnum. The failure of the democratizing experiments of the revolutionary Commonwealth and Protectorate during the 1640s and 1650s has often been interpreted as the end of something rather than unfinished business. Christopher Hill's endeavours to recover the radical underground of the English revolution as a precursor to socialism and communism have been subjected to nearly four decades of revisionism, but there have been a few recent attempts to propose the kind of continuities for which Hill argued in 1972. Hill noted the revival of interest during the 1640s and 1650s in the 'Family of Love', or Familists, who 'held their property in common', and 'believed that men and women might recapture on earth the state of innocence which existed before the Fall'.[11] The most consistently proto-communist thinker, according to Hill, was Gerrard Winstanley, who argued that '"once the earth becomes a common treasury again, as it must, [...] then this enmity of all lands will cease, and none shall dare to seek dominion over others, neither shall any dare to kill another, nor desire more of the earth than another"'.[12] In 1989, Nigel Smith cautiously indexed as a 'communist' vision Abiezer Coppe's *A Second Fiery Flying Roll* (1649), in which Coppe 'shouts with a prophetic voice to "have all things in common"'. Smith also devoted a chapter to the influence of Hendrik Niclaes and the Family of Love, beginning in the 1550s, but rediscovered during the Interregnum as a source of transfigurative illumination, an enthusiastic movement of Enlightenment.[13] As David Norbrook reminds us in his recent study of English republicanism, the Restoration Act of Indemnity and Oblivion, banning remembrance of the Interregnum, continues to signify a deliberate forgetting of anti-monarchical traditions that has exacted a price in English political identity. While refusing any easy connection between the republicanism of the Commonwealth and socialist and communist ideas, Norbrook invites a fleeting comparison when he writes: '"Republicanism" presents as many problems for today's historians as "socialism" will for the future.'[14]

With significant regularity, Sarah Fielding both returns to the question of benevolence as indicative of true Christian charity, and appears to go out of her way to reiterate the term 'commonwealth' rather than 'republic'. In *Remarks on Clarissa*, for instance, a discussion of Roman history before the death of Pompey is couched in terms of 'that extensive, powerful, I had almost said unmanageable, Common-wealth', as Mr Johnson puts it, to which Mr Singleton responds by commenting upon 'the Affairs of the greatest Commonwealth that was ever heard of since the Creation of the World'.[15] *A Vision*, the recounting of a dream in which the narrator visits a domain presided over by '*Benevolence, or real Love*', who 'makes it her whole Study hourly to enhance the Pleasure of her Followers', captures the idiom of seventeenth-century enthusiasm perfectly: '[W]hat elsewhere would be called the Height of Friendship, here was but the common Behaviour of every Man to his Acquaintance.'[16] Friendship for Fielding, as we shall see, involves a giving of resources to be shared in common: a commonwealth of mutual affection.

Helpful light is shed on Fielding's intellectual milieu by Donna T. Andrew's study of eighteenth-century London charitable institutions. Andrew describes a major shift in attitudes towards charity occurring between 1650 and 1797, but insists that this shift was in fact a gradual and very uneven one.[17] During the first half of the eighteenth century, ideas of commonwealth, of the polity perceived literally as a common stock to which the poor had as much entitlement as the rich, strongly persisted. In 1650 Jeremy Taylor, chaplain to the late king Charles I, proclaimed that God's design contained an injunction to charity in order to level 'the great inequality which [God] was pleased to suffer in the possessions and accidents of men'; the spirit of charity was a merciful and compassionate one; charity meant giving freely, expecting no returns, and entailing no obligations:

> Against this Rule they offend who give Alms out of custom, or to upbraid the poverty of the other, or to make him mercenary and obliged [...] Give, looking for nothing again, that is, without consideration of future advantages: give to children, to old men, to the unthankful, and the dying, and to those you shall never see again; for else your Alms or courtesie is not charity, but traffick and merchandise.[18]

Repairing inequality through the redistribution of wealth, acting on the basis of empathetic imagining of another's calamity – the politicization of fellow feeling – denouncing obligation, abandoning self-interest for a compassion overriding all hope of return, a direct blow struck against the language of trade in charitable dealings: all these ingredients of active material benevolence will return in Sarah Fielding's *The Adventures of David Simple* (1744), as epitomized in the second epigraph to this chapter. Sarah Fielding will also, in the closing pages of *Volume the Last* (1753), invoke the very phrase, the Family of Love, that provoked such disparate seventeenth-century responses but continued to be associated with enthusiastic illumination or enlightenment (my third epigraph).

By the late eighteenth century, by contrast, charity would be all about the recipient, not the donor; the deleterious effects of charity were its dominant trope, alongside hymns to industriousness. William Sabatier argued:

> Our minds become humbled by receiving charity; we have no longer that ardour, that spring for exertion in youth, or dignity in age, which keeps us from the commission of little actions. When a man is forced to thank, and as it were, to bend the knee for his daily bread, he feels like a slave, and is too apt to act the part of one.[19]

Rather than levelling the inequality that immiserated so many, as Taylor and other clergymen argued, charity, according to Sabatier, undercut the very principle of equality that was crucial to the 'happiness of a state'.[20] Sabatier proposed equality under the law, coupled with political economic faith in the market's ability to guarantee prosperity. All charity sabotages this regimen, according to Sabatier, introducing slavish dependence, rather than countering existing inequality.

Between Jeremy Taylor and William Sabatier, then, a major change occurred in the structure of feeling. A crucial figure in the battering suffered by charitable benevolence was Adam Smith. On the one hand, Smith argued that a certain kind of mutual fund of social sympathy helped to knit society together; the division of labour entangled the various social ranks in reciprocal dependency. Yet Smith also claimed that human subjectivity was comparatively isolated and distanced; social sympathy could only go so far in projecting fellow feeling. In his *Theory of Moral Sentiments* (1759), Smith opined that people could only imagine the suffering of others by imagining what they themselves might feel in the same situation, assimilating another's pain and adapting it to their own imaginative capacities:

> As we have no immediate experience of what other men feel, we can form no idea of the manner in which they are affected, but by conceiving what we ourselves should feel in the like situation. Though

our brother is upon the rack, as long as we ourselves are at our ease, our senses will never inform us of what he suffers [...] [I]t is by the imagination only that we can form any conception of what are his sensations.[21]

Binding together these atomized, but still potentially sensible and sympathetic subjects, was the market. Whereas Shaftesbury had argued for an intrinsic fellowship of feeling, Smith emphasized self-interest, which imaginative sympathy ameliorated but could never fully overcome. The Mandevillian strain so sceptical of human capacities for genuine charity and benevolence loomed large in Smith's formulations. In *The Wealth of Nations* (1776), Smith expounded how self-interest was negotiated in socially productive ways through the interdependencies ensured by the division of labour:

It is not from the benevolence of the butcher, the brewer, or the baker, that we expect our dinner, but from their regard to their own self interest. We address ourselves, not to their humanity but to their self-love, and never talk to them of our own necessities but of their advantages.[22]

Charitable benevolence had little place in a politically economic world in which the market regulated distribution fairly, if not entirely equitably. According to Smithian economics, if each performed his or her necessary labour with diligence and sobriety, each would prosper and the wealth of the nation be assured. Charity would then be largely beside the point.

Such views did not achieve widespread popularity until rather late in the eighteenth century. Until mid-century at least, Anglican clergymen continued to preach that charity *was* the property of the poor, to which they had every entitlement. Ideas of a communist commonwealth continued to be entertained within ecclesiastical thinking. Before 1740, powerful voices within the Church of England defended the importance of charitable redistribution in English society.[23] Daniel Waterland (1683–1740), vice-chancellor of Oxford University and archdeacon of Middlesex, suggested that property was only held by divine leasehold, and that the rich were obliged to give to the poor the rent that was their due.[24] In 1712, Waterland preached to the congregation at St Mary's in Cambridge that charity was the essence of Christianity: 'To feed the hungry, and clothe the naked, is kind and Christian, though the persons so relieved be strangers and aliens, and even useless or ill-deserving.'

For Waterland the goodness or social utility of the objects of benevolence were never at issue (although by the end of the century, only the respectable, industrious, and grateful poor would be suitable recipients; the 'useless' and 'ill-deserving' would have to shift for themselves). Given his university audience, Waterland concluded predictably with a fundraising pitch: 'Of all the methods and contrivances of doing good, there is none more excellent and praiseworthy than that of founding schools and universities for the propagation of religion and sound learning.'[25] When during the mid-eighteenth century nationalist imperatives began to dominate discussions of benevolence, to schools and universities would be added other institutions, as Donna Andrew has shown.[26]

That England was at war with France during the 1740s and 1750s had a profound effect on contemporary social theory and practice. The London Foundling Hospital, the General Lying-in Hospital, the Marine Society, the Lock Hospital for venereal diseases, and the Philanthropic Society were founded during these decades throughout which the fate and future of the nation were fervently debated. Concerted efforts to increase the population and improve the health and strength of the labouring force that fed the navy, army, and colonial settlement, as well as trade and industry, produced charities devoted to preserving life and promoting fecundity. By the century's end, very different demographics would be animating the debate, inspiring the political economists' concern with overpopulation, not underpopulation, and with managing the work force to extract maximum productivity through moral reformation.[27]

Like Andrew I will propose that there was far more intellectual continuity between Taylor and Winstanley in 1650, and that of the first half of the eighteenth century, than has often been supposed. Sarah Fielding, like Waterland and the founders of London charities, evinces this continuity. Sentimental female novelists who figured charity as pounds, shillings, and pence, and who pictured acts of almsgiving and other forms of benevolence in their fiction, were active agents in mid-century debates about the role of philanthropy in regulating society. A distinctly religious ethics pervades mid-century sentimental fiction, with the benefits of charity being equally distributed between the giver and the receiver. There is a persistent return to ideas of commonwealth; the poor are not bound to reveal themselves as deserving. That they are poor is reason enough, because the poor are entitled to a redistribution of wealth. This levelling view of charity is elegantly formulated in the 'Preface' to the anonymous compilation of fictionalized narratives by penitent prostitutes, *The Histories of Some of the Penitents in the Magdalen-House, as Supposed to be related by Themselves* (1760): 'Virtue alone can merit our esteem; but misery deserves our pity, and indigence may claim our bounty.'[28]

Picturing benevolence with Sarah Fielding, to Henry's embarrassment

Sarah Fielding herself says of her hero David Simple, that the point of him is his possession of 'more of what *Shakespear* calls the *Milk of Human Kind* [...] than any other among all the Children of Men'.[29] As Linda Bree notes in her Penguin edition, 'Fielding's use of "Kind" for "Kindness" subtly alters the meaning of the phrase.'[30] Shakespeare's Lady Macbeth fears that Macbeth's nature will prove 'too full o' th' milk of human kindness / To catch the nearest way' to the throne of Scotland (*Macbeth* I.v.14–15). The switch from 'kindness' to 'kind' here opens up David Simple's possession of this attribute from mere kindliness towards others into a recognition of what Marx called species being, a kinship with humanity as a species.

The milk of human kind intimately corporealizes what is represented otherwise more abstractly as an exchange of money. I think that here, as elsewhere, *David Simple* provides a necessary gloss on one of the strangest moments in that highly unpopular later work (unpopular because too formally innovative), *The Cry*, written with Jane Collier and possibly others, as Carolyn Woodward has suggested.[31] When in *The Cry* the profligate Nicanor desperately seeks funds to keep his mistress Cylinda out of jail for debt, after she has been swindled out of her entire fortune by her agent, he seeks out his kind and dutiful daughter Cordelia. Before Nicanor can ask Cordelia for money, she offers him a gift to lift his melancholy spirits: a watercolour she has painted after Rosa Alba entitled the *Roman Charity*, in which a daughter suckles her father to keep him from starving to death in prison. She has predicted – metaphorically speaking – exactly what her father is about to extract from her – her monetary, rather than bodily, substance for his sustenance. Bleak irony lurks here, lodged in the exchange of breast-milk for paternal gratitude, and Cordelia's already shrunken, and now terribly small, fortune, for Nicanor's incorrigible sense of entitlement. Cordelia will offer him her entire substance – the milk of human kind-ness indeed – and never be thanked for such selfless expenditure.[32]

Fielding does not pull her punches regarding the necessity for active charity; woolly feelings of sympathy in themselves cannot alleviate distress. Like many other eighteenth-century heroes, David Simple feels and sheds tears on behalf of others, but unlike them he also gives money unhesitatingly to all those in need. And with those whose need is greatest, and to whom he has become closest, he is willing to share his entire fortune. In Fielding, we return to Winstanley's idea of 'a common treasury', and the Family of Love's notion of all property to be held in common. I think that Sarah Fielding's benevolence should be read as communist, or proto-communist in the light of nineteenth-century developments.

The radical nature of these ideas disturbed, among others, Sarah's brother Henry. As is well known, Henry edited Sarah's text for the second edition, to which he attached his own preface, while also changing quite a number of passages. The altered moment in *David Simple* that I find most significant occurs during the embedded narrative of the tragic French character, Isabelle. As Linda Bree comments, Isabelle's story is 'a distorted, nightmare version of the stories enacted in the rest of the novel', replete with associations between French Catholic absolutism and the inevitable degeneration of chivalric romance.[33] When Isabelle's brother, the Marquis de Stainville, is reunited with his boyhood friend Dumont, his delight knows no bounds, and his expression of friendship takes the form of relieving the poverty of Dumont and his widowed mother by offering to share his fortune equally with them. In the first edition, Sarah Fielding wrote:

> The Marquis would by no means admit him to go any farther; but said, I beg, my dear *Dumont*, you will talk no more of such Trifles, you shall share my Fortune with me; and, from this time forward, the only Favour I beg of you, is to make my House your own, nor shall you accept of that pitiful thing the Duke *de* —— designed for you.[34]

Henry's emendation in the second edition limits the Marquis's generosity to offering merely to share his house with Dumont:

> The Marquis would by no means admit him to go any farther; but said, I beg, my dear *Dumont*, you will talk no more of such Trifles, from this time forward, the only Favour I beg of you, is to make my House your own, nor shall you accept of that pitiful thing the Duke *de* —— designed for you.[35]

Peter Sabor comments that this interference with matters of money in Sarah's text is part of a larger pattern; here Henry insists on 'modifying

Sarah Fielding's depiction of male comportment', 'watering down' the Marquis de Stainville's communal and egalitarian desires.[36] Even Malcolm Kelsall, who accepts Henry's changes as the basis of his Oxford World's Classics edition, comments that 'there is something a little dull in Henry's refusal to let the Marquis [...] offer to share his fortune, then his house, then his estate with his friend'.[37] Throughout, Henry indulges in what Sabor calls 'unwarranted tampering' with Sarah's text when it comes to money, increasing David's original inheritance from his uncle from £7000 to £10,000, 'making the size of the legacy accord with his own concept of wealth', as Sabor puts it.[38] Later, Henry increases the landlady's bill owed by Valentine and Camilla from a guinea to two guineas, comments Sabor, 'as though the original sum were somehow unbecoming'. Finally, Sabor remarks, 'by reducing the £15,000 that David's father-in-law possesses after the death of Livia to £10,000, Henry creates a tidy parallel with David's original legacy that has no counterpart in Sarah's text'.[39] The effect of Henry's emendations, then, is to render the question of money rather more mythic and less messily material, as well as to inflate the sums, thus raising David's economic and social milieu. And any question of communal and equitable wealth-sharing is written out of the narrative completely.

As if anticipating the charitable downturn of subsequent decades, the emphasis on labouring-class self-help, and the growing insistence on humble, cheerful gratitude for any benevolence shown, Sarah Fielding attacks 'obligation' as the enemy of true charity. This is a preoccupation common to *David Simple, Volume the Last*, and *The Cry*. In *The Cry*, Portia denounces obligation, revealing in the process that the Cry, Fielding's figure for hypocritical English society, resembles nothing so much as a pack of hounds 'in full cry' who will hound to death anyone who deviates from pack behaviour:

> The word *obligation* is very seldom in my thoughts, and consequently very seldom is it utter'd by my tongue; for I am satisfied, that whoever hath the word obligation continually in his mouth, hath the love of tyranny steadily fixt in his heart [...] Portia could not have thrown amongst the *Cry* any bone so hard as a thought of hers wherein the two words *obligation* and *gratitude* were to be found. Yet it was a subject which set them a quarrelling amongst themselves, too much to suffer them to attempt giving any answer to *Portia*.[40]

Given to snarling as well as growling and fighting amongst themselves, the Cry cannot understand anything but rude self-interest. For them benevolence in-curs, if you will, obligations. True charity, by contrast, according to Fielding's scheme must be offered without constraint. If gratitude for charitable acts is expected and exacted, a new form of tyranny is exercised. Charity, far from levelling inequalities or restoring to the poor their just portion of the common treasury, would in that instance be perverted into an exercise of domination.

In *Novel Relations*, Ruth Perry has brilliantly shown how, during the later decades of the eighteenth century, 'the emotional capital' of kinship was being rewritten, and the extended family displaced by the conjugal couple and its offspring.[41] I would argue that both the symbolic and real, material capital of charitable benevolence similarly underwent profound changes, and that as with the extended family, so also with the family of mankind: an abrupt lopping off of previously deserving branches occurred, in keeping with the dictates of economic productivity and the social modernizing attendant upon it. Nowhere is this change anticipated more vividly than in the fiction of Sarah Fielding, inspiring numerous imitators.

The milk of human kindness in Sarah Fielding's female contemporaries

Elizabeth Justice, Mary Collyer, Elizabeth Griffith, and Sarah Scott are as unembarrassed as is Fielding to record pounds, shillings, and pence when it comes to active benevolence. Justice's novel *Amelia, or, The Distress'd Wife: A History Founded on Real Circumstances* (1751) appeals to readers' sympathies on behalf of a female protagonist, a Londoner of reasonably genteel background, determined to do the charitable thing despite her hostile husband, Mr Johnson of York. One of the pleasures of this text is its staging, long before Elizabeth Gaskell's, of a confrontation between North and South. For blunt love of money, one should travel to Yorkshire, it would seem, as is revealed when her father-in-law gives Amelia a present of twenty guineas:

> This Present surpris'd her, Money being his darling Passion; therefore it was as much as a thousand from one of a nobler Way of Thinking: For his Advice to his Son was, *Get Money honestly, if you can; but be sure you get Money.*[42]

The affect generated by money in this text is remarkable: libidinally charged, but also redolent of religious enthusiasm. The mystical dimension of money as characterized by Justice would have delighted Marx: 'When her Father came to see her, he made her a Present of five broad Pieces, which gave her inexpressible Joy.'[43] This strange energy derives from money's ability to do good to those who are suffering from its lack. Charity is the sole justification for its possession:

> [T]he first step she took, was to teach [her children] true Humility, and frequently observed to them, the several poor Objects in the Street, charging them to speak courteously, and to be sorry if they had not any thing to give; and when they passed by any Prison, always made them stand, and look at those that begged, to see how they were affected at the Sight. They would then say, Mamma, may I give them my Money that was to buy Playthings? Which gave *Amelia* singular Pleasure, to see Charity, at four Years old, should so strongly shew itself.[44]

The climax of Justice's novel is a revelation of perpetually impoverished Amelia's plan for charitable lending as she explains it to her wealthy friend Mrs Sweet:

> Why Madam, answer'd she, there are many Hundreds in the World, that for want of thirty, forty, or a hundred Pounds, at a low Interest, are inevitably ruin'd; now I would upon their Bonds or Notes, let them have such a Sum, without Interest, and take it again at so much a Month, or Quarter, as they could best spare it; for was I to give it I should be a Bankrupt, and that might prevent their Industry, and render me incapable of being more useful.[45]

After desertion by her wastrel husband, Amelia's acute sense of economic necessity, inspiring meticulously detailed strategies for getting by whilst supporting an extended family, friends and neighbours, and occasional penitent prisoners, is consolidated here as a philanthropic programme.

Mary Collyer's *The History of Betty Barnes* (1753) is similarly preoccupied with financial infrastructure and how it determines social life. Betty, born in a barn, hence the surname Barnes, is introduced wittily, at age five, by the narrator's 'only telling you in general, that she was a fine forward girl, and tho' much sunburnt, far from disagreeable'.[46] When Betty, a ward of the parish, fights in the road with a fellow orphan over some money thrown from a coach and is struck by a carriage horse's hoof, she provokes compassion in Lady Benson, owner of the offending horse, on the grounds that being called to be charitable is a mark of providential favour:

> '[A]s the child would not probably have been hurt, at least not by a horse of mine, had not providence made a kind distinction in my favour; I should, I think, but ill deserve that distinction, if I did not endeavour to alleviate the misfortune I was unwillingly the cause of.'[47]

The novel's conclusion reunites Lady Benson with Betty, now happily married to the gentlemanly Mr Marshall, restored to her missing sailor father, and in a position to dispense charity of her own.

> Young Mrs. Marshall would not suffer her to proceed, but cried out, 'Madam, you were always kind and good; Betty Barnes would never have been what she now is, if it had not been for your charity and compassion'. Her ladyship expressed a good deal of surprise at this discovery, but far from treating her with less respect, on account of her former obligations, she caressed her with great tenderness, and still honours her with her favour and friendship.[48]

Here Collyer, like Fielding, seeks to displace the onerous associations acquired by 'obligation' in the course of the eighteenth century. Lady Benson, if portrayed as a more conventional figure of the type belonging to Fielding's Cry, would have held Betty at a distance because of the girl's indebtedness. Betty's having been *obliged* to Lady Benson for her relatively genteel upbringing would have marked an unbridgeable social gap between them. But Collyer's upholding of fellow-feeling and social sympathy over such rigid distinctions of rank is democratically levelling. Lady Benson's taking the injured Betty into her household to be brought up by her housekeeper Mrs Evans establishes a chain of benevolence, as Mrs Evans was herself the recipient of a similar style of charity. Deserted by her husband, a merchant's clerk, the well-born Mrs Evans finds refuge with former servants of her late mother, where she receives charity from the West Indian merchant Mr Gibbons in the guise of a small gift to her son:

> [T]o her great surprise she found her son's penny was no less than a couple of three pound twelves. It is hard to say whether this relief, seasonable as it was, gave her more pleasure or pain; for tho' she

looked on it as a kind interposition of Providence in her favour, and felt the highest gratitude on the account; yet as it was the first time she had received an obligation that could be called by the mortifying, the self-abasing word, CHARITY, it set before her view all the misery of her situation.[49]

Charity can appear unbearably humbling to gentlewomen. Yet in the fiction of Sarah Fielding and her contemporaries, protagonists, unlike reprobate minor characters, willingly recognize their commonality with the lower orders rather than with unfeeling people of rank. Mrs Evans thus remains in the employ of Lady Benson for the duration of the novel, but in a way that is far from mortifying.

Charity guarantees Betty Barnes's survival from beginning to end, and the novel's conclusion returns to the question of benevolence. Active charity is once again pictured. Mr Gibbons endows Betty with a fortune equal to Mr Marshall's, but insists there shall be no such thing as pin-money in the settlement; he will provide her with her own money for pins, at fifty pounds a quarter. Such benevolence is repaid by Betty to the community at large. Some merit is expected from the indigent, but not a mortifying justification of themselves; and preventative action is also taken:

As heaven has put into her hands the power of relieving the distressed, it has also given her a large heart to scatter its bounties. The poor, the industrious poor, fly to her as to a common benefactress; she relieves the wants of indigent merit, without forcing the unhappy on the mortifying detail of their miseries, and often, by a seasonable, tho' unask'd supply, prevents the ruin of families.[50]

Collyer, like Elizabeth Justice, perpetuates the advocacy of materially grounded benevolence pioneered by Sarah Fielding.

Elizabeth Griffith, within a hermetically sealed world of minor aristocracy, also insists that benevolent feeling be materially grounded. When, in *The Delicate Distress*, Lord Straffon's sister Lucy inherits £12,000, she not only insists on endowing her little niece Emily, but also on providing for the impoverished Sir James Miller, who had previously jilted her. Her rationale for this beneficence is that in abandoning her, Sir James has contributed to her happiness, leaving her free to marry the much nicer, and much richer, Lord Mount Willis. Lucy declares: 'Sir James is poor, and wretched; [...] I now consider him, as my benefactor; and the saving him from the miseries of extreme poverty, will relieve my mind, from a sort of mental debt.' Lucy's generosity is substantial, not begrudging; she intends to lay out 'four thousand pounds, in an annuity, for Sir James, which, if he continues to live abroad, may support him decently'. [51] One third of her fortune to pay this 'sort of mental debt' is radically redistributive, especially as Lucy intends that Sir James Miller never know the name of his benefactor; there is to be no sense of obligation attached to this relief. [52]

Benevolence: insufficiently Picturesque?

Later eighteenth-century refusals to picture benevolence confused contemporary audiences. When, in 1799, Dr Charles Burney reviewed *Lyrical Ballads*, he appeared to be frustrated by the lack of proposed solutions to the misery portrayed. Of 'The Last of the Flock', Burney wrote, as in my first epigraph: 'No oppression is pointed out; nor are any means suggested for his relief. If the author be a wealthy man, he ought not to have suffered this poor peasant to part with *"the last of the flock"*.' [53] Mary Jacobus comments that Burney's literalism here 'naïvely' suggests 'Wordsworth's success in making us respond to the poetry of passion as if to passion itself'. [54] But how naive was Burney's reading? Had he not learned to read in a more benevolent, politically mobilized tradition than the one to which Wordsworth was appealing? Nicholas Roe is on firmer ground than Jacobus in suggesting that when read in the light of contemporary agrarian politics, Burney's 'comment is the less simplistic' for indicating Wordsworth's 'success in realizing the imaginative potential of protest in his poems of 1797–8'. [55] Unfortunately, Wordsworth was growing increasingly intent upon frustrating the expectations of readers like Burney, turning deliberately from protest poetry to a poetry that would transcend the 'political and social focus of that genre', as Roe puts it. [56] Wordsworth's project was to create a poetry of emotion in which 'the feeling therein developed gives importance to the action and situation, and not the action and situation to the feeling'. [57] Despite his criticism of the Picturesque as encouraging the tyranny of the eye over the other senses, Wordsworth appears to have internalized the Picturesque tendency to suppress the economic in favour of the purely aesthetic, severing what had once been, in print at least, an affective inclination towards their inseparability. [58]

Did Charles Burney misunderstand Wordsworth's project in *Lyrical Ballads*? Was Wordsworth perhaps not so much acquiescing in the shepherd's suffering or exploiting it but rather observing a delicate decorum that silently advocated not only fellow-feeling but active charity, that pictured want rather than its relief, and left the ravishing experience of benevolence to the imagination of readers? Or was Burney, well schooled by his daughter, that admirer of Sarah Fielding, rightly insisting that without a graphic picture of the social good of benevolence, the poor would inevitably be left to their own devices, resulting in complete destitution, the final expenditure of all their meagre stock, even unto the last? Wordsworth's refusal to picture active charity of any sort, whether directed towards the shepherd of 'The Last of the Flock', the old Cumberland beggar, the discharged soldier, the leech-gatherer, or any other deserving case, appears to have been at odds with his defence of almsgiving.[59] Should we read his failure or refusal to picture charity as participating in a higher radicalism of feeling that could more effectively transform the world than any individual acts of almsgiving?

Whatever one's conclusions regarding the efficacy of Wordsworth's poetic programme, Sarah Fielding, and the other women writers of mid-century that I have investigated in this essay, thought differently. For them, the burgeoning wealth of the nation was in itself an irresistible call to redistribute wealth more equitably than the structure of English polite society permitted. By century's end, however, the picturing of charitable acts had become not only unfashionable but positively contentious. Amidst the violent disruptions of rural life wrought by the capitalization of agriculture, the effects of commercial wealth and colonial slavery on country and city alike, and increasing admonitions to the poor to behave themselves within the rigours of the division of labour, the merest intimations of charitable relief constituted a protest against economic inequality and social injustice. Within the turbulent currents of Romanticism at the turn of the century, what had become of the vision of human emancipation – the Pantisocratic dream? The progress of Enlightenment stripped to economic improvement and technological innovation had overtaken it. Acts of material benevolence, as they were pictured in *David Simple, Volume the Last, The Cry*, and other mid-century texts by women, could suggest an alternative – that there remained something meaningful in the ideal of commonwealth and the earth as a common treasury for all.

Notes

1. See Adam Smith, *The Theory of Moral Sentiments* (1759), ed. by D.D. Raphael and A.L. Macfie (Oxford: Clarendon Press, 1976), and *An Inquiry into the Nature and Causes of the Wealth of Nations* (1776), ed. by R.H. Campbell, A.S. Skinner, and W.B. Todd, 2 vols (Oxford: Clarendon Press, 1976).

2. Jean-François Lyotard, *The Postmodern Condition: A Report on Knowledge*, trans. Geoff Bennington and Brian Massumi (Minneapolis: University of Minnesota Press, 1984), pp. 31–7.

3. This chapter has greatly benefited from Nigel Smith's essay 'Enthusiasm and Enlightenment: Of Food, Filth, and Slavery', in *The Country and the City Revisited: England and the Politics of Culture, 1550–1850*, ed. by Gerald MacLean, Donna Landry, and Joseph P. Ward (Cambridge and New York: Cambridge University Press, 1999), pp. 106–18.

4. Peter Sabor, ed., 'Introduction', Sarah Fielding, *The Adventures of David Simple and The Adventures of David Simple, Volume the Last* (Lexington: University Press of Kentucky, 1998), pp. xxiii, xxiv.

5. Sabor, 'Introduction', p. xxv. As Sabor notes, the list, from the *Hampshire Chronicle* for 15 January 1776, is reproduced by Park Honan, 'Richardson's Influence on Jane Austen', in *Samuel Richardson: Passion and Prudence*, ed. by Valerie Grosvenor Myer (London: Vision Press, 1986), p. 173.

6. I owe this formulation to conversation with Alessa Johns, with whose admirable chapter on Fielding I am in enthusiastic agreement; see *Women's Utopias of the Eighteenth Century* (Urbana and Chicago: University of Illinois Press, 2003), pp. 67–90. Other indispensable readings include Harriet Guest, *Small Change: Women, Learning, Patriotism, 1750–1810* (Chicago and London: University of Chicago Press, 2000), pp. 30–49, and Felicity Nussbaum, 'Effeminacy and Femininity: Domestic Prose Satire and *David Simple*', *Eighteenth-Century Fiction*, 11 (1999), 421–44.

7. Raymond Williams, *Marxism and Literature* (Oxford and New York: Oxford University Press, 1977), pp. 128–35.

8. Johns, *Women's Utopias*, pp. 89–91.

9. Frances Burney, *Diary and Letters of Madame d'Arblay* (1778–1840), ed. by Austin Dobson (London: Macmillan, 1904–05), I, 409; quoted in Sabor, 'Introduction', p. xxxi, n. 3.

10. Frances Burney, *Evelina, or the History of a Young Lady's Entrance into the World*, ed. by Edward A. Bloom and Lillian D. Bloom (Oxford and New York: Oxford University Press, 1968; rpt 1990), pp. 214–15.

11. Christopher Hill, *The World Turned Upside Down: Radical Ideas during the English Revolution* (1972; London and New York: Penguin, 1975), p. 27.

12. George H. Sabine, ed., *The Works of Gerrard Winstanley* (Ithaca: Cornell University Press, 1941), pp. 262, 253–4; quoted in Hill, *World Turned Upside Down*, p. 139.

13. Nigel Smith, *Perfection Proclaimed: Language and Literature in English Radical Religion 1640–1660* (Oxford: Clarendon Press, 1989), pp. 93, 4, 144, 84.

14. David Norbrook, *Writing the English Republic: Poetry, Rhetoric and Politics, 1627–1660* (Cambridge and New York: Cambridge University Press, 1999; rpt 2000), pp. 1, 15.

15. [Sarah Fielding], *Remarks on Clarissa, Addressed to the Author. Occasioned by some critical Conversations on the Characters and conduct of that Work* (London: Printed for J. Robinson, 1749), pp. 6–7.

16. [Sarah Fielding], *Familiar Letters between the Principal Characters in David Simple, And Some Others. To which is added, A Vision*, 2 vols (London: printed for the author; and sold by A. Millar, 1747), II, 390.

17. Donna T. Andrew, *Philanthropy and Police: London Charity in the Eighteenth Century* (Princeton: Princeton University Press, 1989).
18. Jeremy Taylor, *The Rule and Exercise of Holy Living*, 11th edn (London: printed by Roger Norton for Richard Royston, 1676), pp. 245–9.
19. William Sabatier, Esq., *A Treatise on Poverty, its Consequences, and the Remedy* (London: printed for John Stockdale, 1797), pp. 71–2. This pamphlet was collected by Jeremy Bentham, whose annotated copy in the British Library evidences his approval of the arguments.
20. Sabatier denounces the 'equal division of property' and the 'extinction of all rank', which suggests how ideas of commonwealth, proto-socialist and communist, continued to circulate alongside Paineite republicanism; *Treatise on Poverty*, p. 71.
21. Smith, *Theory of Moral Sentiments*, p. 9. On Smith, see Markman Ellis, *The Politics of Sensibility: Race, Gender and Commerce in the Sentimental Novel* (Cambridge and NY: Cambridge University Press, 1996), pp. 13–14.
22. Smith, *Wealth of Nations*, I, 26–7.
23. Thomas Secker (1693–1768), archbishop of Canterbury, preached that: '[W]e have two Sorts of love: one of Esteem, founded on the Opinion that men are deserving; the other, of mere Benevolence, founded on the Knowledge that they are capable of Pleasure and Pain. The former we may justly be expected to have for all we can: the latter, for all absolutely'; Thomas Secker, *Sermons on Several Subjects*, 7 vols (London: printed for F. and C. Rivington, and B. and J. White, 1795), II, 86–8.
24. Daniel Waterland, *The Works of The Rev. Daniel Waterland, D.D.*, 2nd edn, 6 vols (Oxford: At the University Press, 1843), V, 566.
25. Waterland, 'The Duty of doing Good, A Sermon preached before The University of Cambridge, at St. Mary's Church, On Commemoration Sunday, Nov. 2, 1712', *Works*, V, 307, 308.
26. Andrew, *Philanthropy and Police*, pp. 54–5.
27. Andrew, *Philanthropy and Police*, pp. 149, 153, 199.
28. Jennie Batchelor and Megan Hiatt, eds, *The Histories of Some of the Penitents in the Magdalen-House, as Supposed to be related by Themselves* (1760) (London: Pickering & Chatto, 2007), p. 3. The authorship of the *Histories* remains indeterminate, but Fielding has been proposed as a likely suspect, along with Sarah Scott.
29. Sabor, ed., *David Simple*, Book 2, chapter 9, p. 100.
30. Sarah Fielding, *The Adventures of David Simple And The Adventures of David Simple, Volume the Last*, ed. by Linda Bree (London and New York: Penguin, 2002), p. 427, n. 6.
31. Carolyn Woodward, 'Who Wrote *The Cry*?: A Fable for Our Times', *Eighteenth-Century Fiction*, 9 (1996), 96.
32. [Sarah Fielding and Jane Collier], *The Cry: A New Dramatic Fable*, 3 vols (London: printed for R. and J. Dodsley, 1754), I, 225–6.
33. Bree, ed., *David Simple*, 'Introduction', pp. xi–xxxvi; this passage p. xxx.
34. M. Kelsall, ed., S. Fielding, *The Adventures of David Simple Containing an Account of his Travels through the Cities of London and Westminster, in the Search of a Real Friend* (Oxford and New York: Oxford University Press, 1987), Book 3, chapter 9, p. 219.

35. Kelsall, ed., *David Simple*, Book 3, chapter 9, p. 219.
36. Sabor, ed., 'Introduction', *David Simple*, p. xxx.
37. Kelsall, ed., 'Introduction', *David Simple*, p. xxi.
38. Sabor, ed., 'Introduction', *David Simple*, p. xxix.
39. Sabor, ed., 'Introduction', *David Simple*, p. xxix.
40. S. Fielding, *The Cry*, I, 55–6.
41. Ruth Perry, *Novel Relations: The Transformation of Kinship in English Literature and Culture, 1748–1818* (Cambridge and New York: Cambridge University Press, 2004), p. 97.
42. [Elizabeth Justice], *Amelia, or, The Distress'd Wife: A History Founded on Real Circumstances* (London: printed for the authoress, 1751), p. 30.
43. Justice, *Amelia*, p. 45.
44. Justice, *Amelia*, pp. 49–50.
45. Justice, *Amelia*, p. 227.
46. [Mary Collyer], *The History of Betty Barnes*, 2 vols (London: printed for D. Wilson and T. Durham, 1753), I, 10.
47. Collyer, *Betty Barnes*, I, 13.
48. Collyer, *Betty Barnes*, II, 293.
49. Collyer, *Betty Barnes*, I, 25–6.
50. Collyer, *Betty Barnes*, II, 297.
51. Elizabeth Griffith, *The Delicate Distress* (1769), ed. by Cynthia Booth Ricciardi and Susan Staves (Lexington: University Press of Kentucky, 1997), pp. 162, 163.
52. Sarah Scott's *Millenium Hall* has received far more critical attention than any of the other novels treated in this chapter, including Fielding's, and for that reason I shall not analyse it here. See, for instance, Johns, *Women's Utopias*, pp. 91–109; Guest, *Small Change*, pp. 41–8, 95–8, and Gary Kelly, ed., 'General Introduction', *Bluestocking Feminism: Writings of the Bluestocking Circle, 1738–1785*, 6 vols (London: Pickering & Chatto, 1999). May it suffice to note that Scott, although in a more piously moralizing tone, and with considerably more complacency about the obligations incurred by those who receive charity than Sarah Fielding would have countenanced, reiterates something of her predecessor's valorization of 'all property laid in one undistinguished common' as the signifier of 'true friendship'. Sarah Scott, *A Description of Millenium Hall* (1762), ed. by Gary Kelly (Peterborough, Ontario: Broadview Press, 1995; rpt 2004), p. 93.
53. Dr Charles Burney, *Monthly Review*, 29 (June 1799), 207.
54. Mary Jacobus, *Tradition and Experiment in Wordsworth's Lyrical Ballads* (1798) (Oxford: Clarendon Press, 1976), p. 205.
55. Nicholas Roe, *Wordsworth and Coleridge: The Radical Years* (Oxford: Clarendon Press, 1988), pp. 140–1.
56. Roe, *Radical Years*, p. 140.
57. Wordsworth, *'Preface to Lyrical Ballads, with Pastoral and Other Poems* (1802)', in *William Wordsworth: The Major Works*, ed. by Stephen Gill (Oxford and New York: Oxford University Press, 1984; rpt 2000), p. 599.
58. On this aspect of Picturesque aesthetics, see Donna Landry, 'Ruined Cottages: The Contradictory Legacy of the Picturesque for England's Green and Pleasant Land', in *Green and Pleasant Land: English Culture and the Romantic Countryside*, ed. by Amanda Gilroy (Leuven: Peeters, 2004),

pp. 1–17; John Barrell, *The Birth of Pandora and the Division of Knowledge* (Basingstoke: Macmillan, 1992), pp. 96–7; Stephen Copley, 'Gilpin on the Wye: Tourists, Tintern Abbey, and the Picturesque', in *Prospects for the Nation: Recent Essays in British Landscape, 1750–1880*, ed. by Michael Rosenthal, Christiana Payne, and Scott Wilcox (New Haven and London: Yale University Press, 1997), pp. 133–55.

59. Andrew, *Philanthropy and Police*, pp. 149, 153, 199. Wordsworth himself noted that 'The Old Cumberland Beggar' was composed when 'The political economists were [...] beginning their war upon mendicity in all its forms, and by implication, if not directly, on Almsgiving also'; quoted in Gill, ed., *Wordsworth*, p. 687, n. 49.

8
Women Writers and Abolition

Deirdre Coleman

The years 1787–88 mark the high tide of popular abolitionism. What had begun as a small-scale protest, with Quakers submitting their first public petition to Parliament in 1783, was soon to culminate in a sudden and widespread outburst of humanitarian revulsion against the 'abominable' and 'indefensible' trade. There have been many attempts to explain the speed and breadth of the national mobilization against the slave trade. In a recent contribution Seymour Drescher dismisses arguments that attribute the new popularity to 'chastened anxiety or national humiliation' at the loss of the North American colonies. Nor does Drescher see abolitionism's coming of age as a response to heightened internal class conflict, or to an economic decline in the value of the British slave trade. Without offering much explanation himself, apart from the great expansion of print media in this period, what Drescher does note is that popular abolitionism emerged at one of the most shining moments in British history, when the nation revelled in its 'prosperity, security and power'.[1] This means that, while abolitionists might express strong sentiments of outrage, the underlying premise of their protest involved a degree of complacency. As Drescher puts it, 'how could the world's most secure, free, religious, just, prosperous and moral nation allow itself to remain the premier perpetrator of the world's most deadly, brutal, unjust and immoral offences to humanity? How could its people, once fully informed of its inhumanity, hope to continue to be blessed with peace, prosperity and power?'[2]

Several women's poems discussed in this chapter demonstrate precisely this mixture of indignation and patriotic complacency, but there are significant differences too, many of which can be related to differences in age, class, religion, and national identity. For instance, one poet

172

examined here is an Irish Quaker, another an English Evangelical; one is a renowned radical Dissenter, another is fiercely critical of Christianity, worshipping a secular 'social love' instead. In the single year 1788, poems urging abolition were published by the elder Evangelical writer Hannah More, her milkwoman protégé Ann Yearsley, the teenage sisters Harriet and Maria Falconar, and the sentimental novelist and poet Helen Maria Williams. Of this group it is only the labouring-class Yearsley who ventures out beyond a 'safe' focus on faraway Africa, boldly building direct connections between injustice and oppression abroad and the sufferings of the labouring poor at home. Entirely absent from Yearsley's poem is any patriotic sentiment about Britain as a chosen nation with a special role to play in abolitionism, a tactic which kept protest 'safe' from charges of subversion or (later) Jacobinism. Similarly, as we shall see, the Irishness of the Quaker poet Mary Birkett makes for some interesting deviations, such as when, alluding to Oliver Goldsmith's *The Deserted Village* (1770), she insinuates a parallel between the eviction of Irish villagers and the kidnapping of Africans into slavery.

One composite picture that does emerge from this period of national mobilization is the expanded opportunity for women to be politically active and engaged. Women's enlarged roles in the public sphere can be seen in their fund-raising, their organization of petitions, and their pivotal role, as household managers, in boycotting West Indian sugar.[3] That women were highly visible in the campaign can be seen in Wilberforce's ambivalence about their 'private exertions', going 'from house to house stirring up petitions', behaviour which he felt to be 'unsuited to the female character as delineated in scripture'.[4] We can only wonder at his reaction to Anna Laetitia Barbauld's Amazonian and unpatriotic vehemence when initial confidence in the imminent collapse of the slave trade passed over into the national anguish and shame of the repeated failure of the abolition bills before Parliament in 1791–92. Addressing Wilberforce directly in 1791, Barbauld soars above the national disgrace by envisioning 'th' account of vengeance yet to come'. As we will see below, Barbauld's exchange with Wilberforce is just one of women abolitionists' many fascinating dialogues with contemporary male politicians and fellow-poets.

First phase, 1788–90

Hannah More's *Slavery, A Poem* (1788) is a long verse epistle written to assist William Wilberforce in his opening of the parliamentary campaign against the slave trade. It combines appeals to spiritual equality

('Does the immortal principle within / Change with the casual colour of a skin?') with vivid snapshots of enslavement:

> I see, by more than Fancy's mirror shewn,
> The burning village, and the blazing town:
> See the dire victim torn from social life,
> The shrieking babe, the agonizing wife![5]

The emancipatory rhetoric is, however, cautious, with 'Liberty' invoked as a 'sober Goddess' rather than as an 'unlicens'd monster of the crowd'. Furthermore, a hidebound set of binaries underscores the incompatibility of slavery with Britain's norms of civilized life; while Britain basks in the 'full blaze of light' afforded by liberty, 'sad Afric' lies 'quench'd in total night'. Since the Africans' only sin appears to lie in 'a darker skin', More urges:

> Barbarians, hold! Th'opprobrious commerce spare,
> Respect *his* sacred image which they bear:
> Tho' dark and savage, ignorant and blind,
> They claim the common privilege of kind;
> Let Malice strip them of each other plea,
> They still are men, and men shou'd still be free.

(p. 3)

On the whole Africans remain abstractions for More, removed to a discreet and safe distance. Her denunciation of the British slave trader as a 'WHITE SAVAGE' may on the surface appear daring (one editor has described it as 'slashing rhetoric'[6]), but reversed dichotomies of this kind were standard fare. The phrase 'white savage' also occludes more than it reveals. In the same year that her poem appeared, More's close friend the Reverend John Newton, ex-slave trader, published his *Thoughts upon the Slave Trade* (1788), a pamphlet that made explicit the brutality of the middle passage. In a chilling passage, almost certainly known to More, 'white savages' are white rapists: 'When the women and girls are taken on board a ship, naked, trembling, terrified, perhaps almost exhausted with cold, fatigue, and hunger, they are often exposed to the wanton rudeness of white savages [...] In imagination, the prey is divided, upon the spot [...] Where resistance or refusal would be utterly in vain, even the solicitation of consent is seldom thought of.'[7]

More keeps her distance from such enormities. Africa and Africans are topics for condescension, as can be seen towards the conclusion of her poem where Britain's temperate Christian cherub, 'Mercy', descends upon the dark continent, dispensing light and freedom to the grateful 'dusky myriads' who crowd the sultry plains below:

> She bears, exulting, to the burning shore
> The loveliest office Angel ever bore;
> To vindicate the pow'r in Heaven ador'd,
> To still the clank of chains, and sheathe the sword;
> To cheer the mourner, and with soothing hands
> From bursting hearts unbind th' Oppressor's bands;
> To raise the lustre of the Christian name,
> And clear the foulest blot that dims its fame.

> (p. 19)

At the forefront of the poem is the Evangelical mission to wipe clean Britain's slate of sin and export Christianity to the 'dark and savage, ignorant and blind'. Indeed, as far as More is concerned, Mercy's enfranchising mission to Africa is already accomplished:

> She tears the banner stain'd with blood and tears,
> And, LIBERTY! thy shining standard rears!
> As the bright ensign's glory she displays,
> See pale OPPRESSION faints beneath the blaze!
> The giant dies! no more his frown appals,
> The chain untouch'd, drops off; the fetter falls.
> Astonish'd echo tells the vocal shore,
> Opression's fall'n, and Slavery is no more!

> (p. 20)[8]

Helen Maria Williams, as ardent in her liberalism as More was in her Evangelical conservatism, struck the same optimistic note in her 1788 poem 'On the Bill which was passed in England for regulating the Slave-Trade'. The bill to which Williams refers was the Dolben bill, designed to regulate conditions aboard slave ships. As her title suggests, Williams believed that the abolition of the slave trade was imminent. Accordingly, deploying tidy rhyming couplets and a refrain intoning 'No more', her poem (prematurely) bids farewell to various atrocities connected with the trade before singing a paean of praise to Britain:

> O, first of Europe's polish'd lands
> To ease the captive's iron bands;

> Long, as thy glorious annals shine,
> This proud distinction shall be thine![9]

Pride in their nation's clamour for abolition meant that women poets were keen to make their own distinctive contribution. They did so by focusing on the destruction of African families – the annihilation of the tender ties of 'social love' – through the kidnapping which drove the trade. We see the theme at work in the poems of Harriet and Maria Falconar, two young prodigies aged fourteen and seventeen respectively, each of whom published, like More, a work entitled *Slavery: A Poem* in 1788.[10] Peace, plenty, 'liberty, the right of man' and social joy inform the Africans' lives before Oppression's 'hireling minions' descend, rupturing and trampling upon the bonds of parent, husband, wife, lover, and child.[11] The Falconar sisters are typical in their focus on the kidnapped male slave, with the wife or lover left behind to grieve in Africa. William Cowper's 'The Negro's Complaint' (1788) provided an extremely popular instance of this stereotype, but he had already prepared the way by the following passage in his long poem *Charity* (1782):

> The tender ties of father, husband, friend,
> All bonds of nature in that moment end [...]
> The sable warrior, frantic with regret
> Of her he loves, and never can forget,
> Loses in tears the far receding shore,
> But not the thought that they must meet no more [...].[12]

While many women poets stayed with the dominant Cowperian model, More's poem actually switches the focus to the brutal separation of an enslaved mother and infant:

> By felon hands, by one relentless stroke,
> See the fond links of feeling nature broke!
> The fibres twisting round a parent's heart,
> Torn from their grasp, and bleeding as they part.

(p. 8)

Helen Maria Williams's poem touches the same chord, but her vignette is more highly coloured emotionally, painting an enslaved mother so crazed by suffering that she appears to commit suicide, killing her baby at the same time.[13] In the cry of 'No more' the poet is determined to find comfort in the thought that the worst is over. There is even comfort in the thought that this enslaved woman, unlike her more passive sister victims, has displayed agency in the midst of despair:

> No more, in desperation wild,
> Shall madly strain her gasping child;
> With all the mother at her soul,
> With eyes where tears have ceas'd to roll,
> Shall catch the livid infant's breath,
> Then sink in agonizing death![14]

It is not until Eaglesfield Smith's 'The Sorrows of Yamba; or, the Negro Woman's Lamentation' (1795) that we again see such a powerful portrait of the suicidal slave mother.[15]

If much of the women's verse under discussion is characterized by a willed optimism and sentimentality – the language of the heart – there are also passages that, surprisingly, directly challenge key arguments in the abolitionists' arsenal.[16] The fourteen-year-old Harriet Falconar, for instance, boldly contradicted the much publicized claim of Thomas Clarkson and others that there was not a great deal of difference between the sufferings of slaves and of sailors press-ganged into the African trade.[17] The British youth 'torn from his much-lov'd home' may suffer the terror of storms aboard his slaver, Harriet concedes, but 'the friendly ray / Of hope' always returns for him. The passage continues:

> Not so the slave; oppress'd with secret care,
> He sinks the hapless victim of despair;
> Or, doom'd to torments that might even move
> The steely heart, and melt it into love;
> Till worn with anguish, with'ring in his bloom,
> He falls an early tenant of the tomb![18]

In terms of single-minded, independent argumentativeness, one of the most impressive poems of 1788 is Ann Yearsley's *A Poem on the Inhumanity of the Slave-Trade* (1788).[19] Yearsley frames the inhumanity of the trade through the sentimental vignette of the separated lovers, Luco and Incilanda. The kidnapping of Luco is presented as a crime against his parents and his 'faithful maid', with Yearsley arraying the 'universal good' of 'social love' against the inhumanity of Luco's dreadful torture and death in the West Indies:

> Hail, social love! true soul of *order*, hail!
> Thy softest emanations, pity, grief,

> Lively emotion, sudden joy, and pangs,
> Too deep for language, are thy own [...]

> (p. 28)

Social love is empathy, the 'sympathy unseen' that collapses all distinctions of self and other so that we feel the slave's suffering and the desolation experienced by his grieving family. The liberating effects of social love resemble the divine afflatus of Yearsley's native city of Bristol, invoked at the beginning of the poem as a power strong enough to stretch the 'shackled souls' of 'Christian slaves [...] along the course of *Freedom*' as well as to release the 'crude ideas' of poets from their 'panting state' so that they 'fly in wide expansion' (p. 2).

Expressions of national pride and confidence that abolition would be achieved by Britain, sentiments voiced by More and Williams, arise from their exclusive focus on Africa. Yearsley, on the other hand, takes a comparative view, denouncing with fury not just slavery in Africa but the hypocrisy of Christianity and a British justice system gone awry. Inconsistencies abound. While the murderer at home is condemned to die, the slave trader abroad is licensed to wreak havoc wherever he goes:

> Say, doth this law, that dooms the thief, protect
> The wretch who makes another's life his prey [...]
> Is this an English law, whose guidance fails
> When crimes are swell'd to magnitude so vast,
> That *Justice* dare not scan them?

> (p. 27)

Yearsley also plays upon what Marcus Wood has described as an 'inverse colonial demonology'[20] in which other forms of imperialism pale alongside Britain's version. To Yearsley, whereas Christian slave-owners conceal knowledge of their religion from their slaves, the Mussulman 'frees his slave / Who turns to Mahomet' and the Spaniard baptizes his into Catholicism (pp. 22–3).

Second phase, 1791–92

As abolitionism moved from its first optimistic phase into the political doldrums of the 1790s, women stepped forward as activists, fund-raising and organizing the many petitions which were presented to Parliament during the period 1791–92. Petitions were a new force in politics in this period, widening the boundaries of the political nation, but while women coordinated and assembled many of them, only adult males were allowed to sign. Even without women's signatures, the names of more than 400,000 petitioners flowed into London just in time for the opening of Wilberforce's second motion in early 1791,[21] but despite the unprecedented outcry, the abolition bill failed again.

The most powerful intervention at this point was Anna Laetitia Barbauld's *Epistle to William Wilberforce, Esq. On the rejection of the bill for abolishing the slave trade.*[22] Lofty, magisterial, scornful, apocalyptic: Barbauld's verse captures the shame of this moment when, despite so much evidence and so much knowledge, Britain permitted the trade to continue:

> She knows and she persists – still Afric bleeds;
> Unchecked, the human traffic still proceeds;
> She stamps her infamy to future time
> And on her hardened forehead seals the crime.

(p. 181)

The rhetorical drama unveiled before the House of Commons – a drama of rattling chains, deep groans, bloody scourges, and constant tears – has counted for nothing; and none have been more deceived in their campaign than her fellow poets. In what may well be a pointed barb at Hannah More's cherub 'Mercy', Barbauld the rational Dissenter scoffs: 'The muse, too soon awaked, with ready tongue / At mercy's shrine applausive paeans rung' (p. 181). Even Wilberforce, the great man himself, does not escape Barbauld's sharp tongue. Given the futility of his efforts, and those of his fellow Saints, Barbauld unceremoniously urges them all to desist: 'But seek no more to break a nation's fall, / For ye have saved yourselves, and that is all' (p. 184). The great public ambition to save the nation from sin dwindles into the mini-drama of individual salvation.[23]

Barbauld's authoritative eye ranges from Britain to the West Indies then home again. In the West Indies she moves from the slave-owning planter to the planter's wife and on to the poet who, instead of roving through pastoral scenes of rural pleasure, finds his 'palmy walks and spicy groves' echoing to the sound of 'shrieks and yells' (pp. 182–3). In an allusion to Thomas Gray's *Elegy* (1751), 'Far from the madding crowd's ignoble strife', Barbauld concludes: 'Far from the sounding lash the muses fly / And sensual riot drowns each finer joy' (p. 183). The

West Indian scene is then boldly linked to Britain through the metaphor of contagion, a soft and luxurious 'spreading leprosy' which 'taints ev'ry part' of England's 'rosy bowers' and 'smoky towers'. Britain is doomed, the vengeance already come: 'By foreign wealth are British morals changed, / And Afric's sons, and India's, smile avenged' (p. 183). While the parliamentary movement stalled in the early 1790s, there was another strategy gathering momentum, one which was peculiarly suited to ease the frustration of women activists keen to make their mark in the extra-parliamentary arena. This was the consumer boycott of West Indian produce, a campaign which grew dramatically in the wake of Parliament's failure to pass an abolition bill in 1791. The beginnings of this campaign, and its particular application to women abolitionists, can be seen in the work of the Quaker Thomas Wilkinson of the Lake District. In 1789 Wilkinson published a poem 'on behalf of the abused Africans' which concludes with pointed appeals to 'men of pow'r' such as the king, clergymen, educators, and politicians, and all 'free and favour'd Britons'.[24] Also addressed are:

> Ye *British Dames!* Whose tender bosoms know
> To melt with pity o'er the couch of woe:
> How must your hearts commiserate his woes,
> Whose lot nor home, nor couch, nor country knows!
> These sacred rights he never must regain,
> Oh plead for such! – you seldom plead in vain.[25]

The idea that female sentiment and sympathy might have its own role to play in abolitionism was being demonstrated all round him in the many poems published by women on the topic. What is new is Wilkinson's focus on the tea ceremony as a sanguinary banquet:

> Would it not spoil the flavor of thy tea,
> Mingled with tears and blood the cup to see?
> From blood and tears thy sweeten'd cups are drawn;
> Still drink they sweet, these circumstances known?[26]

Wilkinson probably took inspiration for these lines from Cowper's 'The Negro's Complaint' (1788). In this much reprinted poem, set to a popular tune and commonly surtitled 'A Subject for Conversation at the Tea Table',[27] Cowper's slave asks:

> Why did all-creating nature
> Make the plant for which we toil?

> Sighs must fan it, tears must water,
> Sweat of ours must dress the soil.
> Think, ye Masters iron-hearted
> Lolling at your jovial boards;
> Think how many backs have smarted
> For the sweets your Cane affords.[28]

It was a young female Quaker, the seventeen-year-old Mary Birkett, who brought into dramatic conjunction Wilkinson's direct appeal to women's sentiment and the sanguinary tea ceremony. Her abolitionist poem is not as well known as it should be, so the next section is devoted to it.

The Irishwoman and the African slave

Living in Dublin, Mary Birkett published her *Poem on the African Slave Trade* in two parts in 1792.[29] Seizing the dramatically widened public sphere offered by the sugar boycott, her poem is explicitly *Addressed to her own Sex*. In the three years between Wilkinson's poem and Birkett's own, the gruesome theme of sugar as a sweetener composed of blood, tears, and sweat had gathered powerful momentum, issuing in a boycott of slave-produced goods, especially sugar and rum.[30] As a Quaker, emboldened by a belief in the equality of all people, regardless of class, race, or gender, Birkett felt no shyness in translating her religious convictions into the public authority of the poet on this issue. Drawing upon a strong tradition of women's preaching, backed up by autonomous quarterly and annual meetings composed solely of their own sex, Quaker women like Birkett enjoyed unusual public confidence in bearing testimony against political and social evils.[31]

Addressing the poem to her tea-drinking 'sisters', Birkett urges them to leave off their guilty complicity with the trade:

> How little think the giddy and the gay
> While sipping o'er the sweets of charming tea,
> How oft with grief they pierce the manly breast,
> How oft their lux'ry robs the wretch of rest,
> And that to gain the plant we idly waste
> Th'*extreme of human mis'ry* they must taste!
>
> (Part I, p. 2)

In an ironic turn on the conventional topic of romantic love, 'the manly breast' pierced by the 'giddy and the gay' is not that of the slighted beau but that of the male plantation slave. Birkett's enthusiasm for the expanded sphere of activity offered by abstention is captured in the lines:

> Say not that small's the sphere in which we move,
> And our attempts would vain and fruitless prove;
> Not so – we hold *a most important share*,
> In all the evils – all the wrongs they bear [...]

(Part I, p. 15)

Rejecting the construction of the female sphere as narrow and belonging solely to the private realm, Birkett wants to argue for the public and central role of women's economic power. In a rousing passage towards the end of Part I, Birkett turns to her 'sisters' – the 'Hibernian fair, who own compassion's sway' – and urges:

> Scorn not a younger sister's artless lay;
> To you the Muse would raise her daring song,
> For Mercy's softest beams to you belong;
> To you the sympathetic sigh is known,
> And Charity's sweet lustre – all your own;
> To you gall'd Mis'ry seldom pleads in vain,
> Oh, let us rise and burst the Negro's chain!
> Yes, sisters, yes, to us the task belongs,
> 'Tis we increase or mitigate their wrongs.

(Part I, p. 13)

At this point Birkett invokes the more graphic and visceral rhetoric of the boycott pamphlets, which played on the dreadful imagery of an obscene Eucharist in which white consumers ingest the blood and flesh of suffering Africans. Urging her sisters to 'push the plant away' from their lips, she describes sugar as a 'blood-stain'd lux'ry', a phrase reminiscent of William Cowper's short poem 'An Epigram', also published in 1792: 'No nostrum, planters say, is half so good / To make fine sugar, as a *Negro's* blood'.[32]

As an Irishwoman, conscious of her nation's subjection to British rule (Birkett was ten years old when her family moved to Dublin from

Liverpool), she rejects Thomas Wilkinson's blanket appeal to *'British Dames'*, substituting instead the more poetical 'Hibernian fair' or 'daughters of Ierne'. Appealing to 'Ierne's gentle daughters', Birkett asks them to prove 'The kindling force of sympathetic love [...] And plead for those "who have no power to plead"' (Part I, p. 15). At issue here, in a poem that constantly invokes the sister island of Albion, is the Irish poet's patriotic contrast between Ireland's refusal to deal in slaves and the crime of her 'sister kingdoms':

> For Ireland, when her sister kingdoms rose,
> And heap'd on Afric Misery's piercing woes;
> When link'd in vice, they plough'd the faithless main,
> With hearts impure – and souls intent on gain;
> Then firm in Innocence – supremely good
> In Virtue's awful dignity – she stood,
> Stood as a rock, which boisterous waves assail,
> Unmov'd by every loud and threatning gale,
> The all seducing lure of gold – she dar'd,
> And when she weigh'd the crime, she spurn'd the base reward.

(Part II, pp. 3–4)

A year later, Blake published his powerful *Visions of the Daughters of Albion* (1793), a poem which has at its heart the sufferings of a Celtic woman, Oothoon, a name glossed by the poet as 'the soft soul of America'.[33] In the poem Oothoon appeals across the water to her sisters, the daughters of Albion. It is possible that, through Quaker connections in London, William Blake came upon Birkett's's rousing Irish poem.[34] His poem touches on a raft of intertwined injustices, such as the sexual ownership and enslavement of women, blacks, and children, all of which crimes are inflicted by church and state and an oppressive patriarchal order. A choral audience of Englishwomen, themselves enslaved, hear Oothoon's rousing call to action but they respond supinely: 'The Daughters of Albion hear her woes, & echo back her sighs.'[35] In Blake's poem the contrast is striking between the Celtic woman's energetic, bold and liberated voice and the ineffectual echo of her compromised English sisters.

It is clear that Birkett read many of her women contemporaries on slavery, and that she places herself in a tradition of sister poets. Her arguments are especially close to those of Yearsley. For instance, Birkett picks up on Yearsley's hard-hitting comparison of British slavery with the slavery inflicted by other nations and creeds:

> The Turk to Mah'met would convert his slave;
> He gives him freedom and his soul would save:
> The Spaniards to the mine their vassals send,
> But first the rites of baptism them attend:
> Our Albion, when opprest her captives lie,
> Shews not the way to suffer and to die [...]
>
> (Part I, p. 11)

Birkett also engages with Yearsley's concept of 'social love' at the very start of her poem. Social love is what African families enjoy, before their lives are ripped apart by the kidnapping and murder associated with the slave trade. At the heart of this Quaker poem stands a conception of Africa as a country of rustic simplicity and virtue, underpinned by a well-integrated social and familial life. This idealized picture of Africa has many sources, including Birkett's own family connections with the Swedenborgians.[36] More direct authority for this view could be found in Olaudah Equiano's autobiography, *The Interesting Narrative of the Life of Olaudah Equiano* (1789). Equiano toured Ireland for nine months, between May 1791 and January 1792, promoting his book. He began his tour in Dublin, gathering enough new subscribers by the end of his first month to warrant a fourth, enlarged edition. Altogether he boasted that his sales in Ireland amounted to just under two thousand copies.[37] The most moving section of his biography is the tale of his kidnapping along with his sister, and their later enforced separation.[38] It is likely that this moving story helped to shape the sentimental family vignettes which lie at the heart of Birkett's poem. Following Cowper, the slave for Birkett is a 'father, husband, brother, son or friend'. The husband is snatched from wife and children, the son lost to ageing parents, the entire family group destroyed, generating 'deep distress and disappointed love'. Birkett's lament for the damage done to an innocent Africa by rapacious and greedy fellow-Christians is reminiscent of Oliver Goldsmith's *The Deserted Village* (1770), with its nostalgic grief for a vanished 'bold peasantry' and the lost Irish village of his youth: 'Sweet Auburn! Loveliest village of the plain'.[39] Auburn symbolizes rural simplicity, innocence and happiness, a peaceful agrarian economy of 'humble bowers' and untutored villagers, all uprooted by the tyrant's greedy hand:

> Dear lovely bowers of innocence and ease,
> Seats of my youth, when every sport could please,

> How often have I loitered o'er thy green,
> Where humble happiness endeared each scene;
> How often have I paused on every charm,
> The sheltered cot [...][40]

Invoking this famous Irish scene, Birkett imagines an idealized young
African man enjoying his ancestral home:

> Rear'd in the lap of innocence and ease,
> Him simple Nature's genuine bounties please.
> For him no palace rears its costly head,
> Contented with an humble turf-built shed;
> On him no fawning lacqueys proudly wait,
> In all the pamper'd insolence of state [...]
>
> (Part I, p. 5)

Here, in the close verbal allusions to Goldsmith's poem, Birkett insinuates a parallel between the dispossessed Irish peasant and the African
kidnapped into slavery.

Apart from skin colour (the Negro's 'sable tincture'), there is, for
Birkett, no difference between the African and the European. Going
further than More's assertion of spiritual equality – the 'immortal principle within' – Birkett insists upon physical sameness as well, urging her
fellow Christians to look up close: 'Examine well each limb, each nerve,
each bone, / Each artery – and then observe *thy own*' (Part I, p. 4). This
is an unusual invitation; and if the African seems in any way inferior, is
not this the result of his suffering? Can the Negro's 'sable frame'

> Th'internal value of his soul proclaim?
> Ingulph'd in misery – with pain depress'd,
> These harrow up the feelings of his breast [...].
>
> (Part II, p. 16)

How would the greatest British orators and politicians have fared 'If o'er
their heads did Slavery's mandates roll, / And freeze the gen'rous current
of their soul' (Part II, pp. 16–17)? In posing this question Birkett boldly
alludes to Gray's *Elegy Written in a Country Churchyard* (1751) where
the narrator, referring to the churchyard's unlettered and unhonoured

dead, declares: 'Chill Penury [...] froze the genial current of the soul'. Birkett continues Gray's theme:

> Torn from his friends, bereav'd of every joy,
> Which might his mental faculties employ,
> Degraded, and dishonour'd – where, ah! where
> Shall sense and reason's blooming flowers appear?
> Where would the eloquence of Grattan shine?
> Where Sheridan's address? – where Pitt divine?

(Part II, p. 17)

This roll-call of a trio of great statesmen and orators, two of whom were Irishmen, is directly modelled on the *Elegy*'s reflections on how one or other of these anonymous dead, with education and opportunity, might have been a Hampden, a Milton, or a Cromwell:

> But Knowledge to their eyes her ample page
> Rich with the spoils of time did ne'er unroll;
> Chill Penury repressed their noble rage,
> And froze the genial current of the soul.
>
> Full many a gem of purest ray serene
> The dark unfathomed caves of ocean bear:
> Full many a flower is born to blush unseen
> And waste its sweetness on the desert air.[41]

Birkett is not the first woman poet to re-imagine Gray's famous poem in an anti-racist, abolitionist framework. The argument that we are all born equal, but that difference arises from access to knowledge and wealth, can also be seen in Mary Deverell's 'On reading the poems of Phillis Wheatley' (1781).[42] Wheatley, the 'African poetess', achieved celebrity status during her brief life. Born in Africa in 1753, sold into slavery as a child, then transported to America, her Bostonian owners not only noticed her native genius but nurtured it through private tuition in various subjects, including Latin and Greek. Unable to find a publisher in New England, Wheatley travelled to London in 1773 where she was taken up by abolitionists as a literary prodigy.[43] Deverell writes of her as 'a lowly maid' of 'sable charms':

> By fortune doom'd to languish in the shade;
> Till Britain call'd the seeds of genius forth,
> Maturing, like the sun, her native worth.

Though no high birth nor titles grace her line,
Yet humble PHILLIS boasts a race divine;
Like marble that in quarries lies conceal'd,
Till all its veins, by *polish*, stand reveal'd.[44]

In lines that bear a remarkable parallel to these, Birkett adopts the metaphor of education as a transforming polish, a power capable of transmuting a neglected chunk of marble into the finest statuary:

'Tis education gives the polish'd gloss,
Refines the metal from the worthless dross:
Prunes, with careful hand, the opening shoot,
And tends, with anxious care, the promis'd fruit [...]
Improves wild nature's nursling – gives the soul
The seal which stamps a value on the whole.
And as the marble in the quarry lies,
Its hidden worth conceal'd from human eyes [...].

(Part II, p. 16)

The hidden worth of Africans, symbolized by the valuable black marble buried out of sight in deep quarries, is paralleled by a conviction, widely held by Birkett's contemporaries, of the great wealth of Africa itself, particularly its natural productions such as ivory, beeswax, palm-oil, pepper and other spices, and assorted gums, timbers, and dye-woods. Leading abolitionists argued strongly for a new, purified type of commerce with Africa, one that substituted a legitimate trade in things for an obscene and illegitimate commerce in persons. Birkett picks up on this theme in her injunction to traders travelling to Africa:

Search her fertile land,
Let the mild rays of commerce there expand;
Her plains abound in ore, in fruits her soil,
And the rich plain scarce needs the ploughman's toil.

(Part I, p. 12)

In common with many other abolitionists, including Equiano himself, Birkett's idealization of Africa goes hand in hand with a zeal to Christianize and civilize the country through trade and colonization. At the time of the poem's publication, John Clarkson was en route to Freetown, Sierra Leone with almost twelve hundred loyalist ex-slaves from Nova Scotia. Originally founded in 1788 as an anti-slavery 'Province of Freedom', within two years Freetown had been razed by local African chiefs, so the plan in 1791–92 was to import black loyalists to rebuild and secure the settlement.[45] Inspired by this bold undertaking, Birkett resoundingly declares: 'Plant there our colonies, and to their soul, / Declare the God who form'd this boundless whole' (Part I, p. 13).[46]

News of the violent slave uprisings in San Domingue (Haiti) in the late summer of 1791 began to circulate in metropolitan centres towards the end of that year. Despite Birkett's Quaker commitment to pacifism, she makes a serious effort to sympathize with African rebellion. Following Anna Barbauld, whose imagination had reached out in 1791 to embrace an image of Africa goaded to revenge and slaughter – 'injured Afric, by herself redressed, / Darts her own serpents at her Tyrant's breast'[47] – Birkett pronounces: 'No wonder if fierce passion aims the blow' at the tyrants who whip and torture their slaves:

> What son of thine, oh Albion, would bow down,
> Would tremble at the upstart planter's frown?
> What son of thine, oh Albion, thus opprest,
> Nor feel revenge inflame his haughty breast?

> (Part I, p. 11)

Birkett also follows Barbauld in denouncing each 'flimsy sophistry' adduced by the supporters of slavery.[48] But where the elder poet does not deign to rehearse any of these specious arguments, Birkett covers most of them, including the claim that slavery solved Africa's problem with overpopulation. Nor does Birkett have much patience with the ameliorationist argument or the figure of the 'mild master'. Drawing on a tradition stemming from *Oroonoko* (1688), which imagined the slave as a noble African, Birkett believes no amelioration is possible for those 'once chieftains in their native land' (Part I, p. 9).

Part II of Birkett's poem appeared shortly after the publication of Part I. Buoyed up by several factors – the warm reception of her poem by female compatriots, France's recent abolition of slavery (Part II, p. 7), and yet another abolition bill going forward across the Irish sea – Birkett opens Part II with vows of loyalty and love towards Albion (England). At the same time, as we have seen, she embarks upon a denunciation of England (together with Wales and Scotland) for embruing their hands 'in gore' and 'foul crimes'. With her childhood lessons in the glorious history of English deeds now tarnished, disillusion with England and her 'sister kingdoms' is offset by a new-found patriotic pride in Ireland and in those 'Sisters' to whom the poem is addressed, those 'mild and fair' daughters of Ireland who share her pride in Ireland's spotless history where slave-trading is concerned: 'No – never were her peaceful vessels mann'd / To ravage helpless Afric's guiltless land' (Part II, p. 4). In general the discourse of Part II is more elevated. Gone is the rebellious slave of Part I. In Part II Birkett surrenders herself 'unrestrain'd' to the muse of Fancy as she pictures to herself African men and women, not just liberated from their sufferings but in ecstasy at the prospect of freedom unfolding before their eyes:

> Oh with what transport, with what rapturous fear
> Will they the great, the Heav'n-sent blessing hear
> How will the varied passions of their soul
> With bliss too high for speech their acts controul?
> The swimming tear! big throb! the speaking eye!
> And all th'unutterable extacy!
> Even now methinks the melting scene I see,
> And every passion struggling to get free;
> His feet they kiss who did the news impart,
> Embrace his knees, and clasp him to their heart:
> Lost in a flood of rapture [...]
>
> (Part II, pp. 10–11)

Unfortunately the Africans' rapture takes the form of undignified gratitude. No doubt with the Wedgwood medallion in mind ('Am I not a man and a brother?'), which her Quaker uncle George Harrison had helped to design in 1787, Birkett substitutes for the original kneeling supplicant the 'wild effusion' of grateful Africans, kissing the feet of the first white man who bears tidings of their liberation. The rapture eventually settles down into 'a flow of gratitude and love', but only because of 'British learning' which will, by imparting light,

> Dispel the chaos of the Negro's heart;
> Diffuse fair knowledge, scientific lore,
> And *to the rights of Men* their souls restore;
> When Gospel truths shall dart an heav'nly ray,
> And slaves enfranchis'd own a Saviour's sway [...]
>
> (Part II, p. 12)

Birkett's allusion to '*the rights of Men*' invokes two of the great revolutionary tracts of her time: the feminist Mary Wollstonecraft's *Vindication of the Rights of Men* (1790), and Tom Paine's *Rights of Man* (1791). The invocation of Paine, the son of a Quaker corset-maker, was particularly daring, as he had been accused of seditious libel for his *Rights of Man*, and by 1792 was living in exile in France. But the rights invoked here are not unequivocally radical and egalitarian. As Birkett's full line suggests – 'And *to the rights of Men* their souls restore' – these rights belong to the spiritual as well as to the political domain, an equivocation strengthened by the poem's concluding vision of a liberated but subjugated Africa, where slaves are only 'enfranchis'd' to the extent that they bow to the yoke of 'a Saviour's sway'.

Conclusion

For a brief moment in April 1792 it looked as though the parliamentary defeat of the previous year might be reversed, but it was not long before abolition fell under the same odium as all other reform movements. By 1793, Britain was at war with revolutionary France and the opportunity was lost. Women poets did not fall silent, however. In a number of heartfelt poems Mary Robinson continued to urge the lesson of Enlightenment reason: that all races were equal, regardless of 'clime, / Estate or colour'. The blood which flowed in the African's veins was 'As pure, – as clear, as Europe's Sons can boast'.[49] In this same poem, entitled 'The African' (1798), Robinson also touches on the taboo topic (for her sex) of the violation of black women by their new owners, the very topic that More had carefully eschewed a decade earlier. Chief of the enslaved African's sufferings is to see

> The darling of his heart, his sable love,
> Selected from the trembling timid throng,
> By the wan Tyrant, whose licentious touch
> Seals the dark fiat of the Slave's despair![50]

In the year of her death, Robinson published another abolitionist poem, *The Negro Girl* (1800). This romantic tale, set on a West Indian beach, is narrated by the 'love-lorn' Zelma as she watches her beloved Draco transported to another island. Zelma's white owner, who wants her as his mistress, has taught her to read and write. Ironically, he has even taught her the lesson of racial equality: 'in the Soul to find / No tint, as in the face'.[51] Although this device means that Zelma's voice sounds no different from that of the white abolitionist woman poet, the act of ventriloquism should not detract from Robinson's serious innovation in attempting to explore, as Helen Maria Williams had begun to do, the suffering of black women under slavery. The abolitionist movement granted women poets new opportunities for making their voices heard in the public sphere. The agitation arising out of the much publicized horrors of the slave trade also afforded women writers a new legitimacy, both economically in their roles as managers of the household and affectively as defenders of social love in all its manifestations of pity, grief, joy, and love. The clampdown on protest during the counter-revolutionary 1790s did not deter them from pursuing their campaign, nor were they deterred by the definitive closing of all avenues to national self-complacency on the issue of abolition.

Notes

1. Seymour Drescher, 'Public Opinion and Parliament in the Abolition of the British Slave Trade', in *The British Slave Trade: Abolition, Parliament and People*, ed. by Stephen Farrell, Melanie Unwin, and James Walvin (Edinburgh: Edinburgh University Press, 2007), pp. 42–65.
2. Drescher, 'Public Opinion', p. 47.
3. See Clare Midgley, *Women Against Slavery: The British Campaigns, 1780–1870* (London and New York: Routledge, 1992).
4. See Robin Blackburn, *The Overthrow of Colonial Slavery, 1776–1848* (London: Verso, 1988), p. 153.
5. Hannah More, *Slavery, A Poem* (London: T. Cadell, 1788), p. 3. Subsequent references to this poem are given parenthetically in the text.
6. See James G. Basker, *Amazing Grace: An Anthology of Poems about Slavery, 1660–1810* (New Haven and London: Yale University Press, 2002), p. 335. The reference to 'WHITE SAVAGE' appears on p. 15 of More's poem.
7. John Newton, quoted in Marcus Rediker, *The Slave Ship: A Human History* (New York: Viking, 2007), p. 241.
8. Over the past few years more sympathetic readings of More's politics have emerged. Notable are Anne Stott's *Hannah More: The First Victorian* (Oxford: Oxford University Press, 2003) and Harriet Guest's 'Hannah More and Conservative Feminism', in *British Women's Writing in the Long Eighteenth Century: Authorship, Politics and History*, ed. by Jennie Batchelor and Cora Kaplan (Basingstoke: Palgrave Macmillan, 2005), pp. 158–70.
9. Basker, *Amazing Grace*, p. 372.
10. *Poems on Slavery: by Maria Falconar, aged 17, and Harriet Falconar, aged 14* (London: Egertons, Murray and J. Johnson, 1788).
11. *Poems on Slavery*, pp. 14–17.
12. Basker, *Amazing Grace*, p. 294.
13. For an illuminating discussion of slave suicide and infanticide in this and other poems, see Debbie Lee's *Slavery and the Romantic Imagination* (Philadelphia: University of Pennsylvania Press, 2002), pp. 194–200.

14. Basker, *Amazing Grace*, p. 372.
15. For the complicated textual history of this poem and its appearance in Hannah More's *Cheap Repository Tracts* (1795), see Alan Richardson, ' "The Sorrows of Yamba" by Eaglesfield Smith and Hannah More: Authorship, Ideology, and the Fractures of Antislavery Discourse', *Romanticism on the Net*, 28 (November 2002) <http://www.ravon.umontreal.ca/>. For the text of 'The Sorrows of Yamba' see Marcus Wood, ed., *The Poetry of Slavery: An Anglo-American Anthology, 1764–1865* (Oxford: Oxford University Press, 2005), pp. 110–16.
16. For sensibility in abolitionist writing, see Brycchan Carey's *British Abolitionism and the Rhetoric of Sensibility: Writing, Sentiment, and Slavery, 1760–1807* (Basingstoke: Palgrave Macmillan, 2005).
17. For a recent study of this nexus, see Emma Christopher, *Slave Ship Sailors and their Captive Cargoes, 1730–1807* (Cambridge: Cambridge University Press, 2006).
18. *Poems on Slavery*, pp. 19–20.
19. Ann Yearsley, *A Poem on the Inhumanity of the Slave-Trade* (London: G.G.J. and J. Robinson, 1788). Subsequent references to this poem are given parenthetically in the text.
20. Wood, *The Poetry of Slavery*, p. 120.
21. See Drescher, 'Public Opinion', p. 54.
22. Anna Laetitia Barbauld, *Epistle to William Wilberforce, Esq. On the rejection of the bill for abolishing the slave trade* (1791). The text used here and subsequently cited by page number in the text is the one reproduced in Marcus Wood's *The Poetry of Slavery*, pp. 181–4.
23. Wood, *The Poetry of Slavery*, p. 180, has commented on these lines that 'not many abolitionists would dare to stand up and say [this] straight out to Wilberforce'.
24. Thomas Wilkinson, *An Appeal to England, on behalf of the Abused Africans. A Poem* (London: James Phillips, 1789), pp. 27–9.
25. Wilkinson, *An Appeal to England*, p. 29.
26. Wilkinson, *An Appeal to England*, p. 17.
27. See Thomas Clarkson, *The History of the Rise, Progress, and Accomplishment of the Abolition of the African Slave-Trade*, 2 vols (London, Longman, Hurst, Rees and Orme, 1808), I, 188.
28. Basker, *Amazing Grace*, p. 300.
29. Mary Birkett, *A Poem on the African Slave Trade. Addressed to her own Sex*, Parts I and II (Dublin: J. Jones, Grafton Street, 1792). The full text of Birkett's poem is available in *Irish Women Poets of the Romantic Period*, ed. Stephen Behrendt (Alexandria, VA: Alexander Street Press, 2007–) <http://asp6new.alexanderstreet.com/iwrp/> [accessed 15 April 2008]. Both parts of the poem are also available on Brychhan Carey's website, which is the source for the extracts from the poem cited in the text <http://www.brycchancarey.com> [accessed 29 March 2008]. For critical commentary see Nini Rodgers, 'Two Quakers and a Utilitarian: The Reaction of Three Irish Women Writers to the Problem of Slavery, 1789–1807', in *Proceedings of the Royal Irish Academy*, vol. 4 (2000), pp. 137–57, and Josephine Teakle, 'The Works of Mary Birkett Card 1774–1817, Originally Collected by her Son Nathaniel Card in 1834: An Edited Transcription with an Introduction to her Life and Works', unpublished doctoral thesis, University of Gloucestershire, 2004.

30. See Deirdre Coleman, 'Conspicuous Consumption: White Abolitionism and English Women's Protest Writing in the 1790s', *English Literary History*, 61 (1994), 341–62; Elizabeth Kowaleski Wallace, *Consuming Subjects: Women, Shopping, and Business in the Eighteenth Century* (New York: Columbia University Press, 1997), pp. 37–51.

31. See Phyllis Mack, 'In a Female Voice: Preaching and Politics in Eighteenth-Century British Quakerism', in *Women Preachers and Prophets through Two Millennia of Christianity*, ed. by Beverly Mayne Kienzle and Pamela J. Walker (Berkeley and London: University of California Press, 1998), pp. 248–63.

32. Basker, *Amazing Grace*, p. 302.

33. Scholarly consensus derives the name Oothoon from 'Oi-thona', a character in one of James Macpherson's supposed translations from Ossian, a Scottish Gaelic bard; see *Blake's Poetry and Designs*, ed. by Mary Lynn Johnson and John E. Grant (New York and London: Norton Critical Edition, 1979), p. 69.

34. For Birkett's biography, including information concerning her uncle George Harrison and his 1792 incendiary pamphlet against the bishops, see Deirdre Coleman, 'Mary Birkett', in Behrendt, *Irish Women Poets of the Romantic Period*. See also Harrison, *An Address to the Right Reverend the Prelates of England and Wales, on the Subject of the Slave Trade* (London: J. Parsons and Ridgway, 1792).

35. *Blake's Poetry and Designs*, pp. 70–80.

36. Coleman, 'Mary Birkett'.

37. Olaudah Equiano, *The Interesting Narrative of the Life of Olaudah Equiano* (1789), ed. by Vincent Carretta, rev. edn (Harmondsworth: Penguin, 2003), p. 358.

38. Equiano, *Interesting Narrative*, pp. 51–2.

39. Roger Lonsdale, ed., *The New Oxford Book of Eighteenth Century Verse* (Oxford and New York: Oxford University Press, 1984), p. 523.

40. Lonsdale, *Eighteenth Century Verse*, p. 523.

41. Lonsdale, *Eighteenth Century Verse*, p. 356.

42. Mary Deverell, *Miscellanies in Prose and Verse, mostly written in the epistolary style* (London: printed for the author by J. Rivington, 1781). The text used here is reproduced in Basker's *Amazing Grace*, p. 293.

43. Wood, *The Poetry of Slavery*, pp. 404–5.

44. Basker, *Amazing Grace*, p. 293.

45. For a reassessment of this colonial experiment, see Isaac Land and Andy Schocket, eds., 'New Approaches to the Founding of the Sierra Leone Colony, 1786–1808', *Journal of Colonialism and Colonial History*, 9 (Winter 2008). <http://muse.jhu.edu/journals/cch> [accessed 5 January 2009].

46. For colonization plans in this period, see my *Romantic Colonization and British Anti-Slavery* (Cambridge: Cambridge University Press, 2005).

47. Wood, *The Poetry of Slavery*, p. 182.

48. Wood, *The Poetry of Slavery*, p. 181.

49. Basker, *Amazing Grace*, p. 264.

50. Basker, *Amazing Grace*, p. 264.

51. Wood, *The Poetry of Slvarey*, p. 51.

9
Charlotte Smith, Mary Wollstonecraft, and the Romance of Real Life

Stuart Curran

In the autumn of 1784, Charlotte Smith, having managed to extricate her husband from London's King's Bench Prison where he had been confined for his debts, repaired with him and her large number of children to the safety of Normandy. There, with the fluent French she had learned in school, she settled on two important French texts to translate into English with the aim of earning sufficient means to secure her family against her husband's improvidence. The first was the Abbé Prévost's *Manon Lescaut*, which, however, on its appearance in 1786 was quickly withdrawn as already existing in translation and as being, besides, rather too scandalous for British moral tastes. The second was a two-volume selection from an enormous archive of French court cases called *Les causes célèbres*. Among these was the now-famous account of 'Le faux Martin Guerre' (commonly known in English as 'the return of Martin Guerre'), and its concentration on female powerlessness before the law and male abuse of women sets the tone for the cases Smith included in a collection she entitled *The Romance of Real Life*, which was published early in 1787. Unlike the earlier translation, this one was a best-seller, and it gave Smith the financial security she had set out to achieve. Already a poet of repute, she now found standing as a writer of prose, which would lead her soon to embark on a career as a novelist that would quickly render her the most influential writer of fiction in Britain during the 1790s. It would appear, however, that her influence was immediately felt even from the translated French court accounts. For in 1788, the year following their publication, Mary Wollstonecraft published her second educational tract, one in which she established the characteristic voice that would make her a major intellectual force in British culture for the ensuing decade. She called this book *Original Stories from Real Life, with Conversations Calculated*

to Regulate the Affections, and Form the Mind to Truth and Goodness.
Although unacknowledged then, we may see in this quiet doubling of
titles – *The Romance of Real Life, Original Stories from Real Life* – a paradoxically important moment in the development of fiction in English,
for that intrusion of 'real life' into the world of romance marks the
beginning of a reconstituted literary realism markedly distinct from
that of Richardson, Fielding, and Smollett, though perhaps akin to that
created by Defoe, a realism that would eventually inundate the novel
during the nineteenth century. That its source is clearly within the
orbit of literary women has been overlooked by most chroniclers of the
development of fictional realism.[1]

Smith and Wollstonecraft appear to have met only once, on 25 July
1787, nine days after Smith had first become acquainted with William
Godwin and scant weeks before Wollstonecraft gave birth to the future
Mary Shelley, which occasioned her own death. Before this they had
not moved in the same cultural orbits. Charlotte Smith for the most
part lived in Sussex near the English Channel and within miles of
Bignor Park, the estate where she was raised; and Mary Wollstonecraft,
aside from her experience as a governess in Ireland, was an inveterate
Londoner. But beginning in that summer of 1797 Smith became closely
acquainted with Godwin, for whose tragedy *Antonio* she supplied the
spoken prologue and whom she reconfigures as Armitage, the sceptical
voice of reason in her last conventional novel, *The Young Philosopher*
(1798). In its preface Smith notes a similarity of plot devices between
her and Wollstonecraft in these words:

> I may just mention, that the incident of the confinement in a
> mad house of one of my characters was designed before I saw the
> fragment of 'The Wrongs of Woman,' by a Writer whose talents
> I greatly honoured, and whose untimely death I deeply regret; from
> her I should not blush to borrow, and if I had done so I would have
> acknowledged it.[2]

Loraine Fletcher, Smith's most trustworthy biographer, notes another
gesture toward Wollstonecraft in this novel, where the ideal of female
education is described in terms that echo both Wollstonecraft's
Vindication of the Rights of Woman and the beginning of *Original Tales
from Real Life*.[3] For her part, Wollstonecraft had earlier reviewed five of
Charlotte Smith's novels in the progressive *Analytical Review*, though
she did not particularly distinguish Smith's own radical perspectives in
these notices, except to praise the import of *Desmond* where 'the cause

of freedom is defended with warmth'.[4] Perhaps, her restraint was strategic, as a novel that was not adversely criticized in these pages bore an implicit seal of approval. Certainly, Smith, conscious as she was of the closeness of conception between her fiction and Wollstonecraft's *Maria, or the Wrongs of Woman*, would have recognized there Wollstonecraft's clear borrowing from *Desmond* (1792), Smith's novel set in the midst of the French Revolution in which the dissolute Richard Verney, to satisfy his mounting debts, attempts to prostitute his wife Geraldine, a circumstance that Wollstonecraft returns to in George Venables's treatment of his wife Maria.

Even if these two writers had no further personal contact than what is noted here, such a shared, deeply felt, and ultimately transgressive concern with the vulnerability of women suggests the cultural ties that bind them. The realism with which they confront the world they create in their writings is a testimony to a fundamental honesty that both of them attained first-hand, Wollstonecraft having grown up with a drunken and abusive father and Smith having been married off at sixteen to a husband who squandered a fortune between gambling and other women and whom Smith eventually left to earn a living for herself and her children by means of her pen. Neither of them was content to rest comfortably within the conventions of the female romantic fictions they inherited. Their politics are similarly radical, but in both their cases radicalism goes far beyond a simple political or social programme; rather, it should be understood in its basic sense, as a concern with the actual structural roots of a late Enlightenment order undergoing a deservedly revolutionary assault.

To understand how this realism functions, we might begin with Wollstonecraft's *Original Stories*, a work that has no pretensions as a great piece of literature, but that nonetheless, in a genre whose usual attribute is a bland sweetness, is remarkable for its sharpness of attention and tone. Derived from Wollstonecraft's own Irish experiences, the plot revolves around Mrs Mason, a new governess to Mary and Caroline, respectively fourteen and twelve years of age, who have up to this point been thoroughly spoiled rather than educated. The opening of the first chapter sets the tone as Mrs Mason leads her charges outdoors on a conventionally lovely spring morning that Wollstonecraft immediately undercuts: 'every prospect smiled, and the freshness of the air conveyed the most pleasing sensations to Mrs. Mason's mind; but the children were regardless of the surrounding beauties; and ran eagerly after some insects to destroy them'.[5] Mrs Mason sets out to teach the children a basic humanity and succeeds so well that they quickly veer to the other extreme, indulging in an undifferentiated sentimentality. She tells them the story of 'crazy Robin', who lived with his dog in a cave. The dog, who had a habit of chasing and barking at horses, one day was almost responsible for having a young gentleman thrown from his mount. In his anger this man shot the dog, and Robin was so distraught at his loss that he too soon expired. 'Was that the cave? said Mary. They ran to it. Poor Robin! Did you ever hear of anything so cruel! Yes, answered Mrs. Mason [...]' (IV, 376). The remainder of this work unfolds with a like refusal to sentimentalize and a continuing impulse of reality, or what Mrs Mason simply calls 'truth'.[6] Although there could be no significant crossover to a children's book from Smith's volume of French trials for murder, bigamy, impersonation, and the like, Wollstonecraft's emphasis on the real does not skirt matters of social justice, class pretension, and mistreatment of dependants. Nor does it hide the darker aspects of existence to preserve the putative innocence of young girls. Behind Mrs Mason's own solitude are hints of connections lost and sorrows overcome by sheer resolve, a most unusual centring device for a children's book.

'I like to use significant words', Wollstonecraft proclaims in *A Vindication of the Rights of Woman*.[7] 'I declare against all power built on prejudices, however hoary' (IV, 170). In the present context what is important is not the audacity of her language, her pose as an army of one, or the uncompromising stance of her principles, but rather Wollstonecraft's reliance on unvarnished truth to undercut the status quo, venerable as it might seem to be. Today her cultural analyses, however radical and viciously attacked in her own time, seem obvious and scarcely overstated. But what should be emphasized in this context is not the correctness of her social vision, but its realism. That is to say, what she confronts in her famous polemic is an interlocking series of sentimentalized assumptions – what in a later time we call a cultural imaginary – by which she saw eighteenth-century women being kept in an intellectual and cultural prison. Concentrated on the definition of women as avatars of sensibility, these are likewise the assumptions governing the principal subgenres of fiction geared to a female audience: the female *Bildungsroman*, the courtship novel, domestic fiction. What from this perspective needs to change is the very way in which women are characterized, and in her last great works that is essentially the task Wollstonecraft undertakes.

Wollstonecraft's *Letters Written during a Short Residence in Sweden, Norway, and Denmark* (1796) is her most polished piece of writing. Godwin famously said of it, 'If ever there was a book calculated to make a man fall in love with its author, this appears to me to be the book.'[8] And, of course, he did indeed fall in love with her. But his characterization of its tone as one of 'melancholy', 'tenderness', 'softness', 'gentleness', though suggestive of the earnestness of a lover, rather misses the mark of what distinguishes the book. There is only one prominent travel memoir written by a woman in English before Wollstonecraft's work, Lady Mary Wortley Montagu's letters from Constantinople (published 1763), where her husband was the British Ambassador. These are the work of an aristocratic woman of the world who has access to its principal centres of power. Wollstonecraft's letters, in contrast, are the product of a middle-class businesswoman who happens to have a refined imagination, travelling by herself with her infant and a maidservant, uncommonly alone but also strikingly alert. She casts herself as a unique, unprecedented voice, who, though a woman and a mother, is somehow beyond the claims of class or gender roles even as she continually registers her awareness of their complex interactions in the cultures she visits.

Appreciation of the natural vistas through which she passes is one of Wollstonecraft's hallmarks in this work, but again and again she conspicuously subverts the Kantian gendered opposition of the masculine sublime and the feminine beautiful by locating them within the same perspectival frame,[9] and she does not retreat before the nominally non-aesthetic but rather allows it equally to intrude.

> Advancing toward Quistram, as the sun was beginning to decline, I was particularly impressed by the beauty of the situation. The road was on the declivity of a rocky mountain, slightly covered with a mossy herbage and vagrant firs. At the bottom, a river, straggling amongst the recesses of stone, was hastening forward to the ocean and its grey rocks, of which we had a prospect on the left, whilst on the right it stole peacefully forward into the meadows, losing itself in a thickly wooded rising ground. As we drew near, the loveliest banks of wild flowers variegated the prospect, and promised to exhale odours to add to the sweetness of the air, the purity of which you could almost see, alas! not smell, for the putrifying herrings, which they use as manure after the oil has been extracted, spread over the patches of earth, claimed by cultivation, destroyed every other.
>
> (VI, 261)

Wollstonecraft's focus on the rotting herrings here seems a deliberate deconstruction of the simplistic aesthetic code – a world abstracted into the sublime and beautiful – that, though she employs it, she knows stands in for – substitutes as – the real, in a manner similar to the way in which class and gender roles function to abstract social reality.

She likewise continually juxtaposes her acute sensibility, which she represents in a highly feminized manner, with a discourse that refuses to remain within that bounded realm. In the very first letter she notes, 'At supper my host told me that I was a woman of observation, for I asked *men's questions*' (VI, 248). As the *Letters* unfold, her 'observations', thus licensed, self-consciously intrude into such areas as women's wrongs – 'Still harping on the same subject, you will exclaim' (VI, 325) – the mistreatment of social inferiors (VI, 253, 283), the effects of political equality (VI, 272–3, 287), the Norwegians' sympathy with the revolutionists of France (VI, 302), and the ill effects wrought by unbridled commercial exploitation (VI, 304, 340, 344). As she re-enters Quistram, she even broaches the subject of human animality, perhaps as an analogy with the rotten herrings she encountered on the road into the town: a local fair has ended with 'men, horses, carts, cows, and pigs huddled together' (VI, 313) at the door of the inn; and as she finally departs, she sees 'drunken men [...] like weary cattle [...] fallen by the road side' and a large party of men and women 'drinking, smoking, and laughing' (VI, 314), from which she foresees a night of debauchery. '[M]en's questions', it would appear, are thus defined as 'real' questions, forcing issues of social organization, cultural heritage, and primal urges upon Wollstonecraft's reactions to the natural landscape and competing with them for attention. Realism here inhabits a much larger world than that which characterizes the norms of literary representation Wollstonecraft inherits from her predecessors.

It might thus almost be anticipated that in her last, unfinished piece of writing Wollstonecraft would take this realistic strain to an unprecedented extreme. In *Maria* her most powerful rendering of the real is a descent into the lower depths, the autobiographical narrative of Jemima, the madhouse guard, in chapter 5, for which previous fiction in English offers no full model. The illegitimate child of a maidservant, Jemima describes herself as like 'an egg dropped on the sand [...] who belonged to nobody',[10] as one who has gone through life 'hunted from hole to hole [...] like a beast of prey' (V, 84). Put to hard work as soon as she was able to labour, she sees herself more as a slave than a servant, and, after a childhood of abuse, in her early adolescence she is raped by her master and finds herself pregnant. She is forced into an abortion, then turned out onto the streets, where she makes a living as a prostitute. Eventually Jemima becomes the mistress of an educated man with whose male company she mingles freely, becoming at once educated and liberated: 'I had the advantage of hearing discussions, from which, in the common course of life, women are excluded' (I, 113–14). But her independence is an illusion: with the man's death she is back on the streets making shift as she can. Eventually after much more brutalization and some time working over a washtub from one in the morning until eight at night, she is lucky to have found employment in the shady madhouse where Maria, though perfectly sane, has been confined on orders of her husband.

Such a view into the life of an existential proletariat one thinks of as the province of the later nineteenth century, not the end of the eighteenth century. But something akin to this recital of degradation, though lacking the extremity of its terms, can be found eight years earlier, in Charlotte Smith's third novel, *Celestina*. There the eponymous heroine, herself a displaced orphan, shares a coach with a young servant being sent in to the country and hears Jessie Westbourne's life story. Grown inured to a life of 'hard, and [...] dirty work in our dismal kitchen',[11] she has fallen in love with Frank Cathcart, her master's clerk, who over-strains his frail constitution in order to provide support for his sister Sophy and her four children. His other sister Emily is already beyond the pale: seduced at fifteen, she has had no recourse but to become a prostitute. This entire account casts an oblique shadow across the novel inasmuch as Celestina is, like all these young people, educated but stateless, wholly dependent on the kindness of an upper-class family of which she is not a legitimate member.

To read Charlotte Smith's fiction in the context of Mary Wollstone-craft's writings is to see a similar project undertaken from a more conventional novelistic positioning and extending far beyond Wollstonecraft's focus on the dependent situation of women in contemporary culture. That is to say, Smith, needing financial security for her children above all other considerations, in her early novels sets herself wholly within the framework of the popular female *Bildungsroman*, but she does so only to subvert its conventional terms from within. Her young, handsome, virtuous heroines move in high society, but they are either apparently illegitimate like Emmeline and Celestina, the protagonists of the first and third novels, or they are of impoverished younger stock like Ethelinde, the protagonist of the second. The figures central to these novels, then, are on the periphery of their society, and their very presence casts the pervading codes through which it operates into serious question.

The matter of legitimacy haunts these novels, and it resonates against a sexual ambiguity that no other woman novelist of this period, except Wollstonecraft, would attempt (and even Wollstonecraft, in her reviews, questioned the propriety of some of Smith's episodes). In the forefront of the novels the female protagonists are of impeccable character, though often they are thought otherwise by men inflamed by jealousy; but in the background the situation is markedly different. In the first four novels Smith's affront to the customary moral constructions of the genre is conspicuous. In *Emmeline* the secondary heroine Lady Adelina Trevelyan, married off to a dissolute and inebriate likeness of Charlotte Smith's own husband, has an affair with the dashing Fitz-Edward (who bears his own Irish family's illegitimate origins in his divided name), and she becomes pregnant. Emmeline and her friend Mrs Stafford conceal her and her baby and, after the death of her husband, manage to reconcile her family to her second marriage. Thus, a collaborative and secretive woman's perspective built on compassion triumphs over public social structures created to reinforce male possessiveness. In *Ethelinde* the hero Charles Montgomery is descended from a grandmother who was a nobleman's mistress; his uncle likewise kept a mistress whose daughter by him runs away from a convent with the heroine's brother.[12] The wife of the secondary hero, having flirted with a dissolute aristocrat throughout the novel, at last deserts her husband and her children to live with him on the continent. In *Celestina*, as already noted, the heroine is thought illegitimate, until we learn late in the novel that she is actually heiress to the estate and fortune at the novel's centre: her father and mother did at some point exchange vows, though it would appear to have been after her conception. In the fourth novel *Desmond*, the only contemporary British novel set directly within the turmoil of the French Revolution, the heroine Geraldine Verney is married to another scoundrel modelled on Smith's husband who, as noted before, attempts to prostitute her. The hero, against all standard propriety, is desperately in love with her and continually shadows her with the aim of protection. His older counsellor Bethel, who admonishes that behaviour, lives alone, having been deserted some years earlier by his high-spirited wife. While in France Desmond is wounded in a duel and is seduced by his friend Montfleuri's sister, a wholly unnecessary plot device that drew strong admonition from critics of the novel and still provides shock to today's readers. In the end the husband dies, and after a period of mourning Desmond and Geraldine are to marry and incorporate her three children and his illegitimate one within a renewed and cosmopolitan family. Doubtless, there is more to reality than sexuality; but what is here tracked through Smith's early novels is the most explicit treatment of transgressive heterosexual mores in the English novel until well into the twentieth century.

Although some readers thought it unseemly for Smith continually to reintroduce her irresponsible husband as a character type in her novels, the fact that the circumstances of her life were made so publicly apparent authorized her, as a married woman with a number of children, boldly to intrude upon territory that none of her contemporaries would enter. It is not just in the realm of personal desire, moreover, that she forces the novel to a new level of realism. On political and social planes, as well, Smith continually tests her readers to accommodate unsettling truths and distasteful circumstances. And in this she goes far beyond Wollstonecraft's concentration on the plight of women in her society and a pointed deconstruction of its codes (though it might be argued, as with the crossing noted earlier between *Desmond* and *Maria*, that her own example furnished Wollstonecraft with an impetus for her focus on women's wrongs).

First, the political. Smith's early novels are rife with aristocrats who are unconcerned with society as a whole or refuse to confront their responsibility for upholding its inequalities. With a few exceptions (who only prove that exceptions change nothing), the upper classes lead lives of fruitless, selfish dissipation in which gambling and duelling are the abiding metaphors for a society that preys on its own denizens, with egos, mainly male, reinforcing themselves through a fundamentally self-destructive code of behaviour. Gambling was, indeed, a major social problem in England during the late Enlightenment, and such spendthrift and heedless aristocrats likewise constitute an aspect of the contemporary fictional repertory. But no one else among Smith's contemporaries, except Godwin, turns the fictional discourse into so blunt a political attack. This stance surfaces intermittently during the first three novels, but comes directly to the fore in *Desmond* where Smith carefully lodges within its plot a sustained defence of the ideals of the French Revolution and a sharp critique of contemporary British inequalities or such common, inhumane practices as the flourishing slave trade. On an even subtler level, in *Ethelinde*, Smith's second novel, the money that both corrupts the rich and salvages virtuous impoverishment has the same source in the slave culture of West Indies plantations. Whatever your moral character, you are already compromised if not quite thoroughly corrupted by the circumstances of the commerce in which you are necessarily engaged. In that novel a second source of accruing wealth is promised by Britain's emerging empire in India, but it is equally venal: the young hero, because of his basic honesty, earns nothing from his experience in Asia and almost loses his life. Literally at the centre of this novel is the same King's Bench Prison from which Charlotte Smith had escaped a few years earlier, and that site is at once powerfully symbolic of society's reduction of all of the novel's characters to their financial rather than moral worth and graphically described from the inside. This same prison will return as a symbolic centre to which the plot inexorably drives a virtuous family in the later novel, *Marchmont.*

The injustice of Britain's political system and the debilitating effects of commerce lead to a continual focus on middle-class venality that, once again, takes Smith far beyond the inheritance she owes to Smollett and especially Burney among her predecessors. Throughout her fiction, on a social level, she discriminates a scramble to better oneself within the determinants of the class system, with those who become agents of its power resorting to dishonest means to further it and their attachment to it. Foremost among these agents are lawyers, who assume an uncommon importance in Smith's fiction, as they did in her life, for the inheritance from her father-in-law which was to have provided for her children was disputed for decades in chancery and was not resolved until after her and her husband's deaths. Lawyers thus become the abiding prototypes of a society in which the law is manipulated and justice sacrificed. The fact that most of her heroines have been robbed by such scheming of a legitimate inheritance or denied their just deserts by conniving family members underscores her own sense that in such a clawing capitalist society it is women who are always victimized. Although her principal heroines manage in the end to evade the chicanery to which they are subject, there are many secondary younger women characters who are willing goods in the marriage market, with designing mothers who are indistinguishable except by their social position from bawds.

This entire complex of a corrupt and corrupting society in Smith's novels depends upon the physical instrument that supports all its inter-connected links, state violence. War, which Britain entered upon in early 1793, is, remarkable as it is for a woman novelist of the time, another focus of several of Smith's novels. The counter-revolutionary violence current in the French countryside is powerfully enacted in *Desmond*; but the political censorship that descended on Great Britain after the declaration of war, although it made it impossible from that point on for Smith so candidly to voice her political opinions, did not deter her continuing to confront the nature and effects of political violence. In *The Old Manor House*, her next novel, she forces her hero into the American War of Independence, where he is witness to the gruesome savagery perpetrated by native Americans allied with the British against their own settlers. In the ensuing novel, *The Banished Man*, Smith nominally changes sides, beginning her work within a French countryside being ravaged by marauding bands of *sans culottes*. But, in truth, there is no 'side' to be on in this novel: whether revolutionary or counter-revolutionary, both are equally destructive, grinding characters, whatever their ideologies or national allegiances, within the abstract machinery of state power.

The arenas enumerated here extend far beyond the customary resort of contemporary women novelists, and there are likewise few men of the time with either the skill or the interest to paint so broad a social landscape. Smith is in this sense the palpable link between her eighteenth-century predecessors and the next generation of male novelists. Edgeworth and Austen owe much to her, it is true, as their heroines try to weave their way through the treacherous straits of upper-bourgeois society.[13] But the line of realism traced here leads most directly to two distinctly different novelists, who nevertheless owe much to Smith's example, Walter Scott (who generously admitted it[14]) and Dickens, who, a generation further along, may never have been wholly conscious of it (though the unending chancery suit of *Bleak House* might easily have been modelled on Smith's own).

Where Smith made her most conspicuous effort to forge a new realism for fiction in English, however, and where it could be argued that she had her greatest impact – certainly so for Scott and Dickens – may be in the realm of language. That she was highly attuned to stylistic differences in gendered discourse can immediately be discerned from the exchanges of letters in the epistolary novel *Desmond*. The whole of the first volume of that novel is rendered from the epistolary perspective of her male protagonists. When suddenly, with the second volume, the discourse moves to Geraldine Verney and her sister Fanny, it is accompanied by an entire spectrum of altered colouration that ranges from verbal nuance to a shift of distinctive references, both those of experience and in literature. In the early novels the characters, conversant with the expectations of the day, are largely drawn from the same upper-class social setting. But even with the second, *Ethelinde*, Smith develops a secondary plot where the impecunious heroine is forced to enter the family of an aunt who has married a Bristol tradesman. What we encounter is not simply a collision between classes, levels of education, and cultural expectations, but also between social and professional ideolects. From this point on Smith continually experiments with clashes of idiolect and dialect. *The Old Manor House*, generally thought her finest accomplishment, is in this respect also her most elaborate linguistic experiment. Virtually every character is conceived of in linguistic terms, even to the point of Smith's being able to differentiate between lower-class regional dialects in the south of England.

Charlotte Smith's experimentation with language and her capturing of distinctive dialects and ideolects, with their idiosyncracies of pronunciation and idiom, enormously amplify the range of voices that English fiction will be able to accommodate. A decade after her death Scott will begin to incorporate Scots vocabulary and experience in dialectical interplay with English to form a new sense of what constitutes Britishness in fiction, and by the time of Dickens's first masterpiece, *The Pickwick Papers*, the Cockney locutions of Pickwick's 'man', Sam Weller, and the dexterous verbal games of Jingles, who speaks in a kind of rapid-fire outline, demonstrate that the nineteenth-century English novel has found a new and greatly expanded language in which to configure itself and its interests.

The crucial development of the late eighteenth-century novel was the commitment to a literary (and linguistic) realism by Charlotte Smith and, less influentially because of her sudden death, Mary Wollstonecraft. Although one can certainly see the woman's novel of the eighteenth century that Smith and Wollstonecraft inherited reaching its climactic realization in the work of Edgeworth and Austen, as Ian Watt argues, Charlotte Smith was equally the empowering force for the broad social landscapes of Scott and Dickens. In this sense she was, indeed, the most influential writer of fiction in the 1790s, who, as her contributions become more generally known, will occupy an increasingly prominent position in British literary history.

Notes

1. Ian Watt's *Rise of the Novel* (1957) is generally credited with establishing 'formal realism' as the governing principle for the development of fiction in English, but he scarcely alludes to any women writers until introducing Burney and Austen in his final brief chapter. In describing *Robinson Crusoe*, for instance, he quotes Clara Reeve on the subject of the work's originality, but he does not refer to her own highly germane definition of the novel as 'a picture of real life and manners, and of the times in which it is written': see, *The Progress of Romance, through Times, Countries, and Manners*, 2 vols ([Colchester:] Keymer, 1785), I, iii. It is certainly possible that this definition, in the first crucial canonization of the English novel, prompted both Smith and Wollstonecraft's choice of titles. Most historians of the late Enlightenment novel of manners, however, eschew the subject of realism. The one, highly valuable exception is Michael Gamer, 'Maria Edgeworth and the Romance of Real Life', *Novel: A Forum for Fiction*, 34 (2001), 232–66, to which this chapter is indebted. Another influential literary voice, that of Joanna Baillie, in her 'Introductory Discourse' (1798) to her *Plays [on the] Passions* (London: Cadell and Davies, 1798), continually invokes the 'real' as the object of dramatic representation (see pp. 19, 34n, 47, 52, 54).

For the extensive resonance of Smith's collection and its title over the next sixty years, see Michael Gamer's Introduction to its reprinting in *Works of Charlotte Smith*, general editor Stuart Curran, 14 vols (London: Pickering & Chatto, 2005), I, xxxvi–xxxvii.

2. *The Young Philosopher*, ed. by A.A. Markley, in *Works of Charlotte Smith* (London: Pickering Chatto, 2006), X [3]. Markley concentrates on this novel in its relation to Godwin and Wollstonecraft in 'Charlotte Smith, the Godwin Circle, and the Proliferation of Speakers in *The Young Philosopher*', in *Charlotte Smith in British Romanticism*, ed. by Jacqueline Labbe (London: Pickering and Chatto, 2008), pp. 87–99.

3. Loraine Fletcher, *Charlotte Smith: A Critical Biography* (Basingstoke and New York: Macmillan, 1998), p. 279.

4. *Analytical Review*, 13 (August 1792), 428.

5. *Original Stories from Real Life*, in *Works of Mary Wollstonecraft*, ed. by Janet Todd and Marilyn Butler, 7 vols (New York: New York University Press, 1989), IV, 367.

6. One of Mrs Mason's educational strategies is repeatedly to juxtapose the imaginary and the real: for example, Jane Fretful who 'without any real misfortune [...] was continually miserable' (IV, 381); Mrs Mason's older charge Mary is 'fond of ridicule ... but seldom in the right place; real cause for it [she] let[s] slip' (IV, 409); Mrs Mason wants the girls to learn to discriminate between claims on their charity and 'give but a trifle when you are not certain that the distress is real' (IV, 441).

7. *Works*, V, 126.

8. *Memoirs of the Author of A Vindication of the Rights of Woman*, ed. by Richard Holmes (Harmondsworth: Penguin, 1987), p. 249. It should be noted that Charlotte Smith had read this work carefully, for she quotes from it in sending condolences to Godwin on Mary Wollstonecraft's death: see Pamela Clemit, 'Charlotte Smith to William and Mary Jane Godwin: Five Holograph Letters', *Keats-Shelley Journal*, 55 (2006), 29–40 (p. 34).

9. See, for instance, *Works*, VI, 247, 251, 265.

10. *Works*, I, 110.

11. *Celestina*, in *Works of Charlotte Smith*, ed. by Kristina Straub (London: Pickering and Chatto, 2005), IV, 55.

12. In this novel Smith calls attention to her realistic mode by invoking the customary fantasies found in novels. When Ethelinde finds herself attracted to Montgomery, she is 'dismayed to find herself thus strongly and suddenly attached to a person of whom, she knew so little [...], exactly that romantic infatuation which she had so often condemned as weakness when it had occurred in real life and as of dangerous example when represented in novels' (*Works of Charlotte Smith*, III, 81). Later, her worldly brother berates her for the 'nonsense' she believes about 'inviolable friendship and everlasting love: stuff that you have picked up from the novels and story books you are eternally reading. In real life such *things are not*' (III, 454).

13. See, for instance, Jacqueline Labbe, 'Narrating Seduction: Charlotte Smith and Jane Austen', *Charlotte Smith in British Romanticism*, pp. 113–28.

14. See *The Lives of the Novelists* (1821), in *Miscellaneous Prose Works* (Edinburgh: Robert Cadell; and London: Whitaker, 1834), vol. 4.

10
Charlotte Smith, Mary Robinson and the First Year of the War with France

Harriet Guest

In April 1797 Charlotte Smith wrote to her publisher urging him to restrict the circulation of her engraved portrait, intended for the forthcoming edition of her *Elegiac Sonnets*.[1] She asked him to 'take such precautions as are in your power to prevent its being exhibited in Magazines "with anecdotes of *this* admir'd *Authoress*" like M[rs] Mary Robinson & other Mistresses whom I have no passion for being confounded with'.[2] Smith was not habitually generous about her contemporaries and competitors, but her eagerness to distance herself from Robinson may be accentuated by a tacit recognition that there were clear points of comparison between their careers, and by an implicit acknowledgement that her reputation might already be linked too closely for her comfort with that of her more scandalous contemporary; for Smith's comment alludes to Robinson's notoriety as the former mistress of the Prince of Wales, Charles James Fox, and other prominent men. While no suggestion of sexual impropriety tinged Smith's personal reputation, her liberal social and political connections and the politics of her work nevertheless associated her quite closely with Robinson, whose career as a poet and novelist at least in its broad outline shadowed her own.

In 1794 the *Morning Post* had paired Smith and Robinson as exemplary liberal victims persecuted for their democratic views by the 'Aristocratical Reviewers'. The paper, which was sympathetic to the cause of political reform, and had also frequently championed Robinson, reported that while the *Anti-Jacobin* and other loyalist monthly journals enthusiastically extol 'the wretched trash of State Puffers', they 'endeavour to crush all enlightened productions, even from pens of the most acknowledged Literary Fame', such as those of Robinson and Smith.[3] Hostile conservative commentators such as Robert Bisset, who reviewed Robinson's work for the *Anti-Jacobin*, liked to hint that the two writers

207

were almost partners in their literary crimes, and both T.J. Mathias and Richard Polwhele shared his opinion.[4] Robinson might well have been happier with this pairing than Smith; she had celebrated Smith's poetry in a sonnet of 1793 as well as in the Preface to her *Sappho and Phaon* (1796), and in *Walsingham* (1797) a female character of reliable judgement praises all of Smith's works, confessing that she admires 'some of them to enthusiasm'.[5] In the eleventh of the *Sylphid* essays which Robinson published in the *Morning Post* at the end of her life she praised the 'sweetly plaintive SMITH' as one of the select group of 'enlightened females for which this country is so justly celebrated'.[6]

There is no evidence that the two women ever met, though they had friends in common. Both expressed admiration in their printed work for Mary Wollstonecraft. Robinson met her and William Godwin in 1796, and the two women 'often took tea together' before Wollstonecraft's controversial marriage.[7] Smith also met Wollstonecraft as well as Godwin in London in the summer of 1797. She wrote to him expressing her sense of personal as well as intellectual bereavement following Wollstonecraft's death, and continued on friendly terms with him for the rest of her life.[8] In the imaginations of the reviewers of the *Anti-Jacobin* at least, the three women formed a coterie, a hothouse for the pathological excrescences of affect, in which Wollstonecraft embodied and acted out the libidinized implications of the passions which Smith and Robinson cultivated in their heroines. A review of Robinson's *The False Friend* (1799), probably by Bisset again, commented that her favoured characters possessed the kind of 'morbid sensibility' that Wollstonecraft had regarded as sufficient justification for her 'concubinage and [...] attempted suicide', and which posed a threat 'to morality, to order, and to every thing valuable in society'.[9] A later review observed that Wollstonecraft's actions seemed to her defenders to be justified by moral standards such as those Smith attributed to her heroines.[10] In the eyes of conservative critics such as these, the three women shared a sensibility prone to lax sexual morals and worse political judgement.

Wollstonecraft's response to events in France was, however, much more mixed than her critics acknowledged, as Janet Todd and Barbara Taylor have recently argued; and both Robinson and Smith also reflected on what they saw of the changing nature of revolutionary society there, and on its effects in Britain, in complex and perhaps unexpected ways.[11] Though they may have shared aspects of their political beliefs, and though similarities, even echoes, may occasionally be apparent between their works, their differences are also significant. The political landscape changed with extraordinary rapidity in the 1790s, and they travelled through it by different routes. Robinson's 'Sonnet to Mrs. Charlotte Smith, on hearing that her son was wounded at the siege of Dunkirk', published on 17 September 1793 in the *Oracle*, made explicit her sympathy for the older writer. I will use it as a way into thinking about relations between their work, in the context of the habitual caution and wariness that characterized both women's responses to events in Europe in 1793, particularly after the execution of Louis XVI in January.

> FULL many an anxious pang, and rending sigh,
> Darts, with keen anguish, through a MOTHER's breast;
> Full many a graceful TEAR obscures her eye,
> While watchful fondness draws her SOUL from rest.
>
> The clang of ARMS! triumphant VALOUR's wreath!
> Startle, yet fascinate the glowing mind!
> For, ah! too oft the crown by FAME entwin'd,
> Conceals the desolating lance beneath!
>
> Yet HOPE for THEE shall bend her soothing wings,
> Steal to thy breast, and check the rising tear,
> As to thy polish'd mind rapt Fancy brings
> The GALLANT BOY, to BRITAIN's GENIUS dear!
> And, while for HIM a LAUREL'D Couch SHE strews,
> Fair TRUTH shall snatch a Wreath, TO DECK HIS PARENT MUSE![12]

For Robinson, the sonnet functioned most obviously as a form of advertisement. The *Oracle* had carried a large announcement of her *Poems* extending almost the full length of a column on its front page on 13 September, and on the following day reported that she had recovered from illness and would 'render her usual Offerings to APOLLO through the medium of his ORACLE'.[13] She was an adept self-publicist, and the *Oracle* was eager to second and benefit from her efforts. The sonnet was perhaps also offered as a reminder of her poetic skills, tempting readers to buy her volume, and pursue her career in the columns of the paper – which might perhaps have gone some way to explaining the disdain Smith later expressed for her.[14] It is therefore worth exploring what it advertised, and what Robinson might have thought she had to gain from associating herself publicly with Smith at this point.

The sonnet was framed as a response to and reflection on the news and comment which surrounded it, which that week focused on the inglorious retreat of the army led by the Duke of York from the siege of

Dunkirk. The injury to Ensign Smith, 'son of the famous Mrs. CHARLOTTE SMITH', who had his foot shot off early in the fighting and subsequently lost his leg, was widely reported on 11 September.[15] On the following day, the *Oracle* reported that the army besieging Dunkirk had been 'driven away with infinite loss',[16] and by the 13th all of the papers were full of news of its ignominious retreat and the failure of the campaign. Robinson's poem is dated 15 September, by which time the press had been able to reflect on the causes of what was seen as 'the most unfortunate [event] for this Country that has occurred since the commencement of the present War'.[17] The opposition papers tended to concentrate their criticism on government policy in general, and on the conduct of Pitt and his ministers in particular, rather than on the generals of the combined armies. Francis Plowden accurately reflected their reports in his observation that the negligence of the ministers who should have ordered naval and artillery support had caused widespread public outrage. 'Such gross delay and neglect', he wrote, 'cannot have existed without the most criminal responsibility in some departments.'[18] Though the opposition papers largely exonerated the Duke of York, the better to concentrate their fire on Pitt and his ministers, his military leadership was questioned in papers subsidized by the Treasury and supportive of the government, and he was also ridiculed in popular songs which mocked his incompetent management of the retreat and the abandonment of valuable supplies and equipment.[19] Throughout the autumn and winter of 1793–94 prints appeared mocking the Duke's role in the Flanders campaign, and emphasizing the discrepancy between the comforts he enjoyed and the miserable conditions of his army.[20] The ignominious failure of the siege was used to taunt the Duke for decades, and the image of him as 'first jockey at the fam'd Dunkirk races' continued to be current till at least the 1820s.[21]

It is therefore striking, even pointed, that Robinson's sonnet avoids any comment on the furore surrounding the retreat from Dunkirk, or indeed on the progress of the war. There is here no hint of the anger at political incompetence and waste – both of troops and scarce resources – which embittered humane grief for lives shattered or lost, and which Plowden saw as the irrepressible public response to the news (p. 333). Instead, the poem draws on the traditional notion that what women contribute to the national effort is their private anguish and grief, but elegantly turns this to suggest that patriotic feeling admires and celebrates Smith as the 'PARENT MUSE'. Smith was of course primarily famous as the poetess who wrote what were seen as extraordinarily tender and pathetic sonnets, and Robinson here uses the sonnet form to show both profound and sympathetic feeling for Smith as a mother, as well as admiration for and emulation of Smith's achievements as a poet. But the way Robinson's poem turns away from and remains silent about the siege and its failure, which was the immediate occasion for its writing, indicates, I think, something about the difficult politics of sensibility which can be explored by thinking about the sonnet in relation to Smith and Robinson's other poetical publications of 1793.

For Smith herself Charles Smith's injury was no doubt primarily a private source of sorrow and worry, though her letters make it clear that his plight appeared to her 'the more afflicting' because he had entered 'this trade of Death' as a result of the loathed trustees' refusal to provide the money necessary to support his education for the church.[22] She admitted to a degree of reluctant pride, writing to Charles Burney that her son had 'acquitted himself with so much honor that if I had much of the Spartan or the Roman about me might make me proud rather than miserable'.[23] But it is significant that her apparent hesitation here is about the conflict between the maternal impulses of public-spirited pride and suffering sensibility, rather than about the morality of the war. For by mid-1793, the enthusiasm for the Revolution which Smith had expressed in *Desmond* (1792), and more cautiously in the first book of *The Emigrants* (1793), had, like that of many liberal supporters in Britain, apparently been tempered by events in a complex process which the two books of her long poem attempted to chart. An early review, printed first in the *St James's Chronicle*, and reappearing within the week in an edited form in the *Kentish Chronicle*, praised the representation in *The Emigrants* of changing responses to the Revolution. It was, the reviewer wrote, 'perhaps as strong a picture as can any where be found, of that progress which the French Revolution has made in every feeling mind'. The review calls attention to the dates of the books of the poem, which situate the first – but not the second – before the execution of the king or the onset of war, but after the reporting of the September Massacres, and notes that: 'The first book, where the scene is laid on the cliffs near Brighton, in November, 1792, though containing some poetry, sweet and interesting, savours, perhaps a little too much of that *political mania*, which, while it is blameable in men, is to be pitied in a lady. To this, however, ample atonement is made in the second book, dated in April, 1793.'[24]

Smith was well aware that the pace and unpredictability of events meant that timing was critical in writing on France, and dated her poem accordingly. Her correspondence shows that she had not finished writing the first book in late February 1793, though its date indicates that it is written from the imagined perspective of the preceding November.[25] She dated her dedication to Cowper 10 May 1793, and sent 'the whole poem' to Cadell and Davies on 12 May, but though an advertisement of 25 May announced publication 'in a few days' the poem did not appear that month, and she wrote to her publisher on 18 June expressing her impatience at the delay apparently caused by the loss of an earlier letter of corrections from her:[26]

> I have many reasons for wishing, tho pecuniary considerations are at present out of the question, that the Poem may be publishd this season however late – Mr Cadell was once pleas'd to tell me that it signified not at what time any work of mine was publish'd – As that however was before I had been compelled to write so many – perhaps the case may be changed – However the World has not been satiated with my poetry – & I have reason tho I am no longer very sanguine to believe that there will be a considerable demand for this Poem if it is directly publishd.[27]

On 2 July, the day publication of the poem was announced in the *Morning Chronicle* and *True Briton*, Smith wrote again to her publishers anxious to know when it would appear, and within the week it was advertised in a range of Treasury and opposition papers.[28] The dating of the books of the poem signals its structure as a chronology of affective response, as the books chart the change of sentiment produced by the execution of Louis XVI and the declaration of war against Britain and the Netherlands. The dedication to William Cowper calls attention to the process of retrospective rereading that the poem enacts, noting that the events of the summer of 1792 – Smith has in mind the massacre of the king's Swiss Guards on 10 August, and of the inmates of the Paris prisons in early September – have renewed English prejudice against the French people in general, and worked to confound the 'original cause' of liberty 'with the wretched catastrophes that have followed its ill management'. As a result, the genuine defenders of liberty have become confused with 'promoters of Anarchy, and enemies to the prosperity of their country' (*Emigrants*, dedication, p. 122). The private letter urging that the poem be 'directly publishd' suggests that Smith saw it as a timely intervention because of the instability of the situation in France in the early summer of 1793, when it looked as though much of the country had turned against the Convention in Paris, and because of the increasing suspicion and resentment with which emigrants were received in Britain.

Smith was certainly at work on the poem late in 1792, and was concerned with the plight of the emigrants early in November, when she wrote to the radical Joel Barlow, on the eve of his departure for Paris to address the National Convention on behalf of the Society for Constitutional Information. Smith told Barlow that though she thought the exiles should lose 'a very great part of their property & all their power', a reconciliation with them brought about by the 'glorious Government' of the republic would be a sign of its moral strength and political confidence. It would show that the republic could afford to be magnanimous towards them, 'considered as Men & Frenchmen' – and the resonance of the phrase may imply respect for their rights as well as humane tenderness.[29] But probably the most important context for the poem was provided by the parliamentary debates between 21 December 1792 and 4 January 1793 on the Alien Bill, which was intended to control the presence and movements of immigrants, and which was to provide one of the grounds for the declaration of war by republican France in February. The Bill built on and contributed to public fears about the influx of emigrants from France in the wake of the September Massacres, fears which many liberals would have liked to see calmed, as opposition newspapers pointed out.[30] The Lord Chancellor, Lord Loughborough, set the tone of much subsequent discussion in his claim that there were 'two classes of Frenchmen now in this country: one who came here by necessity to take refuge; they should of course be treated with tenderness and humanity: – another class who came hither for the purpose of, and who were active in doing all they could to create confusion; they of course were the proper objects of this Bill, and ought to be of much greater severity.'[31] French emigrant clergy absorbed the 'tenderness and humanity' of High Church Tories and loyalists, and even of those conservative Evangelicals, like Hannah More, who had doubts about the war.[32] Debate on the Bill magnified the idea of lay emigrants as a 'host of emissaries, and agents' of revolution who 'infested the streets of the metropolis' like a plague, as Josiah Dornford argued in his alarmist analysis of the *Motives and Consequences of the Present War* (1793); and of course the Bill inevitably increased suspicions of those whom even the government claimed to believe deserved compassion. It was intended to respond to what John Bowles colourfully imagined as 'numbers of desperate and blood-stained Frenchmen [...] daily flocking here for the most mischievous and horrid purposes', and it worked to suggest that all Frenchmen nourished such purposes.[33] Smith's poem addressed the anxieties of liberal Whigs, who, by the time the poem was finished in early May 1793, were increasingly concerned by the alarmism nurtured by legislation such as the Alien Act, as well as by the Traitorous Correspondence Act of a few months later.

The first book of the poem asserts the poet's sympathy for the emigrants, and, in extended sentences that wind down the page, explores the circumstances and qualifications that make that sympathy possible and attenuate its force. The syntax of the poem's long verse-paragraphs becomes increasingly elaborate as the first book progresses. It concludes with a verse-paragraph of eighty-six lines, for example, which is initially addressed to 'Poor wand'ring wretches! whoso'er ye are, / That hopeless, houseless, friendless, travel wide / O'er these bleak russet downs'. She goes on to compare the isolated and alienated condition of these wanderers to that of French emigrants:

> Poor vagrant wretches! outcasts of the world!
> Whom no abode receives, no parish owns;
> Roving, like Nature's commoners, the land
> That boasts such general plenty: if the sight
> Of wide-extended misery softens yours
> Awhile, suspend your murmurs! – here behold
> The strange vicissitudes of fate – while thus
> The exil'd Nobles, from their Country driven,
> Whose richest luxuries were their's, must feel
> More poignant anguish, than the lowest poor,
> Who, born to indigence, have learn'd to brave
> Rigid Adversity's depressing breath! – [34]

The poet explicitly suggests in these lines that the sufferings of the vagrant poor, isolated from any form of social support, may be ameliorated by their knowledge of and perhaps sympathy for the plight of the emigrants, whose situation is even more pitiable because unlike the poor they are not inured to adversity. But that suggestion may be difficult to accept – the poet has insisted quite forcefully at the beginning of the book that 'never yet could I derive relief, / [...] / From the sad thought, that others like myself / Live but to swell affliction's countless tribes!' The lines also make it clear that England has its own homeless outcasts, internal exiles whose condition may be more desperate, and in the lines immediately following these sympathy seems to be withdrawn abruptly from the French exiles, as the poet continues: 'Ah! rather Fortune's worthless favourites! / Who feed on England's vitals – Pensioners / Of base corruption' (I, ll. 61, 63–4, 315–17).

At first glance, the poet seems in these lines to turn on the emigrants and to paint them, in the most hostile language of the debate on the Alien Bill, as parasites sapping England's strength and virtue, and it does not become clear for perhaps another dozen lines that these 'worthless favourites' are the corrupt British courtiers and placemen whom Smith conjures to learn from the fate of the emigrants:

> Ye venal, worthless hirelings of a Court!
> Ye pamper'd Parasites! whom Britons pay
> For forging fetters for them; rather here
> Study a lesson that concerns you much;
> And, trembling, learn, that if oppress'd too long,
> The raging multitude, to madness stung,
> Will turn on their oppressors; and, no more
> By sounding titles and parading forms
> Bound like tame victims, will redress themselves!

(I, ll. 315, 329–37)[35]

The parallel implied by the initial difficulty of identifying fortune's favourites in this long verse-paragraph allows Smith to suggest the ways in which her sympathy for the emigrants is qualified, and to turn around the apparent complacency of her suggestion that 'vagrant wretches' console themselves by contemplating the emigrants' lot. But the dangerous suggestion that oppressors may earn the punishment meted out to them by the wretches they oppress is itself diluted or defused in the lines that follow these on the bloody confusion of France. The complex verse-paragraphs of the first book of *The Emigrants* enable the poet to articulate a difficult politics which must constantly shift its ground, and repeatedly qualify its position. She must be able to express admiration for the initial ideals of revolution, while distancing herself from aspects of their working out, as well as humanitarian sympathy for the sufferings of the emigrants, qualified by disapprobation for their support for the oppressive pre-revolutionary regime and the 'German spoilers' led by the Duke of Brunswick who intended to restore it. Above all, the extended syntactical structures of the first book allow the poet to make the case for domestic political and social reform by invoking and yet denying a direct or explicit link between the movement for reform and revolutionary politics.

In the second book, Smith contrasts the principle of Liberty which had initially animated the Revolution, with 'Freedom's name, usurp'd and misapplied', a debased ideal which could mislead men into imagining that monarchical tyranny was preferable, despite the 'wasted lives' it demanded. Much of the book turns on the careful distinction between tenses, as the poet and the emigrants of whom she writes 'From fairer hopes and happier prospects driven, / Shrink from the future, and regret the past'; and that notion of regret hovers ambiguously between longing for the apparent security and familial warmth of the past, and the shame the poet implies the exiles might feel for their part in the despotic regime which Book I had represented as the cause of the revolution (II, ll. 81, 92, 15–16, and see I, ll. 273–81, 333–5).[36] As the *Monthly Review* pointed out in December 1793, the poet had 'judiciously confined her attention to those particulars in the case of the emigrants, which have excited sympathy in the minds of the humane of all parties'.[37] In a present briefly isolated from the 'dark retrospect' of 'human follies' and 'human woes' – from both the bloodshed of the Revolution and the 'regal crimes' that caused it – the poet makes the humane case for the emigrants, and invites her readers to sympathize unreservedly with their private and individual sufferings, with the fears for their families that torment both the aristocratic exiles and, she imagines, the imprisoned French queen, without condoning the errors her 'boundless power' had led her into (II, ll. 41, 42, 88, 158).[38]

The *Analytical Review* praised the caution and precision of Smith's writing, commenting that

> Without attempting the entire justification of the political conduct of the French emigrants, she draws several interesting and affecting pictures of their misfortunes, and applauds that generous sympathy, which ministers relief to a brother in distress, without listening to the chilling remonstrance of national or political prejudice.[39]

As the reviewer recognized, the poet distinguishes carefully between sympathy for the plight of the emigrants, and support for their politics, and between her initial admiration for the revolutionary ideal, despite the upheaval it might threaten, and her present disapprobation for the violence the Revolution wreaks on familial and affective ties. That destructive conduct is epitomized in Louis XVI's kinsman, the former Duc d'Orléans, now known by the revolutionary name of Philippe-Égalité, who had worked relentlessly to secure the throne to his own branch of the royal family. He is pictured here 'Wading, beneath the Patriot's specious mask, / And in Equality's illusive name, / To empire thro' a stream of kindred blood' (II, ll. 124–6).[40] It is worth noting that Smith's lines echo Robinson's condemnation of him in her 'Fragment, supposed to be written near the Temple, at Paris, on the night before the execution of Louis XVI', published in the *Oracle* on 2 February 1793. As a deputy to the Convention, Philippe-Égalité was one of those who in January 1793 voted for the death sentence for Louis, and Robinson commented that:

> Retiring HOPE beholds, subdu'd,
> The fatal mandate sign'd with blood,
> WITH KINDRED BLOOD! OH! HORRIBLE AND BASE,
> To stigmatize with shame, a LONG, ILLUSTRIOUS RACE![41]

Both poets regard with horror the former duke's violation of the bonds of kinship and class loyalty, which they suggest characterize what is most disturbingly anarchic and inhuman in revolutionary Paris. Condemnation of his actions, however, was perhaps a sign of humane sensibility rather than of particular political affiliation. Wollstonecraft, for example, expressed disgust and contempt for his knavish depravity, while loyalist caricatures and newspapers also condemned him as a 'Parricide Monster'.[42]

The emphasis in Smith's poem on humanitarian sympathy for the emigrants, based in shared notions of private and familial feeling, may, as the reviewer for the *St James's Chronicle* suggested, provide atonement for the '*political mania*' of the first book, and make the concerns of the poem appropriate to an idea of polite and sentimental femininity, at the same time as it echoes the opinions of the Foxite Whigs. Fox had argued in his speech on the Alien Bill that though he regarded the Bill itself as an example of 'abuses and encroachments of the Executive Power', he wished to 'protect those who had fallen a sacrifice to their opinions in favour of the old government of France, not because he approved their principles, but because he respected their misfortunes'.[43] Like Smith, he is careful to distinguish between the circumstances of the emigrants, which attract humane sympathy, and their political principles. The language of humane and familial feeling, in this context, is not necessarily excluded from public or political debate – it does not necessarily mark the poetry of Smith's *Emigrants* or indeed of Robinson's sonnet to Smith as that of feminine privacy, but, as the *Analytical Review* suggests, of a liberal sentiment which side-steps 'national or political prejudice'.

* * *

Mary Robinson's *Sight, The Cavern of Woe, and Solitude. Poems* (1793) was published shortly after Smith's *Emigrants*, and her advance publicity was juxtaposed with notices for Smith's ambitious work.[44] It might have been particularly galling to Smith that the *Oracle* should suggest, so soon after her own significant intervention, that the blank verse of two of Robinson's 'elegant novelties' – 'Sight' and 'Solitude' – gave the form its best chance of becoming fashionable again.[45] Reviews of the work of the two poets appeared, often in close proximity, in a range of periodicals from August 1793. Smith's poem is evidently taken seriously, and usually discussed in considerable detail, whereas reviews of Robinson's poetry almost invariably take the form of lengthy extracts, and imply that it is slight, but still Robinson's work attracted at least as much attention as Smith's. After the reference to Robinson in the letter I cited earlier, Smith advised her publisher to prevent her work from 'getting into Newspapers or being printed "with beauties of Poetry, or elegant selections"'.[46] She suggested that this kind of circulation damaged sales, but perhaps there was also an element of sour grapes about Robinson's ability to manipulate the market and promote her work. For Robinson in contrast, association with Smith enhanced the status of her poetry – Richard Phillips's *Public Characters*, for example, later suggested that Robinson's poetry, and her sonnets in particular, entitled her to share the 'Sapphic throne even with a Smith and a Seward';[47] and it might also have suggested that both writers participated in or drew their inspiration from a particular kind of sensibility, of feminine and maternal suffering, that contributed to the prestige and authority of Smith's work, and to its oblique relation to political debate.

By the summer of 1793, Robinson's personal and political reputation was complex. Jon Mee has written, in his illuminating essay on Robert Merry and Della Cruscanism, that the poetic exchange between Robinson and Merry, in which her *Ainsi va Le Monde* (1790) replied to his *The Laurel of Liberty* (1790), was an 'explicitly politicized extension of the flirtations of Della Cruscanism', mixing 'eroticism with political radicalism'. Mee argues that Merry's work of this period is distinguished by a language of enthusiastic rapture which identifies the political discourse of liberty with the 'delirium of sensation', with an unregulated and potentially democratized sociability and sensibility.[48] By responding positively to Merry's celebration of the spirit of liberty animating revolution in France, Mee suggests, Robinson engaged in an exchange that characterized her own sensibility as similarly unrestrained, even promiscuous.

There clearly is a sense in which Robinson's participation in newspaper culture in the late 1780s and 1790s did tacitly produce or accept a poetic identity characterized by its sensitivity to events, its responsiveness and availability to exchange – an identity that expressed an accessible and unrestricted sensibility. In the *Memoirs* that Robinson produced in some degree of collaboration with her daughter at the end of her life, she emphasized that *Ainsi va Le Monde*, like other poetry she produced in these years, was an extempore performance, dashed off within twelve hours of her receipt of Merry's poem. The *Memoirs* record that Robinson's 'Lines to him who will understand them', first published in the *World and Fashionable Advertiser* in October 1788, were largely improvised on the spot in a conversation on the 'facility with which modern poetry was composed'. The most extreme example of this method is the composition of 'The Maniac' (1793), which was apparently produced despite or because of a large dose of opium – the *Memoirs* are ambivalent about the effects of the drug. While under its influence, Robinson's 'spirit of inspiration was not to be subdued', though her daughter attempted to calm her, and she dictated the whole poem, 'much faster than it could be committed to paper'.[49] Robinson clearly prided herself on a poetic discourse and mode of production which was enthusiastic, uncontrollable, and which in the case of 'The Maniac' in particular, involved a kind of ecstatic dissolution of the poetic subject; and that 'facility and rapidity', in the *Memoirs*, is closely bound up with commercial success. The text juxtaposes wonder at the speedy composition of *Ainsi va Le Monde* with admiration for the voracity of her public, who, on the strength of her celebrity and the 'favourable impression' made by her poetry, showed an enthusiasm which matched her own, and bought up the whole of the first printing of her romance, *Vancenza* (1792), in a day.[50] This libidinized and rapid reciprocity of composition and consumption involves Robinson in a kind of commercial ecstasy, in which reader and writer together marvel at the miraculous processes of commodity exchange.

The politics of Robinson's response to Merry in 1790 were, however, more cautious, and less uncontrolled than her later account of the composition of the poem might suggest. On one hand the poem celebrates freedom as an expansive and unifying force, reminiscent of Merry's notions of universal benevolence. Robinson writes:

> Thro' all the scenes of Nature's varying plan,
> Celestial Freedom warms the breast of man;
> Led by her daring hand, what pow'r can bind
> The boundless efforts of the lab'ring mind.
> The god-like fervour, thrilling through the heart,
> Gives new creation to each vital part;

Throbs rapture thro' each palpitating vein,
Wings the rapt thought, and warms the fertile brain; [...][51]

Freedom here is both idea and sensation, diffused through each 'vital part' of nature's plan in an eroticized rapture of the material and ideal, of reason and association. It is worth noting that these are among the lines reprinted in 1796 in the *Moral and Political Magazine of the London Corresponding Society*, which also reproduced much of the poem's closing address to Freedom.[52] On the other hand, the *Critical Review* noted in its review of Robinson's poem that while her 'poetical talents are no way inferior' to Merry's, 'her *patriotism*, or rather political sentiments' are 'more just and rational'.[53] The first extract from the poem printed in the magazine of the radical London Corresponding Society carefully excluded lines in which the poet suggested that in Britain Freedom 'adorns the throne' and 'Gives [...] Worth command' (*Ainsi*, ll. 174, 176). Robinson's poem celebrates a sensationalist and apparently unrestricted, universal idea of freedom, but suggests that this may – and the conditional 'may' and 'when' convey the only hint of reservation here – be personified in the British monarchy, for 'When Virtue rules – 'tis Rapture to obey', and '*love* may bind – when *fear* has lost its pow'r' (*Ainsi*, ll. 312, 314).

As a number of critics, Anne Janowitz and Judith Pascoe perhaps most prominent among them, have pointed out, Robinson actively defended the cause of the French queen in a series of texts published after the flight to Varennes in June 1791, and those texts also chart the progressive narrowing of Robinson's revolutionary sympathies.[54] In her *Impartial Reflections on the Present Situation of the Queen of France* (1791) she praised the Revolution as the cathartic expression of freedom, 'bursting through the bonds of galling subjection by an effort of celestial energy', but her sympathy was limited to 'those who are really and dispassionately devoted to the interests of their country', and denied to those she represented as 'the illiterate, unsteady, factious multitude'.[55] Her *Monody to the Memory of the Late Queen of France* (1793) represented the progress of the Revolution in the analogy of a stable landscape, bestowed by 'celestial bounty', suddenly overwhelmed by an orgasmic torrent which is 'by no barrier in its course confin'd'. After the flood, 'No sweet diversity enchants the eye; / One liquid space reflects the low'ring sky!'[56] Robinson's expansive notions of freedom, and admiration for the universal benevolence praised in Merry's work of the early 1790s, are increasingly cautious and confined, careful of the need to preserve social diversity, particularly after the reporting of the September Massacres of 1792. Her 'Ode to Humanity. Written during the Massacres at Paris', for example, expresses an abstracted idea of humanity which inspires no shared 'celestial energy' or revolutionary ardour, but laments the blood spilt in France from the comfortable vantage of 'Britannia's lucid zone; / Where in calm majestic pride / Her conqu'ring NAVIES proudly ride', while art and commerce flourish.[57] The *Oracle* noted approvingly that writers who initially welcomed the Revolution now 'shudder with horror [...] and are ready to exercise their pens in defence of the GLORIOUS CONSTITUTION of their native Country'. Implicitly numbering Robinson among these, it remarked with satisfaction that her ode 'is not so popular with the Revolution Writers as some of her former works. Sensible minds are always open to conviction, and ever swayed by the admonitions of Reason.'[58]

Her *Poems* of 1793 were still perceived by reviewers to be marked by what were regarded as the distinctive characteristics of her earlier, Della Cruscan poetry. The *Analytical Review*, for example, commented on the 'extravagance' of her poetic language, and remarked that she 'still retains too much predilection for that artificial phraseology which sacrifices sense to sound, or for those pretty embellishments which turn upon a play of words'.[59] But the poetry explicitly turned away from the delirious sensationalism and enthusiastic rapture of Merry's work of the late 1780s and early 1790s. 'Solitude' narrates the story of an old warrior and his son living in retirement, where the father reminisces about old feuds over the public good, fought by 'sturdy HINDS whose bosoms soar'd sublime, / On heav'n-born LIBERTY's immortal wing'. As the son listens 'growing rapture glisten'd in his eye, / Till every fibre throbb'd with proud applause!' He becomes dissatisfied with a life of 'base inglorious ease' and leaves to take part in the Wars of the Roses. When his father follows in search of him the son unfortunately shoots him dead and then sacrifices himself on the battlefield. The moral seems to be that even the virtuous are misled by the 'burning ardour' of ambition for glory achieved through public action or political reform, when they should be content to remain sequestered in familial solitude, cherishing a limited and exclusive notion of liberty – a moral that echoes that of the sonnet to Smith.[60]

The first of the *Poems*, on 'Sight', is largely a meditation on sensory deprivation, and while the discussion of the implications of blindness does involve praise for what the poet represents as the redeeming and intellectual powers of vision, much of the poem focuses on the inability of poetic language to mimic or reproduce sense, on the necessarily abstract and arbitrary status of its 'artificial phraseology'. Robinson writes that the inability of fancy to 'give the rainbow's lustre pure / To the cold vacuum of the sightless eye', or to remedy its insensibility to 'colours, space, or form', leaves man an 'isolated being' who 'wanders still, / Sad, unillum'd, disconsolate, and lost!' (ll. 67–8, 69, 74–5). Her diction indicates, as it laments, the impotence or artificiality of language that it discusses:

> Can FANCY paint,
> With all the vivid magic of her pow'r,
> The spangling legions of the sphery plains;
> The gaudy-vested SUMMER's saffron glow,
> When proudly gilded by its parent SUN,
> As through the flaming Heav'ns his dazzling car,
> Burnish'd with sparkling light, sheds liquid gold
> O'er seas ethereal; [...]

(ll. 57–64)

The inability of this language to lend some kind of imaginative substance to the visions of fancy contrasts strongly with the idea of effective poetry invoked in the opening lines of Merry's *The Laurel of Liberty*:

> GENIUS, or Muse, whate'er thou art! whose thrill
> Exalts the fancy, and inflames the will,
> Bids o'er the heart sublime sensation roll,
> And wakes extatic fervour in the soul; [...]

Poetic language, Merry claims, will 'Wake the true throb, the living flame impart, / Usurp his mind, and seize upon his heart!'[61] It possesses an affective power which, in Robinson's poem, is deferred to sight itself, as a property capable of socializing man, and which there marks the difference and distance between the language of fancy and the act of intellectual perception or physical sensation.

In addressing her sonnet to Smith, then, Robinson perhaps indicated that her conception of herself as a poet had moved on from the heady mixture of eroticism and political radicalism of her exchanges with Merry earlier in the decade. Robinson's use of the sonnet form might suggest that it was Smith's success in this genre that she wished to emulate, but she could not fail to have been aware of the critical reception accorded to Smith's *Emigrants*, which jostled with reviews of her own *Poems* in the periodical press. What Smith's long poem in particular might have offered her was the model for a feminine and poetic sensibility that was expansive and socially inclusive, but that did not share the political radicalism which was, by 1793, making Britain inhospitable to Merry.[62]

The style of Smith's poem contrasted markedly with the extravagance of Della Cruscan verse and of Robinson's poetry; several reviewers found the language of the *Emigrants* 'seldom highly poetical, and sometimes [...] nearly prosaic'.[63] But aspects of the poem's narrative form, as well as of the sensibility it expressed, might have influenced Robinson's *Monody* on Marie Antoinette, published in mid-December 1793. As Smith acknowledged in her dedication, the *Emigrants* was indebted to the model of William Cowper's *The Task* (1785). It borrowed from the formal characteristics of Cowper's long meditative poem, where the unity of the digressive and episodic structure depended on the presence of the narrator, reflecting or wandering through the landscape, a figure whose very marginality and idiosyncrasy – his self-proclaimed retirement and inconsequence – underwrote his poetic authority. The speaker of Smith's poem follows the poet of the *Task* in using the rural workers and social outcasts she encounters on her rambles as an index of the moral and political health of the nation, and in calling, Jeremiah-like, for reform. The *European Magazine* implicitly alluded to these characteristics in suggesting that Smith's poem could be 'considered as a soliloquy', in which the poet 'by a liberty usually allowed to the servants of the Muses, is the subject of a part of her Poem', though the reviewer expressed some doubt about the successful use of complaint as the unifying theme of a poem of this length.[64] The conservative *British Critic* was more overtly hostile to the use of this style by a female poet, deploring her 'egotism' and 'affectation of a criminal singularity', and suggesting that she should 'have been herself more concealed'.[65] In Robinson's *Monody* the first person is directly used only once, in the Burkean passage of reminiscence that begins 'OH! I have seen her, like a sun, sublime!' But the monodic form uses the narrator's impassioned grief to license and lend coherence to the passages of extended simile and anguished reflection that make up the poem, and to justify the extravagance of, for example, the fantastic vision of the bleeding spectre of the French queen returning to comfort her imprisoned offspring with thoughts of their father's 'IMMORTAL CROWN' (ll. 159, 336, and see 307–46).

The *Monody* represents Marie Antoinette as a 'BEAUTEOUS MARTYR' distinguished by philanthropy and wonderful powers of mind. Though the poem acknowledges that the Revolution is a response to oppression, which 'Drove weeping FREEDOM from the GALLIC land', these wrongs are distanced not just to the pre-revolutionary past, as in Smith's account of the queen, but across centuries as well as national boundaries. They are the 'crimes LONG PAST' of the French monarchy, for which the poet suggests that the queen, as an Austrian, should have no responsibility; she asks, 'Was it for THOSE, an ALIEN's heart was torn / With taunting Insult's agonizing thorn!' (ll. 139, 248, 247, 261–2; and see ll. 8, 513–45). In the opening verse paragraphs of the *Monody* the narrator shares the vatic position of justice, personified as an 'HOLY EXILE', 'wand'ring on some distant shore', who is able to forget his own sorrows in recollecting those of the dead queen. The narrator seems to adopt his idealizing retrospect in representing the queen's early days at court, when she was adorned with 'DOMESTIC VIRTUES, glitt'ring round THE THRONE.' Robinson then sketches the descent into revolution before returning to the figure of the exiled 'PIOUS PASTOR', still 'wand'ring o'er the earth', who now provides the opportunity to consider what is for the poem the central tricky problem of the relation between worth derived from rank or virtue. Robinson's discussion of this issue is distinctly equivocal. The emigrant priest is first and foremost 'Of MIND enlighten'd, and of noblest birth!', and it seems a proof of his nobility that he values virtue more highly, so that with his 'proud race, the proudest VIRTUES came, / To prove their *rank*, their SECONDARY claim' (ll. 13, 11, 42, 115, 116, 117–18).[66] It is then again ambiguously from the perspective of the emigrant priest that the narrative returns to the queen as the 'Epitome of ALL – to worth ally'd!' and marks her altered appearance and blanched hair.

Charlotte Smith described *The Emigrants*, while she was still at work on it in February 1793, as 'not a party book but a conciliatory book'.[67] The success of the poem depended on its use of the language of sensibility to suggest, for example, a partial sentimental identification of the poet with the emigrants and outcasts of the poem. The delicate politics of her support for what she recognized as the newly controversial idea of liberty, on the one hand, and of the suffering of the French queen and her children on the other, was negotiated through a complex understanding of the relation between private sympathy and public political judgement which did not engage directly or explicitly with party political debate. In Robinson's *Monody* the narrator also identifies partially with the emigrant priest as well as with the alien queen. But here this works to emphasize notions of moral worth that seem distanced from partisan political debate, as though the poet, like the exile, 'Shrunk from the clamours of domestic strife' (l. 120). This is a language which endorses private sympathy for Marie Antoinette's suffering as a mother and widow, but where it acknowledges the queen's public role it is also and perhaps unexpectedly hospitable to the language of courtly deference and respect for rank, represented as the appropriate affective response to the queen's personal merits. Thus Marie Antoinette is admirable because of her superior qualities of mind and of feeling, her appeal to private sensibility rather than political judgement.

Neither Smith nor Robinson in their poetry of 1793 engaged in everyday political skirmishes, or in the kinds of detailed controversies that arose from, for example, the retreat from Dunkirk. Perhaps their conceptions of the proprieties of their social stations, their class positions, had as much to do with this as their gender. Their understandings of relations between private and political sentiments and events might have made participation or commentary inappropriate. I have suggested that Robinson's praise for Smith as a poet and mother implied her admiration for the complex implications of the language of sensibility in her poetry of 1793, though in Robinson's own poetry of that year private sympathy works to soften the ambiguities of her political opinions. After war was declared in February 1793, Smith's efforts as a mother included encouraging her son Charles to purchase an Ensigncy because, as she explained, 'nothing could be more distressing to him & to me than his being at home with[t] any plan of Life'.[68] By the late spring he was active in the disastrous campaign in Flanders. In the summer of that year, Smith was at pains to smooth the way to the marriage between her favourite daughter and one of the emigrants they had entertained in Brighton – the wedding took place in early August. It was, I have suggested, the complex relation between Smith's private and familial sympathies and her political opinions that resulted in poetry capable of embracing both sympathy for the French emigrants and support for reform in Britain.

Notes

1. *Elegiac Sonnets*, vol. 2, was published by Cadell and Davies in 1797 with a preface dated 15 May.
2. Charlotte Smith to William Davies, Oxford, 25 April 1797, in Judith Phillips Stanton, *The Collected Letters of Charlotte Smith* (Bloomington: Indiana University Press, 2003), p. 268.
3. *Morning Post*, 14 October 1794. A letter to the editor of 18 October 1794 identifies the *Critical Review* and other monthly publications as particularly biased and incapable of 'Impartial Criticism'. On the politics of the *Morning Post*, and its praise for Robinson's work, see Lucyle Werkmeister, *A Newspaper History of England, 1792–1793* (Lincoln: University of Nebraska Press, 1967), pp. 311–12, 333–6. The paper appointed Robinson 'poetical correspondent' (with S.T. Coleridge) in 1797.

4. See [Robert Bisset], *Anti-Jacobin*, 1 (1798), 160–4, in Appendix A, Mary Robinson, *Walsingham; or, The Pupil of Nature*, ed. by Julie A. Schaffer (Peterborough, Ontario: Broadview Press, 2003), pp. 502–3. See also Robert Bisset, *Douglas; or, The Highlander*, ed. Richard Cronin, vols IV and V in W.M. Verhoeven, *Anti-Jacobin Novels*, 10 vols (London: Pickering & Chatto, 2005), V, 18; and [Thomas James Mathias], *The Pursuits of Literature: A Satirical Poem in Dialogue with Notes. Part the First* (3rd rev. edn, London: T. Becket, 1797), ll. 99–106, and p. 14, n. zz. The reference does not appear in earlier editions. See also Richard Polwhele, *The Unsex'd Females. A Poem, Addressed to the Author of the Pursuits of Literature* (London: Cadell and Davies, 1798), ll. 93–6.

5. For Robinson's comments on Smith in the preface to *Sappho and Phaon* see Judith Pascoe, ed., *Mary Robinson: Selected Poems* (Peterborough, Ontario: Broadview, 2000), p. 145 n. 2; Robinson, *Walsingham*, p. 238 and see p. 248.

6. Mary Elizabeth Robinson, ed., *Memoirs of the Late Mrs. Robinson, written by herself. With some posthumous pieces*, 4 vols (London: R. Phillips, 1801), III, 61, 60; Robinson revised the essays which had first appeared in the *Morning Post* between October 1799 and February 1800 for inclusion in these volumes.

7. Janet Todd, *Mary Wollstonecraft: A Revolutionary Life* (London: Phoenix, 2000), p. 382. On the colder relations between Robinson, Godwin, and Wollstonecraft following the marriage, and the lack of clarity about their cause, see Todd, pp. 419–10; see also Paula Byrne, *Perdita: The Life of Mary Robinson* (London: Harper Perennial, 2004), pp. 351, 407; and Pascoe, ed., *Robinson*, pp. 38–47.

8. See Pamela Clemit, 'Charlotte Smith to William and Mary Jane Godwin: Five Holograph Letters', in *Keats-Shelley Journal*, 55 (2006), 29–40. Godwin's friend, the surgeon, Sir Anthony Carlisle, visited Smith at Tilford during her last illness, perhaps at Godwin's instigation, and reported to him on her health. See A. Carlisle to Godwin, 11 December 1805, in Bodleian Library, Abinger Dep. b. 214/3.

9. [Robert Bisset], 'Review of *The False Friend: a Domestic Story*, by Mary Robinson', *Anti-Jacobin*, 3 (1799), 39–42. See the review's references to Bisset's earlier review of *Walsingham*, and Bisset's reference to the review in his *Life of Edmund Burke*, 2nd edn, 2 vols (London: G. Cawthron, 1800), II, 243 n.

10. Review of *A Defence of the Character and Conduct of the late Mary Wollstonecraft Godwin* (1803), in *Anti-Jacobin*, 15 (1803), 186.

11. See Todd, *Wollstonecraft*, pp. 218ff., and Barbara Taylor, *Mary Wollstonecraft and the Feminist Imagination* (Cambridge: Cambridge University Press, 2003), esp. ch. 5.

12. *Oracle*, 17 September 1793. The sonnet appeared above the pseudonym 'Oberon', which readers had been reminded was one of Robinson's signatures in an advertisement in *Oracle*, 13 September 1793. See also Pascoe, ed., *Robinson*, p. 290.

13. *Oracle*, 14 September 1793, and see 13 September 1793. The advertisement appears to be for a reissue of the *Poems* published by J. Bell in 1791, rather than for the second volume of *Poems* printed in 1793 by T. Spilsbury and Son

and sold by J. Evans and T. Becket, which is mentioned as ready for publication in the paper the following day. The column includes substantial extracts from the reviews of the 1791 edition. Robinson was ill following the death of her mother in early August 1793. See Byrne, *Perdita*, p. 312.

14. The poem did not however reappear in any collection of Robinson's verse published in her lifetime.

15. *Morning Chronicle*, 11 September; see also, for example, *Oracle*, 11 September, *St James's Chronicle*, 10–12 September. A more detailed report appeared in *The Times*, 11 and 12 September (all 1793).

16. *Oracle*, 12 September 1793.

17. *Morning Post*, 13 September 1793.

18. Francis Plowden, *A Short History of the British Empire during the last twenty months; viz. from May 1792 to the close of the year 1793* (London: G.G. and J. Robinson, 1794), pp. 330–1.

19. See for example *The Times*, 12 September 1793; *St James's Chronicle*, 14–17 September 1793. See also 'Europe Embattled', in *Literary Remains of the United Irishmen of 1798, and selections from other popular lyrics of their times, with an essay on the authorship of 'The Exile of Erin'*, ed. by R.R. Madden (Dublin: James Duffy, 1887), p. 135; 'Dunkirk Races', Bodleian Library Broadside Ballads, Harding B 22 (71).

20. See, for example, James Gillray, *Pantagruel's Glorious Return to the court of Gargantua* (London: H. Humphrey, February 1794) BMC 8425; *Fatigues of the Campaign in Flanders* (London: H. Humphrey, May 1793) BMC 8327; Isaac Cruikshank, *The Wet Party or the Bogs of Flanders* (London: S. Fores, December 1793) BMC 8351.

21. A New Song, called The Duke done by the Upholsterer' (H. Price: London, ?1821), in Bodleian Library Broadside Ballads, Johnson Ballads, fol. 147. The Allegro Catalogue at http://www.bodley.ox.ac.uk/ballads/ballads/htm suggests a date of 1810, but Hanbury Price's libel on the Duke of York, mentioned in the publication details printed with the ballad, was reported in *The Times*, 6 January 1821.

22. Smith to Joseph Cooper Walker [9 October 1793], *Letters*, p. 78; Smith to James Upton Tripp, 15 September 1793, *Letters*, p. 73.

23. Smith to Dr Charles Burney, 15 October 1793, *Letters*, p. 83.

24. *St James's Chronicle*, 16–18 July 1793, and *Kentish Chronicle*, 23 July 1793. The poem was advertised in *St James's Chronicle*, 9–11 July 1793. The dating of the books of the poem is also discussed in John Barrell and Harriet Guest, 'Thomson in the 1790s', in *James Thomson: Essays for the Tercentenary*, ed. by Richard Terry (Liverpool: Liverpool University Press, 2000), p. 232, and in Simon Bainbridge, *British Poetry and the Revolutionary and Napoleonic Wars: Visions of Conflict* (Oxford: Oxford University Press, 2003), pp. 60–4, and more briefly in Jacqueline M. Labbe, 'The Exiled Self: Images of War in Charlotte Smith's "The Emigrants"', in *Romantic War: Studies in Culture and Conflict, 1793–1822*, ed. by Philip Shaw (Aldershot: Ashgate, 2000), pp. 39, 44–5. See also Jacqueline Labbe's introduction to her edition of Smith's poetry, in *Works of Charlotte Smith*, general editor Stuart Curran, 14 vols (reprinted in 3 vols; London: Pickering and Chatto, 2005–07), XIV, xii–xv.

25. See Smith to Walker, 20 February 1793, in *Letters*, p. 61.

26. Smith to Thomas Cadell, 13 May 1793, in Charles Thomas-Stanford archive, Royal Pavilion, Libraries and Museums, Brighton & Hove, ESRO ACC 8997, L/AE/68. *Morning Chronicle*, 25 May 1793.

27. Letter from Smith to William Davies, 18 June 1793, in *The Extra-Illustrated Hutchins' History of Dorset* (1904) 51; vol. VIII, pp. 370, 91 on renumbered page, Dorset County Archives.

28. See Smith to Cadell, 2 July 1793, ESRO ACC 8997, L/AE/73. The earliest advertisements announcing the publication of *The Emigrants* that I have seen are those in the *Morning Chronicle*, *True Briton*, and *Morning Herald* on 2 July, and *The Times*, 4 July, *London Chronicle*, 4–6 July, and *St James's Chronicle*, 9 July (all 1793).

29. Smith to Joel Barlow, 3 November 1792, in *Letters*, p. 49. In this letter Smith, like Tom Paine and Horne Tooke, urged that Louis XVI should be exiled rather than executed. See Smith to Walker, 16 December 1792, in *Letters*, p. 3.

30. Werkmeister, *A Newspaper History*, pp. 151–7, 179–86.

31. 'Substance of the Speech of the right Honourable Lord Loughborough in the House of Lords, on the third reading of the Bill for establishing certain Regulations respecting Aliens, December 26, 1792', in *Publications printed by order of the Society for Preserving Liberty and Property against Republicans and Levellers. Number VI* (London: J. Downes, 1793) pp. 14–15. See also the parliamentary debates on the Alien Bill, in *Parliamentary History*, XXX, pp. 146–70, 174–238; and Jennifer Mori, *William Pitt and the French Revolution, 1785–1795* (Edinburgh: Keele University Press, 1997), p. 177, on the Alien Office.

32. On More's support for emigrant clergy, and doubts about the war, see Anne Stott, *Hannah More: The First Victorian* (Oxford: Oxford University Press, 2003), pp. 147–9, 199.

33. [Josiah Dornford], *The Motives and Consequences of the Present War Impartially Considered* (London: J. Pridden, 1793), p. 46; John Bowles, *The Real Grounds of the Present War with France* (London: J. Debrett, 1793), p. 56.

34. Charlotte Smith, *The Emigrants, A Poem. In Two Books*, Bk I. ll. 296–8, 303–14, in *Works*, XIV. Subsequent citations are given in parentheses in the text.

35. See Labbe's thoughtful comments on Smith's syntax in her 'The Exiled Self', pp. 39–40.

36. See the review in *St James's Chronicle*, 16–18 July 1793.

37. *Monthly Review*, n.s. 12 (1793), p. 375.

38. For discussion of the representation of Marie Antoinette in the poem, see Judith Pascoe, *Romantic Theatricality: Gender, Poetry, and Spectatorship* (Ithaca: Cornell University Press, 1997), pp. 104–10; and Jacqueline Labbe, 'Towards an Ungendered Romanticism: Blake, Robinson and Smith in 1793', in *Women Reading William Blake*, ed. by Helen Bruder (Basingstoke: Palgrave Macmillan, 2007), pp. 118–26.

39. *Analytical Review*, xvii (London: J. Johnson, 1794), September 1793, 91.

40. Compare Wollstonecraft's comments on the ambitions of Philippe-Égalité, and on his 'decided preference for the grossest libertinism', in her *An Historical and Moral View of the Origin and Progress of the French Revolution; and the effect it has produced in Europe* (1794), in Janet Todd and Marilyn Butler with the assistance of Emma Rees-Mogg, *The Works of Mary Wollstonecraft*,

7 vols (London: Pickering, 1989), VI, 207. On reports of his desire for the throne circulating in late 1792, see William Doyle, *The Oxford History of the French Revolution*, 2nd rev. edn (Oxford: Oxford University Press, 2002), p. 221. He was executed in November 1793.

41. Robinson, 'A Fragment, supposed to be written near the Temple, at Paris, on the night before the execution of Louis XVI', ll. 81–4, in Pascoe, ed., *Robinson*.

42. *Sun*, 14 December 1793. See Wollstonecraft, *French Revolution*, in *Works*, VI, 198–9, 206–7. See, for example, I. Cruikshank, *The Near in Blood, The Nearer Bloody* (London: S.W. Fores, 26 January 1793) BMC 8292; I. Cruikshank, *The Martyr of Equality* (London: S.W. Fores, 12 February 1793) BMC 8302.

43. C.J. Fox, *Speech of the Right Hon. Charles James Fox, in the House of Commons, Jan. 4, 1793. On the Alien Bill* (London: J. Ridgway, [1793]), pp. 10, 12.

44. Notices were juxtaposed on the front page of *The Times*, which advertised *Emigrants* on 4 and 6 July, and Robinson's 'Three Poems' (as they were usually named) on 5 July. The publication of Robinson's volume on 16/17 July was trailed in numerous and widespread pre-publication advertisements, as well as in the more common post-publication advertisements. See, for example, *Sun*, 28 June, *True Briton*, 17 July, *Morning Herald*, 27 June, *Morning Post*, 12 and puffed 17 July, *Morning Chronicle*, 17 July, and *Star*, 18 July (all 1793).

45. *Oracle*, 18 July 1793.

46. Smith to Davies, 25 April 1797, in *Letters*, p. 268.

47. 'Mrs. Robinson', in *Public Characters of 1800–1801*, ed. by Richard Phillips (1801; this edn London: R. Phillips, 1807), p. 343. Anna Seward was celebrated for her sonnets.

48. Jon Mee, '"Reciprocal expressions of kindness": Robert Merry, Della Cruscanism and the Limits of Sociability', in *Romantic Sociability: Social Networks and Literary Culture in Britain, 1770–1840*, ed. by Gillian Russell and Clara Tuite (Cambridge: Cambridge University Press, 2002), p. 112.

49. *Memoirs of the late Mrs. Robinson, written by herself. With some posthumous pieces*, 4 vols (London: R. Phillips, 1801), II, pp. 116, 131, and see 127.

50. *Memoirs*, II, 129, 127.

51. *Ainsi va Le Monde*, ll. 157–64, in Pascoe, ed., *Robinson*. Subsequent citations are given in parentheses in the text. Compare Mee's discussion of Merry's account of universal benevolence, in '"Reciprocal expressions"', pp. 112–13.

52. *Ainsi*, ll. 157–72, 179–84 appeared in the *Moral and Political Magazine of the London Corresponding Society*, August 1796, pp. 239–40; ll. 319–28, 331–41 were printed in the magazine for November 1796, pp. 332–3.

53. *Critical Review*, January 1791, pp. 73–5.

54. See Anne Janowitz, *Women Romantic Poets: Anna Barbauld and Mary Robinson* (Tavistock, Devon: Northcote House, 2004), pp. 78–80; Amy Garnai, '"One Victim from the Last Despair": Mary Robinson's Marie Antoinette', *Women's Writing*, 12(3) (2005), 381–98; Pascoe, ed., *Robinson*, pp. 117–27.

55. [Mary Robinson], *Impartial Reflections on the Present Situation of the Queen of France* (London: Bell, 1791); Brown Women Writers Project first electronic edition, 2002 <http://www.brown.edu/texts/robinson.reflections.html> [accessed 10 November 2004].

56. Robinson, *Monody to the Memory of the Late Queen of France* (London: J. Evans, 1793), ll. 89, 81, 85–6.

57. 'Ode to Humanity. Written during the Massacres at Paris, in September, 1792', in *Poetical Works of the late Mrs. Mary Robinson: including many pieces never before published*, 3 vols (London: R. Phillips, 1806) I, 168. On the reception of the ode, see Byrne, *Perdita*, p. 309. Merry, in contrast, seems to have been willing to defend the uprising of 10 August 1793, when the king's Swiss Guards, having opened fire on the crowd, were attacked and 600 of them hacked to death. Jon Mee has pointed out to me that *The Times* for 11 September 1792 advertised a pamphlet by Merry defending the uprising, which may have been published with the unambiguous title of *A Circumstantial History of the Transactions at Paris on the Tenth of August; plainly shewing the perfidy of Louis XVI. and the general unanimity of the people, in defence of their rights* (London: R. Thomson, R. Lyttlejohn, and H.D. Symonds, 1792).

58. *Oracle*, 26 January 1793.

59. *Analytical Review*, xvii, September 1793, 93, 95.

60. Robinson, 'Solitude', in *Sight, The Cavern of Woe, and Solitude. Poems* (London: J. Evans, 1793), ll. 157–8, 159–60, 173.

61. Robert Merry, *The Laurel of Liberty, A Poem* (London: John Bell, 1790), ll. 1–4, 25–6.

62. See Mee, '"Reciprocal expressions"', p. 114. *World*, 15 July 1793, commented: '"Mr. MERRY *has escaped from* FRANCE," so says a MORNING PRINT. Can this be possible? ESCAPE! and from a Government he has admired so much. "Leaves any Man the thing he much admires!"'

63. *Monthly Review*, xii, September–December 1793, 375; see also, for example, *British Critic*, 1 August 1793, 405.

64. *European Magazine and London Review*, xxiv, July 1793, 42.

65. *British Critic*, 1 August 1793, 405.

66. On Robinson's advocacy of feminist meritocracy in the *Monody* see Adriana Craciun, *Fatal Women of Romanticism* (Cambridge: Cambridge University Press, 2003), pp. 89–91.

67. Smith to Walker, 20 February 1793, in *Letters*, p. 62.

68. Smith to Walker, 20 February 1793, *Letters*, p. 62. This essay was submitted for publication in 2007, and I have therefore been unable to acknowledge recently published work.

Part III
1800–1830: Worlds of Writing

11
The Porter Sisters, Women's Writing, and Historical Fiction

Devoney Looser

Throughout the nineteenth century, the Porter sisters (or the 'Misses Porter', as they were called) were mentioned alongside the likes of Jane Austen, Frances Burney, and Maria Edgeworth in accounts of celebrated women writers. Claiming such critical prominence for the Porters may now seem exaggerated. If so, it is because their careers have not been fully assessed, despite the burgeoning of feminist scholarship in this pivotal period for the professional woman writer. It was, as Cheryl Turner puts it, the era of 'the emergence of female literary professionalism' as well as 'the rise of women's prose fiction', interrelated phenomena in which the Porters played a central role.[1] Recent criticism has laid the groundwork for further attention to their fiction, but few attempts have been made to trace the contours of their remarkable lives or their innovative novels.[2] In this chapter, I argue for the prominence of Jane Porter (bap. 1776–1850) and Anna Maria Porter (1780–1832) in the history of women's writings from this period. Returning the achievements of both women to literary history is not only a project of recovery; it also provides us with the opportunity to revisit long-held assumptions about the origins of historical fiction and the role of the professional woman writer in the flowering of the genre.

Assessing the accomplishments of the Porter sisters is a task that deserves more extended treatment, but in what follows, I consider their positions as professional women writers, using them to focus on the fate of that group during the years 1800–30. Starting from the Porters' own sense of their literary contributions, I also explore their contemporaries' perceptions of their originality, drawing conclusions about the ways in which gender played a role in these debates. Following up on scholarship by Ian Dennis, Fiona Price, Gary Kelly, and Thomas McLean, I further the project of describing how the Porter sisters' historical fiction

233

broke new ground.[3] I consider the ways in which they were invested in branding themselves as originators, examining and contextualizing Jane Porter's claims of having created a 'new species' of writing. The Porter sisters' use of sensitive male warrior-protagonists whose military careers and domestic lives were closely intertwined was groundbreaking and ought to make us look differently at Sir Walter Scott's *Waverley* (1814). As McLean rightly puts it, Jane Porter's 'significance in the development of the historical novel and national tale has been seriously undervalued'.[4]

England produced several sets of sister-novelists before the Brontës, but none were perhaps more famous than the Misses Porter. Children of an Irish army surgeon who died when they were very young, the Porters were raised in Durham, Edinburgh, and London by their widowed mother. Anna Maria, the younger sister, emerged as a prodigy as a teenager with her *Artless Tales* (1793) and would become a prolific fiction writer. Elder sister Jane published less but enjoyed greater fame, as two of her novels became bestsellers: *Thaddeus of Warsaw* (1803) and *The Scottish Chiefs* (1810). The sisters ultimately published two dozen novels, as well as poetry, short stories, and non-fiction. Their historical fiction – some of which they published jointly – frequently centres on perfect war heroes, features strong women, and stresses morally uplifting qualities. Together, Jane and Anna Maria and their artist and travel-writer brother, Sir Robert Ker Porter (1777–1842), became international celebrities in the early 1800s.

For much of their lives, the Porters travelled in elite artistic, theatrical, literary, and political circles. Despite their father's death, theirs was in some ways a storybook (if hardscrabble) youth, but it was not followed by the happy endings dominant in domestic novels of the day. Instead, the sisters endured an exhausted and anxious middle and old age, as each remained single, desperately worried about supporting their elderly mother and themselves by the pen. The sisters also tried to manage their brother Robert's troubled financial affairs. Even the event that was to have saved them – Robert's marriage to an orphaned Russian princess – did not bring the financial stability it seemed to promise. When Robert turned from the arts to foreign service in search of respectability (and to flee his debts), the Porter women drew modest amounts from his salary as a Venezuelan diplomat. At the same time, Jane tried to get the family out of the red by negotiating with their publisher for advances of fifty or a hundred pounds on her or her sister's next work of fiction. Jane and Anna Maria were, of necessity, unusually active in their negotiations in the literary marketplace. They were also, for a time at least, quite savvy in creating new fictional combinations of history and romance that appealed to readers and critics alike. The Porters deserve to be brought back into our literary histories and to the historical record. Their lifetime impact and posthumous legacies suggest the need for a series of literary and biographical studies, much less a first one.

Assessing the 'Misses Porter'

The genealogy of the historical novel in Great Britain remains subject to debate. It is a story of the literary past that has not yet been adequately reconstructed. Nevertheless, contemporary scholars have shown that female authors played a more central role than is traditionally credited. As Clara Tuite argues, the early nineteenth century saw 'the consolidation of the genre of the historical novel in the context of the emergence of a vast diversity of historical fiction'. Among that diversity she names the Jacobin and anti-Jacobin novels engaging the French Revolution, the Gothic novel, the national tale, the regional novel, tales of village life, the futuristic romance, and the historical romance, concluding that 'Women writers were at the forefront at experimentation in these forms and in consolidating the genre of the modern historical novel.'[5] Others have made similar arguments. Katie Trumpener, for example, in tracing the interrelations of the national tale and the historical novel, describes the signal contributions of Sydney Owenson (Lady Morgan), Charlotte Smith, and Maria Edgeworth. Anne Stevens charts the rise of historical fiction from the 1760s to its flowering in the 1790s and beyond, listing subtitles of novels that reveal a historical focus. The preponderance of these volumes (among those that are signed) indicate female authorship: Anna Maria MacKenzie, Cassandra Cooke, Sophia Lee, Mrs E.M. Foster, Mrs F.C. Patrick, Anna Millikin, and Ann Yearsley among them. As Stevens puts it, 'By the time Walter Scott came to publish *Waverley* in 1814, he was working within an already established genre.'[6]

That genre – not just the novel but the *historical* novel – was for several decades in the late eighteenth and early nineteenth centuries a feminized one. That it would later mistakenly come to be seen as originally a masculine genre is due, no doubt, to the popularity of Scott, as well as to the dominance of male-centred and partial twentieth-century accounts like Georg Lukács *The Historical Novel*.[7] Of course, the tide would turn again. As Diana Wallace demonstrates, the historical novel returned to its roots as a feminized genre in the early twentieth century and thereafter, when 'male writers were moving away from the genre, with the result that it has come to be seen as a "feminine" form'.[8]

However, at the time that the Porters were writing, in the 1800s and 1810s, when the novel was gaining respectability and the historical novel was beginning to change its gendered associations, such shifts could hardly have been anticipated. It was only later in their lives that the Porters perceived that literary history was being written in ways that would sell their work short.

One need not go far into the periodicals of the early 1800s to establish that the Porter sisters were cast as central figures in a burgeoning tradition of women's fiction. As one reviewer put it in 1830, 'Novel writing, until these last few years, was a species of composition that seemed solely vested in the female part of the community', naming as prominent Miss Edgeworth, Mrs Opie, the Misses Porter, Mrs Inchbald, and Mrs 'Ratcliffe' (Radcliffe).[9] What prompted the reviewer's caveat, 'until these last few years', was undoubtedly Scott's anonymously published and celebrated historical fiction of the 1810s and 1820s, dubbed the Waverley novels. As Peter Garside puts it, 'the Waverley novels first emerged at a time when male authorship was at an unusually low ebb; though from 1820 the position changes sharply, and by the later 1820s, no doubt partly because of Scott's influence, male novelists are dominant'.[10] The Porter sisters were among those women able to maintain a foothold in the world of letters, thanks to their earlier fame and to newly published editions of their best-regarded earlier works. The research of Garside, Terry Lovell, and others, however, makes it clear that the 1820s to 1830s were challenging years for many women trying to make a living by fiction writing.[11] What was once their field to dominate had contracted; it had come to be understood as masculine territory.

Some contemporaries noticed that male novelists, in the wake of Scott, had effectively muscled women out of the market. At least one saw it as a sad state of affairs, writing, 'We are inclined to hazard a conjecture, that one cause of the present low state of English literature, is the invasion the stronger sex has made into the legitimate province of the weaker.'[12] More customary was the opposite opinion – that men's 'invasion' (or women's 'disappearance') prompted the novel's *progress* as a genre. A piece in the *Monthly Review* from 1824 makes the claim that in the previous fifteen years, all of 'the popular novelists of the day, with a very few exceptions, prefixed Mrs. or Miss to their names'.[13] The *Monthly's* reviewer lists among them 'Miss Edgeworth, Miss Austen, Miss Benger, Miss Owenson, the two Misses Porter, Mrs. West, Mrs. Brunton, Mrs. Opie, &c. &c'. The reviewer then suggests that these women writers have been supplanted by men, principally because the women have not produced (or cannot produce) new work:

> Since that period [the 1800s and 1810s], however, the ladies have been almost driven from the field of fiction by the hosts of power-ful writers of the masculine gender who have occupied it. The most serious incursion has been made by our neighbors the Scotch, the well-known 'Unknown' [Sir Walter Scott] leading the way [...] These masculine writers have at length almost entirely superseded their feminine predecessors. Even Miss Edgeworth's pen has been idle since the publication of her Patronage; and Miss Anna Maria Porter's romantic heroes now seldom make their appearance. Mrs. Opie's Tales have become 'few and far between,' and if we except the fair writer of 'The Favorite of Nature' [Mary Ann Kelty], no new female writer has for some years past appeared before the public with any claims to celebrity as a novelist.[14]

Despite the reviewer's perspicacity in noting the shift in gender domi-nance in the production of the novel, some of his assertions must raise eyebrows – particularly the idea that novels by once-celebrated women authors had become 'few and far between'. Austen, dead since 1817, could not have produced new work. But even among the female authors who were named by this reviewer, few had had *idle* pens. A handful had indeed taken a hiatus from publication; Jane West brought out no new novels between 1816 and 1827. Edgeworth, however, had published several works after *Patronage* (1814), including *Ormond* (1817) and *Harrington* (1817), additional writing for children, and a continuation of her father's memoirs.

The *Monthly's* reviewer also suggests that Jane and Anna Maria Porter too had gone silent, but in each case, he was inaccurate. Anna Maria Porter (whose 'romantic heroes' were said by the reviewer to 'seldom make their appearance') had published many signed novels in the 1810s and early 1820s, including 1814 (*The Recluse of Norway*), 1817 (*The Knight of St. John: A Romance*), 1819 (*The Fast of St. Magdalen: A Romance*), 1821 (*The Village of Mariendorpt: A Tale*), and 1822 (*Roche-Blanche: or, The Hunters of the Pyrenees: A Romance*). For her part, Jane Porter's two most famous novels, published in 1803 (*Thaddeus of Warsaw*) and 1810 (*The Scottish Chiefs*), continued to appear in new editions through the 1810s, and she published two more novels. One saw print in 1817 (*The Pastor's Fire-Side*). Her *Duke Christian of Luneburg: A Tale from the Hartz* (1824) made its debut in the month before the *Monthly Review* pronounced her fiction's disappearance.[15]

Across the span of her more than 30-year publishing career, Anna Maria Porter brought out new novels every two to four years on average; Jane Porter was less prolific but more critically and commercially successful.[16] One way we might measure each sister's respective powers is by the inclusion of her works in Henry Colburn and Richard Bentley's Standard Novels series of the 1830s and 1840s. That series of 'the cheapest library of entertainment ever published' set out to include 'the best works' of the 'most distinguished modern novelists'.[17] Jane Porter's *Thaddeus of Warsaw* appeared as volume four (1831), *The Scottish Chiefs* appeared as volumes seven and eight (1831), and her *Pastor's Fire-Side* as volumes eighteen and nineteen (1832). Anna Maria Porter's *Hungarian Brothers* (1807) is the only novel from her corpus to appear – posthumously – as volume eleven (1832).

Despite their separate achievements in multiple genres across their careers, the Porters' contemporaries often referenced them in one breath. In this way, the 'Misses Porter' experienced on an individual level (or rather a dual level) what women writers as a group faced during this period – the phenomenon of being lumped together, to be handled en masse. We see this above in the phrasing of the *Monthly Review*'s 1824 reviewer, and we can glimpse this phenomenon at work in the same periodical in 1828. There, the reviewer claims to be thankful to the 'Misses Porter for putting us into this excellent humour with female novelists'.[18] The two come to stand in for the many. While such homogenizing impulses meant that a newly successful female novelist entered an established 'group' through which her works could be evaluated and marketed, she might, by this means, be dismissed in one stroke as well.

The Porters benefited and suffered from this tendency to homogenize women novelists and to bracket their works off from those of men. The Porter sisters may even have consciously contributed to the sense of their own interchangeability to try to increase the attention they were paid. Their sister-novelist predecessors and contemporaries, Harriet Lee (1757/8–1851) and Sophia Lee (bap. 1750–1824) (the 'Misses Lee'), had enjoyed success in doing so. Perhaps the Porters, too, sought thus to double their market share. Early editions of *Thaddeus of Warsaw* were published as by 'Miss Porter', allowing for potential confusion as to which sister was responsible for the work. That at least a few readers were confused is evidenced by a review of *The Hungarian Brothers*, which lists the name of its author on its title page as 'Miss Anna Maria

Porter'. Although the *Critical Review* offers a positive assessment of *The Hungarian Brothers*, it concludes, 'On the whole, we think the work inferior to "Thaddeus of Warsaw," but not unworthy of its author' – as if the two works were by the same person.[19] In the late 1820s, the Porter sisters joined forces, publishing two co-authored novels, *Tales Round a Winter Hearth* (1826) and *Coming Out; and the Field of Forty Footsteps* (1828).[20] Both works received warm, if not precisely enthusiastic, notice. As one reviewer concluded, 'it would probably be difficult to keep the names of Jane and Anna Maria Porter very distinctly apart'.[21]

The Porter sisters as innovators in historical fiction

Attempts to market themselves as two-for-one may have increased the attention the Porters' works received, but it did not necessarily help others to recognize the depth of their achievements. Today most continue wrongly to imagine Sir Walter Scott as the inventor of the historical novel, despite some years of scholarship working to unseat this view. Once we investigate the use of the term 'historical novel' or 'historical romance' on the title pages of eighteenth-century fiction, we discover that the label (if not the genre *tout court*) pre-dates Scott and the Porters by decades. The terms are used as the subtitle of dozens of productions of the 1790s, but they appear on occasion much earlier.[22] In fact, 'historical novel' is featured as a subtitle in fiction translated from the French as early as 1725.[23] Though the meaning of 'historical novel' no doubt changed across the period, the use of the term to identify fiction of a historical hue nearly a century before Scott ought to give us pause.[24] If we cast a wider net, we find that fictional works billing themselves as 'historical romance' or 'founded on facts' appear in significant numbers from the 1760s on but particularly after the late 1780s. Until Scott's *Waverley* novels, however, few rivalled in popular success Jane Porter's contributions to the genre.[25] *The Scottish Chiefs*, which may have been the source text for Mel Gibson's film *Braveheart* (1995), was arguably the most enduring among them.[26] But when it came time for Jane Porter to stake her claim as an originator of the historical novel, it was to *Thaddeus* that she turned to make her case.

Thaddeus of Warsaw is the story of a fictional Polish war hero, Thaddeus Sobieski, whose ancestor was said to be King John Sobieski (1624–96). Porter's hero was loosely based on General Thaddeus Kosciusko (1746–1817), identified in the story as the hero's namesake and himself a character in the novel. Kosciusko was known in England as the stalwart defender of Poland in its 1792–95 invasion by

Russia, during which Poland was partitioned. In the novel, Thaddeus Sobieski loses his illustrious family – his mother (Therese Sobieski) and his grandfather (the Palatine of Masovia) who raised him – but not before they reveal that his father was an Englishman who mysteriously deserted his mother shortly after marriage. Defeated in his battle against the Russians, Thaddeus is encouraged to flee, gives up his faithful steed, and escapes to England, incognito and destitute. The bulk of the novel describes his adventures as a man with a secret, using an alias, trying to make his way in a foreign country by trading on his knowledge and artistic talents, rather than using his former identity. He discovers that an English friend is actually a younger brother and locates his father. Thaddeus, now an acknowledged son, is given a fortune, reunites with his horse, and marries his worthy first cousin.

The plot of the novel may sound conventional; more innovative are the techniques Porter uses to combine martial and familial action, particularly in her early battle scenes. As McLean argues, Porter 'crafted and pioneered many of the narrative tools most commonly associated with both the national tale and the historical novel'.[27] Her story alternates between imaginary domestic stories and historically-based military ones, particularly in *Thaddeus of Warsaw*'s first volume. The two strands – the domestic and the martial – occasionally intertwine through inserted letters and through the character of Thaddeus's grandfather, represented as both a war hero in battle and as an anxious father-figure. But it is Thaddeus's mother, Therese Sobieski, who is at the centre of the early chapters of the work. Therese tells Thaddeus, as he is about to return to battle, 'You must forgive me, Thaddeus, I have nothing of the soldier in my heart; it is all woman. But I will not detain you longer, my dear boy, from that rest which you require; go to your room, and try to recruit yourself for the dangers, which I expect tomorrow will bring forth.'[28] Thaddeus, 'consoled to see any composure in his mother, withdrew' (p. 186). Porter makes a distinction between the hearts of women and soldiers, but Therese's words open up the possibility that a woman *could* have 'the soldier' in her heart. We might say that Porter did so in her pen. It would not be until *The Scottish Chiefs* that Porter realized this potential, crafting the character of a woman who cross-dresses as a soldier. Porter presents a domestic story (the 'fiction') as it is enveloped by and envelops war, its grand historical event (the 'truth'), which, despite its idealized characters and settings, offers in its combination an original if idealized proto-realism.

Indeed, near the end of the first volume, the home and the battlefield become one and the same. The violence in *Thaddeus of Warsaw*'s first volume (a fictional rendering of the Battle of Praga or Battle of Warsaw, 1794) was bloody and revolting. At least one military man, General Gardiner, was said (by Porter herself) to have found it impossible that the novel's war scenes were written by someone who had not been an eyewitness.[29] Porter's battle depicts complete, repellent disorder:

> In an instant, the field before Prague [Praga] was filled with women and children, flying in all directions, and rending the sky with their shrieks. 'Father Almighty!' cried Thaddeus, wringing his hands, 'canst thou suffer this?' Whilst he yet spake, some straggling Cossacks, from the town, who were prowling about, glutted, but not sated with blood, seized the poor fugitives, and with a ferocity as wanton as unmanly, released them at once from life and affliction.
>
> (pp. 192–3)

Thaddeus sees the 'hideous spectacle', and it 'brought his mother's defenceless state' in the palace before his eyes (p. 193). He flies across 'heaps of dead bodies' to his home, where he finds a general guarding the palace. Thaddeus discovers his mother on her deathbed, proclaiming that she will die before their 'cruel murderers' arrive (p. 195). She kisses his bloody forehead and tells him she has not uttered a complaining word, despite finding him covered in wounds. She orders him to leave defeated Poland for England, 'a free country', giving him a miniature of his estranged English father (pp. 196–7).

Again, the military and the domestic fold together as 'a volley of fire arms made Thaddeus spring upon his feet', and as the women rush into the room to announce that the ramparts are stormed. His mother (conveniently) dies a natural death as the cannons are fired into the palace. Thaddeus escapes, plunges into a stream 'amidst a shower of musket balls from the enemy' and is 'assisted out of the river, by some of the weeping inhabitants of Warsaw' (p. 201). Seeing his home in flames, he proclaims to the general, 'with a smile of agony', 'See what a funeral pile, Heaven has raised to the manes of my dear mother!' (p. 201). As Thaddeus recovers, the narrator informs us that 'Prague [Praga] was not only razed to the ground: but upwards of thirty thousand persons, besides old men, women, and defenceless infants, perished by the sword, in the river, and the flames' (p. 203). We might argue that *Thaddeus*, like *The Scottish Chiefs*, imagines 'the whole of the [...] landscape as a site of struggle and emphasizes the mass activity of the [...] people', adding that the landscape under construction here often blends exteriors and interiors, masculinity and femininity, and truth and fiction, allowing for significant – and often groundbreaking – traffic between them.[30]

Anna Maria Porter's *The Hungarian Brothers* (1807) provides a good point of comparison with Jane Porter's techniques. Like *Thaddeus of Warsaw*, *The Hungarian Brothers* is set in the late 1790s, against the French Revolutionary conflicts, and treats domestic and military contests as intertwined. Many of the domestic conflicts are between the two brothers (Count Charles Leopolstat and his younger sibling, Dimitrius), orphan sons of a Hungarian nobleman, and their lovers or would-be lovers. This novel's battle scenes are not nearly as extended, detailed, or movingly narrated as those in *Thaddeus*. Even so, the sisters' novels share a sensibility about the relationship – and the proximity – of the home fires to the war front. Anna Maria Porter demonstrates her sense of their connection through philosophizing letters and comments from the older to the younger brother. Both siblings distinguish themselves in separate battles. The elder brother, Charles, fighting the French in Switzerland, writes to his brother, fighting them in Italy, the following comments: 'The man that studies the military art, for any other purpose than that of saving lives, is unworthy the name of man. We must never get enamoured of what we ought to detest: for war should be our aversion; though the study of it is our duty, and the glory attached to it our reward.'[31] After having indicated that war should be anathema, Charles goes on to defend the idea of standing armies, as a way to protect freedom but also to prevent the slaughter of the brave (those drawn into war without training – the volunteer soldier and the civilian) versus the potential 'bloodless conquest of whole battalions' (II, 201).

As Charles concludes, 'When the subject is thus contemplated, I am astonished at the odium which our profession incurs from many enlightened classes of society. If they believe, preposterously believe, that there would be no wars, if there were no disciplined soldiers, of course they are justified in denouncing us: but I think they might as well go to prove that there would be no diseases, if there were no physicians' (II, 201–2). Charles speaks of war as arising from passion and of soldiers as a small body of men who 'take the whole portion of humanity's worst affliction, upon themselves' (II, 202). He calls for someone to write a history of war as a science, from 'when it first ceased to be a blind slaughter' to the present day, when 'a new system has suddenly risen above the military sphere, like a lawless comet', threatening the return of the slaughter (II, 210). Charles then abruptly shifts to tell Dimitrius that he must be surprised that the letter has been filled with 'professional remarks' rather than comments on the beautiful scenery.

Charles admits that the scenery moves him, though 'every new discovered charm, only makes me witness with greater horror, the seas of blood which even now deluge its majestic beauties' (II, 210). That this philosophical lecture is delivered in a private letter, from the wise older brother to the impetuous (but educable) younger one, heightens its force as a domestic and martial object. Christian soldier brothers, Anna Maria Porter suggests, risk death for our human sins.

Charles's long letter is dated August 1799, from the 'Valley of the Reusse'. This was contemporaneous with the defeat of General Joubert at the Battle of Novi in Italy and a few months prior to Napoleon's overthrow of the Directory and establishment of the Consulate, details that would have been well known to Anna Maria Porter's readers. She does not highlight them in her text, except through the familiar letters and through the narrator's descriptions of battles in particular locations. Just as we saw in *Thaddeus*, in *The Hungarian Brothers* the focus is on the ways in which military and familial lives intertwine. The heroes' complicated relationships offer a behind-the-scenes view of grand-scale history, in all of its domestic and martial difficulties. We might conclude that domesticating the masculine sphere of war functioned as a compensatory conservatism in the Porters' novels, making palatable the notion of a woman having entered the territory. Conversely, however, we could see the mixing of masculine and feminine settings and subjects as a kind of gender progressivism. Regardless, the Porters' mixings presented political and romantic material in a new vein for eager readers seeking moral truths and true history in fiction.

A 'new species' of fiction

We are only now beginning to assess and catalogue the specific ways in which the Porters were innovators in the genre of the historical novel before Scott, but the question of 'newness' has applied to Jane Porter's fiction almost from the first. Late in her life, as we shall see, she suggested that she invented the genre of the historical novel.[32] From today's vantage point, such a claim seems as much of a stretch as giving the honour solely to Scott. But Jane Porter could make strong claims to having successfully popularized the blending of true history and romance, as well as to having blazed the trail in the narrative combinations we saw above. Significantly, arguments for the newness of her fictional contributions circulated prior to the publication of *Waverley*. As early as 1810, one writer refers to Jane Porter's *Thaddeus of Warsaw* (1803) as 'a new species of composition, an harmonious union between the heroic matter of ancient romance, and the domestic interest of a modern novel' and notes her 'many imitators'.[33] The Porter sisters themselves also believed they had broken new ground in fiction writing. However, despite the merit in some parts of their claims, after protracted battles over branding themselves the originators of historical fiction, the Porters ultimately lost the literary war.

From the mid-1810s forward, the Porters felt that they were not being given their due by fellow authors. The sisters believed their original ideas and methods were being remodelled (without credit) by highly regarded male authors, both poets and novelists. There is no suggestion that the Porters saw it as a case of crytomnesia. On the contrary, they seem to locate intentional theft at every turn. Their sense that their works had been victimized crops up several times in unpublished letters in the 1810s, as well as in Jane Porter's anonymous and then signed published writings in the 1830s and 1840s. In 1819, Anna Maria writes in a private letter to Jane that the Waverley author (Scott) 'evidently uses *our* novels as a sort of store house' from which

> he draws unobserved whatever odd bit of furniture strikes his fancy for his own pompous edifice. I do not say he steals the thing itself, but the idea & fashion of it, and if he had the honesty to shew that he thought well of our writings, by a hand or two of such commendation as he liberally gives to works that have no resemblance to his own, I should say the conduct was fair and allowable. But I quarrel with the self-interestedness of working the hints we give him, yet never owning that he does.[34]

Despite her claims of the Waverley author's quasi-theft, Anna Maria wrongly predicts that his works' popularity will be fleeting, once the 'temporary taste for antiquarianism passes away'. She praises many aspects of his novels, but she does not echo the periodical reviews of the time, which deemed *Waverley*'s '"variety" of mode, scene, and characterization; and the "fact" and "accuracy" of its historical and cultural representations' to be something new.[35] Such claims must have been galling to the Porters, whose achievements were increasingly being made invisible by those who declared Scott's techniques in blending truth and fiction, imagination and history, to be pioneering.

The Porters' complaints went beyond the novelist, however. In a letter to her sister Jane in 1815, Anna Maria complains that she reads poet Robert Southey's work with a little 'mist-rising' because he has 'rifled' 'unacknowledged' all of the 'best parts' of one of her novels

(HL, POR 728).[36] Another 1815 letter from Jane to Anna Maria shows that she agrees with her sister. Jane writes of Southey having stolen from their novels in his latest poem, complaining, 'there are a thousand situations in the poem like your work & mine', in addition to what she believes are its liberal borrowings from their characters (HL, POR 1707).[37] Jane concludes, 'It is monstrous how these poets play the vampire with our works. – I beg of you to read it. – Some time or other, I think I shall be provoked to give the public the real Genealogy of these matters' (HL, POR 1707).

The Porters are vague about what they see as having been 'rifled' from their works, whether by Scott, Southey, or anyone else. Words such as 'method', 'idea', and 'fashion' are rather inexact. It is nevertheless interesting that the Porters do not seem to blame *female* authors for stealing from their novels, despite occasionally viewing themselves as in competition with other women writers. At the same time, the Porters do not often credit (privately or publicly) male or female predecessors with having inspired their own work – the very thing that they complained was happening to them. They might, for instance, have included among their influences the aforementioned Sophia Lee, whose *The Recess, or, A Tale of Other Times* (1783–85) is said to have 'established the taste for both Gothic and historical fiction, of which it is one of the earliest examples in English literature'.[38] *The Recess* tells the story of the well-born 'orphans' (Matilda and Ellinor, the fictional twin daughters of Mary, Queen of Scots) who were brought up in secrecy, in an underground 'recess' or cave. The novel treats royal personages and actual events alongside fictional ones.

Jane Porter, though perhaps harbouring an exaggerated sense of the *extent* to which she and her sister invented the transformation of historical material into fiction, was undoubtedly perceptive about the evolving fate of their work. The Porter sisters' historical fiction – along with that of the other female authors, from the famous to the obscure – was being subsumed under the mythical story of Scott's invention of the genre. Women writers, as vital contributors to fiction of the late eighteenth century, and as pioneers in Gothic and historical romances, were often trivialized and condescended to by reviewers in the 1810s and thereafter, particularly as the manipulation of historical material became a more mainstream national and literary project.[39] The English vogue for using the past to respond to the present has been dated to the 1790s, which has led scholars to link the flourishing of the historical novel to the French Revolution's 'significance for the very shaping of historical forms, and its wider meaning for English culture and politics' or more generally to the 'emergence of nationalism'.[40] The Porters rode the crest of that wave of interest. Scott's story of having begun *Waverley* around 1805, only to put it into a drawer until 1813, though perhaps true, seems almost too neatly designed to cast doubt on the Porters' rising claims to originality. Two decades after *Waverley*'s publication, under a pseudonym in the late 1820s and in her own name in 1831, Jane Porter began to expend a great deal of energy trying to convince the public that she was the first to combine historical truth and imaginative fiction, as Thomas McLean has shown.[41]

It is possible, however, that Jane Porter sought print to stake her claim even earlier than the late 1820s. For instance, she may have had a hand in one of the reviews of *Duke Christian* (1824), which dubs her the author of 'new species [...] of literary fiction' and refers to Scott as 'only a follower in her wake'.[42] If these claims of having created a 'new species' were not statements from Porter's own pen, it seems to have emboldened or inspired her, because her later claims mirror its rhetoric. In her 'The Author to Her Friendly Readers', a preface to the Standard Novels edition of *Thaddeus of Warsaw* (1831), Jane Porter writes that it was 'Sir Walter Scott who did me the honor to adopt the style or class of novel of which "Thaddeus of Warsaw" was the first: – a class which, uniting the personages and facts of real history or biography, with a combining and illustrative machinery of the imagination, formed a new species of writing in that day'. She reiterates that her *Thaddeus of Warsaw* and *The Scottish Chiefs* were 'both published in England, and translated into various languages abroad, many years before the literary wonder of Scotland gave to the world his transcendent story of Waverley'.[43]

The phrase 'new species' would have been familiar to readers in the early nineteenth century as one that had been at the centre of a previous generation's set of debates about fictional innovation – namely that of Samuel Richardson's claims to fictional originality versus those of his rival Henry Fielding. Richardson (whose *Sir Charles Grandison* was a favourite with Jane Porter and whose name frequently appears in her paratexts) wrote in a 1741 letter to Aaron Hill that he had written *Pamela* (1740) in the hope that it 'might possibly introduce a new species of writing'.[44] Fielding, in his *Joseph Andrews* (1742) also claimed that he was creating a 'species of writing' that he 'affirmed to be hitherto unattempted in our language'. The two novelists, of course, were famous rivals, and their supporters and detractors kept up the debate over who had and who had not created a 'new species' of novel, the phrase being used prominently in works such as *An Essay on the New Species of Writing Founded by Mr. Fielding* (1751) and incidentally in countless others, from the serious to the silly, across the century. In the preface to the second edition of his Gothic novel *The Castle of Otranto* (1764), Horace Walpole, too, laid claim to having created a 'new species of romance'.[45]

Porter's claims of having created a 'new species' of fiction, then, drew on august and still-debated values in the history of the novel. For her to make her claim over and against Scott was received in some quarters with sarcasm and scepticism. As one particularly virulent detractor, 'Peter Puff', put it, when responding to Porter's claims of innovating, 'What is Sir Walter Scott but an imitator of Miss Jane Porter?' Puff ironically dismisses Porter's 1831 claims of having founded a new species of writing:

> Believe us, Miss Porter, when we read this fine passage, we blushed as red as our morocco slippers at our disgraceful ignorance. Well acquainted with your novels as we were, and having a little more intimate acquaintance with Sir Walter Scott's, we assure you we never discovered that Sir Walter had adopted the style of your romances, until you so kindly informed us that such was the case. When the great truth at last flashed on our minds, it is impossible to describe our feelings.

Puff scornfully claims that the world has been in ignorance of the fact that 'Sir Walter Scott has been enjoying the honours rightly due to Miss Porter!'[46] Not all commentators branded Porter a liar, though many more – even when they acknowledged to some extent her claims to originality – declared her a hack. As Henry Bulwer Lytton put it, 'A desire was felt, which no one satisfied, till Sir Walter Scott, succeeding the Misses Porter, who had already feebly attempted the same line of romance, carried his genius into a school, fore-destined to be popular – becoming what he will remain – the Shakespeare of his time – the great popular historian of England.'[47] As traditional literary historical accounts demonstrate all too well, Jane Porter's claims were ultimately dismissed with prejudice and then forgotten. By 1845, five years before her death, one writer could declare, 'Sir Walter Scott, as all the world knows, was the inventor of the historical romance.'[48]

In the year before Jane Porter died, the novelist Thomas Litchfield wrote in a private letter to her that he planned to credit her in a preface to one of his own novels.[49] He tells her that he will name her as an innovator in the genre, calling her 'one of the first who entered upon the untrodden field of Historical Romance'.[50] He included in his letter a draft copy of that preface, which elaborates on this statement and also mentions Sophia Lee. Litchfield writes that Porter 'was the first (if we except Miss Lee who wrote the 'Recess') who entered upon the untrodden field, and how she entered it, and kept possession of it so long, literary records can tell'. Of course, as we have seen, one of the reasons that Porter (and presumably Litchfield himself) was at pains to establish what Porter had once called the 'real genealogy' of the historical novel was that literary records frequently did *not* tell of the Porters' entering the untrodden field – or of Lee's, or other contemporaries, particularly female ones.

Litchfield also quotes from a letter that he indicates Jane Porter sent him in February of 1849, echoing back what he claims are her own words. He says that she wrote that her novels were published a full fifty years ago and that they spawned

> a splendid race of the like Chroniclers of their Country's deeds [...] brightening the track as they have advanced the Author of Waverley and all his soul stirring Tales of My Landlord; then comes Mr. James, with his Historical Romances on British and foreign subjects, so admirably uniting the requisite fiction with the fact, that the whole seems equally veritable.–but my feeble hand will not obey my wish to add more names to this march of British Worthies!

Again, if Porter wrote these words (as seems probable), then she continued, until the very end of her life, to position herself as the inventor of the genre of historical fiction, seeing herself as having passed the torch to male novelists who did not publicly acknowledge her influence.

In addition to Scott, this apparent quotation from Porter also names George Payne Rainsford James (1801–60), a prolific historical novelist. James had been nicknamed the Solitary Horseman, 'because so many of his novels opened with a lone rider dramatically galloping into the foreground'.[51] He prided himself on historical accuracy, quoting directly from sources to add veracity to his fictional work. Though his name, too, is now lost in the literary record, the anecdote adds evidence to the case that Porter believed it crucial to highlight (here more indirectly) the ways that male authors had stolen her literary thunder, whereas for Litchfield, it was most important to highlight Porter in a line of female predecessors. Porter seems to present herself as the rightful and neglected progenitor to a march of male British worthies. Litchfield imagines her as an original literary force with one equally neglected 'foremother'. In these separate moves, each was working to brand – and hand down to posterity – Porter's work in different and perhaps even competing ways.

It is easy to imagine the bind that Porter must have been in. To acknowledge Lee's contributions would have meant that any of Porter's claims to having created a 'new species of writing' would be rendered suspect. But for Porter to suggest that she was the mother of the *sons* of the historical novel would put her work at the pinnacle of what had, by the end of this period, become the most respected work in the genre. Feminist critics some years ago identified and named the modesty topos in the history of British women's writing – the apologies for the weaknesses of one's work – and taught us to view such formulaic statements with scepticism, rather than to accept them as heartfelt sentiments. With Porter, we may have a window opened onto another strain of rhetoric, also likely used to win an audience. We might call this the self-assurance topos, and Jane Porter was not its only practitioner. Some of her female contemporaries, including Sydney Owenson, Lady Morgan, and Harriet Lee, made their own claims of generic originality, with varying degrees of success.[52] In her 1832 introduction to the Standard Novels edition of *The Canterbury Tales*, Harriet Lee (sister of Sophia) wrote that she hoped that she 'may be permitted to observe' that the work she did was 'a novelty in the fictions of the day'. She notes that innumerable tales 'of the same stamp, and adapted in the same manner, have since appeared'. Though she modestly claims that she does not presume to compete with them in merit, she concludes, 'I think I may fairly claim priority of design and style.'[53] The self-assurance topos would seem ripe to appear during an era in which the professional woman novelist experienced a great rise in popularity and status, followed by an equally great and precipitous fall. In this innovation, at any rate, Jane Porter seems inarguably at the forefront.

Notes

1. Cheryl Turner, *Living by the Pen: Women Writers in the Eighteenth Century* (London: Routledge, 1992), p. 2.
2. There is, to date, no book-length study of either Porter sister.
3. See Ian Dennis, *Nationalism and Desire in Early Historical Fiction* (New York: St Martin's Press, 1997); Fiona Price, 'Resisting "The Spirit of Innovation": The Other Historical Novel and Jane Porter', *Modern Language Review*, 101 (2006), 638–51; Gary Kelly, 'Introduction', *Jane Porter's the Scottish Chiefs*, Vol. 4. *Varieties of Female Gothic* (London: Pickering and Chatto, 2002); and Thomas McLean, 'Nobody's Argument: Jane Porter and the Historical Novel', *Journal for Early Modern Cultural Studies*, 7 (2007), 88–103.
4. McLean, 'Nobody's Argument', p. 98.

5. See Clara Tuite, 'Historical Fiction', in *Companion to Women's Historical Writing*, ed. by Mary Spongberg, Ann Curthoys, and Barbara Caine (New York: Palgrave Macmillan, 2005), pp. 240–8 (p. 241).

6. See Katie Trumpener, *Bardic Nationalism: The Romantic Novel and the British Empire* (Princeton: Princeton University Press, 1997); Anne Stevens, 'Tales of Other Times: A Survey of British Historical Fiction, 1770–1812', *Cardiff Corvey: Reading the Romantic Text* 7 (December 2001) <http://www.cf.ac.uk/ encap/corvey/articles/cc07_n03.html> [accessed 19 January 2008].

7. See Georg Lukács, *The Historical Novel*, trans. Hannah and Stanley Mitchell (Lincoln: University of Nebraska Press, 1983).

8. See Diana Wallace, *The Woman's Historical Novel: British Women Writers, 1900–2000* (New York: Palgrave Macmillan, 2005), p. 3.

9. 'Comments of a Reader: The Writings of Mrs. Ratcliffe', *The Olio, or Museum of Entertainment* 6 (1830), p. 329.

10. See Peter Garside, 'Walter Scott and the "Common" Novel, 1808–1819', *Cardiff Corvey: Reading the Romantic Text*, 3 (September 1999) <http://www.cf.ac.uk/ encap/romtext/articles/cc03_n02.html> [accessed 4 May 2008].

11. Terry Lovell, *Consuming Fiction* (New York: Verso, 1987).

12. 'Novels of the Season', *The Monthly Review, Or, Literary Journal*, IX (1828), 311.

13. Review of *Reginald Dalton* [by John Gibson Lockhart], *Monthly Review*, 2nd series, 103 (February 1824), 200. Such an assertion was by no means original to this reviewer. See Ina Ferris, *The Achievement of Literary Authority: Gender, History, and the Waverley Novels* (Ithaca: Cornell University Press, 1991), particularly chapters 1 and 3. See also Stuart Curran, 'Romantic Poetry: The I Altered', in *Romanticism and Feminism*, ed. by Anne K. Mellor (Bloomington: Indiana University Press, 1988), pp. 185–207.

14. These women are Maria Edgeworth (1768–1849), Jane Austen (1775–1817), Elizabeth Benger (bap. 1775–1827), Sydney Owenson, Lady Morgan (bap. 1783–1859), Jane West (1758–1852), Mary Brunton (1778–1818), and Amelia Opie (1769–1853). 'Review of *Reginald Dalton*', p. 200.

15. Though beyond the scope of this chapter, it is important to note that both sisters published anonymous short and full-length fiction, as well as work under their own names in other genres, including poetry, drama, and non-fiction, from the 1790s to the 1830s. On the publication history and circumstances of *Duke Christian of Luneburg*, see my chapter in *Women Writers and Old Age in Great Britain, 1750–1850* (Baltimore: Johns Hopkins University Press, 2008).

16. *Thaddeus of Warsaw* went through at least 84 nineteenth-century editions and printings, while *The Scottish Chiefs* went through roughly 75 editions and printings; see Michael Adams, 'Jane Porter', in *Dictionary of Literary Biography: British Romantic Novelists, 1789–1832*, ed. by Bradford K. Mudge, vol. 116 (Detroit: Gale Research, 1992), pp. 264–270 (p. 264). Even *The Pastor's Fire-Side* (1817) enjoyed some thirteen editions by 1892; see Ann H. Jones, *Ideas and Innovation: Best Sellers of Jane Austen's Age* (New York: AMS Press, 1986), p. 136.

17. See 'Standard Novels' [Advertisement], in *Journey to the North of India by Arthur Connolly*, 2nd edn, 2 vols (London: Richard Bentley, 1838), I, 30.

18. 'Novels of the Season', p. 314.

19. See 'Review of *The Hungarian Brothers* by Anna Maria Porter', *Critical Review* 13 (April 1808), 443.
20. The 'novels' were actually collections of several tales, each sister contributing half the contents, publishing them as one long work. In this choice, too, the Porters followed Harriet and Sophia Lee, who had published a collaborative novella collection, *The Canterbury Tales* (1797–1805).
21. 'Novels of the Season', p. 311.
22. See E.M. Foster, *The Duke of Clarence. An Historical Novel*, 4 vols (London: William Lane, at the Minerva-Press, 1795) and *Jaquelina of Hainault: An Historical Novel*, 3 vols (London: J. Bell, 1798); *Charles Dacres: or, The Voluntary Exile. An Historical Novel, Founded on Facts*, 2 vols (Edinburgh: John Moir, 1797), p. xi.
23. See *The Count de Rethel: An Historical Novel. Taken from the French*, 3 vols (London: T. Hookham, 1779); Louis-Adrien Du Perron de Castera, *The Lady's Philosopher's Stone; or, The Caprices of Love and Destiny: An Historical Novel*, trans from French (London: D. Browne, Junr.; and S. Chapman, 1725); and Claudine Alexandrine Guérin de Tencin, *The Siege of Calais by Edward of England. An Historical Novel*, trans. from French (London: T. Woodward and Paul Vaillant, 1740).
24. On the eighteenth-century novel, genre, and historical change, see Miriam Burstein, *Narrating Women's History in Britain, 1770–1902* (Aldershot: Ashgate, 2004); Lennard J. Davis, *Factual Fictions: The Origins of the English Novel* (New York: Columbia University Press, 1983); J. Paul Hunter, *Before Novels: The Cultural Contexts of Eighteenth-Century English Fiction* (New York: W.W. Norton, 1990); D.R. Woolf, 'Jane Austen and History Revisited: The Past, Gender, and Memory from the Restoration to *Persuasion*', *Persuasions*, 26 (2004), 217–36; and Everett Zimmerman, *Boundaries of Fiction: History and the Eighteenth-Century Novel* (Ithaca: Cornell University Press, 1996).
25. One notable example of historical fiction that pre-dates Porter's is Sophia Lee's *The Recess* (1783–85), discussed later in this chapter.
26. Gary Kelly, 'Introduction', *Jane Porter's The Scottish Chiefs*, p. vii.
27. McLean, 'Nobody's Argument', p. 99.
28. *Thaddeus of Warsaw*, 4 vols, 4th edn (London: Longman, Hurst, Rees, and Orme, 1806), pp. 185–6. Subsequent references will be cited parenthetically in the text.
29. 'The Author to Her Friendly Readers', *Thaddeus of Warsaw* [...] *New Edition, Revised, Corrected, and Illustrated with an Introduction, Notes, by the Author* (London: Henry Colburn and Richard Bentley, 1832), p. xiv.
30. Price, 'Resisting "The Spirit of Innovation"', p. 640.
31. *The Hungarian Brothers*, 3 vols (London: Longman, Hurst, Rees and Orme, 1807), II, 200. Subsequent citations are given in parentheses in the text.
32. Her public statements to this effect are remarkable for many reasons, and some of them are tracked in McLean, 'Nobody's Argument'. To this day, her claims, when not dismissed outright, are gently ridiculed. See, for instance, Dennis, *Nationalism and Desire*, p. 9. The ways in which Scott's claims to originality have been and continue to be treated would provide an interesting study in contrasts.
33. 'Memoirs of Miss Porter', *Monthly Mirror*, 8 (1810), 403.

34. See (HL, POR 819) Jane Porter Papers, Huntington Library, San Marino, CA, quoted by permission. Subsequent references to this collection are cited parenthetically in the text as HL, followed by collection abbreviation (POR) and item number. Anna Maria felt that Scott had 'struck out' to create *Ivanhoe* after reading her 'poor work', *The Knight of St. John*. In particular, she believes that the Waverley author took her narrative workings of a Jew and a knight in crafting his own characters. Interestingly, she also believes that it cannot be just one person, Scott, writing these novels but that it must be a 'manufactory' or a 'firm of writers' (HL, POR 819).

35. Ferris, *The Achievement of Literary Authority*, p. 83. Jane Porter initially recommends *Waverley* to a friend of Anna Maria's, telling her that 'if she does not read "Waverley" before I see her again, I shall think her so great an insensible that I would doom her ever afterwards to read nothing but [Hannah More's] Coelebs [*in Search of a Wife*] for the rest of her life' (HL, POR 1702). After reading *Guy Mannering*, Jane Porter's appreciation does not waver: 'The more I read men's works of this kind, the more I am convinced that theirs is the province of observation, woman's of imagination', she tells her sister (HL, POR 1703).

36. Anna Maria Porter felt that Southey's *Roderick the Last of the Goths* (1814) 'rifled' her *Don Sebastian, or The House of Braganza: An Historical Romance* (1809). Her response to this to her sister, in a line that is surely tongue-in-cheek, is 'see what it is, to be an obscure novelist?'

37. Jane Porter refers to Southey's *Roderick the Last of the Goths* (1814) and, like her sister, believes he has stolen material from Anna Maria's *Don Sebastian* as well as her own *Scottish Chiefs* (1810).

38. April Alliston, 'Lee, Sophia Priscilla (*bap.* 1750, *d.* 1824)', *Oxford Dictionary of National Biography*, Oxford University Press, 2004 <http://www.oxforddnb.com/view/article/16311>. It is Harriet, not Sophia, whose name appears in Jane Porter's letters, but it seems safe to assume that the Porters would have been familiar with *The Recess*. On *The Recess* as the first historical novel, see Devendra Varma's introduction to Sophia Lee, *The Recess: Or A Tale of Other Times*, 3 vols (New York: Arno Press, 1972). See also April Alliston, *Virtue's Faults: Correspondences in Eighteenth-Century British and French Women's Fiction* (Stanford: Stanford University Press, 1996); and Jayne Elizabeth Lewis, '"Ev'ry Lost Relation": Historical Fictions and Sentimental Incidents in Sophia Lee's The Recess', *Eighteenth-Century Fiction*, 7 (1995), 165–84. In her 'Preface' to *The Canterbury Tales*, by Sophia and Harriet Lee (London: Colburn and Bentley, 1832), p. vi, Harriet Lee claims that her late sister's *The Recess* was 'the first English romance that blended interesting fiction with historical events and characters, embellishing both with picturesque description'. Lee indicates that she believes *Cleveland* (1731–39) by Abbé Prévost 'had precedence of all'.

39. See Ina Ferris, *The Romantic National Tale and the Question of Ireland* (Cambridge: Cambridge University Press, 2002), and Nicola Watson, *Revolution and the Form of the British Novel, 1790–1825* (Oxford: Oxford University Press, 1994), particularly chapter 3.

40. Billie Melman, *The Culture of History: English Uses of the Past, 1800–1953* (Oxford: Oxford University Press, 2006), p. 13; Tuite, 'Historical Fiction', p. 241.

41. See McLean, 'Nobody's Argument'.
42. 'Review of Jane Porter's *Duke Christian of Luneburg*', *La Belle Assemblée*, n.s. 29 (April 1824), 170–1. Porter herself was a contributor to *La Belle Assemblée*. See Thomas McLean, 'Jane Porter's Later Works, 1826–1846', *Harvard Library Bulletin*, forthcoming 2010.
43. 'The Author to Her Friendly Readers', p. vi.
44. Quoted in Ian Watt, *The Rise of the Novel* (Berkeley: University of California Press, 1957), p. 208.
45. Horace Walpole, *The Castle of Otranto*, ed. by Michael Gamer (Harmondsworth: Penguin, 2001), p. 13.
46. Peter Puff, 'Letters to Certain Persons: Epistle I: To Miss Jane Porter', *The Aberdeen Magazine* (October 1831), 552, 553. I thank Thomas McLean for bringing this piece to my attention.
47. Henry Bulwer Lytton, *The Monarchy of the Middle Classes*, 2 vols (London: Richard Bentley, 1836), I, 21.
48. Quoted in E.J. Clery and Robert Miles, eds, *Gothic Documents: A Sourcebook, 1700–1820* (New York: St Martin's, 2000), p. 274.
49. Litchfield's novel was *Warkworth Castle: A Historical Romance*, 3 vols (London: T.C. Newby, 1851). He writes in his published preface that he had intended to dedicate the novel to Jane Porter but that her death prevented it.
50. Letter from Thomas Litchfield to Jane Porter (18 May 1849), Jane Porter Papers, Pforzheimer Collection, New York Public Library. References are courtesy of the Carl H. Pforzheimer Collection of Shelley and His Circle, The New York Public Library, Astor, Lenox and Tilden Foundations.
51. Stephanie L. Barczewski, 'James, George Payne Rainsford (1801–1860)', *Oxford Dictionary of National Biography*, Oxford University Press, 2004 <http://www.oxforddnb.com/view/article/14605>.
52. On Morgan's claims to have been a trailblazer in historical fiction, see McLean, 'Nobody's Argument', p. 96. On Lee's claims for innovation in 'Tales', see her 'Preface' and see Anne Mellor, 'A Novel of Their Own: Romantic Women's Fiction, 1790–1830', in *The Columbia History of the British Novel* (New York: Columbia University Press, 1994).
53. Lee, 'Preface', p. viii.

12
Joanna Baillie's Emblematic Theatre

Betsy Bolton

Joanna Baillie, best known as the author of the *Series of Plays: in which it is attempted to delineate the stronger passions of the mind, each passion being the subject of a tragedy and a comedy* (1798–1812), was at once the most respected female dramatist of the early nineteenth century and perhaps the most under-staged. The *British Critic* called her 'one of the brightest luminaries of the present period', and the *Critical Review*, comparing her work with Shakespeare's, agreed that 'Miss Baillie's dramatic powers are of the highest order'.[1] Yet of Baillie's twenty-six plays, only seven were produced during her lifetime, and those achieved at best a moderate success. Thus despite her insistence that she wrote to be performed, Baillie was frequently read as a closet dramatist, a literary figure rather than a playwright. Recent critics, however, have emphasized Baillie's intense theatrical investments, including the way many of her plays specialize in particular theatrical techniques: the use of closet spaces to evoke closet theatre, tableaux displays, mini-dramas foregrounding metatheatrical concerns, and so on.[2] Alan Richardson, addressing the 'neural' theatre of Baillie's plays, highlights a particular use of spectacle, arguing that in Baillie's tragedy of love, 'Basil's inanimate body provides a grisly emblem, as the action closes, of the corporeality that the play has insisted upon all along.' Richardson is most interested in linking Baillie's drama to 'the embodied approach to mind being worked out in Romantic brain science'[3]; I want to suggest the centrality of emblems to Baillie's theatre practice.

Emblem and allegory

In pursuing the emblematic qualities of Baillie's drama, we might consider an analogy between Baillie's *Series of Plays concerning the Passions* and Walter Benjamin's analysis of the *Trauerspiel* in *The Origin of German Tragic Drama*.[4] The historical and geographical distance separating German Baroque tragedy from British Romantic drama allows only a loose comparison of the two forms, but reference to Benjamin's analysis may help unify various paradoxical facets of Baillie's dramatic practice which have been discussed in relative isolation until now: the readerly quality of her plays *and* their insistence on spectacle, their moral investments *and* the cruelty through which those moral investments are pursued, Baillie's meliorative intentions in contrast to her plays' unremitting focus on mental pathology. Even the complex class, gender, and sexual politics of Baillie's plays may come into sharper focus against a more unified backdrop.

British Romantic poetry is more commonly associated with symbolism than allegory, yet the power and difficulty of Baillie's work become more apparent when seen through an allegorical lens. For Benjamin, the *Trauerspiel* registers the theological crisis of its historical moment: the Reformation's attack on good works produces a radical disjunction between the spirit and the material world. This theological situation produces a drama constructed not of symbols, but of allegory: 'Whereas in the symbol destruction is idealized and the transfigured face of nature is fleetingly revealed in the light of redemption, in allegory the observer is confronted with the *facies hippocratica* of history as a petrified, primordial landscape'.[5] Baillie, two centuries later, presents us with a view of human nature as both primordial, constituted by all-powerful archaic passions, and as petrified, fixed and frozen in obsessive forms. For Benjamin, Baroque nature bears the weight of history; in Baillie's work, we see the traces of history even in her insistence that she portrays only human nature.

Baillie's own historical moment contained its own crises: the French Revolution, questions of universal (male) suffrage, changing roles for women. Baillie's work has been read both as a commentary on shifting class relations and as a conservative response to revolutionary ferment; gender politics perhaps inevitably inform the larger political framework of the plays.[6] Baillie's first volume of plays appeared in 1798, the year William Godwin's well-intentioned but scandalous memoir of Mary Wollstonecraft put Wollstonecraft and her *Vindication* of women's rights beyond the social pale.[7] The third volume of the *Series* appeared in 1812, the same year Anna Barbauld published her ambitious 'Eighteen Hundred and Eleven' and was denounced by Croker for failing to realize that 'the empire might have been saved without the intervention of a lady author'.[8] Baillie herself noted of her public reception that 'John *any-body* would have stood higher with the critics than Joanna Baillie.'[9] The women in Baillie's dramas often exemplify the horrific results of what poet Mary Robinson called 'female subordination' or else they quietly rule the men ostensibly ruling them.[10]

While Baillie's 'Introductory Discourse' to her *Series of Plays* stressed the potential moral and political benefits of drama, her ambitions have been framed repeatedly by the medical fame of her brother and uncles.[11] Similarly, Benjamin argues that for a generation of Baroque dramatists, 'the moral intention of the Renaissance poets was complemented by a scientific intention'. The result, as in Baillie's drama, was that 'the representation of the emotions is emphasized increasingly at the expense of a firmly defined action'.[12] Indeed, while Baroque drama indulged in an extravagance of passionate excess, Baillie emphasized the slow and gradual development of fixed (and pathologically extreme) emotional states. Most pertinent for a grasp of Baillie's dramaturgy, however, is Benjamin's account of the allegorist's didactic control of the emblem:

> It is indeed characteristic of the sadist that he humiliates his object and then – or thereby – satisfies it. And that is what the allegorist does in this age drunk with acts of cruelty both real and imagined. [...] The emblematist does not present the essence implicitly 'behind the image'. He drags the essence of what is depicted out before the image, in writing, as a caption, such as, in the emblem-books, forms an intimate part of what is depicted. Basically, then, the *Trauerspiel* [...] is, in its form, a drama for the reader. Although this says nothing about the value or the possibility of its stage-performance. But it does make it clear that the chosen spectator of such examples of the *Trauerspiel* concentrated on them with at least the same thought and attentiveness as the reader.[13]

Benjamin's approach to the emblem unites the elements of cruelty or sadism with a focus on readerly drama, joining two apparently divergent facets of Baillie's own work, allowing us to link Baillie's 'neural theatre' (Richardson) and 'pathology of the passions' (Burwick) with her 'theatre of cruelty' (Myers); her critique of the Romantic stage (Burroughs) with her emphasis on spectacle (Cox, Kucich).[14]

Baillie's contemporaries implicitly grasped the emblematic quality of her work, and the challenge posed for stage production. Francis Jeffrey, Baillie's most influential early critic, complained that Baillie was, like an emblematist, 'a little too eager to obtrude' her 'moral lessons' upon the notice of her audience. His specific complaints against *Ethwald* encompass both the cruelty and the readerly quality described by Benjamin: Jeffrey moves rapidly from noting that 'There is a good deal too much fighting and slaughtering in these tragedies' to complaining that 'The story goes on a great deal too slowly and it goes on a great deal too long.'[15] Elizabeth Inchbald – actress, dramatist, and critic herself – privately found Baillie's *De Monfort* flat onstage, yet maintained her enthusiasm for the play as written: 'its very charm in the reading militates against its power in the acting'.[16] Baillie's drama demands readerly attention.

Objections to Baillie's dramatic method intensified in response to her comedies – in part, I would argue, because her emblematic method is more at odds with the conventions of comedy. When *The Election* was staged as a musical drama in 1817, William Hazlitt complained that Baillie's handling of her characters 'makes moral puppets of them'; she 'pulls the wires, and they talk virtue and act vice, according to their cue [...] not from any real passions of their own'.[17] (Shorn of condescension, the description might be apt: Benjamin identified puppet-theatre as a legitimate offspring of the *Trauerspiel*.) But Baillie is more interested in form than character: staging the purification of comedy, its abjection of deceit and disrespect, Baillie's *Election* enacts the changes required to make comedy a moral and implicitly political form. While Jeffrey argued against the systematic 'trammel[ing]' of drama by such moral constraints, Baillie's comedy remains theatrically focused and informed, recalling the strategies of contemporary female playwrights. Elizabeth Inchbald remarked of Baillie's *De Monfort* that 'no one critic so good as herself has ever written a play half so good at the following tragedy', and the same might be said of its comic partner *The Election*.[18] Reading Baillie's comedy through its allegorizing of theatrical concerns helps clarify both the respect her plays achieved and the difficulties she experienced in staging them.

Allegorizing comic form: *The Election*

Baillie's plot encapsulates the historical drama of shifting class boundaries. Baltimore, a country gentleman of decayed fortune, opposes Freeman, a wealthy clothier, in the local election. Having bought most of Baltimore's ancestral lands, Freeman, naively ostentatious, offends Baltimore with friendly gestures. Despite his hatred for the man, Baltimore saves Freeman from drowning, but Freeman's wife then stoops to buying Baltimore's debts in order to have him jailed during the election. Freeman attempts a rapprochement, then pays Baltimore's debts anonymously and sacrifices the election to his opponent. Still, in the fifth act, egged on by solicitors, Freeman and Baltimore are about to duel with pistols; the duel is prevented only at the last moment by the revelation that the two men unwittingly share a father, and that their mothers treated each other with gracious liberality. The 'triumph' over Baltimore's unreasoning hatred is based on the female solidarity of the previous generation, replicated in the present day by the friendship between Baltimore's young wife and Freeman's daughter, Charlotte, who knew each other at school.

As *De Monfort* is the play which most nearly encapsulates Baillie's model of tragedy, so its partner *The Election* enacts her reform of comedy in almost every point. The first three acts offer up distinct episodes of lying, deceit, mockery of age, and domestic authority – all standard procedures of eighteenth-century comedy – only to insist on the pernicious effects, within the play, of each of these strategies. Baltimore's servant Peter, for instance, specializes in lying to his master with stories ridiculing Baltimore's hated rival. At first rewarded for his fictions, he glories in feeding his master's low desires: 'Fiddle faddle with all that! Do you think one gets on the blind side of a man to treat him with respect?'[19] But Baltimore eventually discovers Peter's lies, shakes him in fury and throws him against a wall, after which Peter remarks ruefully, 'Well, I sees plainly enough that a body who tells lies should look two or three ways on every side of him before he begins' (p. 44). Without actually repenting of his actions or promising a fresh start, Peter nonetheless registers Baillie's comic abjection of lying: he vanishes from the play. And while other characters – notably solicitors – will lie later in the action, they profit no more than Peter from their deceit.

With the figure of Isabella Baltimore, Baillie struggles to distinguish mockery of a misguided passion from mockery of a person. When Isabella first discovers the depth of her husband's hatred for Mr Freeman, she repeatedly bursts into laughter. Her husband denounces his rival even to 'the very gait and shape of his legs' (pp. 9–10), and Isabella is startled into laughter, for she and others have noted a distinct resemblance between the two men. Baltimore responds to the idea of similarity even more ferociously – 'I could kick my own shins if I thought they had the smallest resemblance to his' (p. 10) – and Isabella responds by laughing once again at the excess of his passion. Sketching a kind of psychological laughing cure, Baillie's 'Introductory Discourse' had suggested that some individuals could be teased or mocked out of a fixed passion, though noting that such a strategy will frequently fail: 'to those with whom such dangerous enemies [as the passions] have long found shelter, exposing them in an absurd and ridiculous light, may be shooting a finely-pointed arrow against the hardened rock'.[20] Mrs Baltimore's laughter seems oddly involuntary as well as ineffective: she twice asserts the distressing reality of the situation yet also insists she could not help but laugh. Indeed, laugh she must: the incident not only underscores Baltimore's fixed passion, hatred; it also invites Isabella to disavow her involuntary mockery of age and domestic authority. When Baltimore remarks bitterly, 'I was a fool to expect a wife so many years younger than myself would have any sympathy with my feelings', his wife insists 'you wrong me, unkindly' (p. 12), and she is careful to refrain from laughing at him throughout the rest of the play. An idealized figure of feminine restraint, Isabella Baltimore seldom stumbles in the play, and her failing here is notably that of comedy itself: ridiculing absurdity when distress is also involved.

Indeed, Isabella's simple elegance and freedom from absurdity make her something like an embodiment of comedy: certainly, she is the comic character most like the exemplary Jane de Monfort – a role written expressly for Sarah Siddons, famously painted by Sir Joshua Reynolds in 1784 as the Muse of Tragedy. The similarity between the tragic Jane de Monfort and the comic Isabella Baltimore is underscored by a similar scene of closet instruction in both plays – a scene which further highlights the emblematic quality of both characters. Baillie's 'Introductory Discourse' argues that 'To Tragedy it belongs to lead them [great men] forward to our nearer regard', and Baillie pictures that intimacy most frequently as an entry into the great man's 'secret closet'.[21] In *De Monfort*, Jane explicitly claims the space of the closet for moral reform. Jane, having discovered with horror her brother's uncontrollable hatred of Rezenvelt, urges de Monfort,

> Come to my closet; free from all intrusion,
> I'll school thee there; and thou again shalt be
> My willing pupil and my generous friend.[22]

But the closet 'schooling' is less effective than Jane intends. De Monfort's intellectual grasp of the reading Jane sets him leaves him untouched morally and emotionally; his summary of his 'schooling' ends with the unrepentant demand, 'what is this to me?' (p. 348).

Conversely, the comic closet of *The Election* fails to reach one young man's mind. When Charles Baltimore, cousin to Mr Baltimore and raised in his house, comes to Isabella complaining of boredom, she tells him, 'try, for once in your life, what kind of a thing reading quietly for an hour to one's self may be'. Even though she suggests he'll gain 'some little insight into the affairs of mankind' through reading, he refuses (p. 47). As in *De Monfort*, Baillie carefully *stages* this rejection of closet instruction, giving extensive directions for Charles's fidgeting refusal to read.[23] Charles's effective resistance to achieving 'some little insight into the affairs of mankind' suggests he would take little moral benefit from a staged comedy either.

Young Charlotte, his pointedly named female counterpart, conversely seems eager to learn, though her reception of Mrs Baltimore's instruction also leaves something to be desired. Both Charlotte and Isabella see their relationship as educating Charlotte in a manner both natural and effortless. Mrs Baltimore tells her husband that Charlotte 'is a girl that will very much improve by any reasonable intimacy, and very soon become like the people she is with' (p. 55), and Charlotte remarks to her mentor that 'When I am with Mama, I think it will be so difficult to become amiable and accomplished [...]; but when I am with you, it appears so pleasant and so easy' (p. 52). Mrs Baltimore's promise to Charles of 'insight into the affairs of mankind' is implicitly on offer to Charlotte – not through reading, but through Mrs Baltimore's modelling of mature, restrained feminine behaviour. Charlotte, unlike Charles, hungers for the lessons Mrs Baltimore has to offer, but she understands those lessons only in the most superficial terms: 'Well, and if it depended upon me, [...] I should go wherever you go and do whatever you did, and wear the same caps and gowns that you wear, and look just as like you as I could' (p. 51). Baillie's 'Introductory Discourse' grants that 'the dress and the manners of men, rather than their characters and disposition are the subjects of our common conversation, and seem chiefly to occupy the multitude'. But Baillie also suggests that 'the multitude' can be led beyond this focus on caps and gowns, claiming that drama's appeal is always partly philosophical and psychological, feeding a deep hunger for self-knowledge, for 'a more enlarged and connected view' of 'the varieties of the human mind'.[24] Unlike Charles, Charlotte seems to register the multitude's capacity for deeper understanding, but we don't see her actually exhibiting the enlarged and connected view that Baillie promises her audience.

Rather, Baillie's Charlotte, embodying both the energy and the perils of childish rebellion, exemplifies both the appeal and the shortcomings of immature comedy. With support from the Baltimores, Charlotte provides 'that ambushed bush-fighting amongst closets, screens, chests, easy-chairs, and toilet-tables' which recalls the beating heart of youthful hide-and-seek.[25] Charlotte, having snuck into the house, is about to be caught by Baltimore in his wife's 'closet'; she hides or more specifically *'skulks behind the door of an open cabinet and Mrs. B stands up close by her to conceal her completely'* (p. 54). Eavesdroppers, of course, hear no good of themselves, and Baltimore proceeds to abuse Charlotte's behaviour to his wife. When Mrs Baltimore speaks up for her, Charlotte *'catches hold of Mrs. B's hand and kisses it'* (p. 54); and when Mrs Baltimore affirms her attachment to the girl, 'Charlotte, *behind, catches Mrs. B's hand again and kisses it very gratefully'* (p. 56).[26] But this dumb-show of affection between the two young women is merely prelude to a very different performance. Mr Baltimore, disgusted with his wife's disagreement,

> *turns upon his heel in anger to go away, whilst* Charlotte *springs from her hiding-place, and slipping softly after him, makes a motion with her foot as if she would give him a kick in the going out; upon which* Balt. *turns suddenly and sees her. She stops short quite confounded* [...]. Balt. *then turns upon his heel angrily and exit.* (p. 56)

Baillie seems to present Charlotte's action as simultaneously innocent, comic, and socially scandalous. The stage directions demurely confuse Baltimore's action of 'going out' with a periphrasis for buttocks (she 'gives him a kick in the "going out"'). Charlotte, telling her mother what happened, similarly searches for a polite expression:

> Charl.   (*much embarrassed.*) I did but give him a little make-believe kick with my slipper as he went out at the door. [...]
> Mrs. F.   A make-believe kick! what do you mean by that?
> Charl.   La! just a kick on— on—
> Mrs. F.   On what, child?
> Charl.   La! just upon his coat behind as he went out at the door.

> (p. 62)

Baillie writes both scenes to stress the unspeakable nature of Charlotte's target and action: Charlotte's embarrassment shows what happens when comic slapstick goes too far for maidenly mores, even if a kick in the 'going out' was mild indeed by the standards of the Samuel Foote farces Baillie herself enjoyed as a girl.

Charlotte's gesture here seems to encapsulate the mockery of domestic authority Baillie finds so pernicious in circumstantial comedy.[27] Refusing to underwrite such mockery, Baillie transforms the comic potential of the scene into sentimental reform. After Baltimore's departure, Charlotte exclaims, sobbing,

I shall never be able to look up again as long as I live. [...] I shall be
so scorn'd and laugh'd at! – I'll never enter this house any more –
Oh! – oh! oh! [...] I'll go home again and never come a visiting any
more. Oh! oh! oh! I am so disgraced!

(p. 57)

If Baltimore is proof against having his hatred exposed in a ridiculous
and absurd light, Charlotte is the model of how characters less fixed in
their ways respond to ridicule. If anything, she is excessively chastened:
grateful to Mrs Baltimore for her continued friendship, Charlotte can
only articulate her own self-loathing: 'It is so good in you to say that
you love me; for I shall never love myself any more' (p. 57). Even after
reflection, self-loathing remains dominant. She sees no possibility for
change – 'I know I shall be a blundering creature all my life, getting
into scrapes that no body else gets into; I know I shall' – and demands
of her mother and governess, 'Why need I study my carriage, and pin
back my shoulders, and hamper myself all day long, only to be laughed
at?' (p. 61) In short, why should Charlotte bother to grow up? Or, in this
allegory of comic form, why should circumstantial comedy, with all its
immature delights, bother to mature into characteristic comedy?

The Election answers this last question only indirectly by bringing
Charlotte back on stage as a part of the final, semi-political denouement.
After her humiliated self-chastening, Charlotte vanishes from the play,
to reappear only in the last scene, brought forward as ever by Isabella
Baltimore. In the meantime, the antagonism between Baltimore and
Freeman has been brought to a boil by their corrupt solicitors, and a
duel between the antagonists averted only by Truebridge's news that
they share a father. That fact alone, however, would not have brought
the two men together. Freeman's first response is outrage on his mother's
behalf: 'She was seduced and betray'd?' The resolution of conflict thus
depends upon the quiet heroism of both mothers:

True.　The late Mrs. Baltimore discovered [Freeman's mother] some
　　　years afterwards, sympathized with her misfortune, and from
　　　her own pin-money, for the family affairs were even then very
　　　much involved, paid her a yearly sum for the support and
　　　education of her son, which laid the foundation of his future
　　　wealth and prosperity.

Balt.　(*stepping forth with emotion.*) Did my mother do this?

True.　Yes, Baltimore, she did; till Mrs. Freeman, informed of the state
　　　of your father's affairs, [...] toiled day and night to support the

aspiring views of her son, independent of a bounty which she would no longer receive, tho' it was often and warmly press'd upon her.

Free. (*with emotion.*) And did my mother do this?

(pp. 101–2)

Symmetry and female heroism matter more than male autonomy in this conclusion: the men move forward by identifying with their mothers. Truebridge's phrasing – 'the family affairs were even then very much involved' – suggests the overlapping of patriarchal and matrilineal stories here. The failure of patriarchy, the Baltimores' lost fortunes, is expressed through this phrase, this 'involvement' of family affairs; yet the success of the two mothers, working to aid each other, is also clearly confirmed here, as their joint involvement in this affair of the family is finally recognized.

Revising the form of the patriarchal family, Baillie also returns to her reform of comedy. Once Baltimore and Freeman have made their peace as brothers, the women reappear to corroborate the peace. Welcoming Freeman as her brother and reconciling graciously with Mrs Freeman, Mrs Baltimore exclaims, 'But there is something wanting for me still' (p. 106). Predictably, that 'something' is the reconciliation of Charlotte with her 'uncle' Baltimore, now the MP for the borough. In her theatre theory, Baillie asserts that the man schooled by her psychologically 'characteristic' drama 'will prove for it the better Judge, the better Magistrate, the better Advocate: and as a ruler or conductor of other men, under every occurring circumstance, he will find himself the better enabled to fulfil his duty, and accomplish his designs'.[28] A reformed ruler of other men, Baltimore as newly elected lawmaker binds himself in this final scene to 'cheerfully submit to whatever correction' Charlotte, a similarly reformed figure of comedy, 'may think proper to inflict upon [him]' (p. 107). Baillie's narrative resolution submits her ruling men to the behavioural model of their mothers and the formal control of a feminized comedy.

Baillie's insistent allegory of dramatic form results most clearly in 'a drama for the reader'; using Benjamin's framework to explore that drama emphasizes its historical investments, even as reading *The Election* in relation to contemporary women's comedies highlights its theatrical self-consciousness. Jeffrey's implied moral critique, for instance, questioning *The Election*'s inclusion of illegitimacy, might remind us of a far more scandalous example: Elizabeth Inchbald's highly successful *Lovers' Vows* (1798), loosely translated from Kotzebue, which outrageously presented a Baron marrying the maidservant he had seduced and abandoned twenty years earlier. The moral outrage which greeted *Lovers' Vows* had focused on the immorality of the fallen woman; publishing *The Election* a mere four years later, Baillie skates over the question of the woman 'seduced and betray'd': 'We will not, if you please, enter into that part of the story at present' (p. 101). Baillie straightforwardly presents Mrs Freeman's morals through her maternal labours and her collaboration with the gentlewoman who married her son's father: her sexual fall is only relevant, ironically, because it establishes closer bonds between rivals, transforming the cantankerous gentleman and tradesman into brothers. As a commentary on the furore created by Inchbald's scandalous but successful comedy, the resolution of *The Election* is far sharper than has yet been recognized.

Tenuously balanced at the intersection of poetry, science, and (political) history, Baillie's drama has an allegorical force inseparable from its gendered investments. In place of the transcendent Wordsworthian sublime or the organic form Coleridge attributed to the symbol, Baillie quietly accumulates allegorical fragments, sketching the historical ruins of patriarchal power. 'For it is common practice in the literature of the baroque to pile up fragments ceaselessly, [...] to take the repetition of stereotypes for a process of intensification.'[29] The artifice of Baillie's conclusion draws attention to her non-naturalistic intentions throughout the play. The problem posed by *The Election* – Baltimore's hatred of Freeman – is persuasive primarily as a statement of class relations, and its resolution comes, as Benjamin describes in the *Trauerspiel*, 'in a flash, like the appearance of the print when a page is turned'. But if Benjamin's emblematist 'drags the essence of what is depicted out before the image', 'humiliat[ing] his object and then – or thereby – satisfy[ing] it',[30] Baillie as emblematist insists on the inseparability of image and essence, character and theatrical form. In *The Election*, Charlotte's humiliation fuses her character with the essence of comic form, devaluing the particularities of her individual character while empowering a feminized vision of comedy. Charlotte's humiliation at the Baltimores' transforms her into an emblem of comic correction and constraint; having chastened herself, she is authorized by her identification with comedy to monitor others' behaviour. By contrast, her male counterpart, Charles, remains pointedly impervious to insight, even in the last scene.

Baillie's fusion of character and comic form allows for a striking inversion of social structure, as an older male legislator 'submits' himself to the judgement of a young girl. On a larger scale, Baillie's career followed a trajectory not unlike that created for her character. Like Charlotte, Baillie suffered 'humiliation', describing 'the mortification' of discovering that as her plays 'are not acted in the London Theatres, they are considered as not adapted to representation',[31] only to find herself transformed into a potent emblem of drama per se. Hannah Cowley and Elizabeth Inchbald enjoyed far more commercial and professional success than Baillie, but Baillie, her works seldom staged, became the genius of drama, the Shakespeare of the age. Inchbald's preface to Baillie's *De Monfort* quietly draws attention to the critics' construction of Baillie as emblem of dramatic genius: 'Amongst the many female writers of this and other nations, how few have arrived at the elevated character of a woman of genius! The authoress of "De Monfort" received that rare distinction, upon this her first publication' (p. 3). Inchbald carefully refrains from joining the emblematizing chorus: drawing attention to the host of female writers not yet granted 'the elevated character of a woman of genius', Inchbald goes on to treat Baillie as a promising playwright rather than an established genius. For *Blackwood's* and others, however, Baillie's failure to attain success onstage paradoxically confirmed her intimate power over 'the heart and mind' of her readers, her command over 'the poetic literature of our nation'.[32] Allegorizing drama's historical investments, Baillie's career offers its own allegory of the female playwright at the turn of the century.

Notes

1. 'Miss J. Baillie's *Series of Plays. Vol. II'*, *British Critic*, 20 (1802), 194; 'Miss Baillie's *Series of Plays'*, *Critical Review*, 37 (February 1803), 212. Poet and dramatist, Joanna Baillie (1762–1851) was daughter to a Presbyterian minister and scholar of divinity as well as niece and sister to three eminent medical researchers and royal physicians; her sister-in-law was a published poet. Living quietly on the outskirts of London with her mother and sister, Baillie theorized a model of drama based on pathological states of emotion; her work and character were admired by all the leading literary figures of the day.
2. See especially Catherine Burroughs, *Closet Stages: Joanna Baillie and the Theater Theory of British Romantic Women Writers* (Philadelphia: University of Pennsylvania Press, 1997); Thomas Crochunis, ed., *Joanna Baillie, Romantic Dramatist: Critical Essays* (New York: Routledge, 2004); and Marjean Purinton, 'Women's Sovereignty on Trial: Joanna Baillie's Comedy *The Tryal* as Metatheatrics', in *Women in British Romantic Theatre: Drama, Performance, and Society, 1790–1840*, ed. by Catherine Burroughs (Cambridge: Cambridge University Press, 2000), pp. 132–57.
3. Alan Richardson, 'A Neural Theatre: Joanna Baillie's Plays on the Passions', in, *Joanna Baillie, Romantic Dramatist*, ed. by Crochunis pp. 145, 140.

4. Walter Benjamin, *The Origin of German Tragic Drama*, trans. John Osborne (New York: Verso, 1985).
5. Ibid., p. 166.
6. See Daniel Watkins, '"The Gait Disturb'd of Wealthy, Honour'd Men": Joanna Baillie's *De Monfort*', in his *A Materialist Critique of English Romantic Drama* (Gainesville, FL: University Press of Florida, 1993), pp. 39–59; Jeffrey Cox, 'Baillie, Siddons, Larpent: Gender, Power, and Politics in the Theatre of Romanticism', in *Women in British Romantic Theatre*, ed. by Burroughs, pp. 23–47.
7. William Godwin, *Memoirs of the Author of A Vindication of the Rights of Woman* (London: J. Johnson, 1798).
8. John Wilson Croker, *Quarterly Review*, 7 (1812), 309.
9. Joanna Baillie, *The Collected Letters of Joanna Baillie*, ed. by Judith Slagle, 2 vols (Cranbury, NJ: Associated University Presses, 1999), I, 439.
10. Mary Robinson, writing as Anne Frances Randall, *A Letter to the Women of England, on the Injustice of Mental Subordination* (London: Longman and Rees, 1799).
11. Joanna Baillie, 'Introductory Discourse', *A Series of Plays in which it is attempted to delineate the Stronger Passions: each Passion being the Subject of a Tragedy and a Comedy*, 3 vols (London: T. Cadell and W. Davies, 1798–1812), I, 1–72. For medical connections, see especially Dorothy McMillan, 'Dr Baillie', in *1798: The Year of the Lyrical Ballads*, ed. by Richard Cronin (New York: St. Martin's, 1998), pp. 68–92; Richardson, 'A Neural Theatre'; and Frederick Burwick, 'Joanna Baillie, Matthew Baillie, and the Pathology of the Passions', in *Joanna Baillie, Romantic Dramatist*, ed. by Crochunis, pp. 48–68.
12. Benjamin, *The Origin of German Tragic Drama*, p. 99.
13. Ibid., p. 185.
14. See, in addition to those already cited, Victoria Myers, 'Joanna Baillie's Theatre of Cruelty', in *Joanna Baillie, Romantic Dramatist*, ed. by Crochunis, pp. 87–107; Jeffrey Cox, 'Staging Baillie', in ibid., pp. 146–67; Greg Kucich, 'Joanna Baillie and the restaging of history and gender', in ibid., pp. 108–29.
15. Francis Jeffrey, *Edinburgh Review*, 4 (July 1803), 277, 279–80.
16. Elizabeth Inchbald, quoted in James Boaden, *Memoirs of Mrs. Inchbald*, 2 vols (London: Bentley, 1833), II, 34.
17. William Hazlitt, *The Complete Works of William Hazlitt*, ed. by P.P. Howe, 21 vols (London: J.M. Dent, 1930–34), V, 147.
18. Elizabeth Inchbald, ed., 'Remarks' [on *De Monfort*], in *The British Theatre, or, A Collection of Plays*, 25 vols (London: Longman, Hurst, Rees, and Orme, 1808), XXIV, 3. Baillie's De Monfort is an aristocrat defined by his uncontrollable hatred for his bourgeois rival, Rezenvelt. Unable to escape Rezenvelt's presence or overcome his hatred, and spurred on by the mistaken belief that his rival is engaged to De Monfort's own sister Jane, De Monfort eventually kills Rezenvelt and then, shut up with the corpse of his victim, dies himself in remorse.
19. Joanna Baillie, *The Election*, in *A Series of Plays* (1802), II, 1–108. Subsequent references are given parenthetically in the text.
20. Baillie, 'Introductory Discourse', p. 57.
21. Ibid., pp. 29, 31; see also pp. 11, 18.

22. Joanna Baillie, *De Monfort*, in *A Series of Plays* (1798), I, 344. Subsequent references are given parenthetically in the text.
23. See Burroughs, *Closet Stages*, p. 130, for a less critical reading of Charles in this scene.
24. Baillie, 'Introductory Discourse', p. 3.
25. Ibid., p. 49.
26. See Purinton, 'The Sexual Politics of *The Election*: French Feminism and the Scottish Playwright Joanna Baillie', *Intertexts*, 2 (1998), 119–29, for a French feminist reading of this episode and relationship.
27. Baillie complains that circumstantial comedy's 'mockery of age and domestic authority [...] has a very bad effect on the younger part of an audience' ('Introductory Discourse', p. 49).
28. Baillie, 'Introductory Discourse', p. 15.
29. Benjamin, *The Origin of German Tragic Drama*, p. 178.
30. Ibid., p. 185.
31. Baillie, *Collected Letters*, p. 283.
32. *Blackwood's Edinburgh Magazine*, 16 (August, 1824), p. 162.

13
National Internationalism: Women's Writing and European Literature, 1800–30

Diego Saglia

Woman and the nation constitute a powerful ideological binary in the Romantic period, when women writers are active contributors of domestic, local, and regional kinds of literature that ultimately feed into, expand, and enhance the store of national culture. Thus Mary Robinson is hailed as the 'English Sappho', Anna Laetitia Barbauld repeatedly takes on the controversial role of educator and 'mother' of the nation, while in 1819 *Blackwood's Edinburgh Magazine* triumphantly announces that 'Scotland has her Baillie – Ireland her Tighe – England her Hemans'.[1] Simultaneously, however, women writers transgress the boundaries of a national culture that is anything but cohesive in order to explore foreign traditions, past and present, and enmesh their own production, and British literature at large, in an increasingly complex web of intercultural exchanges.[2] And a clear testimony of this vocation appears in Letitia Elizabeth Landon's remark on the cosmopolitanism of Felicia Hemans's poetic inspiration – 'Mistress both of German and Spanish, the latter country appears to have peculiarly captivated her imagination' – as well as her practice, since her verse is comparable to 'the finest order of Italian singing – pure, high, and scientific'.[3]

   The early nineteenth century, and especially the period after Waterloo, sees a remarkable increase in the interest in foreign cultures which counters the widespread resistance to Continental literatures during the war years. Indeed, this renewed attention corrects and reverses the rampant cultural Europhobia of the 1790s which, as Peter Mortensen indicates, is rooted in the belief that 'Britain is essentially different from and superior to its Continental neighbour-nations', and is aggravated by 'the suspicion or indeed conviction that such Europeanization is *already* taking place, and that it is proceeding apace'.[4] Such hostility, however, never brings about a complete interruption of intercultural exchanges.

Although the war with France seemingly hinders travels abroad and international contacts, in actual fact interactions continue undeterred in the context of a European and global conflict that greatly expands the scope of Britain's foreign policy and its international outlook. Thus, in the 1790s, the number of novels translated into English does not dramatically decrease, while stage productions of foreign drama reach an unprecedented and, to many, disturbing high, as in the craze for the plays of August von Kotzebue.[5]

In the same period, women writers and intellectuals continue to produce translations and adaptations, cultivate links with Continental cultures (for instance, Mary Wollstonecraft and Helen Maria Williams in France) and spread knowledge about other lands (again, Wollstonecraft in Scandinavia is an exemplary case). As central players in these uninterrupted relations, women facilitate contacts, build bridges, and mediate between different languages and literatures. This chapter seeks to sketch out some of the main manifestations of these cultural intersections by focusing on the diverse uses of European literatures by women writers between 1800 and 1830.

A crucial figure in this context is that of Madame de Staël for the exemplary role she plays in defining the scope of the female contribution to cultural intersections at a European level. Transporting the Enlightenment idea of the 'republic of letters' into the Romantic age, Staël makes it a European reality in her literary *salon* at the Castle of Coppet on Lake Geneva. An eminently public character, she is an object of controversy and idolatry on a Continental scale, and the Italian literati fête her in Milan in 1804, while the British lionize her in London in 1813 after her escape from Napoleonic persecution in France. Significantly, on 3 October 1810 Anne Savary, Duke of Rovigo, Napoleon's notorious Minister of Police, writes to her on the subject of *De l'Allemagne* (*On Germany*): 'It has seemed to me that the air of this country did not agree with you at all, and we are not yet reduced to looking for models among the peoples you admire. Your latest work is not French at all.'[6] The bureaucrat turns Staël's cultivation of intercultural exchanges into a serious incriminating charge, and his accusation is even more deeply distressing to the author, as this practice is much more than a mere intellectual programme. Indeed, as Staël confesses to a friend in a letter of 1806, 'being born French with a foreign character, with French tastes and habits, and the ideas and feelings of the North, is a contrast that destroys one's life'.[7] That the links between Staël's cosmopolitan origins and international upbringing and her desire to interweave different traditions are crucial to her cultural project is as clear to her admirers as to her detractors. When, in 1821, Mary Russell Mitford retrospectively reveals to a friend her aversion to Staël, she writes: 'To tell you a secret, I had some sympathy with the dear Emperor in his dislike of that Germanized Frenchwoman, whose example as to conduct has done great harm, and her example in literature has done no good.'[8]

Staël's works confirm the inseparability of her hybrid cultural experience from her intellectual identity, as they variously advocate the need for intercultural comparison, exchange, and transmutation. From *De la littérature* (*On Literature*, 1800) through *Corinne* (1807) to *De l'Allemagne* (1813), her fictional and critical discourse develops within the extremes of deeply entrenched national cultural identities and transnational aspirations, giving actual shape to a desire for the transgression of boundaries that is widespread in European literatures of the Romantic period.[9]

Such complex cross-cultural operations are especially significant for British women writers at a time when the transformation and expansion of national literature overlaps with an intensified literary commerce with foreign traditions. Caught in the drawn-out process of establishing their own cultural credentials, women indefatigably open up new paths to foreign literatures in order to ground their own cultural authority and enlarge the scope of the national *belles lettres*. It is also by promoting international connections and locating their literary practice in a cross-cultural terrain that women qualify and strengthen their position in the national culture.

Other voices: women writers and foreign language learning

It is a largely uncontested fact that in Romantic-period Britain middle- and upper-class women are the designated recipients of foreign-language tuition. French and, to a lesser degree, Italian feature in the customary array of female accomplishments, and the learning of modern languages is subject to the prescriptive regulations of conduct books. Thomas Gisborne's *An Enquiry into the Duties of the Female Sex* (1797) recommends competence in Italian and French for a young woman in order 'to supply her hours of leisure with innocent and amusing occupations'.[10] And, in *Strictures on the Modern System of Female Education* (1799), Hannah More concedes that 'A young lady may excel in speaking French and Italian' also because a knowledge of these languages may improve accuracy and precision in her native language: 'since many English words take their derivation from foreign languages, they cannot be so accurately understood without some knowledge of those languages'.[11] If foreign languages are essential to the correct upbringing of a young lady, they may also be put to good use in the competitive social world of Regency Britain, as Ugo Foscolo caustically remarks in an essay of 1821: 'the study of the Italian language [...] is now indispensably necessary for all young ladies, who ought to vie in accomplishments, with their equals and their superiors, in rank and fortune'.[12]

As for the practical aspects of language learning, one general problem is the limited presence of competent native tutors both in London and in the provinces. Although French teachers had been a common presence in Britain since the eighteenth century, the number of Italian teachers begins to increase only after the failed patriotic rebellions of 1820–21 force many into exile, and the same conditions obtain for Spaniards after 1823. However, self-teaching is the norm and British learners may resort to a sizeable number of grammars, readers, and dictionaries for a variety of modern languages.[13] And since language learning is aimed both at polite conversation and the development of reading skills, anthologies of literary passages (such as Antonio Panizzi's 1828 *Extracts from Italian Prose Writers*) are the most common tools to develop the latter ability. In addition, foreign-language books are regularly published in Britain (a volume of *Quindici tragedie di V. Alfieri* appears in Edinburgh in 1806, and the four-volume *Teatro Español*, edited by Angel Anaya, is published in London in 1817–21), while London booksellers specializing in foreign books include Joseph de Boffe for French books (in Gerrard Street and then Nassau Street in Soho), Vaughan Griffiths for German books (in Paternoster Row) and Thomas Boosey (in Old Bond Street) who stocks publications from different countries and sheet music by foreign composers.

Although it is impossible to generalize on the level of competence attained by female learners, an interesting testimony in this respect appears in Rose Lawrence's memoir of Felicia Hemans, usually characterized as the polyglot poet of the Romantic period thanks to her knowledge of Spanish, Italian, French, German, and Portuguese. In *The Last Autumn at a Favourite Residence* (1836), Lawrence remarks that

> [Hemans] possessed a rare industry, and her knowledge of languages was perfectly self-acquired: it was not, perhaps, very extensive or accurate, but she seized upon whatever it communicated with the habitual quickness of intuitive talent, and gave back their poetical imagery with a truth and a beauty which was rather the achievement of the 'freemasonry of mind' than the result of previous study

or application. This purpose of appropriating or subduing a subject to our purposes is one of the faculties, or, perhaps, one of the minor characteristics of genius.[14]

If the reference to the poet's self-taught skills reveals nothing unusual, Lawrence's celebration of her linguistic competence on the basis of its lack of extensiveness or precision is rather surprising. In fact, Lawrence praises Hemans's spontaneous linguistic abilities as yet another trait of her innate genius, whilst also stressing that linguistic competence is a genteel accomplishment and, in the poet's case, the manifestation of a natural artistic *penchant*, rather than an aspect of hard-edged professionalism.

Mitford's letters, quoted in Harness's biography, offer further insights by throwing light on the different status of classical and modern languages. Indeed, in 1802, she writes to her mother from school expressing her intention to learn Latin and reassuring her that 'It is so extremely like Italian, that I think I shall find it much easier than I expected' (I, p. 14). Although her parents oppose this decision on the grounds that 'it is perfectly unnecessary, and would occasion you additional trouble', Mitford continues her study of the language, but she is an impatient reader and cannot resist plunging into the classics in translation (Dryden's versions from Homer and Pope's *Iliad*, in particular) (I, pp. 14–15). Simultaneously, she advances in her study of French and its literature, a passion that will accompany her until the end of her life, as well as acquiring a tolerable knowledge of Italian. Yet she also gradually abandons the more demanding Latin and, on 15 October 1811, writes to a friend, Sir William Elford: 'I do not wish to affect a knowledge I do not possess' (I, p. 157).

Nonetheless, classical literature (in translation) remains a fixed point of reference for Mitford during her long career, retaining a fascination that is all the more poignant as it implies cultural exclusion and personal defeat. In November 1821, after seeing the pupils at Reading School perform Euripides' *Orestes*, she tellingly confesses, again to Sir William Elford:

Ever since the Greek play I have been trying as well as I can, in French and English and Italian translations, to get at the Greek dramatists, and am so in love with Aeschylus and Sophocles (Euripides, though very fine, is rather in a lower style – more pathetic than sublime) that I can really hardly think or talk of anything else.–

(II, p. 141)

Shot through with a sense of undeserved exile from classical originals, similar remarks abound in Mitford's letters, but are usually accompanied by *revanchist* references to the modern-language translations offering her an alternative access. Writing to Benjamin Robert Haydon, on 28 October 1824, she remarks: 'although I have no knowledge of Greek, I have read these plays very often in translations, both French and English' (II, p. 193).

Inevitably, when Mitford meets the young Elizabeth Barrett in 1836, she writes to her father that her new friend 'reads Greek as I do French, and has published some translations from Æschylus, and some most striking poems', and also that she 'has translated the most difficult of the Greek plays (the "Prometheus Bound")' (III, pp. 46, 47). Barrett, as unusual in her classical training as Elizabeth Carter in the eighteenth century, has achieved what Mitford did not, and thus embodies the possibility for women to encroach successfully on a prestigious and jealously guarded cultural preserve. Yet, what is at stake is not that women are debarred from this fund of cultural capital. For Mitford's case reveals how, as in the more familiar instance of John Keats, they access the classics through modern-language versions which transform the ancient texts into mediated documents caught up in a dialogue between different cultures. Accordingly, the loss of the original brings about a hybrid and comparative approach to the origins of Western literature and its evolution, a reinterpretation that intensifies women writers' attunement to cross-cultural contaminations, as well as their intimate 'affiliation' to a notion of literature as a texture of intersections and admixtures.[15]

Women and translation

As modern languages are a crucial component in the cultural background of middle-class women, their ranks inevitably provide a sizeable number of translators between the eighteenth and nineteenth centuries. Indeed, the names appearing in published translations indicate that these women mainly 'belonged to the middle or upper classes [...], enjoyed a high standard of education, moved in cultivated circles, and chose to translate intellectually challenging texts', although a number of them also 'depended on the income they received from their translations'.[16] Of course, many Romantic-era women writers are also translators, and a brief checklist of excellent names and titles might include Charlotte Smith's version of the Abbé Prévost's *Manon Lescaut* (1785, 1786), Helen Maria Williams's translation of Bernardin de Saint-Pierre's

Paul et Virginie (1795), Elizabeth Inchbald's translation of August von Kotzebue's *Das Kind der Liebe* (1798), Mariana Starke's paraphrases of Carlo Maria Maggi's poems (1811), Hemans's *Translations from Camoens and Other Poets* (1818), and Landon's English verse translations of Corinne's 'rhapsodies' for Isabel Hill's version of Staël's *Corinne* (1833). For these writers, as for the more obscure professionals, translating does not aim at a careful reproduction of an original, but is far closer to adaptation and recasting, and usually affects both the formal and the cultural-ideological features of the source text. Particularly revealing instances of this practice are Charlotte Smith's translations from the French, *Manon L'Escaut* and *The Romance of Real Life* (1787) from Gayot de Pitaval's *Causes célèbres et interessants* (1735–45). In the former, Smith takes Prévost's narrative and deliberately 'writes it anew in English', whilst also mitigating the morally dubious contents of his 1753 revision of the even more contentious 1731 edition; whereas, in the latter, her translation is also a formal intervention that edits and rearranges the original material into new narrative formats.[17]

Given the proximity between translation and literary composition, women writers also create fictional versions of female translators by placing their characters in situations of interlinguistic and intercultural mediation, often in order to help men access another culture. In Lady Morgan's *The Wild Irish Girl* (1806), for instance, as the English protagonist H.M. embarks on the study of Gaelic, it is the daughter of the Prince of Innismore, the beautiful Glorvina, who acts as his language instructor. In *Corinne*, Madame de Staël makes her heroine a paradigmatic cultural mediator who has a native-speaker command of Italian and English, masters French with great ease and naturalness, and interprets the language and culture of Rome for the benefit of Lord Nelvil – 'Rome interpreted by imagination and genius.'[18] Moreover, female authors concentrate on their heroines' use of foreign languages in delicate situations, as they negotiate the traps and pitfalls of their social environments. For example, at the beginning of Frances Burney's *The Wanderer* (1814), the heroine Elinor, still *incognita*, tries to escape from Terror-stricken France and strategically alternates between French and English to confuse her fellow-travellers and evade their potentially damaging enquiries. Similarly, the connection between a foreign language and the ability to navigate the treacherous waters of society appears in Jane Austen's *Persuasion* (1818), when the protagonist Anne Elliot attends a musical evening in Bath's Octagon Room. Here, her powers of translation are called upon by her cousin, the seductive but untrustworthy William Elliot, who asks her to render the words of an Italian aria into English and thus removes her from the attentions of Captain Wentworth. Since Anne's skills in linguistic mediation become dangerously entangled with her ability to negotiate this embarrassing situation, this and similar scenes also seemingly imply a reflection on the emblematic social and ideological value of the act of translation.

As with these fictional characters, the female translators of this period are cultural mediators who contribute to the introduction and diffusion of foreign literary works and thus expose British literature to an ever-increasing range of different cultural phenomena. This is the case of Sarah Austin, who establishes herself as a major translator from the German (an all but male preserve) and who, in a volume of *Minnesinger* verse (1825), also produces a series of translations of troubadour poetry from the Provençal. A comparable case is that of the critic Mary Margaret Busk who regularly includes extensive translated excerpts in her articles for the *Blackwood's Magazine* series of 'Horae Germanicae', 'Hispanicae', and 'Italicae' (from 1825) and then in her pieces for the *Foreign Quarterly Review* (from 1828).[19] In both cases translation contributes to a wider operation of cultural construction and reappraisal that promotes forgotten or marginalized traditions as well as the latest foreign literary developments. In other words, women are instrumental in making translation the crucial vehicle for what David Simpson has called the 'sense of significant otherness' pervading Romantic-period culture and for its exposure to the profitable 'impasse of blocked communication' underlying intercultural contacts.[20]

While Austin and Busk exemplify women's contribution to translation as a means of cultural expansion, reconstruction or comparison, Barbarina Brand, Lady Dacre, testifies further to the relevance of translation in defining the place of women in the contemporary cultural field. A celebrated London hostess and a central figure in the art world of the Regency, Dacre was well known as a sculptor, dramatist, and translator, and counted Catherine Fanshawe, Joanna Baillie, and Mitford among her closest female correspondents. An accomplished linguist proficient in French and Italian, in 1821 she published two volumes of *Dramas, Translations and Occasional Poems*, the epigraph to which – 'Per desio di Lode / Non canto io, no; ben per chi m'ama e m'ode' – is taken from an illustrious forebear, the Italian Renaissance poet Vittoria Colonna, and rehearses the familiar notion of the female artist's rejection of fame.[21] In particular, Dacre belonged to the group of Italianists gravitating around the Whig circle of Holland House, including William Stewart Rose, the translator of Ariosto's *Orlando Furioso*, and John Herman Merivale.

Her specialization was Petrarch, and the 1821 volumes regularly feature several translations (already privately printed at an earlier date) from his poems. In addition, the second volume concludes with a Petrarchan sonnet 'To Ugo Foscolo, with a snuff-box' dated November 1820, where Dacre addresses the exiled Italian poet by admiring his literary masterpieces and confining herself to the more mundane reality of everyday sociability represented by the gift of the snuff-box. Yet, notwithstanding this act of textual self-effacement, Dacre mixes freely with the world of genius and creativity and, thanks to her social connections, London salon and translating skills, enjoys a central position in the contemporary cultural scene.

In 1823 John Murray brings out a second edition of Foscolo's celebrated *Essays on Petrarch* (the first limited and numbered edition had appeared in 1821) aimed at a general readership and featuring a sizeable number of translations by Dacre, both as excerpts in the essays and as complete texts in an appendix of 'Translations from Petrarch'. Accordingly, in 1821–23, the correspondence between Dacre and Foscolo features countless discussions of her versions, as she explains her doubts and dissatisfactions and he provides interpretations of obscure lines. In his answers Foscolo is unswervingly appreciative of Dacre's work and, on 29 October 1821, praises 'the soul you have infused' into her rendition of Petrarch's political song 'Italia mia'.[22] Half-jokingly Dacre considers the finished volume a joint effort, and on 5 January 1823 writes to Foscolo about '*notre* livre' ('*our* book').[23]

The poet significantly dedicates the 1823 *Essays* to Dacre, and in his preface acknowledges the universal plaudits given to her translations by 'those distinguished Literary Characters, whose kind assistance, surpassed only by yours, has enabled me to present my Essays to the English reader', and who 'With one voice and with national pride [...] pronounce, that your poetry has preserved the very spirit of Petrarch with a fidelity hardly to be hoped for, and certainly unattained by any other translation.'[24] Indeed, when it comes to the 'distinguished Literary Characters' of the Holland House set, by this time Dacre has established a fruitful literary exchange with the polemical Whig intellectual and lawyer Henry Brougham, one of the founders of the *Edinburgh Review* and later first Baron Brougham and Vaux, for whom she translates a political sonnet, 'Per la Pace di 1814' ('Tradito e vinto per virtude o inganno') attributed to Vincenzo Monti, and who urges her to try her hand at Dante as he finds Henry Francis Cary's versions of the *Divina commedia* particularly unsatisfactory. In another letter from this period, Brougham informs her that he has 'arranged so as to enable

Foscolo occasionally to give a course of lectures on Italian Literature and Poetry'.[25]

In her recollections of her artistic grandmother, Dacre's granddaughter remarks that Foscolo probably 'became acquainted with Lady Dacre through Mrs. Lawrence of Liverpool', an intriguing connection that, however, is not substantiated by Foscolo's biographers.[26] Nevertheless, the figure of Rose Lawrence (née D'Aguilar), author of *The Last Autumn at a Favourite Residence*, discloses a further series of literary links. A friend of the Liverpool Whig, banker, author, and benefactor William Roscoe, Lawrence is the wife of the Whig mayor of Liverpool, a close friend of Dacre and, later in life, of Hemans. The suggestion that she may have introduced Foscolo to the former emphasizes the importance of this circle of Whig relations and of women's role in promoting connections and exchanges. As an apposite conclusion to this female-centred web of relations, in a letter of 3 August 1823 Dacre invites Foscolo to read Hemans (probably *The Siege of Valencia … with Other Poems*, published in June of the same year): 'Pray read Mrs Hemans's book of poems – They are beautiful.'[27]

Placed at the heart of this intricate set of connections, Dacre throws light on the role of translation within the knot of sociability, ideological allegiances, and cultural exchanges typical of Regency literary circles. If in this period women translate for very practical reasons, their translating activities are also an essential component of a cultural field characterized by curiosity and experimentalism, a marked tendency to renovation and countless links with foreign literatures.

Women's plays and foreign drama

As with the novel and poetry, Romantic women's drama engages in an intense commerce with other traditions based on a well-established practice, from the Restoration onwards, of importing and adapting foreign plays and plots. The extent to which translation and adaptation inform the composition of a dramatic text is the object of some relevant remarks in Inchbald's preface to *Lovers' Vows*, perhaps the most prominent such case in the Romantic-period canon. Here, she both points out the need for textual interventions – 'I was compelled, on many occasions, to compress the substance of a speech of three or four pages, into one of three or four lines' – and the inevitability of ideological revision – 'in no one instance, I would suffer my respect for Kotzebue to interfere with my profound respect for the judgment of a British audience'. She emphatically vindicates the right to such revisionist and adaptative work by adding that, as for 'the dull admirer of mere verbal translation, it would be vain to endeavour to inspire with taste by instruction'.[28] Less well known than Inchbald's, albeit more wide-ranging, is the translating work of Fanny Holcroft, daughter of Thomas Holcroft, for her father's short-lived periodical *The Theatrical Recorder* (1805). Its issues regularly feature profiles of foreign playwrights and their works, as well as discussions of foreign dramatic traditions, often in comparative perspective, in addition to Fanny Holcroft's translations, all of them probably based on intermediate French versions. Among these are Vittorio Alfieri's *Philip II*, Pedro Calderón de la Barca's *From Bad to Worse* and *Fortune Mends*, and Gotthold Ephraim Lessing's *Emilia Galotti* and *Minna von Barnhelm*, both of which belong in a running series on the 'Rise and Progress of the German Stage'.

Women playwrights, moreover, develop and reflect on their own productions through the lens of foreign drama. Thus, for instance, while composing *The Vespers of Palermo*, Hemans is aware of the existence of a French play on the same subject, Casimir Delavigne's *Les Vêpres siciliennes* (staged in 1819 at the Parisian Théâtre de l'Odéon), and of a translation of it into English. Both facts lead her to change the title of her own tragedy, as she writes to Henry Hart Milman on 12 October 1821: 'with regard to the translation from the French Sicilian Vespers, as I have determined upon changing the name of mine (which is to be simply "Procida,") I trust they will not materially interfere with each other'.[29]

Mary Russell Mitford's development as a playwright offers an additional angle, combining dramatic composition and critical comparatism, since the impact of foreign drama on her production is remarkably strong from the outset. In a letter to Sir William Elford of 22 March 1821 she asserts that, while writing for the magazines, she is also busy composing a tragedy on the sixteenth-century conspiracy led by Count Fieschi against the Genoese despot Doria. She knows of Friedrich Schiller's *Die Verschwörung des Fiesco zu Genua* (*Fiesco; or, the Genoese Conspiracy*, 1783), 'but I have neither seen nor sought for it [...] for fear that Schiller should "put me out"' (Harness, II, pp. 123–4). Yet when *Fiesco* is sent to the actor William Charles Macready, who rejects it as unsuitable for performance, no more is heard of it. From this moment Mitford begins to apply insistently to her correspondents, such as Haydon and Barbara Hofland, asking them for foreign materials for a play. In a long letter to Macready of April 1823 she runs through a whole series of subjects in an attempt to gauge the actor's inclinations: 'the story of Garzia de Medici', an enigmatic 'intense but terrible tragedy of "Alfieri"', Procida ('but then – would that be quite right?' she asks, possibly aware of Hemans's play), Francesca da Rimini (drawing on Dante but also 'beginning with the scene of Phaedra from Euripides'), Rienzi or Masaniello. 'Am I likely to find anything to the purpose in Froissart?', she also asks Macready.[30]

In the end, Mitford begins work on the medieval tale of Cola di Rienzo which will result in the tragedy *Rienzi*, her most resounding theatrical success when, after innumerable delays, it is eventually staged at Drury Lane in 1828. The influence of foreign drama and literature exerts a lasting hold on the development of the play much beyond the mere choice of its subject. Aware that Mitford is about to begin her new tragedy, her friend the poet Eleanor Porden enquires: 'Are you at work on "Rienzi" yet? And does Ugo Foscolo help you with Petrarch?'[31] The Italian poet is evidently a much sought-after authority for British women writers in the early 1820s. Unfortunately, however, there is no trace of any actual exchange between Mitford and Foscolo, just as it seems improbable that Rose Lawrence had introduced him to Lady Dacre. A further intercultural component in the composition of *Rienzi* is that it draws both on Edward Gibbon's *Decline and Fall of the Roman Empire* (1776–88) and on 'the second volume of l'Abbé de Sade's "Mémoires pour servir à la Vie de Pétrarque"' (translated by Susannah Dobson in 1775) as a source of biographical information on Rienzi's close connection with the Italian poet.[32]

In addition, Mitford's interest in foreign dramaturgy is not limited to the adoption and re-elaboration of foreign materials – which is, after all, a rather common occurrence in this period. Rather, it also affects her reflections on the nature and practice of drama, as she constantly interleaves her remarks on Shakespeare with references to an extensive list of foreign dramatists comprising the Greek tragedians, Pierre Corneille, Molière, Alfieri, and Schiller. And in the 'Introduction' to her *Dramatic Works* (1854) she specifically invokes and discusses Kotzebue, Molière, Alfieri, and Jean Racine, while her letters testify to her keen interest in foreign literature and drama, especially French, until the end of her life. Deeply embedded in the English tradition and in the world of the London patent playhouses of her day, Mitford's dramatic practice also evolves through an ongoing dialogue with other dramaturgies, both classical and modern. Indeed, her varied engagements with foreign drama confirm that, if Romantic women's playwriting works within the national tradition to explore national concerns, its focus is also importantly complicated and refracted through the lens of a composite international dramatic heritage.

Cross-cultural lines and hybrid verses

Romantic women's poetry is a particularly fertile area for an examination of intercultural contacts and 'foreignizing' strategies, and several instances may serve to illustrate the different ways in which female poets thread their lines through with a variety of foreign intertexts. Charlotte Smith's *Elegiac Sonnets* is an obvious case in point thanks to its interpolated series of poems 'from Petrarch' and 'Supposed to be written by Werter'. Another, less familiar, instance is that of the Scottish poet Anne Bannerman who contributes translations to Joseph Cooper Walker's *Historical and Critical Essay on the Revival of the Drama in Italy* (1805) and whose *Poems* (1800) include seven versions of Italian sonnets (six by Petrarch and one by Giovanni della Casa) and ten 'Sonnets from Werter' with notes detailing the exact passage from Goethe's novel that each sonnet is meant to gloss. Similarly, Mary Tighe adapts compositions by the eighteenth-century Italian poet and librettist Pietro Metastasio ('From Metastasio, 1791' and 'To Fortune. From Metastasio', 1811), while Felicia Hemans translates abundantly from, among others, Metastasio, della Casa, Monti, Luis de Camões, Vincenzo da Filicaja, Lope de Vega, Jacopo Sannazaro, Francisco de Quevedo, Bernardo and Torquato Tasso, Solomon Gessner, and Alessandro Manzoni.

Adaptations of Goethe's *Werther*, in particular, indicate that foreign sources are the object of a practice of appropriation and rewriting that results in hybridized texts which 'speak' English yet narrate 'other' tales. And once again, pervaded as it is with foreign texts and themes, Hemans's output offers several relevant, though by no means isolated, examples of this practice. Even a cursory glance at her production reveals poems inspired by Schiller's *Wallenstein* trilogy, the works of J.C.L. Simonde de Sismondi and Claude Fauriel, the biographical myths of Torquato Tasso, Karl Theodor Körner or Mozart, the death of Bartolomeo Sestini, the Spanish legends of the Cid and Bernardo del Carpio, or the Swiss struggle for liberty. This adoption and recasting of foreign materials also extends to Hemans's strategic use of epigraphs from a variety of European sources which often set off multiple echoing effects within her corpus. Thus, for instance, the line from Ippolito Pindemonte, 'Fermossi al fin il cor che balzò tanto', also found in Staël's *Corinne*, first figures as an epigraph to the third canto of *The Abencerrage* (1819) and then to 'Arabella Stuart' in *Records of Woman* (1828).[33] Extracted from its original context, the Italian line becomes a flexible signifier available for insertion in a variety of textual environments in order to emphasize the themes of suffering and death, award Hemans's compositions cultural authority by projecting them on to a broader literary dimension, enrich the internal cohesion of her output, and reinforce its genealogical ties.

Textual hybridizations do not merely feature in single compositions, but may also condition the structure of entire collections of verse, as for instance Hemans's 1823 volume *The Siege of Valencia ... with Other Poems*. In geocultural terms, the texts in this collection design an articulated map ranging from biblical antiquity to present times, from ancient Rome and Greece, to Druidic Britain, medieval Spain, Constantinople, and Wales, and covering the wide expanse of British commercial, imperial, and diplomatic connections in 'England's Dead' (already published in *The Literary Gazette* in 1822). Moreover, the volume features a translation (also already published in *The Edinburgh Magazine* in 1821) of the chorus from Act II of Alessandro Manzoni's tragedy *Il conte di Carmagnola* (1820), while its notes and epigraphs abound with references to, and untranslated excerpts from, Horace, Cervantes, Goethe and Schiller, José Manuel Quintana, Pouqueville's travels in Greece and Chateaubriand's *Génie du Christianisme* (*The Beauties of Christianity*, 1802) among others. And this choir of international voices bears fundamentally on the structure and nature of Hemans's texts. Indeed, *The Siege of Valencia*, with its epigraph from Cervantes's tragedy *El cerco de Numancia* (*The Siege of Numancia*, c. 1580–90), contains a series of interpolated songs that echo and adapt the Spanish tradition of narrative and lyrical poetry, especially the celebrated *romances*; embedded in *The Last Constantine* is the opening couplet of Goethe's 'Mignons Lied' ('Kennst du das land, wo die zitronen blühn'), while in a note to stanza 62 Hemans informs her readers that 'The idea expressed in this stanza is beautifully amplified in Schiller's poem "Das Lied der Glocke".'[34] If in these cases the poet subsumes foreign voices into her texts, she actually draws on and reworks foreign sources in the series of 'Songs of the Cid' (already published in *The Literary Gazette* and *New Monthly Magazine*), which are 'not translations from the Spanish, but are founded upon some of the "wild and wonderful" traditions preserved in the romances of that language, and the ancient poem of the Cid' found in Southey's *Chronicle of the Cid* (1808), Johann Gottfried von Herder's *Der Cid* (1805), and various Spanish-language collections.[35]

The impact of Hemans's eclectic cross-cultural intersections is evident from her friend Rose Lawrence's *The Last Autumn at a Favourite Residence*, where an intricate series of dialogues with foreign and national voices confirms the central role of European literatures in the definition of the female poetic identity and a community of women writers. Hemans is the tutelary figurehead of Lawrence's volume as the dedicatee of some 'irregular stanzas' entitled 'Recollections of Mrs. Hemans' accompanied by prose 'Notes and Fragments', while Lawrence also reminds her readers that she is the dedicatee of Hemans's 1834 *National Lyrics, and Songs for Music*, appropriately a collection of internationally-themed compositions and translations.[36] Accordingly, *The Last Autumn* presents a section of 'Fragments. Imitations from the German, Spanish, Italian, &c. &c.', features a wealth of foreign epigraphs (among which is Pindemonte's 'Fermossi al fin il cor che balzò tanto'), and traces a map of foreign connections that essentially overlaps with Hemans's – from Vincenzo da Filicaja and Adam Ohlenschläger to Schiller and the 'romances' of the Cid.

Hemans and Lawrence's verse collections import and adapt international literary and cultural traditions through operations ranging from paratextual excerpting to translation (and rewriting) and the appropriation and reinscription of foreign voices into their own texts. In addition, these volumes reveal a tendency to produce Anglicized versions of other traditions by importing them into the English-language domain, a practice that Susan Wolfson, following Francis Jeffrey, has defined as Hemans's 'happy Englishing of world literature'.[37] Yet, these collections also effect an 'othering' of English literature by steeping it in foreign lore and cross-breeding it with different linguistic, generic, and thematic traditions. In the resulting hybridized texts, English poetry becomes a space of experimentation aimed at identifying alternative ways of saying and writing reality. And if in this period such operations are not an exclusively female preserve, they effectively offer women writers a space of expressive emancipation that is deeply meaningful to their search for a poetic identity beyond the local and the national.

Intercultural dialogues

The cross-cultural texture of Hemans and Lawrence's poetry is tangible evidence of the multiple linguistic and cultural networks within which the literary labour of women writers situates and manifests itself, as well as of its allegiance to an internationalized idea of literature. As in the examples discussed here, Romantic-period female authors import, adapt, and disseminate foreign literatures through a variety of converging operations, as they extensively translate, exchange, compare, assess, reinvent, gloss, and circulate 'other' cultural materials.

Taken collectively, this array of cultural strategies belongs to what Roger Chartier has termed 'appropriation', a form of transference based on 'differentiated practices and contrasted uses' and resulting in 'diverse readings which are not aimed at or inscribed in the [original] text'.[38] Thus Chartier defines a usefully composite model of the process of cultural acquisition intended not as passive reception but rather as direct intervention, a model which aptly describes Romantic transformative adaptations of foreign materials and their subsequent conversion into new segments of British literary discourse. Specifically, this procedure of cultural transfer relies on what Michel de Certeau defines as 'techniques of re-employment' and Pierre Bourdieu terms 'polythetism', cultural protocols through which the appropriating culture confers different functions and different meanings on the original texts.[39] This definition of appropriation is particularly pertinent to Romantic-period literature in Britain, with its vigorous drives to cultural renovation and attempts by different groups of cultural players, such as women writers, to stake out competing positions of authority in the literary domain.

As Georges Gusdorf has observed, even though Romantic European cultures draw their vitality from the principle of national self-definition, 'national claims in no way imply a dissociation from the European sphere', so that different cultures share in a joint 'internationalism of geographical and historical specificities'.[40] Therefore, what comes into view is 'a Europe of borders and differences', a transnational culture which 'delights in being several' and nurtures itself through what Gusdorf calls a 'romantic transference from one mental space to another'.[41] Stuart Curran has stressed the literary effects of this shift by observing that, in the Romantic period, 'Everywhere in European literature the observed canons were revealed as inadequate to encompass the burden not just, as a strictly historical overview might have it, of startling new material and creative conditions, but of a revived heritage. And after the first wave, national recovery, came its sharing through translation', and, we may add, the many forms of appropriation that reach unprecedented intensity in early nineteenth-century women's writings.[42]

A decisively emancipatory operation, women's incorporation of foreign literatures into the flow of national culture responds to this distinctive Romantic tendency. As cultural mediators, women writers have to respect the demands of the literary market and its ideological mandates, and thus import figures, texts, and issues that may be adapted to indigenous cultural expressions. Yet these imports, which effectively enable female writers to accumulate cultural capital and authoritativeness, insinuate literary discourse and thus potentially modify its national qualities. As Patrick Vincent has remarked of Romantic women's poetry, 'transnational connections among women poets, critics, and other cultural agents were crucial to how women poets imagined themselves'.[43] In this perspective, appropriation and adaptation are more than a mere nod to the exotic or a mechanical exploitation of unfamiliar literary and cultural sources in pursuit of novelty. Instead, these practices bring about an expansion of the boundaries of English-language literature by enmeshing it in cultural and linguistic difference. Between 1800 and 1830, yet on the strength of much earlier impulses, women writers produce national literature even as they appropriate foreign materials and assemble resonantly cross-cultural texts. Through a recovery of women's restless work of literary acclimatization, British Romanticism becomes visible as the space of an interplay of foreign voices and themes that coexist and interact with an equally compelling impulse to delimit and define the national literary heritage.

Notes

1. 'Meeting of Wallace and Bruce', *Blackwood's Edinburgh Magazine*, 5 (September 1819), 686. See also Anne K. Mellor, *Mothers of the Nation: Women's Political Writing in England, 1780–1830* (Bloomington and Indianapolis: Indiana University Press, 2000), pp. 78–80.
2. In this chapter the term 'intercultural' will be employed to refer to the network of relations (such as exchanges, contacts, comparisons, and mediations) between different cultures, whereas 'cross-cultural' will be used to describe the actual contaminated and hybridized representations resulting from these relations.
3. 'On the Character of Mrs. Hemans's Writings' (*New Monthly Magazine*, 44, August 1835), in Felicia Hemans, *Selected Poems, Prose and Letters*, ed. by Gary Kelly (Peterborough, Ontario: Broadview, 2002), pp. 472, 473. On Romantic-period cosmopolitanism, see Amanda Anderson, *The Powers of Distance: Cosmopolitanism and the Cultivation of Detachment* (Princeton and Oxford: Princeton University Press, 2001); David Simpson, 'The Limits of Cosmopolitanism and the Case for Translation', *European Romantic Review*, 16 (2005), 141–52; and Michael Scrivener, *The Cosmopolitan Ideal in the Age of Revolution and Reaction, 1776–1832* (London: Pickering and Chatto, 2007).
4. Peter Mortensen, *British Romanticism and Continental Influences: Writing in an Age of Europhobia* (Basingstoke and New York: Palgrave Macmillan, 2004), p. 20.
5. On the translations of foreign novels into English in the 1790s, see James Raven, 'Historical Introduction: the Novel Comes of Age', in *The English Novel 1770–1829: A Bibliographical Survey of Prose Fiction Published in the British Isles*, general editors Peter Garside et al., 2 vols (Oxford: Oxford University Press, 2000), I, 56–65. On Kotzebue, see Lionel Field Thompson, *Kotzebue: A Survey of his Progress in France and England* (Paris: Honoré Champion, 1928).

6. 'Il m'a paru que l'air de ce pays-ci ne vous convenait point, et nous n'en sommes pas encore réduits à chercher des modèles dans les peuples que vous admirez. Votre dernier ouvrage n'est point français.' Quoted in Georges Gusdorf, *Le Romantisme I: Le savoir romantique* (Paris: Payot, 1993), p. 291 (my translation).
7. '[N]aître Française avec un caractère étranger, avec les goûts et les habitudes françaises, et les idées et les sentiments du nord, c'est un contraste qui abîme la vie.' *Mme de Staël, ses amis, ses correspondants: Choix de Lettres (1778–1817)*, ed. Georges Solovieff (Paris: Klincksieck, 1970), p. 328 (my translation).
8. [William Harness], *The Life of Mary Russell Mitford*, ed. by A.G. L'Estrange, 3 vols (London, 1870), II, 136. Subsequent references are given parenthetically in the text.
9. See John Claiborne Isbell, *The Birth of a European Romanticism: Truth and Propaganda in Staël's 'De l'Allemagne'* (Cambridge: Cambridge University Press, 1994).
10. Thomas Gisborne, *An Enquiry into the Duties of the Female Sex*, 11th edn (London, 1816), p. 84.
11. Hannah More, *Strictures on the Modern System of Female Education*, intro. Jeffrey Stern, 2 vols (London: Routledge/Thoemmes Press, 1995), I, 96, 198.
12. Ugo Foscolo, 'Learned Ladies', *New Monthly Magazine*, 1 (1821), 223.
13. See, for instance, the case of Italian as detailed by C.P. Brand in *Italy and the English Romantics: The Italianate Fashion in Early Nineteenth-Century England* (Cambridge: Cambridge University Press, 1957), pp. 36–45.
14. Mrs. [Rose D'Aguilar] Lawrence, *The Last Autumn at a Favourite Residence, with other Poems; and Recollections of Mrs. Hemans* (Liverpool and London, 1836), pp. 313–14.
15. On affiliation, see Edward Said, *The World, the Text and the Critic* (London: Vintage, 1991 [1984]), pp. 19–20, 174–7.
16. Susanne Stark, 'Women', in *The Oxford History of Literary Translation in English*, ed. Peter France et al., 5 vols, IV: 1790–1900, ed. by Peter France and Kenneth Haynes (Oxford: Oxford University Press, 2006), p. 125. Some information on the payments women received for translations is in Cheryl Turner's *Living by the Pen: Women Writers in the Eighteenth Century* (London and New York: Routledge, 1992), pp. 122–3.
17. *Manon L'Escaut: or, the Fatal Attachment* (1786) and *The Romance of Real Life* (1787), ed. by Michael Gamer, in *The Works of Charlotte Smith*, general editor Stuart Curran, 14 vols (London: Pickering and Chatto, 2005–07), I, 5 (and pp. xxix–xxxvii more generally).
18. Madame de Staël, *Corinne, or Italy*, trans. Sylvia Raphael (Oxford, New York: Oxford University Press, 1998), p. 57.
19. On Busk, see Eileen Curran, 'Holding on by a Pen: The Story of a Lady/Reviewer: Mary Margaret Busk (1779–1863)', *Victorian Periodicals Review*, 31 (1998), 9–30.
20. Simpson, 'The Limits of Cosmopolitanism', pp. 148, 151.
21. 'I do not sing for praise, no, but rather for those who love and listen to me'. On Dacre's linguistic proficiency, see *A Family Chronicle Derived from Notes and Letters Selected by Barbarina, the Hon. Lady Grey*, ed. by Gertrude Lyster (London: John Murray, 1908), p. 9.
22. '[L]'ame que vous avez inspiré', Ugo Foscolo, *Edizione nazionale delle opere*, general editors Mario Fubini and Walter Binni, 22 vols (Firenze: Le Monnier,

1951–94): *Epistolario*, 9 vols, VIII, 328 (my translation). The nine volumes of Foscolo's *Epistolario* are contained within the twenty-two volumes of the complete works.

23. Ibid., IX, 170.
24. Dedication in Ugo Foscolo, *Essays on Petrarch* (London, 1823), n. p.
25. *A Family Chronicle*, p. 47.
26. *A Family Chronicle*, p. 49. E.R. Vincent states that 'They first met on 20 August 1818 at Roger Wilbraham's house at Twickenham, where the old bibliophile had invited them on purpose to effect the introduction.' *Ugo Foscolo: An Italian in Regency England* (Cambridge: Cambridge University Press, 1953), p. 77.
27. Foscolo, *Epistolario*, IX, 260.
28. Quoted in Jane Austen, *Mansfield Park*, ed. by John Wiltshire, in *The Cambridge Edition of the Works of Jane Austen*, general editor Janet Todd (Cambridge: Cambridge University Press, 2005), p. 557.
29. Henry F. Chorley, *Memorials of Mrs Hemans*, 2 vols (London, 1836), I, 69. The French play was reviewed and discussed in a long essay by the playwright Richard Lalor Sheil for Henry Colburn's *New Monthly Magazine* (November, December 1822), a publication to which Hemans would start to contribute in the following year.
30. *Letters of Mary Russell Mitford: Second Series*, ed. by Henry Chorley, 2 vols (London, 1872), II, 158–60.
31. *The Friendships of Mary Russell Mitford as recorded in letters from her literary correspondents*, ed. by A.G. L'Estrange, 2 vols (London, 1882), I, 147.
32. *The Dramatic Works of Mary Russell Mitford*, 2 vols (London, 1854), I, 3.
33. 'It stopped at last, the heart that beat so strongly.' For the reference in *Corinne*, see book 18, ch. 5 ('Fragments of Corinne's Thoughts'), p. 360.
34. Hemans adapts Goethe's lines as 'Know'st thou the land where bloom the orange bowers? / Where through dark foliage gleam the citron's dyes?' Felicia Hemans, *The Siege of Valencia; a Dramatic Poem. The Last Constantine: with Other Poems* (London, 1823), pp. 32, 61.
35. Hemans, *The Siege of Valencia* [...] *with Other Poems*, p. 251. On Hemans's Spanish sources, see Lawrence, *The Last Autumn*, p. 237.
36. Lawrence, *The Last Autumn*, p. 240. Hemans's 1834 volume also contains her 'Prologue to the Tragedy of Fiesco', intended for the translation from Schiller, 'performed at the Theatre Royal, Dublin, December 1832', by Lawrence's brother Colonel George Charles D'Aguilar, Adjutant-General of Ireland, the dedicatee of Lawrence's *Last Autumn*. See Felicia Hemans, *National Lyrics and Songs for Music* (Dublin and London, 1834), p. 328.
37. Susan J. Wolfson, '"Domestic Affections" and "the spear of Minerva": Felicia Hemans and the Dilemma of Gender', in *Re-Visioning Romanticism: British Women Writers, 1776–1837*, ed. by Carol Shiner Wilson and Joel Haefner (Philadelphia: University of Pennsylvania Press, 1994), p. 132.
38. Roger Chartier, *Cultural History: Between Practices and Representations*, trans. Lydia G. Cochrane (Cambridge: Polity, 1988), p. 13.
39. See Michel de Certeau, *The Practice of Everyday Life*, trans. Steven Rendall (Berkeley, Los Angeles, London: University of California Press, 1988 [1984]), pp. xxiv, 54 (on Bourdieu).
40. '[L]a revendication nationale ne consacre nullement une dissociation du domaine européen', 'internationalisme des spécificités géographiques et

historiques'. Georges Gusdorf, *Le Romantisme I*, pp. 289, 290 (my translation).

41. '[U]ne Europe des frontières et des différences', 'se réjouit d'être plusieurs', 'transfert romantique d'un espace mental dans un autre'. Ibid., pp. 290, 293 (my translation).

42. Stuart Curran, *Poetic Form and British Romanticism* (New York, Oxford: Oxford University Press, 1986), p. 213.

43. Patrick Vincent, *The Romantic Poetess: European Culture, Politics and Gender 1820–1840* (Durham, NH: University of New Hampshire Press, 2004), p. xiv.

14
Jane Austen's Critical Response to Women's Writing: 'a good spot for fault-finding'

Olivia Murphy

> any text is constructed as a mosaic of quotations; any
> text is the absorption and transformation of another.
> Julia Kristeva, *Word, Dialogue and Novel* (1969)[1]

Jane Austen's lifetime (1775–1817) coincided with the first serious attempts by literary critics to produce a canon of the novel. In the year before Austen's birth, the House of Lords' decision in *Donaldson v Beckett* ended printers' functional copyright over texts, leading to the widespread reprinting of novels for the first time in English literary history.[2] Various publishers attempted to capitalize on the market for reprinted works with large collections of novels, and James Harrison's *Novelist Magazine* (begun 1780) and Anna Laetitia Barbauld's *British Novelists* (1810) were remarkable for their inclusion of women authors. By the 1820s, however, a narrower, masculinized canon – dominated by Daniel Defoe, Henry Fielding, and Samuel Richardson – was already emerging in the early nineteenth-century narrative of the novel's development. Collections like Walter Scott's *Ballantyne's Novelist's Library* created a canon of the eighteenth-century novel that excluded (most) women writers along with (most) novels from the later decades of the century. At the same time, the selectivity and conscious political and literary bias of reviews like the *Edinburgh Review* and the *Quarterly Review* reinforced the status of a very few novelists at the expense of the majority.

The consequences, in the nineteenth century and beyond, for the eighteenth-century canon of novels were grim. Yet it is important to recognize that this conception of the literary canon, with its bias toward male writers, was in its infancy in Austen's lifetime, and gaining traction only late in her career. She lived to witness only the beginnings of the revisionist attempts of the newly professionalized, male-dominated critical industry to erase the earlier efforts of women writers and commentators on the novel, an industry that seemed entrenched by the beginning of the Victorian period. What little evidence we have suggests that Austen was beginning to resent the appropriation of the novel by 'masculine' writers. Her response to the publication of *Waverley* has a touch of bitterness: 'Walter Scott has no business to write novels, especially good ones. – It is not fair. – He has Fame & Profit enough as a Poet, and should not be taking the bread out of other people's mouths.'[3] The evidence of Austen's own writing suggests that her personal literary canon treats men and women writers equally and flattens the traditional hierarchies of genre. Pursuing such textual evidence can allow Austen's readers to reconstruct this canon, and in doing so to guess at Austen's critical and creative processes.

The half-century of criticism following Ian Watt's *The Rise of the Novel* has led to the construction of a new canon of eighteenth-century novels, one that has particularly benefited, in the 1970s and after, from the work of feminist critics.[4] Considering the selections made by Barbauld in her *British Novelists*, however, this 'new' canon appears after all to be closer to a *re*construction of a canon already in existence at the beginning of the nineteenth century, and including not only the works of women authors, but also a wide range of stylistic and generic differences, all understood as inherently and coherently novels. These are the texts that critics such as Marilyn Butler, Claudia Johnson, Margaret Kirkham, and Jocelyn Harris have identified as forming the literary matrix within which Austen's works should be read.

As the novel grew in importance and cemented its legitimacy as a literary genre during the Romantic period, the production and criticism of novels was steadily appropriated by professional, male writers. As Terry Castle writes, in the major contributions made to novelistic criticism at the turn of the nineteenth century by French women of letters

> Genlis and Staël defended women's writing and predicted that female authors, and especially female critics, would play an increasingly prominent role in the literature of the future. [...] [However,] for most of the nineteenth century, literary criticism remained a predominantly male-identified activity: [...] the works of Behn, Montagu, Riccoboni, Inchbald, Barbauld, Genlis and even Staël herself (not to mention those of lesser figures) were consigned to oblivion.[5]

The first critics and theorists of the novel were, of course, novelists themselves. In their dedications and prefaces, they advertised and (often simultaneously) apologized for their work, in the process gradually developing a vocabulary for defining and discussing the genre. This chapter argues for Jane Austen's pre-eminence as such a creative critic: a writer who forms new and sophisticated fiction out of her response to the fiction of other writers.

Austen's critical and creative practice can be seen in her earliest juvenilia and throughout her mature fiction. In this chapter I focus on the examples of Austen's technique provided by *Mansfield Park* (1814), and in particular its responses to the conservative domestic fiction of Hannah More and Maria Edgeworth. 'The more closely nineteenth century fiction asks us to focus on domestic life and the personal experience of women', Nancy Armstrong writes, 'the more it will also insist that the information at hand is natural and universal and hence removed from political history.'[6] Recognizing this, Austen's acute critical attention was drawn to the sexual politics of other women writers, influencing her efforts to demonstrate the ways in which texts form opinions, and ultimately ideologies. The first of Austen's novels to be begun and completed in the nineteenth century, *Mansfield Park* shows Austen's ongoing preoccupation with the literature of the eighteenth century. Just as importantly, the novel evinces Austen's interest in the rapidly changing nature of literary culture in England. As I have mentioned above, Austen was not alone in her attempts to assert, and ultimately to define, the novel as a genre. These efforts to raise the profile of the novel amongst other literary genres deployed those very genres in their arguments. Often the simple act of declaring the novel's legitimacy as a genre was made with reference to forms of literature such as classical epic, religious texts, lyric poetry or (mostly Shakespearean) drama: genres whose respectable, canonical status might be helpful in enhancing the novel's standing among contemporary readers and critics.

What sets Austen's practice apart from that of her contemporaries is the use she makes of this allusive strategy. She does not deploy frequent quotations in order to inflate her novel's gravitas, to assert its political, literary or philosophical kudos, or to advertise her own wide reading, as is the tendency of writers as diverse as Mary Hays, Ann Radcliffe, and Walter Scott. Rather, Austen's literary references are used as much to demonstrate the ways in which her characters' thoughts are led by their remembered reading into predetermined pathways (such as when, like *Persuasion's* Anne Elliot, they 'fall into a quotation'[7]), as they are used to embed Austen's own fiction in an extended literary tradition. The tentativeness – and in some egregious cases, deliberate blindness – with which critics of Jane Austen tend to respond to the presence of outside literary influences in her novels can be excused, to an extent, by the way in which, by integrating their traces so deeply into the text, she renders them deliberately obscure or ambivalent.

Austen's superficially self-deprecating, tongue-in-cheek comment to the Prince Regent's librarian that 'I may boast myself to be [...] the most unlearned, & uninformed Female who ever dared to be an Authoress',[8] serves as a reminder that in the repressive social and political climate of the late eighteenth and early nineteenth centuries, a woman's knowledge, once acquired, ought not to be openly displayed. 'A woman especially, if she have the misfortune of knowing anything', the narrator wryly comments in *Northanger Abbey*, 'should conceal it as well as she can.'[9] Many eighteenth-century authors took care to emphasize their heroines' modest concealment of their (inevitably prodigious) learning. The unobtrusive nature of Austen's literary allusions may be seen, then, as a pre-emptive defence against any imputation of unladylike pedantry or exhibitionism. Fanny Price certainly tends to recite her quotations 'in a low voice'.[10] The eponymous pedant of Walter Scott's 1816 novel *The Antiquary* suggests that male writers could be forgiven virtuosic or even tedious displays of learning, provided they couched such displays in a self-deprecatingly comic framework. Austen's contemporary Germaine de Staël, however, warned that 'when women write, the public, generally assuming that the primary motive is to show their cleverness, only reluctantly bestows its approval'.[11]

Austen's unostentatious use of quotation and allusion also sets her apart from those of her contemporary novelists who tend to wear their poetic mottoes and other literary allusions on their sleeves. Mary Hays's *Memoirs of Emma Courtney* (1796), for instance, is immediately recognizable as a novel with sympathies for the radical politics of the French Revolution by its frequent references to Rousseau, Helvétius, Descartes, Godwin, and Wollstonecraft. Maria Edgeworth's conservative novel *Belinda* (1801), in comparison, borrows explicitly from Pope's *The Rape of the Lock*, thereby emphasizing the novel's rationalist, Enlightenment politics, along with the trivial, girlish nature of her unflappable heroine's minor difficulties.[12] Austen, however, rarely signposts the use of the texts she weaves into her fiction. As D.A. Miller has noted, Austen's is the art that – often disturbingly – conceals art,[13] yet it is important to recognize that such concealment achieves political, as well as artistic aims. For Austen, effacing the overt signs of her literary debts has a similar effect to her customary ironic tone, as she keeps her readers guessing.

The structure of *Mansfield Park* identifies it as a novel participating in what Marilyn Butler has called 'the war of ideas', the great ideological and critical battles of the day. The role of the individual within the family, and the political identification of the family as a microcosmic nation, are themes common to ideologically-driven texts such as Edmund Burke's 1790 *Reflections on the Revolution in France* and Mary Wollstonecraft's responses to it, Charlotte Smith's polemic novel *The Old Manor House* (1794), Hannah More's didactic *Cœlebs in Search of a Wife* (1808), Maria Edgeworth's critically acclaimed *Patronage*, and Frances Burney's critically lambasted *The Wanderer*.[14] The latter two novels were both published in 1814, the same year as *Mansfield Park*. Austen's sustained study of a country baronet's family allows her to enter into these debates in a nuanced and strategic fashion, enabling her text to find fault with conservative ideological positions, and to suggest with great subtlety alternative perspectives that, in the year before Waterloo, are still dangerously radical.

Eighteenth-century and Romantic literary criticism sharpened its teeth on the seventeenth-century works of John Milton, and *Paradise Lost* became one of the central unimpeachably canonical English texts around and through which Romantic writers of all genres defined their work. Austen flags her interest in *Paradise Lost* early on in *Mansfield Park*, where she has Henry Crawford refer to marriage as 'Heaven's *last* best gift'.[15] The scene with Henry, Maria, and Fanny at the garden gate in Sotherton recalls the second book of the epic where Satan, on his journey from Hell, stops at its Gates, which are guarded by Sin and Death. Austen's critical interest in *Paradise Lost* takes on new importance when we consider the status of Milton's poem in the Romantic period. As a work of literature *Paradise Lost* was of obvious and enduring significance. Its role as a moral and religious text, however, cannot be overestimated. In Hannah More's *Cœlebs in Search of a Wife*, the entirety of the first chapter is devoted to the narrator's encomium on Milton's epic, and its representations of Eve in particular. More's Cœlebs reflects:

> I early became enamoured of [...] Milton's Eve. I never formed an idea of conjugal happiness, but my mind involuntarily adverted to the graces of that finished picture. [...] It gives an image of that tranquillity, smoothness, and quiet beauty, which is of the very essence of perfection in a wife.[16]

More's heroine Lucilla Stanley is as close to a Regency version of Milton's Eve as can be imagined. Austen, in contrast, takes pains to distinguish Fanny from the heroine of *Paradise Lost*. Milton's Eve is shown amongst roses, 'oft stooping to support | Each flower of slender stalk' (bk.9, ll. 425–8, p. 218), while Fanny's 'stooping' to cut roses in her aunt's garden gives her a headache (p. 72). We might gather from this that Austen is launching a direct attack on Milton's version of idealized femininity. Further clues in the text of *Mansfield Park* suggest that Austen's project is broader and more politically pressing than a simple modernizing revision of a canonical text. Although critics now tend to associate Milton, and particularly *Paradise Lost*, with the revolutionary tendencies of the Romantic era (for example, Wordsworth's frequently cited 'London: 1802', beginning 'Milton! thou should'st be living at this hour'[17]), as More's Cœlebs clearly shows, during the same period the epic poet was being deployed in the most conservative of causes: teaching young women how to behave themselves.

More thus recreates *Paradise Lost* as yet another conduct book for young ladies. To paraphrase Raphael, a woman may 'retain | Unalterably firm his love entire | Whose progeny you are', but only conditionally, that is, 'If ye be found obedient' (bk.5, ll. 501–3, p. 130). For More, however, even more than 'obedience' is demanded of young women – their obedience must be uniformly cheerful, even pleasing – they must be agreeable. Cœlebs calls this *'the positive duty of being agreeable at home'*, and Lucilla's father agrees: 'the absolute *morality* of being agreeable and even entertaining in ones own family circle' (I, p. 347). Austen had earlier spoofed the necessity of being 'agreeable' above all else in her juvenile story 'Frederic and Elfrida', with a young lady named Charlotte 'whose character was a willingness to oblige every one'. When 'an aged gentleman [...] partly by intention & partly thro' weakness was at the feet of the lovely Charlotte, declaring his attachment', the consequences are inevitable:

> Not being able to resolve to make any one miserable, she consented to become his wife; where upon the Gentleman left the room & all was quiet.
> Their quiet however continued but a short time, for on a second opening of the door a young & Handsome Gentleman entered [...] the natural turn of her mind to make every one happy, [Charlotte] promised to become his Wife [...] It was not till the next morning that Charlotte recollected the double engagement she had entered into; but when she did, the reflection of her past folly, operated so strongly on her mind, that she resolved to be guilty of a greater, & to that end threw herself into a deep stream.[18]

Being perfectly agreeable, Austen jokes, can lead only to suicide. She leaves the test of perfect agreeableness to writers like More, but the more widely disputed issue of female obedience is still fodder for Austen's critical investigations.

In *Mansfield Park*, Austen sets up two major tests of Fanny's obedience: the home theatricals and Henry Crawford's proposal. Both have numerous predecessors in Romantic-era fiction, a literary background Austen draws on, and which would have been familiar to her first readers. Private theatricals were familiar holiday entertainment in the Austen household. Nothing as risqué as Elizabeth Inchbald's *Lovers' Vows* (1798, translated and adapted from August Von Kotzebue's 1780 *Das Kind der Liebe*) was ever attempted at Steventon, however, and it is clear that in *Mansfield Park* the nature of the play itself compounds the fault in putting it on. The most vexed issue was that of young ladies' participation in home theatre. More unquestionably disapproves of anything approaching 'display' – even her condemnation of acting is only obliquely mentioned as a metaphor for subtler offences. 'A woman', she writes, 'whose whole education had been rehearsal, will always be dull, except she lives on the stage, constantly displaying what she has been sedulously acquiring' (I, p. 348). In Edgeworth's *Patronage*, the heroine Caroline Percy confirms her admirer's good opinion by refusing to participate in her cousins' home theatricals. 'It would have highly gratified and interested him to have seen Caroline act either the sublime or the tender heroine', writes Edgeworth, 'but he preferred seeing her support her own character with modest dignity [...They] pleaded and pressed in vain; Caroline was steady in her refusal'.[19]

Germaine de Staël sees this as a peculiarly British reticence. In *Corinne, or Italy* (1807), the multi-talented heroine performs the lead role from *Romeo and Juliet* to great acclaim, but her Scottish lover is made thoroughly uneasy: 'he was enjoying the performance [...] but he was also jealous [...] not of any one particular man, but of the public who would be spectators of the talents of the woman he loved'. Staël continues, 'He would have liked to be the only one to know how witty and charming she was; he would have liked Corinne to be as shy and reserved as an Englishwoman and to reveal her eloquence and genius to him alone.'[20] This cultural dissonance – the painful stifling Corinne endures in England, and her lover's inability to reconcile her character with that demanded of respectable English womanhood – leads to the tragedy of the novel's conclusion. Not all private theatricals in literature, however, end with such despair. In Burney's *The Wanderer*, the eponymous heroine, who for much of the novel is also anonymous, is bullied into acting alongside a number of bratty young ladies to whom she teaches music. In spite of her reluctance, her performance is triumphant and improves her standing in a society which can barely tolerate her namelessness and mysterious circumstances. The perform-ance becomes a means of introducing Burney's heroine to her half-siblings and of attracting the attention of the hero.

The inappropriateness of the home theatricals at Mansfield Park is not at issue in the text. Lady Bertram's somnolent approbation is obviously worth little in her husband's absence, and Edmund makes it clear that Sir Thomas, Mansfield's stern paterfamilias, would condemn their fri-volities were he to learn of them. Tom Bertram is unquestionably wrong in his determination to stage such a play in his father's absence, as his flimsy and self-serving attempts at justifying it prove. It is important to recognize that Austen could not have viewed all such entertainment as absolutely beyond the pale; rather, she presents it as being a transgres-sion in the context of the Mansfield Park family. The reasons why this is so lie at the heart of Austen's political project in this novel.

Mansfield Park is, like More's *Cœlebs in Search of a Wife* or Edgeworth's *Patronage*, a study of a family constructed along the conservative, patri-archal model approved by cultural arbiters like Edmund Burke. Austen, like More, demonstrates the way in which such a family is in fact cre-ated by the influence of fiction and other literature on individuals. Where Cœlebs's fantasy wife is explicitly drawn from Milton's Eve, Austen has Fanny inadvertently admit her identification of Edmund with the chivalric heroes of Scott's poetry – 'there is a nobleness in the name of Edmund. It is a name of heroism and renown', she says (p. 211). Other characters reveal views similarly drawn from literature. Sir Thomas's reprimand of Fanny, for example, runs into paraphrase of conservative commentators like James Fordyce or John Gregory: 'I had thought you,' he says,

> peculiarly free from wilfulness of temper, self-conceit, and every tendency to that independence of spirit, which prevails so much in modern days, even in young women, and which in young women is offensive and disgusting beyond all common offence.
>
> (p. 318)

Along with Austen's preoccupation with the literary influences that shape character is an attempt to play with the form that the idealized figures of literature might take when co-opted into a realist setting. Austen's experiment in *Mansfield Park* takes an ideal patriarchal family straight out of the commentary of Edmund Burke, with its strong father, docile mother, intact finances, and handsome children, subjects it to the test of realism, and then observes and reports as the whole structure of the family collapses on itself.

Before the climactic implosion, however, comes a second test, one which demonstrates even more clearly than the home theatricals the process of experimentation to which Austen subjects the Bertram family in *Mansfield Park*. Again, it is female, and particularly daughterly obedience that is at issue. Milton states the case clearly for the conservative side:

> My author and disposer, what thou bid'st
> Unargued I obey; so God ordains,
> God is thy law, thou mine: to know no more
> Is woman's happiest knowledge and her praise.

> (bk.4, ll. 635–8, p. 103)

When Fanny rejects Henry Crawford's marriage proposal, and persists in her rejection even once her uncle has added his recommendation to the suit, then the novel comes closest to revealing the traumatic impact of patriarchal power even on an 'agreeable' young lady like Fanny. Conservative novelists of Austen's period tend to represent patriarchal power as wholly benevolent, and fathers act as a sort of domesticated personification of divine authority, placing great emphasis on their daughters' exercise of free will. Lucilla Stanley rejects marriage, when 'a girl of eighteen', to 'a young nobleman of a clear estate, and neither disagreeable in his person or manner, on the single avowed ground of his loose principles'. This 'noble rejection of the daughter', More writes, 'was supported by the parents, whose principles no arguments drawn from rank or fortune could subvert or shake' (II, pp. 74–5). The happy Percy family of *Patronage* enjoy the same understanding. On learning from her father of a gentleman's proposal, Caroline Percy

> received from him and from her mother the kind assurance that they would leave her entirely at liberty to accept or refuse Mr. Barclay, according as her own judgment and feelings might dictate. They said, that though it might be, in point of fortune, a highly advantageous match [...] they begged her to decide entirely for herself, and to consult only her own happiness.[21]

Mr and Mrs Percy's equanimity is all the more incredible in light of the fact that they have recently lost their estate and the bulk of their fortune.

For the idealized families beloved of More and Edgeworth, a young woman's rejection of a marriage proposal – even of an acknowledged disinclination to a gentleman – receives the full and unalloyed support of her parents. In less conservative novels, beleaguered heroines are frequently exposed to the unwanted addresses of maniacally persistent suitors, and in Charlotte Smith's *Celestina* (1791), Mary Brunton's *Self-Control* (1810), and Burney's *The Wanderer*, heroines are pursued across country – and even across countries – by obsessed anti-heroes who refuse to take 'no' for an answer.[22] In these texts heroines lack the support of a family: the lone, possibly orphaned heroine is *the* central figure through which novelists of the Romantic period explore social injustice through suffering sensibility. In each of these three texts, the heroines are (if only temporarily) socially and economically marginalized, and thus at the greatest risk from unwanted sexual overtures. Their extreme vulnerability, however, also acts as a kind of liberty, leaving them free from the familial pressure exerted on Richardson's Clarissa Harlowe, and on Fanny Price. Only Austen dares to revive the politically more troubling situation of Richardson's tragedy by positioning her besieged heroine within the circle of a powerful family, and Austen refuses Fanny the special circumstances with which Richardson attempts to ameliorate Clarissa's disobedience.

Henry Crawford is no hideous, miserly Soames, the odious suitor marked out for Clarissa by her family. On the contrary, he is as attractive and charming as the alternative suitor Lovelace, and substantially less of an immoral rake. Richardson has his heroine tormented by an extraordinarily cruel and grasping brother, who has usurped his father's proper authority, but Austen allows Fanny a true friend in Edmond, and an uncle who is genuinely and unselfishly concerned for his niece's prospects. Fanny still says 'no', however, and the text vindicates her decision. Austen's artistic choices in *Mansfield Park* demonstrate the extent to which – in this, the first novel written wholly in adulthood – she structured her text in order to criticize specific novelistic conventions. The 'crisis' of an unwanted proposal is, as we have seen, the focal point of many novels, and its treatment by the novelist is a straightforward indicator of that novel's political agenda. In *Mansfield Park*, however, Austen transforms the staple ingredients of the conservative novel – the grateful daughter, the benevolent patriarch, the submissive matron, the supportive and honourable brother – in the crucible of literary realism.

What the theatrical, 'unhappy mansion' of Mansfield Park shows (*Paradise Lost*, bk.1, l. 268, p. 12) is that the conservative patriarchal ideal of family as it was conceived of by writers like Burke, Edgeworth, and More is inescapably oppressive. Unlike these novelists, and unlike even expressly radical writers such as Charlotte Smith, Austen does not ascribe the systemic defects of domestic patriarchy to the short-comings of individuals. In Smith's *The Old Manor House*, the matriarch Mrs Rayland is a capricious, eccentric, and manipulative old woman – General Tracy, the novel's only other powerful figure, is a scheming, corrupt, and priapic ethical vacuum. Sir Thomas Bertram, Baronet and MP, living up to even a Burkean standard of public and private virtue, and honestly attempting to act in his niece's best interests, nevertheless renders Fanny quite as miserable as the beleaguered hero and heroine of *The Old Manor House*. In *Mansfield Park*, it is not the personal failings of the powerful, nor the ingratitude and vice of the weak, nor even sinister outside influences that cause the suffering of the innocent, but the tra-ditional structure of the family – and by inference the state – itself.

Austen stops short in *Mansfield Park* of outlining any alternative system of human relationships, contenting herself instead with play-ing out the consequences of prevailing conservative ideologies. What she does make wickedly transparent, however, is the seductive cultural apparatus that such ideologies make available to the powerless. Both these artistic decisions set Austen apart from her contemporaries, and render Fanny Price (in 1814) the most complex figure yet to appear in a novel. Fanny has fully imbibed the conservative message that she must be agreeable, quiet, grateful, meek, self-denying: that is, she must be miserable to be good. As Austen points out, however, 'if one scheme of happiness fails, human nature turns to another [...] we find comfort somewhere' (p. 46). In the course of the novel Fanny learns that the 'mind is its own place, and in itself | Can make a heaven of hell' (bk.1, ll. 254–5, p. 11). Her ultimate achievement is not in escaping Mansfield Park, but in coming to love it. This leads to one of the most troubling and masochistic comments in Austen's writing, if not in all Romantic fiction: 'Fanny [...] must have been happy in spite of every thing. She must have been a happy creature, in spite of all that she felt or thought she felt, for the distress of those around her' (p. 461). This is Austen's final criticism of the Burkean model of family, and the conservative ideal of submissive femininity as conceived by Hannah More and other writers whose works expressly trumpeted the oppression of women as 'natural'. It is above all, however, a brilliant analysis of the way in which the ideologically-driven illogic of literature may be uncritically absorbed and even internalized by individuals, who then adopt an author's made-up narrative as their own truth. It took Austen's critical creativity to point out the dangerous nonsense of conservative fiction – indeed the risk inherent in imbibing any fiction unthinkingly. It remains for us to read her criticism well.

Notes

The title quotation is from Jane Austen, *Mansfield Park*, ed. by R.W. Chapman (Oxford: Oxford University Press, 1988), p. 90.

1. *The Kristeva Reader*, ed. by Toril Moi (New York: Columbia University Press, 1986) p. 37.
2. Michael Gamer explains the complex effects of the decision in 'A Select Collection: Barbauld, Scott, and the Rise of the (Reprinted) Novel', in *Recognizing the Romantic Novel: New Histories of British Fiction, 1780–1830*, ed. by Jillian Heydt-Stevenson and Charlotte Sussman (Liverpool: Liverpool University Press, 2008), pp. 155–91.
3. Jane Austen, Letter to Anna Austen, 28 September 1814, in *Jane Austen's Letters*, ed. by Deirdre Le Faye (Oxford: Oxford University Press, 1995), p. 277.
4. This is not to diminish the work of earlier critics such as J.M.S. Tompkins, whose monograph *The Popular Novel in England 1770–1800* remains one of the fullest accounts of the subject available. Tompkins, however, explicitly refrains from attempts at canon-construction, stating instead that her study is of 'tenth-rate fiction' (Lincoln: University of Nebraska, 1961), p. v.
5. Terry Castle, 'Women and Literary Criticism', in *The Cambridge History of Literary Criticism, Volume IV: The Eighteenth Century*, ed. by H.B. Nisbet and Claude Rawson (Cambridge: Cambridge University Press, 1997), pp. 454–5.
6. Nancy Armstrong, *Desire and Domestic Fiction: A Political History of the Novel* (New York: Oxford University Press, 1987), p. 48.
7. Jane Austen, *Persuasion* (1818), ed. by R.W. Chapman (Oxford: Oxford University Press, 1988), p. 85.
8. Letter to James Stanier Clarke, 11 December 1815, in Le Faye, ed., *Letters*, p. 306.
9. Jane Austen, *Northanger Abbey* (1818), ed. by R.W. Chapman (Oxford: Oxford University Press, 1988), p. 111.
10. Jane Austen, *Mansfield Park* (1814), pp. 56, 85.
11. Germaine de Staël, *Literature Considered in Its Relationship to Social Institutions* (1800), in *Politics, Literature, and National Character*, trans. and ed. by Morroe Berger (New Brunswick, New Jersey and London: Transaction, 2000), p. 234.
12. 'Come, a second rape of the lock, Belinda.' Maria Edgeworth, *Belinda* (1801), ed. by Kathryn Kirkpatrick (Oxford: Oxford University Press, 1994), p. 76.
13. See D.A. Miller, *Jane Austen, or the Secret of Style* (Princeton: Princeton University Press, 2003), pp. 2–3.
14. For a discussion of *The Old Manor House* as a source-text for *Mansfield Park*, see Jacqueline Labbe, 'Narrating Seduction: Charlotte Smith and Jane Austen', in *Charlotte Smith in British Romanticism*, ed. by Jacqueline Labbe (London: Pickering and Chatto, 2008), pp. 113–28.
15. Austen, *Mansfield Park*, p. 43 (Austen's emphasis). John Milton, *Paradise Lost*, ed. by Stephen Orgel and Jonathan Goldberg (Oxford: Oxford University Press, 2004), bk. 5, l. 19, p. 116. Subsequent references to both will be cited parenthetically in the text.

16. Hannah More, *Cœlebs in Search of a Wife. Comprehending Observations on Domestic Habits and Manners, Religion and Morals* (1808) 5th edn, 2 vols (London: Cadell and Davies, 1809), I, 1, 3–4. Subsequent references will be cited parenthetically in the text.

17. William Wordsworth, 'London: 1802', in *The Major Works*, ed. by Stephen Gill (Oxford: Oxford University Press, 2000), p. 286.

18. Jane Austen, *Minor Works*, ed. by R.W. Chapman, rev. B.C. Southam (Oxford: Oxford University Press, 1988), pp. 4, 8–9.

19. Maria Edgeworth, *Patronage* (1814) (London: Routledge, 1893), pp. 352–3.

20. Germaine de Staël, *Corinne, or Italy* (1807), trans. and ed. by Sylvia Raphael (Oxford: Oxford University Press, 1998), p. 122.

21. Edgeworth, *Patronage*, p. 199.

22. Celestina's admirer follows her from Devon to the Isle of Skye (in disguise!), *Self-Control*'s Laura Montreville is pursued from Scotland to England before being kidnapped at the impassioned villain's behest and smuggled to Canada, and the heroine of *The Wanderer* is chased from revolutionary France to England by the *sans culotte* who has forced her, unconsenting, to marry him.

15
Mary Tighe and the Coterie of Women Poets in *Psyche*

Harriet Kramer Linkin

In 1805 the Anglo-Irish poet Mary Blachford Tighe privately printed 50 copies of her epic *Psyche; or, The Legend of Love* and distributed them to the friends and family members who comprised her regional literary coterie. More than a few among the circle had already previewed manuscript copies of *Psyche*, including Thomas Moore, whose 1802 tribute 'To Mrs. Henry Tighe, on Reading Her "Psyche"' speaks to the pleasure of that experience; the Ladies of Llangollen, Lady Eleanor Butler and Sarah Ponsonby, whose 1803 copy contains a unique, politically-charged stanza in canto five, a stunning watercolour at the end of canto six, and a proud transcription of Moore's 1802 tribute; and the Irish antiquarian Joseph Cooper Walker, whose admiration for the manuscript prompted him to recommend that Tighe prepare an edition for the public in 1804. She considered that recommendation but declined, preferring to remain a coterie poet in the most classic (or early modern) sense of the term, circulating her works among friends and relatives with no intent to publish them commercially. A year after she died, her family published the first commercial edition of *Psyche, with Other Poems* (1811), which included a lightly edited version of the 1805 *Psyche* and 39 of the nearly 150 poems Tighe circulated in manuscript. *Psyche, with Other Poems* would go through five editions by 1816, sell 5500 copies, and secure Tighe's fame as the posthumous author of *Psyche*, hailed as an 'Irish queen' by Sir James Mackintosh and the 'finest *poetess* of her own or perhaps any country' by Sydney Owenson (Lady Morgan).[1] Why did Tighe decline to publish her own 'Psyche, with Other Poems'? What did it mean for her to position herself as a coterie poet in Dublin and Wicklow in the early 1800s?

If authorship constituted a culturally complex venture for the early modern women writers like Katherine Philips who circulated manuscript copies within their select coteries, it became even more complex in Tighe's time, with the advent of expanded public literacy and printing venues, which dramatically increased potential exposure to an unknown audience. Many women writers wondered how far they could reach before they lost rather than made their reputations, a concern made all-too-concrete through the disciplining example of Mary Wollstonecraft, whose posthumous reputation after William Godwin's notorious 1798 memoir set stern parameters for women contemplating publication in 1800–30. For some, a coterie still offered a safe mode of controlled authorship that occupied a liminal space somewhere between the public and private spheres. Those fortunate enough to write for pleasure rather than profit could bypass the cultural and psychological dilemmas posed by 'the conventional expectation that publishing (or – worse – writing for money) was vulgar and unwomanly'.[2] They also stood to gain a clearer right to their intellectual property than many of the women writers who published commercially, given the constraints of a legal system that only allowed widows and unmarried women over the age of twenty-one to own or manage property (textual or otherwise). Tilar Mazzeo points to the example of Mary Shelley, whose marriage to Percy Bysshe Shelley in 1816 meant that she 'did not own the intellectual property of a work such as *Frankenstein* (1818) except through his goodwill'.[3] Whereas coterie authors typically signed their works with their own names ('M.B. Tighe'), commercial publications by women writers often appear under the sign of Anonymous, 'the Author' (Mary Shelley's case), or a proper legal name ('Mrs Henry Tighe').

While private coterie authorship extended signature or property rights for some women writers, for others a coterie became a means of engaging or transforming the public sphere: Julia Wright notes how the women writers of the LeFanu-Sheridan-Morgan circle used their coterie connections to secure publication; Gary Kelly traces the ways members of the extended Wollstonecraft-Shelley circle enabled one another to advance shared social ideals through coterie novels.[4] In numerous cases coteries provided polite rationales for entering the public sphere: the friends cited in prefaces who urged diffident writers to publish. Thus did Tighe's friends urge her to engage the public sphere, a sphere her lyrics, letters, and journals indicate she might have found attractive, given her professed love of admiration and attention. What seems especially peculiar about Tighe's decision to reserve *Psyche* for her coterie, however, is that the poem explicitly charges Psyche to leave a coterie of women poets she seeks to join in the penultimate canto five and spread the message of that canto to the world. This seeming disparity between Tighe's actions and her poem's outcome points to an intriguing disjunction in her stance on authorship and advocacy. In what follows, I will argue that regional coterie authorship enabled Tighe to circumvent the anxieties of publication but ultimately frustrated her desire for fame; desires and anxieties she expresses with poignancy in her final journal, a set of literary reviews and musings she completed between 1806 and 1809, when she was too ill to move beyond the geographic parameters of her coterie.

Writing for the coterie: 'Oh, you for whom I write'[5]

Determining the actual membership of Tighe's coterie is an imprecise business at best: literary historians tend to centre specific coteries around a great name, shared location, or aesthetic-political ideal, but coteries often operate as intersecting, overlapping circles with fluctuating (yet exclusive) casts of principal, peripheral, and occasional participants. Tighe circulated within a fairly expansive network of literary-social sets in a variety of locations (Dublin, London, Llangollen) and was connected with a range of literary figures (including Joseph Atkinson, Henrietta Bowdler, Henry Boyd, Lady Eleanor Butler, Catherine Maria Fanshawe, William Hayley, Alicia LeFanu, Henry Moore, Thomas Moore, Hannah More, Sydney Owenson/Lady Morgan, William Parnell, Sarah Ponsonby, William Roscoe, Anna Seward, Charlotte Smith, Barbarina Wilmot/Lady Dacre, and Joseph Cooper Walker). Several played very active roles in the primarily Irish Tighe circle – notably Thomas Moore, Lady Morgan, Lady Dacre, and the Ladies of Llangollen – but the most important members of the Tighe coterie were members of the Tighe family: Mary Blachford Tighe (1772–1810) herself, her cousin and brother-in-law William Tighe (1766–1816), her husband and cousin Henry Tighe (1771–1836), her cousin and sister-in-law Caroline Tighe Hamilton (1777–1861), and her cousin George Tighe (1776–1837). Other significant participants included Tighe's brother John Blachford (1771–1817), her mother Theodosia Tighe Blachford (1744–1817), John's first wife Camilla de Brady (m. 1796), and Tighe's mother-in-law Sarah Fownes Tighe (d. 1822), whose father Sir William Fownes infamously propositioned Sarah Tighe's cousin Sarah Ponsonby and thereby precipitated the flight of the Ladies of Llangollen to Wales.

The Tighe family delighted in private intellectual competition at their various Wicklow and Dublin domains. It is probably because the family occupied several great houses that we have significant access to their literary history. As Margaret Ezell observes, 'One reason we associate manuscript author practices with "aristocrats" is because there was, pragmatically, a higher chance of these texts surviving for several generations and thus of being recovered. Manuscript texts have a much better chance of being preserved and passed down if their authors had established family homes.'[6] Three literary albums in particular document the interactions of the Tighe coterie: the Tighe album at Rossana, the Blachford album at Altadore, and the Hamilton album at Hamwood.[7] Caroline Hamilton preserved much of the family history: she kept numerous commonplace books, inherited valuable journals from Sarah Ponsonby and Eleanor Butler, and wrote several family memoirs (including the first biography of Mary Tighe). The memoirs and transcriptions in her commonplace books provide a rich picture of the family coterie: Tighe, the gifted poet who ambivalently displayed or downplayed her intelligence; William Tighe, the poet and statesman still cited for his *Statistical Observations Relative to the County of Kilkenny* (1802); Henry Tighe, the frustrated Latinist; George Tighe, the radical who left Ireland for Italy and marriage to Lady Mountcashell (the pupil of Mary Wollstonecraft who called herself Mrs Mason); and Hamilton herself, the artist and mother who stopped painting to raise her children in Meath but kept her extraordinary literary diaries for them.

One sees the family coterie in action in Tighe's witty 'A Letter from Mrs. Acton to her Nephew Mr. Evans', a celebration of the family's competitive intellectual sociability that was printed in the Rossana album, copied into Hamilton's commonplace book, mailed by Tighe to family friend Susan Butticuz (and others), but, rather tellingly, is not one of the 39 lyrics posthumously published in *Psyche, with Other Poems*.[8] In this 84-line virtuoso poem Tighe assumes the voice of Sidney Acton (of West-Aston) warning her nephew George Evans (of Portraine) that he'd best be ready to deliver an entertaining and erudite performance if he plans to Christmas at Rossana, where one hears 'fifteen languages spoken at table' (l. 18), the servants speak Latin and Greek, the ladies read Arabic and present tea in Chinese, food is prepared to display scientific principles (chemistry, geometry, trigonometry), and, most importantly, everyone is 'a poetical genius' (l. 42):

> When the family, call'd by the bells' silver tine,
> Assembles to supper, each offers his own,
> Whether epic or tragic or comic they choose
> Each worships his favorite appropriate muse.
> Not a person appears in the family circle
> But has verses deserving bays, laurel or myrtle.
> Not with pencil alone is it Caroline's care

> The vices to task, but the persons to spare;
> For tho' on her labours the muses all smile
> Yet the high polish'd satire's her favorite style
> Miss Butticuz modest and timid declares
> That nothing beyond a poor sonnet she dares;
> But it has been whisper'd and I think that the fact is
> She prepares for the press a new system of tactics:
> [...]
> Camilla indeed, as a foreigner, says
> From her lips are expected no vulgar tongued lays,
> But in the Mandingo, or verses Arabic,
> She now and then ventures lines enigrammatic;
> Then Mary sings plaintive in notes elegiac,
> While her brother I'm told prefers the alcaic.

(ll. 49–78)

By assuming Acton's voice Tighe strategically encapsulates her own impressive intellectual performance – limited in the poem to a single line where she describes herself as 'plaintive' (l. 77) – which showcases her participation in the family's competitive sociability by showing off the family showing off. The verbal grandstanding Tighe displays in this coterie poem contrasts sharply with Hamilton's representation of Tighe's silence in non-familial company:

> It was her idea that learning and talents in women, never excited love &, while young, she was willing to pass for having neither. I remember hearing it remarked that Mrs Tighe was very pretty but had not much sense. Indeed, she often chose for her companions those who were very far below the rest of the world in talents if they loved her. She never tried to shine in conversation & was often considered too silent in company.[9]

Hamilton's biography frequently portrays Tighe as torn between her desire to inhabit the comfortable retirement of the family coterie and her attraction to the vainer amusements of fashionable society, a vacillation of desire Tighe's coterie poems enact. In 'La Cittadina: On Leaving Rossana 1798' she delights in the social pleasures of 'Balls, and Concerts, routs and plays / Where the midnight flambeause blaze' (ll. 27–8) but notes the quieter satisfactions of 'home, dear cherished center! / Where no visitors can enter; / From intrusion sweetly free, / Banish'd all formality / .... / Reserves cold frost there melt away / Beneath the social genial ray, / While around the blazing pile / The close contracted circle pile' (ll. 119–32). In 'The Hours of Peace', however, Tighe, employing her coterie name 'Linda', clearly prefers home's 'social hearth' (l. 15): 'I gladly would forego / The splendid circle's idle shew, / Nor sigh for more than you bestow / Dear hours of peace' (ll. 9–12). This poem, in addition to naming Tighe as Linda (the name Sarah Ponsonby uses to address her in a response poem to *Psyche* which parodies the third stanza of canto five[10]), invokes Thomas Moore as 'young Anacreon' (l. 21), a moniker not yet in wide usage. Moore's participation in the Tighe coterie at this early stage of his career in Dublin discloses another form of anxiety that authors experienced as they negotiated the borders of the public/private spheres. For Moore the pressure to perform for the coterie and allow its private circulation of improvised work presented greater anxiety than commercial publication, perhaps because work published commercially could be revised for a permanent printing. He admits the pressure he feels in a letter to Hamilton, in which he apologizes for his not contributing a poem to the Hamwood album before leaving Dublin for England:

> You have every reason to think me very neglectful, but I assure you your album has given me more trouble than you will easily believe. The truth is I had not *courage* to begin it. I tried several subjects and failed in them all. When a man writes a book, he balances the bad against the good, and hopes to atone by what follows for the insipidity of what went before, but to write *one* poem, which was worthy of leading the way, where *you*, Mrs. Tighe, 'e *gli altri* sacri al divo Apollo', were to come after, is a task which I was very inconsiderate in taking.[11]

The poem he encloses in the letter is an unfinished draft of his 'To Mrs. Henry Tighe, on Reading Her "Psyche"' (1802) which he will write and rewrite several times and in several places before he finalizes the version that appears in *Epistles, Odes and Other Poems* (1806).

Despite the anxiety Moore confesses in inhabiting the position Tighe assigns to her friend George Evans in 'A Letter from Mrs. Acton', he invokes the Dublin coterie to support the publication of his pseudonymously titled *Poetical Works of the Late Thomas Little* (1801): 'The Poems which I take the liberty of publishing, were never intended by the Author to pass beyond the circle of his friends [...] if their posthumous introduction to the world be injustice to his memory, or intrusion on the public, the error must be imputed to the injudicious partiality of friendship.'[12] Furthermore, he publishes several poems (as 'Thomas

Little') that emanate from that anxious place, including 'To a Lady. With some manuscript Poems. On leaving the Country', 'Written in the Blank Leaf of a Lady's Common-place Book', and 'To Mrs. —, On Her Beautiful Translation of Voiture's Kiss'. The unnamed 'Mrs. —' is Tighe, whose coterie poem 'The Kiss. – Imitated from Voiture' transforms the amatory metaphysical conceit of Voiture's 1650 *Stances* into her characteristic idiom of desire: 'As I snatched the sudden kiss, / From my lips my heart hath flown; / Ravished by the enchanting bliss, / And resigned its native throne' (ll. 13–16). Like 'A Letter from Mrs. Acton', 'La Cittadina', and 'The Hours of Peace', 'The Kiss' was not published in the posthumous *Psyche, with Other Poems*, but was copied into various commonplace books, including the albums of Reverend Henry and Lucy Moore. Comparable to Mary Robinson outdoing Samuel Taylor Coleridge by citing his unpublished 'Kubla Khan' in her 'To the Poet Coleridge', Moore trades on Tighe's status as an established poet who confined her spirited participation in intellectual competition to her circle, and therein located a safe forum for private publication.

What will prove ironic about Moore's use of Tighe and the coterie argument in the preface to *The Poetical Works of the Late Thomas Little* is the manner in which the preface to this nonexistent poet uncannily anticipates the trajectory of Tighe's publication history: first, Moore takes the identity of the friend who publishes the work posthumously (just as Tighe's family will); second, he offers a justification of the amatory lyrics not unlike the one Tighe will present to her coterie in her 1802 preface to *Psyche*, which claims to offer a verse 'translation' of the bawdy Apuleius (just as Moore translated the *Odes of Anacreon* in 1800); and third, the preface refers to an unpublished novel that might be forthcoming, precisely the status of Tighe's literary work after the posthumous publication of *Psyche, with Other Poems*. (Moore himself advised Henry Tighe not to publish Tighe's manuscript novel *Selena* in 1818.) Perhaps the most important issue of all, however, is the vehemence of the critical response to Moore, who is lambasted in the *Edinburgh Review* for licentiousness in July 1803, the first of a series of attacks or critiques Tighe will note with care, and which will have a considerable impact on her determination to publish within or without the coterie in 1804.[13]

Sociability in *Psyche*: 'Quit the busy circle of the vain' (*Psyche* 2.25)

Up until 1801 Mary and Henry Tighe travelled back and forth between Ireland and England, socializing with various communities in London,

Bath, Bristol, Llangollen, Dublin, Kilkenny, and Wicklow, who provided them with a range of opportunities and venues to enact the social in the literary (and the literary in the social). In 1801 they settled permanently in Ireland, and Tighe 'forsook the Ballroom & Theatre' to turn to the more serious production of literature: her epic poem *Psyche*, a bold retelling of the myth of Cupid and Psyche in 372 Spenserian stanzas.[14] Tighe's rich revision of the myth considers, among other things, the formation of female identity, the nature of romantic love, female eroticism, competitive relations among women, masculine idealizations of women and beauty, female experience of the sublime, the trajectory of a female quest, and the place of women poets in the Romantic era. As I argue elsewhere, Tighe's selection of the Psyche myth resonates with potent self-reflexivity, given her status as a beauty.[15] Throughout the poem Tighe establishes parallels between Psyche and herself, but with an important difference: she contrasts her representation of Psyche as the romanticized object of desire who transgresses when she looks at Cupid with herself as the visionary woman poet who demonstrates her right to look. Tighe expends a good deal of energy differentiating her narrative presence as the poet from Psyche's subject position as a character; indeed Psyche functions as a character whose subjectivity gives pleasure to Tighe as the woman poet who gazes upon her:

> Delightful visions of my lonely hours!
> Charm of my life, and solace of my care!
> Oh! would the muse but lend proportioned powers,
> And give me language, equal to declare
> The wonders which she bids my fancy share,
> When rapt in her to other worlds I fly,
> [...]
> Might I the swiftly glancing scenes recall!
> Bright as the roseate clouds of summer's eve;
> The dreams which hold my soul in willing thrall,
> And half my visionary days deceive,
> Communicable shape might then receive,
> And other hearts be ravished with the strain;
> [...]
> Fond dreamer! meditate thine idle song!
> But let thine idle song remain unknown,
> The verse which cheers thy solitude, prolong;
> What, though it charm no moments but thine own,
> Though thy loved Psyche smile for thee alone,

Still shall it yield thee pleasure, if not fame,
And when escaped from tumult thou hast flown
To thy dear silent hearth's enlivening flame,
There shall the tranquil muse her happy votary claim!

(5.1–27)

In these first three stanzas of canto five – the critical canto where Psyche finds a coterie of women poets but is charged with leaving the coterie to bring its message to the world – Tighe articulates some of the anxiety and ambivalence that will inform her decision not to publish an edition of *Psyche* for the public: here she perhaps disingenuously fears she lacks the power to give full voice to her visions. Although she clearly admits her interest in achieving fame, she protects herself from the risk of failure by claiming to locate pleasure in writing exclusively for herself: 'Though thy loved Psyche smile for thee alone, / Still shall it yield thee pleasure, if not fame' (5.24–5). Surprisingly, despite the distinctions Tighe draws between herself and Psyche, Psyche is also a poet who learns the muse's lore in canto one, but quickly discovers that the life of a solitary visionary poet inspired by the muse fails to suffice. She needs more than invisible voices to teach her, and more than Cupid's embrace: she needs the sociability of a circle, the conclusion Tighe herself will reach after she completes *Psyche* and distributes copies to her friends and family. Given Tighe's identity as a coterie poet, it is significant that part of the journey Tighe scripts for Psyche – within the framework of the myth's requirements that Psyche complete a set of tasks that garner Venus's approval and Cupid's return – entails Psyche interacting with various circles that might or might not satisfy her need for sociability and her potential to participate as a poet in a coterie.

There are at least four episodes among Psyche's numerous adventures that highlight interactions with prospective circles or coteries: the invisible band of female voices who serve Psyche at Cupid's castle in canto one; the family coterie Psyche visits in canto two after her marriage to Cupid; the sycophantic circle that surrounds Varia, the lady of loose delights, in canto three; and the coterie of women poets Psyche seeks to join in canto five when she enters the chaste Castabella's realm. Interestingly, trouble emerges in Psyche's marriage when she expresses desire for community, a desire Cupid recognizes will jeopardize their sequestered idyll. He urges her to 'charm the languid hours of solitude' with 'the Muse's lore' (1.496–7), a pursuit Tighe's narrator approves – 'For none have vainly e'er the Muse pursued, / And those whom she delights, regret no more / The social, joyous hours, while rapt they soar / To worlds unknown, and live in fancy's dream' (1.498–501) – but one that fails to meet Psyche's needs: 'This solace now the lonely Psyche tries, / ... / She learns from lips unseen celestial strains; / Responsive now with their soft voice she vies, / ... / But melancholy poisons all her joys, / And secret sorrows all her hopes depress, / ... / She longs to meet a parent's sweet embrace' (1.508–15). Cupid reluctantly allows Psyche to return home with well-placed trepidation: if Tighe's comfort coterie was her family circle, it certainly isn't Psyche's. Canto two opens with the narrator warning Psyche to 'shun the public eye, / And quit the busy circle of the vain' (2.24–5), which in this instance means the destructive competitiveness of her envious sisters, who respond to Psyche's 'wondrous tale' (2.46) of life with her new husband with counter-tales that depict him as a monster. It's tempting to wonder if Tighe's feelings about the family coterie shifted as her own sisters-in-law prospered: both Camilla Blachford and Caroline Hamilton were considerably wealthier than Tighe in the 1800s and began constructing their own literary circles via their commonplace books. In any event, the envy that mars what Tighe called the 'close contracted circle' of the family coterie ('La Cittadina') materializes as the empty flattery and malicious slander of the 'social circle' ('The Hours of Peace') in canto three, where Psyche has to fly from Varia and her 'white bosomed nymphs' (3.208). They 'sing of love with soft expiring tones' (3.210) when they meet Psyche, but turn on her and transform into serpents with forked tongues when Psyche finds herself unable to accept a portion of their hospitality.[16]

By the time Psyche approaches Castabella's realm at least three models prove unviable: the solitary singer interacting with invisible voices (Cupid's castle), the negatively competitive family coterie (Psyche's sisters), and the sycophantic coterie focused on fashion (Varia's brood). The moment Psyche gazes upon Castabella, however, she recognizes a kindred soul: 'That form majestic might the bravest awe; / Yet Psyche gazed with love unmixed with fear, / ... / Congenial souls! they at one glance appear / Linked to each other by a mutual tie' (5.100–5). Moreover she locates a viable coterie of women poets among Castabella's chaste 'circling nymphs' (5.146) whose 'choral band' (5.183) she seeks to join:

> Psyche with ravished ear the strain attends,
> Enraptured hangs upon the heaven-strung lyre;
> Her kindling soul from sensual earth ascends;
> To joys divine her purer thoughts aspire;
> She longs to join the white robed spotless choir,

[...]
All heedless of her knight, who sad and mute
With wonder hears the strange ungrateful fair,
A prostrate suppliant, pour the fervent prayer
To be received in Castabella's train,
And that in tranquil bliss secluded there,
Her happy votary still she might remain,
Free from each worldly care, and each polluting stain.

(5.334–51)

Here Psyche finally finds a circle that promises to satisfy her need for sociability and potential to participate as a poet in a coterie. But joining Castabella's choir means abandoning the quest for Cupid, a dilemma that Tighe resolves by having Castabella charge Psyche with bearing the message of the coterie to the world: '"Far other services my soul demands / Than those which here in these sequestered lands / Her zeal would pay: no, let her bear my fame / Even to the bowers where Love himself commands: / There shall my votary reign secure from blame, / And teach his myrtle groves to echo to my name"' (5.364–9). Despite Castabella's charge that Psyche teach Cupid's groves to echo to the name of chastity through her songs, when Psyche completes her quest she ceases to speak altogether, uttering no more than a 'softly pleasurable sigh, / That tells unutterable ecstasy!' (6.508–9). While Psyche continues to bear witness to Castabella's fame, she does so through bodily example rather than active voice, a silencing Tighe's narrator mourns in her own grim conclusion, where she speaks to the limitations of writing exclusively for herself:

Dreams of Delight farewell! your charms no more
Shall gild the hours of solitary gloom!
The page remains – but can the page restore
The vanished bowers which Fancy taught to bloom?
Ah no! her smiles no longer can illume
The path my Psyche treads no more for me;
Consigned to dark oblivion's silent tomb
The visionary scenes no more I see,
Fast from the fading lines the vivid colours flee!

(6.532–40)

Of course Tighe rejects the ending she scripts for Psyche as well as the narrator by sharing the poem in manuscript with a few members of her coterie, to see whether 'other hearts be ravished with the strain' (5.15). The postscript to the copy the Ladies of Llangollen receive (an early version of the preface printed in the 1805 edition) opens with a paragraph acknowledging the safe course Tighe takes in presenting her work to interested friends:

> The author who dismisses to the public the darling object of his solitary cares must be prepar'd to consider with indifference the various reception it may there meet with; But from those who write only for the more interested eye of friendship no such indifference can be expected – I must therefore be forgiven the egotism which makes me anxious to recommend to *my* readers the tale with which I now present them, while I endeavour to excuse in it all other defects but that which I fear cannot be excus'd, I mean the deficiency of Genius.[17]

The reception from these interested friends is immediate and immensely encouraging: Moore concludes his unfinished manuscript tribute to Tighe with the words 'Thou soarest — '.[18] Even better, Sarah Ponsonby writes a response poem parodying the third stanza of canto five that urges Tighe not to let her 'song remain unknown' (5.20):

> Sweet Linda! meditate thy charming song,
> Nor let thy charming song remain unknown
> The verse which cheers thy solitude prolong
> To witch the world with beauties all its own,
> Let not thy Psyche smile for thee alone
> Accept the garland which immortal fame
> Of Amaranths in celestial gardens grown
> To crown thy modest brow, doth haste to frame
> The Guerdon meet thy soul-enchanting lay doth claim.[19]

Best of all, the well-connected author Joseph Cooper Walker recommends publication. He first requests permission to show her work to others (such as the British poet William Hayley, who enabled Charlotte Smith's first edition of *Elegiac Sonnets*), which she grants:

> You are very good to receive with such indulgence my compositions but I fear others (to whom your flattering partiality might incline you to show them) cannot be expected to look upon them with the same favoring eye – I hope my vanity of authorship may never conquer the

repugnance I now feel to stand forth to the public & say hear me, but I will not deny that I feel any thing more delightful to self love than to be listen'd to with a smile, nor is that pleasure in any degree lessen'd by a consciousness that I should place the smile to the account of partiality – You have my full leave therefore to impart what ever you may have of mine, whenever your doing so will give *you* the smallest gratification, very certain (from your good heart & good judgement) that you could have none in exposing me to contempt –[20]

But when the results prompt Walker to recommend publication, Tighe declines: 'As to my Psyche – my maternal vanity & fondness for her has been moved alone by your flattery – & I have almost forgotten her in the new fancy of my imagination – but I am a great coward as to publication'.[21]

Tighe satisfies her 'maternal vanity' rather than the 'vanity of author-ship' that would bring her work to the public – for which she claims 'repugnance' but admits cowardice – by printing 50 copies of *Psyche* for the friends and family who belong to her coterie. Each copy bears a specific dedication but each copy bears the same prefatory opening lines, which, in the light of Tighe's decision not to publish commer-cially, reads somewhat differently than it did in the manuscript copies Tighe delivered to friends in 1802: 'The author, who dismisses to the public the darling object of his solitary cares, must be prepared to consider, with some degree of indifference, the various reception it may then meet. But from those, who write only for the more interested eye of friendship, no such indifference can be expected' (p. 53). If repug-nance and fear inform Tighe's decision, so does the inescapable truth of bodily decline: in January 1804 she contracts the consumption that slowly but surely exhausts her energies till her death in March 1810. A letter to Caroline Hamilton dated 27 December 1804 sadly speaks to the 'languor which renders all exertion a misery' and its impact on Tighe's capacity to compose letters much less poetry: 'my spirits are good – far better than they have been at times when "my strength & health had not failed me" – but they are not equal to the *publication* of Psyche – I am going however to print 50 copies & I hope you will honor one with a place in your Hammond library'.[22] Reading the letter to Hamilton against one to Walker on 24 December 1804 tells a slightly different tale about the conflict between body and spirit, however:

I have myself been on the very verge of a most frightful auspice & had almost been persuaded to expose to the mercy of the reviewers,

Edinburg *butchers* & all, my poor little Psyche & a volume of smaller
poems which I was advis'd to add, as I might, to serve like the straw
appendages of a kite, that she might not fall to the ground by her
own weight – however after a few nights agitation I found that I have
not nerves for it, let my stock of self conceit be as great as it may, so
I am very obstinate to the partial solicitations of those who I am sure
are chiefly anxious to provide me with what they think would prove
amusement – but it is too serious a business for that – I have however
resolv'd upon providing a few copies of Psyche only, which I confess
I have great pleasure already in distributing *in idea* –[23]

Tighe precedes her discussion of the frightful auspices of publication by
detailing a visit from 'Anacreon', whose experience with the *Edinburgh
Review* haunts her decision-making and presents a steady topic in her
letters to Walker. More than repugnance, more than ill-health, the
censure – or contempt – of those 'Edinburg *butchers*' keeps Tighe writing
for the coterie.

Too timid to publish, but showing her bluestockings up to the knee

Tighe's coterie responded very enthusiastically to *Psyche*; many of
the recipients wrote coterie poems in response, filled with praise for
her work (including published authors such as William Hayley, Anna
Seward, William Roscoe, and Lady Dacre). Avid readers outside the
select circle of 50 borrowed print (and manuscript) copies and tran-
scribed them, increasing the circulation of *Psyche* in unanticipated ways
and to uncontrolled degrees. In fact several months after the first printing the poem became so much an object of interest that Tighe discovered plans afoot to prepare a second, unauthorized commercial printing,
a project she took quick steps to prevent. In February 1806 she writes
a letter to her printer John Carpenter that warns him 'I have been told
that Psyche is advertis'd in London, & tho' I do not believe it, yet I write
at Mr. Tighe's desire to request, that should this be the case either now
or in future, that you will *immediately* take whatever steps can be taken
towards preventing the publication if possible & if not for commencing
a prosecution.' Interestingly, she follows this warning by suggesting,
a few lines later, that Carpenter print an authorized edition if it is too
late to prevent the rogue edition: 'If it is to be publish'd I would certainly do all in my power that you might be before hand with an edition
of our own, & as you have express'd yourself in so obliging a manner

on the subject I hope for both our sakes that you will not neglect this request, nor allow Psyche to appear with such disadvantage to herself & to us.'[24] Carpenter and Tighe's lawyer John Richardson succeed in preventing the publication of the rogue edition and thus remove the imperative for Tighe to publish 'an edition of our own'. Did Tighe ever regret her decision not to publish beyond the parameters of her coterie? She invites that query through her representation of herself as an important author among published authors in her last extended writing, her 1806–09 journal of literary reviews, where she not only presents herself as a famous author but provides pointed commentary on the women writers who do pursue commercial publication and tracks with care the negative commentary Moore receives from the 'Edinburg *butchers'*.[25]

While Tighe's battle with consumption did take a heavy toll on her poetic production during the last five years of her life, she continued to pursue an active intellectual agenda via her literary salon in Dublin, her correspondence, and her critical commentaries on her reading. Moore actually remarked on Tighe's literary activities with dismay in a December 1806 letter to Mary Godfrey: 'I regret very much to find that she is becoming so "furieusement littéraire:" one used hardly to get a peep at her blue stockings but now I am afraid she shows them up to the knee.'[26] She shows off those bluestockings with abandon in the 1806–09 journal, through sharp critiques of literary contemporaries and predecessors as well as detailed analyses of historical, religious, and scientific texts written in English, French, Italian, and German. The journal's 228 entries cover the roughly 250 works she read between April 1806 and June 1809, beginning with James Raymond's *The Life of Thomas Dermody* and ending with Lord Byron's *English Bards, and Scotch Reviewers*. Entries range in length and depth from a single biting remark on Richard Cumberland's *A Hint to Husbands* – 'An extreme dull comedy in blank verse' (May 1806) – to ten pages on Germaine de Staël's *Influence des Passions* (April 1806). An absorbing portrait of contemporary reading habits, the journal not only reflects Tighe's immersion in antiquarianism, mythology, romance, natural philosophy, spiritual autobiography, and Italian poetry, but also reveals something about the access readers had to literature: the record of Tighe's extensive novel-reading – especially women's novels – neatly correlates with the novels available in circulating libraries.

Perhaps surprisingly, in light of the fondness Tighe expresses for her literary coterie, and the affection she projects through Psyche for the women poets of Castabella's circle, some of the harshest criticism in the journal falls on the commercial publications of women writers, including members of her coterie, such as Mrs Norris, whose *The Strangers* was 'written by an acquaintance so I paid the double tax of purchase & perusal to a most insipid performance totally destitute of all genius' (December 1806); or Sydney Owenson, whose *St. Clair* is 'full of pedantic affectation, absurd principles, forc'd allusions – false sentiments & bad poetry – and yet here & there a trait of true feeling a picturesque description and a happy quotation pleas'd & almost astonish'd me' (April 1806); or Hannah More, whose anonymous bestseller *Coelebs in Search of a Wife* she cuts to shreds: 'I never could have believed that this stupid novel badly written & badly design'd, full of bad taste, bad religion, & bad English was indeed H. More, had I not known from unquestionable authority that she acknowledges it' (March 1809). One wonders whether she writes defensively when she states a preference for Miss Staal's manuscript poems, given her decision to print privately: 'I was quite charm'd by the tender spirit & melancholy grace of these unlabored uncorrected verses. They breathe genius taste & feeling, & inspire me with the utmost compassion for the interesting *Somebody* whose printed poems are inferior to these' (December 1807).

Far more surprising, however, given Tighe's explicit, anxious rejection of 'the vanity of authorship', is the proud regard she expresses for herself as 'the Author of Psyche': after the author of *The Chaplet of Fame* asks her to subscribe to his poem, she declares 'Certainly one of the miseries of authorship is the necessity of receiving the detestable performances which every stupid writer thinks it is honoring you to communicate – This vile nonsense was sent to the Author of Psyche with a demand of a guinea subscription to works which I devoutly pray may never be published' (September 1806). That unexpected hubris emerges again when she comments on John Carr's *Stranger in Ireland*: 'In spite of the honorable mention made of the author of Psyche and several of her friends in this motley work I must say it is a very absurd performance & the views are detestable' (August 1806). Tighe is far from alone in her negative assessment of Carr, but it's surely relevant to note his revealing assessment of her:

> An invincible timidity, and the dread of exciting the animadversions of those who have so much influence upon the public opinion through the channels of criticism, have at present confined to a small circle of friends, a printed poem which, although my perusal of it was limited, would, I can with confidence say, entitle the fair authoress to the admiration, without an appeal to the gallantry,

of the candid reviewer, and would render the name of *Psyche* more memorable, and inscribe the name of Tighe high upon the roll of feminine celebrity [...] If these few remarks should have any influence to induce the fair authoress to a more diffuse publication of a work so interesting, I shall at least make atonement for the errors of that by which it is recommended.[27]

Tighe doesn't copy Carr's remarks directly into her journal, but surreptitiously extracts the most flattering portion of Carr's commentary in the following entry on Edward Dubois's *My Pocket Book*, which cites Dubois quoting Carr: 'This is the age for quizzing & it would have been strange had Carr escap'd – there are some good things in this satire but on the whole it is rather flat & nonsensical – for a sample, a page interesting to myself – "Rosanna the seat of Mrs Tighe is *Arcadian* and she is an *elegant minded lady* [...] Tell her that she ought to publish her MS. Poem"' (June 1807).[28]

If Tighe is tempted to take DuBois and Carr's advice – now two years after the private printing of *The Legend of Love* – she tempers her ambitions and her proud sense of self as 'the author of Psyche' by tracing the consequences of such ambition for fellow Dubliners Moore and Owenson in the pages of the periodical press. She notes of the April 1806 issue of the *Edinburgh Review* that 'They have again dragg'd in the name of Moore in praising the *Lyricks of Smyth* for their amiable innocence' (May 1806); for the next issue (July 1806), which reviews Moore's *Odes, Epistles, and Other Poems* and John Lemaistre's *Travels*, she comments

> Most memorable to me as the occasion of a duel which has prov'd so unpleasant tho' not dangerous to Moore – his work is cruelly abus'd & the personality it contain'd provok'd him to call for the author when Mr Jeffrey came forward – I cannot speak with candour or impartiality of an article which has so much wounded my feelings but of the others I must say I think many of them extremely clever – tho' my friend *LeMaistre* is not attack'd for his morality yet the contempt with which they have treated his *travels thro France &c* will I dare say annoy him as much as Moore.
>
> (September 1806)

A month later she notes of the *Literary Journal* (January to June 1806) that 'a severe attack on Moore was to me the most interesting part of the work' (October 1806). Most interestingly, despite the harsh critiques she consistently offers for all of Owenson's published work, she defends Owenson against a negative review she reads in the periodical *Anonymous* even as she herself disparages *Patriot's Sketches*:

> But what volumes! margins & booksellers list & spaces deducted there may remain about twenty decent pages – this however is not her imposition on the public but her affectation, absurdity, slip slop & false quotations are all her own & hardly she has been handled in a periodical paper W. Kerwin has just sent me the *Anonymous* – very ill-natured & I think unjust – for she has genius, & genius should be kindly treated.
>
> (November 1807)

'Genius should be kindly treated', but Tighe knows too well that it is not, and thus, ultimately, never takes the risk of presenting her work to the public, reserving it, always, for the safe haven of the coterie.

In 1810 Joseph Haslewood published the first formal review of *Psyche; or, the Legend of Love* (1805) for the inaugural issue of *The British Bibliographer* and acknowledges his good fortune in getting access to this rarity in his opening paragraph:

> One hundred copies of the *Legend of Love* have been distributed to the 'chosen few,' while the readers have multiplied above ten fold, and a perusal is only obtained by favour. For the present loan I am indebted to the Rev. Mr. White, of Lichfield, and consider that those who may not have seen the elegant and fascinating numbers of Mrs. Henry Tighe, will feel gratified in the perusal of the following specimens.

Haslewood errs in the number of copies distributed, but not in his allusion to Tighe's publication anxieties as he joins the chorus urging Tighe to publish: 'Let it be hoped that this introduction to extended notice will assist in surmounting the causeless timidity of the writer, and that the fear of periodical critics will no longer keep from the public this pleasing production.'[29] Sadly, by the dedication date of the issue (29 June 1810) Tighe was dead (24 March 1810). But the Tighe family coterie would soon take these words to heart and prepare *Psyche, with Other Poems* 'By the Late Mrs. Henry Tighe' for the world.

Notes

1. See Sir James Mackintosh, *Memoirs of the Life of the Right Honourable Sir James Mackintosh*, 2 vols (London: Moxon, 1835), II, 195; and W.J. Fitzpatrick, *Lady Morgan: Her Career, Literary and Personal, with a glimpse of Her Friends and a Word to Her Calumniators* (London: Charles J. Skeet, 1860), p. 139.
2. Lucy Newlyn, *Reading, Writing, and Romanticism: The Anxiety of Reception* (Oxford: Oxford University Press, 2000), p. 229.
3. Tilar Mazzeo, *Plagiarism and Literary Property in the Romantic Period* (Philadelphia: University of Pennsylvania Press, 2007), p. 52.
4. See Julia Wright, '"All the Fire-Side Circle": Irish Women Writers and the Sheridan-LeFanu Coterie', *Keats-Shelley Journal*, 55 (2006), 63–72; and Gary Kelly, 'Politicizing the Personal: Mary Wollstonecraft, Mary Shelley, and the Coterie Novel', in *Mary Shelley in Her Times*, ed. by Betty Bennet and Stuart Curran (Baltimore: Johns Hopkins University Press, 2000), pp. 147–59. Similarly, Jeffrey Cox demonstrates how the Hunt or Cockney circle sought to advance stylistic and ideological alternatives to the Lake school in a post-Napoleonic society; see *Poetry and Politics in the Cockney School: Keats, Shelley, Hunt and their Circle* (Cambridge: Cambridge University Press, 1998).
5. *Psyche, with Other Poems. By the Late Mrs. Henry Tighe*, 3rd edn (London: Longman, 1811), Canto I, 451.
6. Margaret Ezell, *Social Authorship and the Advent of Print* (Baltimore: Johns Hopkins University Press, 1999), pp. 40–1.
7. See G.H. Bell, *The Hamwood Papers of The Ladies of Llangollen and Caroline Hamilton* (London: Macmillan, 1930), p. 328.
8. For more information, see *The Collected Poems and Journals of Mary Tighe*, ed. by H.K. Linkin (Lexington: University Press of Kentucky, 2005). Unless otherwise stated, all quoted poems by Tighe are from this edition. Subsequent references are given parenthetically in the text.
9. C. Hamilton, 'Mary Tighe', in *Collected Poems and Journals of Mary Tighe*, ed. by Linkin, p. 278.
10. S. Ponsonby, 'Sweet Linda!' IN T448 805, Beinecke Rare Book Room and Manuscript Library, Yale University, New Haven.
11. 12 February 1803; in Bell, *The Hamwood Papers*, p. 334.
12. *The Poetical Works of the Late Thomas Little* (London: Carpenter, 1801), pp. iii–iv.
13. In a review of Moore's *Odes of Anacreon* John Eyre contrasted Younge's translations with Moore's, and concluded that Younge's 'is well fitted for a pot-house; Moore's is much better calculated for a bagnio' (*Edinburgh Review*, 2 (July 1803), 476).
14. The quote is from T. Blachford, 'Observations on the Foregoing Journal by Her Mother', in Linkin, ed., *Collected Poems and Journals of Mary Tighe*, p. 234. Between 1801 and 1803 Tighe completed both *Psyche* and her novel *Selena* (2500 pages in manuscript) as well as a number of lyric poems.
15. See the 'Introduction' to *Collected Poems and Journals of Mary Tighe*, pp. xv–xxxiii.
16. Tighe reiterates the danger of joining such a circle later in canto three when Psyche meets Vanity and Flattery in the woods and finds herself abducted by Ambition.

17. *Psyche; or, the Legend of Love*, MS 22985B, National Library of Wales, Aberystwyth.
18. T. Moore, 'Psyche', in *Psyche; or, the Legend of Love*, MS 22985B, National Library of Wales, Aberystwyth.
19. Ponsonby, 'Sweet Linda', ll. 1–9.
20. *Letters to Joseph Cooper Walker*, MSS 1461/5–7, Trinity College Library, Dublin; here, 1461/5.
21. *Letters to Joseph Cooper Walker*, MSS 1461/5–7, Trinity College Library, Dublin; here, 1461/7.
22. C. Hamilton and Mary Tighe, *Letters*, MS 4239, National Library of Ireland, Dublin.
23. *Letters to Joseph Cooper Walker*, MSS 1461/5–7, Trinity College Library, Dublin; here, 1461/7.
24. 'Letter to John Carpenter, 18 February 1806', Evelyn Papers, UP 12, old folio 58-58V, British Library, London; here, UP 12/58.
25. *Critical Reviews*, MS 4804, National Library of Ireland, Dublin.
26. *The Letters of Thomas Moore*, ed. by Wilfrid S. Dowden, 2 vols (London: Oxford University Press, 1964), I, 111.
27. J. Carr, *The Stranger in Ireland; or, a Tour in the Southern and Western Parts of that Country, in the Year 1805* (London: Richard Phillips, 1806), pp. 146–7.
28. See DuBois, *My Pocket Book: or Hints for a 'ryghte merrie and conceitede' tour, in quarto; to be called 'The Stranger in Ireland' in 1805. By a knight errant*, new edn (London: Vernor, Hood and Sharpe, 1808).
29. J. Haslewood, 'Review of *Psyche; or the Legend of Love*', *British Bibliographer*, 1 (1810), pp. 162, 169.

16
Influence, Anxiety, and Erasure in Women's Writing: Romantic becomes Victorian

Stephen C. Behrendt

When in 1828 Felicia Hemans published *Records of Woman, with Other Poems*, she concluded the first section, the 'Records', with the only poem in that section that documents the life (and death) of a contemporary woman. Significantly, that contemporary woman is the Irish poet Mary Tighe, whose grave Hemans describes, even though she had not yet, in fact, seen the spot personally and would not visit it until 1831. 'The Grave of a Poetess' is delicately positioned between two worlds, two cultural moments. It is at once an elegy on the premature death from consumption in 1810 of the beautiful virtuoso author of *Psyche; or, the Legend of Love* (composed 1801–02, published privately 1805 and republished 1811) and a meditation upon the fate of the woman poet in the emerging Victorian bourgeois world. Writing to John Lodge in 1831 after finally visiting Tighe's grave at Woodstock, Hemans admitted that she 'could not but reflect on the many changes which had brought me to the spot I had commemorated three years since, without the slightest idea of ever visiting it; and though [I was] surrounded by attention and the appearance of interest [in me], my heart was envying the repose of her who slept there'.[1] Hemans was by 1828 a celebrated poet and the object of much public notice throughout the tour during which she visited Tighe's grave, but her comment to Lodge speaks to a perennial private concern among British women poets of the entire Romantic and post-Romantic era: the extent to which a publishing woman poet's life and circumstances belong both to her as a private individual and to her readers as an author – indeed as a very public 'poetess'. The point is as valid for poets from the early part of the period, such as Charlotte Smith, Anna Seward, Mary Robinson, and the then-popular Lady Manners (the former Catherine Rebecca Gray), as it is for later ones such as Hemans, Letitia Landon, Mary Ann Browne, and the Irish poet and travel writer Louisa Stuart Costello.

While British women poets had for more than a century routinely called themselves 'poets', the more narrow term – 'poetess' – was relatively new, having accompanied the advent of the popular late-Romantic genre of the literary annual (and the related occasional volumes typically intended as gifts or keepsakes, for example, *The Keepsake*, which ran from 1828 through 1857). Unlike the poet, whose works were typically conceived as more formal, erudite, and weighty, the 'poetess' was associated with a 'lighter' verse composed on occasional and domestic topics and intended for an audience of primarily middle-class women who constituted a new consumer class. The annuals were widely regarded within the traditional and male-dominated literary culture as possessing little value beyond their token status as physically elegant commodities and as instruments for reinforcing the (often gendered) values and aspirations of conventional moral, capitalist, and imperialist orthodoxy. Only in recent years has this estimate begun to be interrogated,[2] and the resulting reassessment of annuals and poetesses reveals the complex ways in which the period's women poets sought to create – and occasionally to undermine – a sense of 'community' while at the same time working to establish 'names', and therefore legacies of permanence, for themselves.

Ironically, Mary Tighe was not really what Hemans's contemporaries understood as a 'poetess'. Tighe's greatest work, *Psyche*, is anything but light, occasional, or ephemeral; moreover, it is in many respects as detached from the thematic and intellectual preoccupations of much of the poetry of the 1790s and early 1800s with which it is contemporary as it is from the gendered bourgeois domestic ideology of Hemans's generation. This makes all the more remarkable Hemans's comment, recorded by her early biographer Henry Chorley, that '[h]er poetry has always touched me greatly, from a similarity which I imagine I discover between her destiny and my own'.[3] As Paula R. Feldman notes, the similarities included an unhappy marriage, limited recognition as a poetic genius, and a losing battle with illness.[4] But if Hemans envisioned a premature death that would truncate her own 'record' of poetic genius, she also deliberately overlooked some substantial differences: Hemans had already achieved celebrity and undeniable influence, while the well-known circumstances of her own broken marriage (to which her habitual inscription, 'Mrs. Hemans', insistently pointed her readers) served if anything to enhance her stature by underscoring the inhospitable circumstances despite which she had accomplished so much. As for Tighe, nearly twenty years after her death, in 1828, she was still remembered among poets and literary critics, as is evident from her inclusion in contemporary anthologies and literary histories.[5] Hemans's comment seems therefore to have stemmed less from anxiety about premature death than from worries about unfulfilled promise.

Despite her extraordinary productivity, Hemans nevertheless expressed, shortly before her death, her regret at having spent so much time writing about the things that poetesses wrote about and having in the process short-changed her own expectations about what *might* have been, what she *might* have written, had she not faced 'the constant necessity of providing sums of money to meet the exigencies of the boys' education', as she put it to Rose Lawrence in early 1835, adding that 'my wish ever was to concentrate all my mental energy in the production of some more noble and complete work'.[6] Was she saying, in effect, that she had sacrificed being a *poet* in order to become a *poetess*? Hemans had begun her career with undoubtedly ambitious works like *The Restoration of the Works of Art to Italy* (1816) and *Modern Greece* (1817), which struck some contemporary reviewers as so polished and 'academical' as to have been the productions of 'certainly not a female pen'.[7] But by the time of her death Hemans was widely regarded as the epitome of the poetess of hearth, home, and sweet domesticity, qualities that led Frederic Rowton in 1848 to characterize her poetry effusively as 'a perfect embodiment of a woman's soul'.[8] This popular conception, however, was based upon more recent and enormously popular works like the much-anthologized 'Casabianca', 'The Homes of England', and 'Evening Prayer at a Girls' School' (which appeared in 1826 in the popular annual, the *Forget Me Not*[9]). It ignores the problematic nature of much of her work, especially on the subject of women and women's experiences. That work, whose insistent resistance to the conventions of genre and decorum has been recovered in revisionist and feminist reassessments, explores from multiple historical and cultural perspectives the situation of the woman who must accommodate the often conflicting roles that come with being, on the one hand, a private domestic figure – a wife and mother – and, on the other, a public figure – not just a writer but more particularly a *woman* writer. In the historical tales in *Records of Woman*, for example, the often irreconcilable nature of these roles is frequently fatal to the woman, whose death is at once heroic (because it is noble, self-sacrificing, and chosen as an act of defiance or rejection) and ambiguous (because it is the consequence of acting in a fashion traditionally reserved for men, and in a male-oriented public sphere). While the poet*ess* may lament the loss of the woman *as domestic female*, the *poet* necessarily memorializes the woman *as public figure*, as activist in the arena of public affairs.

Tighe's personal and emblematic significance for Hemans is indicated by the fact that Hemans commemorated her on other occasions, and in three other poems.[10] The latest poem, 'On Records of Immature Genius', dates from 1834; there Hemans attempts to reconcile the deaths of those who die 'Ere the soul's flame, through storms, hath won repose / In truth's divinest ether, still and high' (ll. 3–4) with the natural regret of the survivors at what was left unaccomplished. Given Hemans's deteriorating health in 1834, her poem's immediate personal relevance is unmistakable. But, on the broader stage, her poem addresses the subject of the woman writer's fate in a new and faster-paced world in which neither celebrity nor enduring fame is a certainty. Indeed, all four poems make it clear that quite the reverse is the more common fate: 'O Love and Song! though of Heaven your powers, / Dark is your fate in this world of ours' ('Written After Visiting a Tomb, near Woodstock, in the County of Kilkenny', ll. 35–6). To this grim prospect the writer can only oppose an abiding faith in the eternal nature of fame (and the beauty it renders timeless), coupled with a thoroughgoing Christian expectation of an eternal heavenly reward that wipes away the stains of mortal woe.

'The Grave of a Poetess' juxtaposes the living Hemans – both as woman and as poet – with the dead Tighe, who is first represented as cut off from 'all the song and bloom / Thou wouldst have loved so well' (ll. 21–2). Seeking consolation, Hemans observes that while '[t]he shadows of the tomb are here, / Yet beautiful is the earth!' (ll. 367–8) and while in mortal life Tighe gave 'a vain love to passing flowers', in the eternal life which she now enjoys '[t]he sway is not with changeful hours, / *There* love and death must part' (ll. 40–3; Hemans's emphases). Hemans concludes:

> Thou hast left sorrow in thy song,
>   A voice not loud, but deep!
> The glorious bowers of earth among,
>   How often didst thou weep!
>
> Where couldst thou fix on mortal ground
>   Thy tender thoughts and high? —
> Now peace the woman's heart hath found,
>   And joy the poet's eye.
>
> (ll. 45–52)

The mortal woman is 'gone', but the song remains; the artist is dead, but the work of art endures, achieving in the mortal world that Hemans occupies the 'eternal' existence that the dead Tighe is presumed to enjoy. Tighe's lofty 'thoughts' may have been incompatible with 'mortal ground', but the *record* of them – both Tighe's published poetry *and* Hemans's poem – manage at once to inhabit both the temporal present in which Hemans and the reader live and the *eternal* present that inheres in the relationship between books and their readers across time and space. This double inference in Hemans's concluding stanzas suggests another doubling as well. The penultimate line implies that 'the woman' is Tighe, but it points also to the woman who is writing the poem (Hemans) and to the women who read it, while 'the poet' whose eye is animated with joy in the final line may be Tighe but is more certainly Hemans, who also stands in for the poem's (presumably female) reader. It is therefore even more diagnostic of the poem's universal female signification that the article in the title is 'a' and not 'the'. By eschewing 'the' – which would make it a poem about *all* poetesses – and substituting instead 'a', Hemans subtly implies that this happy eternal reward is not assured but only potential. Not every poetess is 'the' poetess; each is, rather, 'a' poetess who may or may not achieve the eternality of fame and heaven, which the poem's rhetoric shrewdly turns into functional cognates.

For Hemans, the poetess's song – both as physical artifact of her art and as song, as performance, as rhetorical and semantic *act* – remains after the poet's death, reminding the survivor (including the surviving *artist*) not only of her achievement but also of what she is now cut off through death from experiencing: both the *natural* world of beauty and sensual enjoyment and the *literary* world of art and aesthetic pleasure. The first of these worlds yields rewards that the artist can enjoy privately, but the latter presumes a public sphere that necessarily extends beyond (and to some extent even excludes) the immediate pleasure experienced by the poet in the private process of composition. It points toward *reputation*, and with reputation come entirely natural concerns about the viability of reputation over time: will 'reputation' become 'fame', or will it pass like the delicate winged creatures in Hemans's Tighe poems, leaving no trace behind?

What will become of me, in other words? What will become of my name? If this sort of question could trouble even so prolific and successful a poet as Felicia Hemans, with what force must it have struck a poet like Mariann Dark, whose name and life are virtually unknown and whose only volume, *Sonnets and Other Poems* (1818), exists in no more than a handful of copies hidden away in research libraries?[11] Tucked away in a rural Wiltshire farm community, befriended by William Lisle

Bowles, the family acquaintance who buried the poet's father in January 1817, and herself widowed at a young age, Dark lived and wrote in obscurity. Given her evident preference for the sonnet form, it is little surprise that she self-consciously declares herself indebted to Charlotte Smith, who (along with Bowles) had been singularly influential in resurrecting the sonnet in Romantic-era Britain. Indeed, in a sonnet called 'On Reading Mrs. Smith's Sonnets', Dark writes that when she reads the catalogue of personal woes in Smith's sonnets, 'I lose remembrance of mine own' (sonnet XII, l. 3, p. 40). 'Yet similar our fates', Dark continues, and so 'why repose / Trust in deceiving hope? so oft abus'd' (ll. 4–5). Abused, that is, by the stark realities of uncertain fortune and untimely personal catastrophe. Musing on Smith's lines, Dark writes, '[m]ethought a kindred flame our bosoms warm'd', so that 'I dar'd aspire to feeling such as thine' (ll. 9–10). This aspiration, she reports, prompted her to '[kneel] again before Apollo's shrine' and take up verse, earnestly praying that 'he would impart the charm / Of thine own melting melody divine' (ll. 9–14). In other words, in linking herself with Smith as another woman sonneteer beset by personal reversal, Dark aspires also to inherit both the voice and the art (and with them, the reputation, or fame) of Smith, who had died in 1806 but whose fame and influence remained considerable in 1818. Interestingly, in appearing in her own sonnets to position Smith as a poetess, Dark unwittingly indicates the cultural shift that had by 1818 begun to transpire in the public acceptability – even the desirability – of the term.

Sadly, however, the woman poet who writes in obscurity, in the shadow of a famous predecessor like Smith, is generally fated to remain obscure, as Dark's next sonnet ruefully admits. Chastizing herself for audaciously assuming parallels between herself and Smith, and between their respective circumstances, Dark confronts her own bleak prospects:

> Charlotte! alas no genial breath of fame,
>   E'er call'd the infant buds of genius forth;
> I strike the lyre unknown! My very name
>   Will soon be blotted from this wretched earth.
> Thine, Charlotte; thine, the bright, the genuine flame,
>   Fosters by fair reward – the mead of worth.
>
> (Sonnet XIII, 'On Reviewing the
> Preceding', ll. 9–14, p. 43)

Fame involves all sorts of circumstances and opportunities; unpraised early on and hidden in rural isolation, Dark was denied access to the (urban) public sphere in which Smith's 'genius' flourished: consequently, she envisions no prospects at all. The bleakness of her prediction, 'My very name will soon be blotted from this wretched earth', contrasts dramatically with Smith's wide celebrity. Dark's suggestion that reward and worth are inevitably connected in literary production and public reputation bears further examination, not just for what it tells us about Dark (and about comparably little-known poets) but also for what it reveals about the ambiguous nature of the 'community' shared by writing women – and specifically by publishing women poets – during the Romantic era. For that community was not always or inevitably as benign as we might expect. It could have an unpleasant side whose uncharitable aspects were often apparent to the participants.

In a recent essay Lucy Morrison has discussed at some length the ambivalent responses to the death of Felicia Hemans that are evident in the writings of Letitia Elizabeth Landon, the famous (or notorious) 'L.E.L.' Fully aware of the circumstances of Hemans's dysfunctional marriage, Landon objected to the popular image of Hemans as the sweetly domestic poetess that Rowton and others (including Hemans herself) cultivated. As Morrison puts it, rather than 'dutifully bemoaning the loss of the exemplary woman poet' as did most of those who memorialized Hemans in the wake of her death in 1835, Landon 'daringly objects to the disjunction between Hemans's life and her public image' and points to an aspect of Hemans's verse that eluded most of her contemporary commentators (and generations of readers that followed): Hemans's calculated 'subversion of assigned [female/feminine] roles in her duplicitous embrace of domesticity'.[12] By 'duplicitous', Morrison (following Landon) means to emphasize the deliberate subterfuge by which this poetess of ruinous marital circumstances successfully positioned her 'public' self (as embodied in her poetry) within the later Romantic and earlier Victorian period's gendered cultural expectations about women as wives and mothers, as representatives of the values and virtues of bourgeois domesticity. Landon situated herself very differently, of course, establishing herself in a publicly successful literary *profession* that combined the ostensibly private role of woman poet with the undeniably public ones of editor, publicist, and celebrity – public roles that Hemans ostensibly eschewed. While Hemans seems not to have explicitly represented herself as a *competitor* – either with Landon or with anyone else – there is no question that she was powerfully aware of the public status and influence enjoyed by other celebrity poets, such as Byron, and that, like her contemporary Melesina Trench, she read in her own personal, domestic circumstances an array of impediments to comparable influence.[13] Playing the role of wife ('*Mrs.* Hemans') and mother, however, much as Smith had done a generation earlier, especially in portraying herself in the prefaces to her novels, allowed Hemans to plead those domestic circumstances as a principal reason for her turn toward the more commercially successful (that is, the more *profitable*) poems that cemented her contemporary reputation. But doing so was not without its personal cost to the *poet*, as Landon explains:

> The meteor wreath the poet wears
>   Must make a lonely lot;
> It dazzles, only to divide
>   From those who wear it not.
>
> Didst thou not tremble at thy fame,
>   And loathe its bitter prize,
> While what to others triumph seemed,
>   To thee was sacrifice?[14]

That Hemans enjoyed a wider and a 'greater' contemporary reputation than Landon reflects the reading public's responses both to what they knew about the authors' private lives and to the strategies of self-representation the two poets employed in engaging their respective publics – which were in fact not quite the same readerships – and in crafting poems according to their assumptions about those audiences. For one thing, Hemans characteristically treats issues and themes involving *permanence*, whether she was writing poems about cultural institutions (for example, 'The Homes of England' or 'The Graves of a Household') or elegiac poems (such as 'England's Dead', 'The Image in Lava', or 'The Grave of a Poetess'). The poems for which Hemans was most popular generally invite their readers to participate in a community of sentiment and national collective consciousness organized around moments and occasions rooted in a familiar and largely quotidian experience. Landon's poems, on the other hand, are often occupied with *impermanence* and with transitory experience. *The Improvisatrice*, for example, not only presents itself as an improvised song but also incorporates within it still other improvised performances. Performativity plays a greater role in Landon's poetic than it does in Hemans's, and it also informs Landon's creative virtuosity with *Fisher's Drawing Room Scrap Book*, where she exercised considerable editorial and artistic control over all aspects of production.

So whether they consciously intended it or not, Landon and Hemans were in fact rivals and competitors, both creatively and professionally, despite the desire they shared with many women writers for a solidarity born of community and mutual interest. As the Romantic era verged into the Victorian, however, this desire was becoming increasingly unrealistic, for the expansion of literary and cultural capitalism inevitably militated against such community and solidarity. Male writers were not pitted against one another – or did not *feel* themselves to be pitted against one another – in quite the same way, since they controlled so much of the age's capital and the means by which it could be wielded, whether in politics, in industry, or in literary production. Women, though, found themselves constrained in new ways by the literary *marketplace*, which was increasingly becoming a public free-for-all. Mariann Dark may lament her authorial powerlessness, her grim prospects for fame and permanence (not to mention fortune), but at least she does not denigrate, misrepresent, or otherwise undermine Smith in order to promote herself. Her complaint reflects her frank though bitter resignation over the extent to which one may fall victim to circumstances that one can neither influence nor control. Dark is not competing with Smith, in other words, so much as she is competing with market forces and the geographical and demographic circumstances that dictate who will succeed and who will fail – whose name will be remembered and whose will be erased. With the expansion of literacy, technological improvements in the publishing industry, and the growing commercial viability of authorship, in other words, the aspiring woman poet of Dark's generation and afterward faced obstacles to community that differed considerably from those faced by her predecessors as little as a generation earlier.

In this light it is therefore useful to consider another troubled poetic relationship in which Smith features prominently, this one from the earlier end of the Romantic era and involving Anna Seward. The publication in 1781 of Seward's *Monody on the Death of Major André* the year after her *Elegy on Captain Cook* (1780) had established her as 'the most famous woman poet in England', almost universally applauded as 'a skilled, professional poet'.[15] Thus an admiring Thomas Park, for instance, did not hesitate in 1797 to call her 'Britain's Muse' and 'the Siren-sister of our Delphic throng',[16] the considerable celebrity of Smith, Mary Robinson, and Lady Manners by that time notwithstanding. Seward regarded herself very much as a 'poet': she took her writing seriously, worked hard and carefully at it, and relished her solid reputation. It is little surprise, then, that she was incensed by the spectacular success that attended the publication in 1784 of Smith's *Elegiac Sonnets*, which evolved through some nine ever-expanding editions during Smith's lifetime. When she finally published her volume of *Original*

Sonnets in 1799, Seward dated many of the poems, as if to document – by assigning them dates before 1784 – that her own sonnets were the 'real' source of the modern sonnet. This fact, taken together with her routine denigration of Smith's poems, both in print and in correspondence, testifies to how fiercely Seward sought to maintain her position as the age's pre-eminent woman poet. Typical is Seward's spiteful reference to 'Mrs. C. Smith's everlasting lamentables, which she calls sonnets, made up of hackneyed scraps of dismality, with which her memory furnished her from our various poets.'[17] With a single stroke Seward accuses Smith of being derivative (if not simply a plagiarist), a shoddy artist, and a shameless melancholic sentimentalist. But Nicola Trott reasonably regards such remarks as nothing more than 'the sort of tribute one author pays to the triumph of another'.[18] My point is not that remarks of this sort reveal Seward as unpleasantly mean-spirited but rather that they demonstrate how seriously Romantic-era women poets took their poetic vocations. It *mattered* to Seward that she devoted herself to her craft and to acquiring both the learning and the worldly experience (and philosophical reflection) that informed what she wrote, and it upset her no end that Smith seemed to have achieved her sensational success through what Seward considered to be short-cuts and gimmicks – a cheap performative sensationalism aimed not at the reflecting intellect but rather at the impressionable imagination. Seward objects to the intrusion into Smith's *Elegiac Sonnets* of what seems an emotionally charged and highly performative personal dimension.

But as Jacqueline Labbe observes, this tactic sold copies while inculcating in the public mind 'the picture of a stricken and needy woman who, in spite of her troubles, proudly brings out the first edition under her own name'.[19] Seward objected to admitting Smith to the community of 'legitimate' writers because she had failed to write 'legitimate' sonnets. Seward could afford, quite literally, to object to Smith's performance on formal and intellectual grounds, but Smith was neither financially nor domestically comfortable in the way that Seward was. Smith had to regard writing not simply as a vocation but as a *profession*, and this meant invoking other standards than merely the formal and the aesthetic. Smith understood that for the woman writer in circumstances like her own, 'there is little currency – in all sense of this word – in differentiating popular success from literary quality'.[20] In effect, Seward proposes before 1800 what Landon proposes in slightly different terms after 1835: that another poet (Smith, Hemans) is not what she seems to be, and that a careful and informed reading will reveal to the reflective reader the nature and extent of that imposture.

Paradoxically, if readers follow the explicit and implicit hints that Seward and Landon provide, they may find that rather than excluding Smith and Hemans from a hypothetical community of women poets because they do not conform to the culturally accepted expectations (to which Seward and Landon direct their readers' attention), the performances of the two poets in fact *admit* them to that community – and for the very same reasons. Certainly this would be the conclusion of much recent revisionist scholarship and critical reassessment. For many contemporary scholars, it is precisely the resistance of poetry and poets to the normative consensus that defines the nature of their 'Romanticism'. This is especially true in the case of women poets and labouring-class poets, both of which groups have historically been marginalized in or excluded from literary-historical discussion.

This is not to minimize the very real forces that worked against women poets in their own lifetimes, of course, nor is it to disregard the fact that their difficulties frequently owed as much to other women as to men. Mary Robinson, for example, explained to her friend Jane Porter in August 1800, only a few months before her death, some of the reasons for her suspicions about other women:

> If I do not enter into the true spirit of Friendship for my own Sex, it is because I have almost universally found that Sex unkind and hostile towards *me*. I have seen the most miserable and degrading, the most contemptible *traits* of false delicacy, glaring through the thin veil of artificial virtue [...] The women whom I have most admired, have been the least prone to condemn [...][21]

Robinson is thinking here specifically about the hypocrisy of those women who had shunned her because they objected to her personal behaviour, including her highly-publicized affairs with the likes of the Prince of Wales and Banastre Tarleton. Labbe plausibly suggests that because she 'feels the sting of social criticism', Robinson 'lashes back at the women she sees as willingly giving her up to her troubles because of her unconventional relationships'.[22] Indeed, Porter herself elected not to publish her memoir of Robinson because she had been warned that if it became known that she and Robinson were friends, 'all the world would cut me'; she reported, for example, that the novelist Mrs Champion de Crespigny told her that she would 'be shunned by all decent people'.[23]

The especially heavy toll that this sort of gender-based malice could exact upon a woman author in particular was apparent to contemporary writers like Mary Hays, who wrote in 1800–01 concerning the still living Charlotte Smith that

> [t]he penalties and discouragements attending the profession of an author fall upon women with a double weight; to the curiosity of the idle and the envy of the malicious their sex affords a peculiar incitement; arraigned, not merely as writers, but as *women*, their characters, their conduct and even their personal endowments, become the subjects of severe inquisition: from the common allowances claimed by the species in general, literary women appear only to be exempted: in detecting their errors and exposing their foibles, malignant ingenuity is active and unwearied.[24]

Both as writers and as women, then, and particularly as *women writers*, authors like Smith (and Robinson) were vulnerable to attacks upon their personal lives that were potentially more damaging than they would be to male authors because more was necessarily at stake for the politically or culturally oppositional woman who depended for her livelihood (and that of her family) upon her literary productions. The author who failed to heed these economic realities of the literary marketplace did so at the peril of both her domestic circumstances and her subsequent reputation. Clearly, it was in women writers' interest to stick together. And yet, to what extent could they really do so, finding both community and common cause?

By 1800 Robinson, for one, was keenly aware of the need for both a *sense* of community among women in general and an actual, *working* community among women writers in particular. This point is central to the four-part essay she published in the reform-minded *Monthly Magazine* only a few months before she died: *Present State of the Manners, Society, Etc. Etc. Of the Metropolis of England*.[25] There, as Adriana Craciun has noted, Robinson argues that urban London 'offers women the professional opportunities that are their only hope for economic and sexual independence' ('Introduction', p. 105). Robinson writes that

> the women of England have, by their literary labours, reached an altitude of mental excellence, far above those of any other nation. The works, which every year have been published by females, do credit to the very highest walks of literature: to enumerate names, will be unnecessary; their productions will be their passports to immortality!
>
> (p. 111)

And yet, as we have seen, not all women poets shared this confidence, and nearly two centuries of literary and cultural history (and scholarship) largely bore out their worst fears about obscurity and erasure. Even now, the recovery of many such writers is hindered and in many cases virtually precluded by the disappearance both of the works they published and of the documentary evidence of their lives and circumstances.

Indeed, even Robinson recognized how hostile the emerging bourgeois culture was to the arts in general and to literature in particular: she attributes this dilemma to the balkanization of culture and taste, largely along class lines, that interposes a lethal gulf between the producers and the consumers (or collectors, or connoisseurs) of art. Not surprisingly, women appear to Robinson to suffer most, in significant part because, in her opinion, women have failed to cultivate the 'community of genius', as she calls it, that would secure both their contemporary and their enduring status:

> England may enumerate, at the present aera, a phalanx of enlightened women, such as no other nation ever boasted. Their writings adorn the literature of the country; they are its ornaments, as they ought to be its pride! But they are neglected, unsought, alienated from society; and secluded in abodes of study; or condemned to mingle with the vulgar. For even among themselves, there appears to be no sympathetic association of soul; no genuine impulse of affection, originating in congeniality of mind. Each is ardent in the pursuit of fame; and every new honour which is bestowed on a sister votary, is deemed a partial privation of what she considers as her exclusive birth-right. How much is genius deceived when it seeks this single, this unconnected species of gratification! How powerful might such a phalanx become, were it to act in union of sentiment, and sympathy of feeling; and by a participation of public fame secure, to the end of time, the admiration of posterity.
>
> (p. 115)

The value of *genuine* fame, in other words, exists in reverse proportion to the extent to which it is sought and enjoyed *personally* (or 'privately') rather than *collectively*. A few years later, writing in about 1804 to Maria Edgeworth, Anna Laetitia Barbauld complained that 'there is no bond of union among literary women [...]; different sentiments and different connections separate them much more than the joint interest of their sex would unite them'.[26] For Robinson and Barbauld alike, women's writing stakes its most powerful claims to both contemporary influence and lasting fame when it articulates a collective 'soul' and vision rather than a private one. The answer to the questions about personal erasure asked by an obscure poet like Mariann Dark, in other words, lies in each poet's understanding that she becomes a member of a perhaps unperceived but nevertheless 'real' community – a 'union of sentiment, and sympathy of feeling' – by virtue both of her private act of composing and her public act of *publishing*. Paradoxically, when an author like Dark *publishes* a poem in which she laments her own obscurity in comparison to a better-known poet and imagines her own erasure, she nevertheless manages in a very real sense to ride that other poet's literary coat-tails into posterity.

Something of this sort is also evident in a sonnet by Martha Hanson, whose two-volume *Sonnets, and Other Poems* (1809)[27] contains several poems that discuss her female poetic forebears, including three sonnets and a long poem concerning Charlotte Smith, and another that involves Mary Robinson. In 'Sonnet XIV. Occasioned by Reading Mrs. M. Robinson's Poems', Hanson seems to celebrate the deceased Robinson at her own expense:

> Daughter of Genius! while thy tuneful lays
> Lift my warm spirit from its mortal clay,
> And bid it soar to realms of endless day,
> In vain I seek thy matchless pow'r to praise.
>
> (ll. 1–4)

While Robinson's verse transfigures and transports Hanson, emotionally and metaphorically, it also reminds the author of her own incapacity – either to praise the power of Robinson's poetry or to praise her memory: Hanson shrewdly leaves the fourth line's actual referent ambiguous. The rest of the sonnet celebrates the surpassing qualities of Robinson's poetry that she feels confident will assure both its immortality and its author's imperviousness to 'base Envy's sting, Detraction's pow'rs' (l. 12). Interestingly, these last terms name the very indicators of the personal malice that are so destructive to women's literary efforts and that Robinson herself identifies in her *Present State* as impediments to community.

The complexities involved in Romantic-era women poets' attempts to reconcile the often conflicting demands of their (public) literary aspirations and their (private) personal circumstances are illustrated in the friendship that developed in the 1790s between the Irish nationalist poet Henrietta Battier and Eliza Ryan. The prolific Battier, whom Andrew Carpenter calls 'the author of the best Irish satirical verse of the late eighteenth century',[28] included at the end of her privately printed 1791 collection, *The Protected Fugitives*, the poignant record of a poetic correspondence which the two women conducted during the 1780s.[29] Ryan was the wife of the learned theologian Revd Edward Ryan, DD, Rector of Donoughmore in County Wicklow and subsequently of St Luke's, Dublin, and author of *The History of the Effects of Religion on Mankind; in countries ancient and modern, barbarous and civilized* (1788).[30] She was also a poet, and Battier opened their poetic correspondence after reading a poem Ryan had published on the subject of 'Contentment'.[31] The women exchanged numerous poems, but their husbands apparently disapproved of their activity. Battier writes that although she is

> [...] pleas'd and proud to see,
> The kind epistle penn'd by thee;
> My husband (now a critic grown)
> Desir'd I'd let my pen alone;
> For in your letter, ev'ry line
> In merit, took the lead of mine;
> I own that what he said is true,
> But tho' I ne'er shall equal You,
> Yet still the humble subjects claim
> A secondary right to fame [...]

Apparently the Reverend Dr Ryan was no more enthusiastic, for Eliza Ryan's response begins by announcing that

> Since both our husbands are agreed,
> That we no longer should proceed,
> I take my pen with grief to tell,
> That now I write a long farewell.
>
> (p. 221; 'To Mrs. Battier')

Both husbands, it appears from the texts of the poems, represented their wives' poetry to them as largely a waste of their (and one another's) time, while in the poems each woman proclaims herself inferior to the other. Ryan finally closes her side of the discussion with the sort of self-deprecation that we have been considering:

> [...] the world may plainly see,
> The garland ne'er was made for me;
> My temples must with truth disown,
> And prove the garland was thy own.

(p. 223)

Battier trumps the compliment in the final poem, though, announcing that it is 'in Eliza's shape' that her own muse comes, so that her own subsequent efforts will reflect back on Ryan:

> Friend of my heart, if what I write
> Obliges you, 'tis my delight,
> Nor will I throw the pen aside,
> Which taste like your's [*sic*] vouchsafes to guide;
> For rest assur'd, my grateful lyre
> Receives from this electric fire.

(pp. 228–9)

So the *private* poetic correspondence concluded, apparently, and that might have been the end of it. But Battier 'went public', as it were, and in publishing both her poems and Ryan's she effectively *prevented* her friend's (and her own) erasure from the poetic records. The published correspondence therefore manages to overcome within the public sphere of the print medium the attempts to silence it that occurred in the private sphere. Furthermore, that correspondence illustrates the social (and gender-based) impediments to women's poetic production (and success) at the same time that it traces one strategy for publicly countering that silencing impulse. It would become harder for women to do this by the 1820s and after, however, because the growth of commercial writing (as in the annuals) worked *against* so intimate a variety of poetic discourse. The personal 'poet' becomes the person-less 'poetess' whose audience is *assumed* to be large, diverse, and largely unknown, unlike the audience for the more 'familiar' poetry that many women wrote thirty years earlier.

Interestingly, Ryan entered the public sphere as a poet herself in 1816, three years after Battier's death, when she arranged for publication of her *Poems on Several Occasions*, which modest collection she announces in her 'Introduction' is intended for her friends alone, none having been printed for sale.[32] Ironically, her volume makes no explicit mention of Battier or their friendship. Her husband Edward, who died two year later in 1818, appears repeatedly in these poems, and in a favourable light, which might suggest why he did not attempt to suppress even their semi-private publication and circulation. And while Ryan offers the familiar formulaic apology for her inferior talents, the mere physical fact of the volume's publication reminds us that the era's women poets were not willing, after all, to descend quietly into obscurity, erased forever from the record, even when they were not always unwilling to erase the names (and works) of those women who had been their familiars.

When we consider that J.R. de Jackson's 1993 bibliography, *Romantic Poetry by Women*, runs to nearly five hundred pages and includes the names of some twelve hundred poets from the period covering 1770 to 1835 alone,[33] it is clear that far from settling for silence and erasure, a remarkable array of women poets from a variety of social and economic backgrounds invested real time, energy, and poetic commitment in *inscribing* their presence upon and within the Romantic and early Victorian literary scene. When we add to the names that Jackson supplies of women who published *volumes* of poetry the names of those many others who contributed only to annuals and other anthologies, and of the still others whose poems appeared only in the periodical press, the numbers become all the more impressive. When she concluded her *Records of Woman* with an image of Mary Tighe as the representative of her age's 'poetess', Felicia Hemans may have meant to suggest – indeed to insist upon – the continuing presence of the woman poet in British culture. Even in death, both as Mary Tighe and as 'a Poetess', she attains iconic status that eerily relates to the figure contained in 'The Image in Lava', also from *Records of Woman*:

> Immortal, oh! Immortal
> Thou art, whose earthly glow
> Hath given these ashes holiness –
> It must, it *must* be so!
>
> (ll. 41–4)

Community and permanence, however difficult to achieve and maintain across time and the fluctuations of fame and celebrity, remain imperatives for the woman poet. We do well to qualify and to re-situate their emblematic presence by measuring it also against the sheer physical evidence of the many volumes of poetry actually published throughout the Romantic and early Victorian period by women, volumes that constitute the fullest and most lasting 'records of *women*'.

Notes

1. Felicia Hemans to John Lodge, July 1831. Quoted in *Felicia Hemans: Selected Poems, Letters, Reception Materials*, ed. by Susan J. Wolfson (Princeton: Princeton University Press, 2000), p. 514. 'The Grave of a Poetess' first appeared in *The New Monthly Magazine* in July 1827, where it was signed simply 'F.H'.
2. See for instance the excellent historical and critical apparatus that accompanies the online edition of *The Keepsake* for 1829, edited by Terence Hoagwood, Kathryn Ledbetter, and Martin M. Jacobsen, available at *Romantic Circles* <http://www.rc.umd.edu/editions/lel/keepsake.htm>.
3. Henry F. Chorley, *Memorials of Mrs. Hemans, with Illustrations of Her Literary Character from Her Private Correspondence*, 2 vols (London, 1836), II, 212.
4. Felicia Hemans, *Records of Woman, with Other Poems*, ed. by Paula R. Feldman (Lexington: University Press of Kentucky, 1999), p. 186.
5. Alexander Dyce's 1825 *Specimens of British Poetesses*, for example, gives fourteen pages to Tighe's poetry, more than any contemporary woman poet except Charlotte Smith (who gets twenty-four) and Anna Seward (twenty-two). *Specimens of British Poetesses: Selected and Chronologically Arranged*, ed. by Revd Alexander Dyce (London, 1825).
6. Felicia Hemans to Rose Lawrence, 13 February 1835. Quoted in *Felicia Hemans*, ed. by Wolfson, p. 521.
7. *The British Review* 15 (January 1820), 299. I have discussed this aspect of Hemans's early reception in '"Certainly not a Female Pen": Felicia Hemans's Early Public Reception', in *Felicia Hemans: Reimagining Poetry in the Nineteenth Century*, ed. by Nanora Sweet and Julie Melnyk (Basingstoke: Palgrave Macmillan, 2001), pp. 95–114.
8. Frederic Rowton, ed., *The Female Poets of Great Britain, Chronologically Arranged with Copious Selections and Critical Remarks*, 1848, rpt. of 1853 American (Philadelphia) edition, ed. by Marilyn L. Williamson (Detroit: Wayne State University Press, 1981), p. 386.
9. *Forget Me Not: A Christmas and New Year's Present for 1826* (London, 1826), pp. 156–8; the poem is accompanied by an engraved illustration of praying girls.
10. The poems are 'Lines Written for the Album at Rosanna' (1829), 'Written After Visiting a Tomb, near Woodstock, in the County of Kilkenny' (1831), and 'On Records of Immature Genius' (1834). They are reproduced in *The Collected Poems and Journals of Mary Tighe*, ed. by Harriet Kramer Linkin (Lexington: University Press of Kentucky, 2005), pp. 277–80. Interestingly, Tighe is not named in the titles, although the epigraphic inscriptions of the latter two cite her by name. Subsequent references to these poems are taken from this edition and are cited parenthetically in the text.
11. Mariann Dark, *Sonnets and Other Poems* (London, 1818). World Cat, for example, lists only six copies in the United States; two additional copies

are in the British Library and the Bodleian Library. Dark's book contains an impressive list of subscribers, including the Marquis and Marchioness of Lansdowne, in addition to Bowles, who was undoubtedly instrumental in getting the poems published. Subsequent references are cited parenthetically in the text.

12. Lucy Morrison, 'Effusive Elegies or Catty Critic: Letitia Elizabeth Landon On Felicia Hemans', *Romanticism on the Net*, 45 (February 2007), para. 1, 36 <http://www.erudit.org/revue/ron/2007/v/n45/015820ar.html> [accessed 15 August 2007]. Morrison considers both Landon's 'Stanzas on the Death of Mrs. Hemans' (1835), which first appeared in *New Monthly Magazine* 44 (1835), 286–8, and her essay, 'On the Character of Mrs. Hemans's Writings', also from *New Monthly Magazine*, 44 (1835), 425–33, as well as the more pointedly personal caption she prepared to accompany a portrait of Hemans that appeared in the 1838 *Drawing-Room Scrap-Book* (1838), pp. 10–11.

13. Trench wrote to Mrs. William Trench, in July 1820 that '[M]y little attempts *can* have no merit but that of showing to those who love me, what I might have done, had I not been deprived of the advantages of classical learning; had I not been flattered in my youth, as one to whom mental acquirements were unnecessary; had I not been the fond mother of nine children, and the troublesome wife of one whom I do not much like to have out of my sight; four very unfavourable circumstances to the cultivation of any art or science whatever.' *The Remains of the Late Mrs. Richard Trench, being Selections from her Journals, Letters, & Other Papers, edited by her Son, The Dean of Westminster*, ed. by Richard Chenevix Trench, 2nd edn, rev. (London, 1862), pp. 432–3.

14. 'Stanzas on the Death of Mrs. Hemans' (ll. 69–76), in *Letitia Elizabeth Landon: Selected Writings*, ed. by Jerome McGann and Daniel Riess (Peterborough, Ontario: Broadview Press, 1997), p. 171.

15. Paula R. Backscheider, *Eighteenth-Century Women Poets and their Poetry: Inventing Agency, Inventing Genre* (Baltimore: Johns Hopkins University Press, 2005), p. 286.

16. T[homas] Park, *Sonnets, and Other Small Poems* (1797; rpt. London, 1803), pp. 5, 20.

17. Anna Seward, *Letters of Anna Seward: Written between the years 1784 and 1807*, ed. by A. Constable, 6 vols (Edinburgh, 1811), II, 162.

18. Nicola Trott, 'Too Good for Them', *TLS*, 5281 (18 June 2004), 3–4.

19. Jacqueline M. Labbe, 'Selling One's Sorrows: Charlotte Smith, Mary Robinson, and the Marketing of Poetry', *The Wordsworth Circle*, 35 (Spring 1994), 68–71, p. 68.

20. Jacqueline M. Labbe, 'Introduction', *The Works of Charlotte Smith: Volume 14*, ed. by Jacqueline M. Labbe (London: Pickering and Chatto, 2007), p. xix.

21. Mary Robinson to Jane Porter, 27 August 1800. Quoted in *Mary Robinson: Selected Poems*, ed. by Judith Pascoe (Peterborough, Ontario: Broadview, 2000), p. 371. Robinson died on 26 December 1800.

22. Labbe, 'Selling One's Sorrows', p. 70.

23. Jane Porter's manuscript diary. Folger Shakespeare Library, Mb 15, fols. 2–3. Porter's memoir was tentatively called 'Character of the Late Mrs Robinson, who is usually stiled the British Sappho, extracted from a letter to a lady'. Quoted in Paula Byrne, *Perdita: The Life of Mary Robinson* (London: Harper Perennial, 2004), p. 420.

24. Mary Hays, *British Public Characters* (1800–01). Quoted in Loraine Fletcher, *Charlotte Smith: A Critical Biography* (New York: St Martin's, 1998), p. 159.
25. Mary Robinson, '*Present State of the Manners, Society, Etc. Etc. Of the Metropolis of England*', ed. by Adriana Craciun, *PMLA*, 119(1) (2004), 103–19. The essay, reproduced in full in *PMLA*, appeared in successive issues of the *Monthly Magazine*, in August, September, October, and November 1800. Subsequent references are taken from Craciun (ed.) and are given parenthetically in the text.
26. Anna Letitia LeBreton, *Memoir of Mrs. Barbauld, Including Letters and Notices of her Family and Friends* (London, 1874), pp. 86–7, quoted in *British Women Poets of the Romantic Era: An Anthology*, ed. by Paula R. Feldman (Baltimore: Johns Hopkins University Press, 1997), p. 54.
27. Martha Hanson, *Sonnets, and Other Poems*, 2 vols (London, 1809), II, 74.
28. *Verse in English from Eighteenth-Century Ireland*, ed. by Andrew Carpenter (Cork: Cork University Press, 1998), p. 464.
29. Henrietta Battier. *The Protected Fugitives. A Collection of Miscellaneous Poems, the Genuine Productions of a Lady. Never before published* (Dublin, 1791). The poems appear on pp. 212–29.
30. Ryan mentions this work by name in the title of the poem that appears on p. 94 of her own collection, *Poems on Several Occasions* (Dublin, 1816): 'On Edward's History of the Effects of Religion on Mankind'.
31. 'Lines, addressed by the Author of the Foregoing. To the Lady of the Rev. Doctor Ryan. On Reading a Poem written by her on Contentment', Battier, *Protected Fugitives*, p. 211. Ryan's poem, 'On Contentment', appears in *Poems on Several Occasions*, pp. 13–14.
32. Ryan, *Poems on Several Occasions*, p. 5.
33. J.R. de J. Jackson. *Romantic Poetry by Women: A Bibliography, 1770–1835* (Oxford: Clarendon Press, 1993). Because Jackson also includes North American writers, the actual number of *British* women poets is in the neighbourhood of one thousand, including poets from Scotland and Ireland.

Select Bibliography

See also individual essays.

Primary sources

Anti-Jacobin Novels, general editor W.M. Verhoeven, 10 vols (London: Pickering and Chatto, 2005).

Austen, Jane, *Mansfield Park*, ed. John Wiltshire, *The Cambridge Edition of the Works of Jane Austen*, general editor Janet Todd (Cambridge: Cambridge University Press, 2005).

——, *Jane Austen's Letters*, ed. Deirdre Le Faye (Oxford: Oxford University Press, 1995).

——, *Minor Works*, ed. R.W. Chapman, rev. B.C. Southam (Oxford: Oxford University Press, 1988).

——, *Northanger Abbey*, ed. R.W. Chapman (Oxford: Oxford University Press, 1988).

——, *Persuasion*, ed. R.W. Chapman (Oxford: Oxford University Press, 1988).

Baillie, Joanna, *Plays [on the] Passions* (London: Cadell and Davies, 1798).

Barbauld, Anna Laetitia, *British Novelists*, 50 vols (London: various publishers, 1810)

Basker, James G., ed., *Amazing Grace: An Anthology of Poems about Slavery, 1660–1810* (New Haven and London: Yale University Press, 2002).

Batchelor, Jennie and Megan Hiatt, eds, *The Histories of Some of the Penitents in the Magdalen-House, as Supposed to be related by Themselves* (1760) (London: Pickering and Chatto, 2007).

Bell, G.H., *The Hamwood Papers of The Ladies of Llangollen and Caroline Hamilton* (London: Macmillan, 1930).

Birkett, Mary, *A Poem on the African Slave Trade. Addressed to her own Sex*, Parts I and II (Dublin: J. Jones, Grafton Street, 1792).

Breen, Jennifer, ed., *Women Romantic Poets, 1785–1832* (London: Dent Everyman, 1992).

Brunton, Mary, *Self-Control* (London: Pandora Press, 1986).

Burney, Frances, *Diary and Letters of Madame d'Arblay (1778–1840)*, ed. Austin Dobson (London: Macmillan, 1904–05).

——, *Evelina, or the History of a Young Lady's Entrance into the World*, ed. Edward A. Bloom and Lillian D. Bloom (Oxford: Oxford University Press, 1998).

——, *Memoirs of Doctor Burney, Arranged from his own Manuscripts, from Family Papers, and from Personal Collections*, 3 vols (London, 1832).

——, *The Journals and Letters of Fanny Burney*, ed. Peter Sabor (Harmondsworth: Penguin, 2001).

——, *The Wanderer, or Female Difficulties*, ed. Margaret Anne Doody, Robert L. Mack, and Peter Sabor (Oxford: Oxford University Press, 2001).

Chapone, Hester, *Letters on the Improvement of the Mind, Addressed to a Young Lady*, 2 vols (London, 1773).

Chorley, Henry, ed., *Letters of Mary Russell Mitford: Second Series*, 2 vols (London, 1872).

——, *Memorials of Mrs. Hemans, with Illustrations of Her Literary Character from Her Private Correspondence*, 2 vols (London, 1836).

Clarkson, Thomas, *The History of the Rise, Progress, and Accomplishment of the Abolition of the African Slave-Trade*, 2 vols (London: Longman, Hurst, Rees and Orme, 1808).

Constable, A., ed., *Letters of Anna Seward: Written between the years 1784 and 1807*, 6 vols (Edinburgh, 1811).

Clery, E.J. and Robert Miles, eds, *Gothic Documents: A Sourcebook, 1700–1820* (New York: St Martin's, 2000).

[Collier, Jane and] Sarah Fielding, *The Cry*, ed. Mary Anne Schofield (Delmar, NY: Scholars' Facsimiles and Reprints, 1986).

Dark, Mariann, *Sonnets and Other Poems* (London, 1818).

Deverell, Mary, *Miscellanies in Prose and Verse, mostly written in the epistolary style*, (London: printed for the author by J. Rivington, 1781).

Duncombe, John, *The Feminiad; or, Female Genius, A Poem* (London, 1754).

Dyce, Revd Alexander, *Specimens of British Poetesses: Selected and Chronologically Arranged* (London, 1825).

Edgeworth, Maria, *Belinda*, ed. Kathryn Kirkpatrick (Oxford: Oxford University Press, 1994).

——, *Patronage* (London: Routledge, 1893).

Equiano, Olaudah, *The Interesting Narrative and Other Writings*, ed. Vincent Carretta (Harmondsworth: Penguin, 2003).

Falconar Maria and Harriet Falconar, *Poems on Slavery: by Maria Falconar, aged 17, and Harriet Falconar, aged 14* (London: Egertons, Murray and J. Johnson, 1788).

Feldman, Paula R., ed., *British Women Poets of the Romantic Era: An Anthology* (Baltimore: Johns Hopkins University Press, 1997).

Ferguson, Moira, ed., *First Feminists: British Women Writers 1578–1799* (Bloomington: Indiana University Press, 1985).

Fielding, Sarah, *The Adventures of David Simple And The Adventures of David Simple, Volume the Last*, ed. Linda Bree (London and New York: Penguin, 2002).

——, *The History of the Countess of Dellwyn*, 2 vols (London: A. Millar, 1758).

——, *The Lives of Cleopatra and Octavia*, ed. R. Brimsley Johnson (London: The Scholartis Press, 1928).

[——], *Familiar Letters between the Principal Characters in David Simple, And Some Others. To which is added, A Vision*, 2 vols (London: Printed for the Author; and Sold by A. Millar, 1747).

——, *Remarks on Clarissa, Addressed to the Author. Occasioned by some critical Conversations on the Characters and conduct of that Work* (London: Printed for J. Robinson, 1749).

Gisborne, Thomas, *An Enquiry into the Duties of the Female Sex* (London, 1816).

Godwin, William, *Memoirs of the Author of A Vindication of the Rights of Woman*, ed. Richard Holmes (Harmondsworth: Penguin, 1987).

Graham, Maria, *Journal of a Residence in Chile during the Year 1822, and A Voyage from Chile to Brazil in 1823*, ed. Jennifer Hayward (Charlottesville: University of Virginia Press, 2003).

Halsband, R., ed., *The Complete Letters of Lady Mary Wortley Montagu*, 3 vols (Oxford: Oxford University Press, 1965–67).

Hanson, Martha, *Sonnets, and Other Poems*, 2 vols (London, 1809).

[Harness, William], *The Life of Mary Russell Mitford*, ed. A.G. L'Estrange, 3 vols (London, 1870).

Haywood, Eliza, *The History of Jemmy and Jenny Jessamy*, ed. John Richetti (Lexington: University Press of Kentucky, 2005).

Hays, Mary, *Memoirs of Emma Courtney*, ed. Eleanor Ty (Oxford: Oxford University Press, 2000).

Hemans, Felicia, *Felicia Hemans: Selected Poems, Letters, Reception Materials*, ed. Susan J. Wolfson (Princeton: Princeton University Press, 2000).

——, *National Lyrics and Songs for Music* (Dublin and London, 1834).

——, *Records of Woman, with Other Poems*, ed. Paula R. Feldman (Lexington: University Press of Kentucky, 1999).

——, *Selected Poems, Prose and Letters*, ed. Gary Kelly (Peterborough, Ontario: Broadview, 2002).

——, *The Siege of Valencia; a Dramatic Poem. The Last Constantine: with Other Poems* (London, 1823).

[Justice, Elizabeth], *Amelia, or, The Distress'd Wife: A History Founded on Real Circumstances* (London: Printed for the Authoress, 1751).

Kelly, Gary, general editor, *Bluestocking Feminism: Writings of the Bluestocking Circle, 1738–1785*, 6 vols (London: Pickering and Chatto, 1999).

Landon, Letitia, *Letitia Elizabeth Landon: Selected Writings*, ed. Jerome McGann and Daniel Riess (Peterborough, Ontario: Broadview Press, 1997).

Lawrence, Mrs [Rose D'Aguilar], *The Last Autumn at a Favourite Residence, with other Poems; and Recollections of Mrs. Hemans* (Liverpool and London, 1836).

Lee, Harriet, 'Preface', in *The Canterbury Tales* by Sophia and Harriet Lee (London: Colburn and Bentley, 1832).

Lee, Sophia, *The Recess, or a Tale of Other Times*, ed. April Alliston (Lexington: University Press of Kentucky, 2000).

Lennox, Charlotte, *The Female Quixote*, ed. Margaret Dalziel, introduction by Margaret Anne Doody (Oxford: Oxford University Press, 1998).

Linkin, Harriet Kramer, ed., *The Collected Poems and Journals of Mary Tighe* (Lexington: University Press of Kentucky, 2005).

Lonsdale, Roger, ed., *Eighteenth-Century Women Poets* (Oxford: Oxford University Press, 1989).

Macaulay, Catharine, *The History of England from the Revolution to the Present Time in a Series of Letters to a Friend* (Bath: R. Crutwell, 1778).

Mahl, Mary R. and Helene Koon, eds, *The Female Spectator: English Women Writers Before 1800* (Bloomington: Indiana University Press, 1977).

McCarthy, William and Elizabeth Kraft, eds, *Selected Poetry and Prose of Anna Barbauld* (Peterborough, Ontario: Broadview Press, 2002).

Mitford, Mary Russell, *The Dramatic Works of Mary Russell Mitford*, 2 vols (London, 1854).

Montagu, Lady Mary Wortley, *Turkish Embassy Letters*, ed. Anita Desai and Malcolm Jack (London: Virago, 1994).

Montagu, Matthew, ed., *The Letters of Mrs. E. Montagu, with Some Letters of her Correspondence*, 4 vols (London, 1809–13).

More, Hannah, *Strictures on the Modern System of Female Education*, intro. Jeffrey Stern, 2 vols (London: Routledge/Thoemmes Press, 1995).

——, *Cœlebs in Search of a Wife. Comprehending Observations on Domestic Habits and Manners, Religion and Morals*, 5th edn, 2 vols (London: Cadell and Davies, 1809).

Parsons, Eliza, *The Castle of Wolfenbach*, ed. Diane Long Hoeveler (Chicago: Valancourt Books, 2006).

——, *The Mysterious Warning: A German Tale*, ed. Devendra Varma (London: Folio Press, 1968).

Pennington, Montagu, ed., *Letters from Mrs. Elizabeth Carter to Mrs. Montagu between the Years 1755 and 1800*, 3 vols (London, 1817).

Pennington, Montagu, ed., *A Series of Letters between Mrs. Elizabeth Carter and Miss Catherine Talbot* (London, 1809).

Porter, Anna Maria, *The Hungarian Brothers*, 3 vols (London: Longman, Hurst, Rees and Orme, 1807).

Porter, Jane, *Thaddeus of Warsaw*, 4 vols (London: Longman, Hurst, Rees, and Orme, 1806).

Radcliffe, Ann, *The Italian*, ed. Frederick Garber (Oxford: Oxford University Press, 1970).

——, *The Mysteries of Udolpho*, ed. Bonamy Dobree (Oxford: Oxford University Press, 1998).

——, *Romance of the Forest* (New York: Arno, 1974).

——, *A Sicilian Romance*, ed. Alison Milbank (Oxford: Oxford University Press, 1993).

Reeve, Clara, *The Old English Baron*, in *The Old English Baron by Clara Reeve and The Castle of Otranto by Horace Walpole*, ed. Laura L. Runge (Glen Allen, VA: College Publishing, 2002).

——, *The Progress of Romance, through Times, Countries, and Manners* ([Colchester]: Keymer, 1785).

Robinson, Mary, *Monody to the Memory of the Late Queen of France* (London: J. Evans, 1793).

——, *Memoirs of the Late Mrs. Robinson, written by herself. With some posthumous pieces*, ed. Mary Elizabeth Robinson, 4 vols (London: R. Phillips, 1801).

——, *Poetical Works of the late Mrs. Mary Robinson: including many pieces never before published*, 3 vols (London: R. Phillips, 1806).

——, *Present State of the Manners, Society, Etc. Etc. Of the Metropolis of England*, ed. Adriana Craciun, *PMLA*, 119(1) (2004), 103–19.

——, *Mary Robinson: Selected Poems*, ed. Judith Pascoe (Peterborough, Ontario: Broadview Press, 2000).

——, *Walsingham; or, The Pupil of Nature*, ed. Julie A. Schaffer (Peterborough, Ontario: Broadview Press, 2003).

——, *Sight, The Cavern of Woe, and Solitude: Poems* (London: J. Evans, 1793).

[——], *Impartial Reflections on the Present Situation of the Queen of France* (London: Bell, 1791).

Rogers, Katherine M. and William McCarthy, eds, *The Meridian Anthology of Early Women Writers: British Literary Women from Aphra Behn to Maria Edgeworth, 1660–1800* (New York: New American Library, 1987).

Scott, Mary, *The Female Advocate; A Poem* (London, 1774).

Scott, Sarah, *A Description of Millenium Hall*, ed. Gary Kelly (Peterborough, Ontario: Broadview Press, 1995; rpt 2004).

Seward, Anna, *Monody on Major Andrè* (Litchfield, J. Jackson, 1781).

Smith, Charlotte, *Elegiac Sonnets* (London: Cadell and Davies, 1797).

——, *Emmeline, or the Orphan of the Castle*, ed. Zoë Fairbairns (London: Pandora, 1988).

——, *The Old Manor House*, ed. Jacqueline M. Labbe (Peterborough, Ontario: Broadview Press, 2002).

——, *The Works of Charlotte Smith*, general editor Stuart Curran, 14 vols (London: Pickering and Chatto, 2005–07).

Stanton, Judith Phillips, ed., *The Collected Letters of Charlotte Smith* (Bloomington: Indiana University Press, 2003).

Tighe, Mary, *Psyche, with Other Poems. By the Late Mrs. Henry Tighe* (London: Longman, 1811).

Uphaus, Robert W. and Gretchen M. Foster, eds, *The 'Other' Eighteenth Century: English Women of Letters, 1660–1800* (East Lansing, MI: Colleagues Press, 1991).

Williams, Helen Maria, *An Ode on the Peace by the Author of Edwin and Eltruda* (London: T. Cadell, 1783).

Williamson, Marilyn L., ed., *The Female Poets of Great Britain, Chronologically Arranged with Copious Selections and Critical Remarks*, ed. Frederic Rowton (1848; 1853) (Detroit: Wayne State University Press, 1981).

Wollstonecraft, Mary, *Mary: A Fiction; and The Wrongs of Woman, or Maria*, ed. Janet Todd (Harmonsdworth: Penguin, 1991).

——, *Letters written during a Short Residence in Sweden, Norway, and Denmark*, ed. T. Brekke and J. Mee (Oxford: Oxford University Press, 2009).

——, *A Vindication of the Rights of Woman. Mary Wollstonecraft: Political Writings*, ed. Janet Todd (Toronto: University of Toronto Press 1993).

——, *The Works of Mary Wollstonecraft*, ed. Janet Todd and Marilyn Butler with the assistance of Emma Rees-Mogg, 7 vols (London: Pickering and Chatto, 1989).

Wordsworth, William, *William Wordsworth: The Major Works*, ed. Stephen Gill (Oxford and New York: Oxford University Press, 1984; rpt 2000).

Yearsley, Ann, *A Poem on the Inhumanity of the Slave-Trade* (London: G.G.J. and J. Robinson, 1788).

Secondary sources

Aaron, Jane, *Nineteenth-Century Women's Writing in Wales: Nation, Gender and Identity* (Cardiff: University of Wales Press, 2007).

Alliston, April, *Virtue's Faults: Correspondences in Eighteenth-Century British and French Women's Fiction* (Stanford: Stanford University Press, 1996).

Armstrong, Isobel and Virginia Blain, eds, *Women's Poetry in the Enlightenment: The Making of a Canon, 1730–1820* (Basingstoke: Macmillan, 1999).

Armstrong, Nancy, *How Novels Think: The Limits of British Individualism from 1719–1900* (New York: Columbia University Press, 2005).

Backscheider, Paula, *Eighteenth-Century Women Poets and their Poetry: Inventing Agency, Inventing Genre* (Baltimore: Johns Hopkins University Press, 2005).

Barash, Carol, *English Women's Poetry, 1649–1714: Politics, Community, and Linguistic Authority* (Oxford: Clarendon Press, 1996).

Barrell, John, *The Birth of Pandora and the Division of Knowledge* (Basingstoke: Macmillan, 1992).

Batchelor, Jennie, 'Woman's Work: Labour, Gender and Authorship in the Novels of Sarah Scott', in *British Women's Writing in the Long Eighteenth Century: Authorship, History, Politics*, ed. Jennie Batchelor and Cora Kaplan (Basingstoke: Palgrave Macmillan, 2005), pp. 19–33.

Batchelor, Jennie and Cora Kaplan, eds, *British Women's Writing in the Long Eighteenth Century: Authorship, Politics and History* (Basingstoke: Palgrave Macmillan, 2005).

Bohls, Elizabeth, *Women Travel Writers and the Language of Aesthetics 1716–1818* (Cambridge: Cambridge University Press, 1995).

Bree, Linda, *Sarah Fielding* (New York: Twayne Publishers; London: Prentice Hall, 1996).

Brennan, Catherine, *Angers, Fantasies and Ghostly Fears: Nineteenth-Century Women from Wales and English-language Poetry* (Cardiff: University of Wales Press, 2003).

Brownstein, Rachel, *Becoming a Heroine: Reading about Women in Novels* (New York: Viking, 1982).

Burroughs, Catherine, *Closet Stages: Joanna Baillie and the Theater Theory of British Romantic Women Writers* (Philadelphia: University of Pennsylvania Press, 1997).

——, ed., *Women in British Romantic Theatre: Drama, Performance, and Society, 1790–1840* (Cambridge: Cambridge University Press, 2000).

Burstein, Miriam, *Narrating Women's History in Britain, 1770–1902* (Aldershot: Ashgate, 2004).

Byrne, Paula, *Perdita: The Life of Mary Robinson* (London: Harper Perennial, 2004).

Chedgzoy, Kate, 'The Cultural Geographies of Early Modern Women's Writing: Journeys across Spaces and Times', *Literature Compass*, 3 (2006), 1–9.

——, *Women's Writing in the British Atlantic World: Memory, Place and History, 1550–1700* (Cambridge: Cambridge University Press, 2007).

Clemit, Pamela, 'Charlotte Smith to William and Mary Jane Godwin: Five Holograph Letters', *Keats-Shelley Journal*, 55 (2006), 29–40.

Coleman, Deirdre, 'Conspicuous Consumption: White Abolitionism and English Women's Protest Writing in the 1790s', *English Literary History*, 61 (1994), 341–62

——, *Maiden Voyages and Infant Colonies: Two Women's Travel Narratives of the 1790s* (London: Continuum, 1999).

——, *Romantic Colonization and British Anti-Slavery* (Cambridge University Press, 2005).

Colley, Linda, *Britons: Forging the Nation 1707–1837* (Yale: Yale University Press, 1992).

Craciun, Adriana, *British Women Writers and the French Revolution: Citizens of the World* (Cambridge: Cambridge University Press, 2005).

——, *Fatal Women of Romanticism* (Cambridge: Cambridge University Press, 2003).

Crochunis, Thomas, ed., *Joanna Baillie, Romantic Dramatist: Critical Essays* (New York: Routledge, 2004).

Curran, Eileen, 'Holding on by a Pen: The Story of a Lady/Reviewer: Mary Margaret Busk (1779–1863)', *Victorian Periodicals Review*, 31 (1998), 9–30.

Curran, Stuart, ed., *The Cambridge Companion to British Romanticism* (Cambridge: Cambridge University Press, 1993).

——, 'Romantic Poetry: The I Altered' in *Romanticism and Feminism*, ed. Anne K. Mellor (Bloomington: Indiana University Press, 1988), pp. 185–207.

——, *Poetic Form and British Romanticism* (New York, Oxford: Oxford University Press, 1986).

Davies, Kate, *Catharine Macaulay and Mercy Otis Warren: The Revolutionary Atlantic and the Politics of Gender* (Oxford: Oxford University Press, 2005).

Davis, Lennard J., *Factual Fictions: The Origins of the English Novel* (New York: Columbia University Press, 1983).

DeLaMotte, Eugenia, *Perils of the Night: A Feminist Study of Nineteenth-Century Fiction* (New York: Oxford University Press, 1990).

Doody, Margaret, 'Deserts, Ruins, and Troubled Waters: Female Dreams in Fiction and the Development of the Gothic Novel', *Genre*, 19 (1977), 529–72.

Eger, Elizabeth, Charlotte Grant, Clíona Ó Gallchoir, and Penny Warburton, eds, *Women, Writing and the Public Sphere, 1700–1830* (Cambridge: Cambridge University Press, 2001).

Ellis, Kate, *The Contested Castle: Gothic Novels and the Subversion of Domestic Ideology* (Urbana: University of Illinois Press, 1989).

Ezell, Margaret, *Writing Women's Literary History* (Baltimore: Johns Hopkins University Press, 1993).

Feldman, Paula and Theresa M. Kelley, eds, *Romantic Women Writers: Voices and Countervoices* (Hanover, NH: University Press of New England, 1995).

Ferris, Ina, *The Achievement of Literary Authority: Gender, History, and the Waverley Novels* (Ithaca: Cornell University Press, 1991).

Festa, Lynn, *Sentimental Figures of Empire in Eighteenth-Century Britain and France.* (Baltimore: Johns Hopkins University Press, 2006).

Fletcher, Loraine, *Charlotte Smith: A Critical Biography* (Basingstoke and New York: Macmillan, 1998).

Gallagher, Catherine, *Nobody's Story: The Vanishing Acts of Women Writers in the Marketplace, 1670–1830* (Berkeley and Los Angeles: University of California Press, 1994).

Gamer, Michael, 'Maria Edgeworth and the Romance of Real Life', *Novel: A Forum for Fiction*, 34 (2001), 232–66.

Garnai, Amy, '"One Victim from the Last Despair": Mary Robinson's Marie Antoinette', *Women's Writing*, 12 (2005), 381–98.

Garside, Peter et al., general editors, *The English Novel 1770–1829: A Bibliographical Survey of Prose Fiction Published in the British Isles*, 2 vols (Oxford: Oxford University Press, 2000).

Gilbert, Sandra and Susan Gubar, *The Madwoman in the Attic: The Woman Writer and the Nineteenth-Century Imagination* (New Haven: Yale University Press, 1979).

Gillroy, Amanda, ed., *Romantic Geographies: Discourses of Travel 1775–1844* (Manchester: Manchester University Press, 2000).

Gramich, Katie, *Twentieth-Century Women's Writing in Wales: Land, Gender, Belonging* (Cardiff: University of Wales Press, 2007).

Guest, Harriet, *Small Change: Women, Learning, Patriotism, 1750–1810* (Chicago: University of Chicago Press, 2000).

Harris, Jocelyn, *Jane Austen's Art of Memory* (Cambridge: Cambridge University Press, 1989).

Hoeveler, Diane Long, *Gothic Feminism: The Professionalization of Gender from Charlotte Smith to the Brontës* (University Park: Penn State Press, 1998).

Homans, Margaret, *Women Writers and Poetic Identity: Dorothy Wordsworth, Emily Brontë, and Emily Dickinson* (Princeton: Princeton University Press, 1980).

Hunter, J. Paul, *Before Novels: The Cultural Contexts of Eighteenth Century English Fiction* (New York: W.W. Norton, 1990).

Irvine, Robert Tate, Jr, 'The Life of Jane Porter', unpublished Master's Thesis, University of Virginia, 1942.

Isbell, John Claiborne, *The Birth of a European Romanticism: Truth and Propaganda in Staël's 'De l'Allemagne'* (Cambridge: Cambridge University Press, 1994).

Jackson, J.R. de J., *Romantic Poetry by Women: A Bibliography, 1770–1835* (Oxford: Clarendon Press, 1993).

Janowitz, Anne, *Women Romantic Poets: Anna Barbauld and Mary Robinson* (Tavistock: Northcote House, 2004).

Johns, Alessa, *Women's Utopias of the Eighteenth Century* (Urbana and Chicago: University of Illinois Press, 2003).

Johnson, Claudia L., *Jane Austen: Women, Politics, and the Novel* (Chicago: University of Chicago Press, 1988).

Jones, Ann H., *Ideas and Innovation: Best Sellers of Jane Austen's Age* (New York: AMS Press, 1986).

Jones, Vivien, ed., *Women and Literature in Britain* (Cambridge: Cambridge University Press, 2000).

Justice, George L. and Nathan Tinker, eds, *Women's Writing and the Circulation of Ideas: Manuscript Publication in England, 1550–1800* (Cambridge: Cambridge University Press, 2002).

Kahane, Claire, 'Gothic Mirrors and Feminine Identity', *Centennial Review*, 24 (1980), 43–64.

Kaplan, Cora, *Sea Changes: Essays on Culture and Feminism* (London: Verso, 1986).

Kelly, Gary, ed., *Jane Porter's the Scottish Chiefs*, Vol. 4, *Varieties of Female Gothic*, ed. Gary Kelly (London: Pickering and Chatto, 2002).

——, 'Politicizing the Personal: Mary Wollstonecraft, Mary Shelley, and the Coterie Novel', in *Mary Shelley in Her Times*, ed. Betty Bennet and Stuart Curran (Baltimore: Johns Hopkins University Press, 2000), pp. 147–59.

Kennedy, Deborah, *Helen Maria Williams and the Age of Revolution* (Lewisburg: Bucknell University Press, 2002).

Keymer, Thomas and Jon Mee, eds, *The Cambridge Companion to English Literature 1740–1830* (Cambridge: Cambridge University Press, 2004).

Kinsley, Zoe, *Women Writing the Home Tour, 1682–1812* (Aldershot: Ashgate, 2008).

Knott, Sarah, *Sensibility in the American Revolution: Self, Society and Independence.* (Chapel Hill: University of North Carolina Press for the Omohundro Institute, 2009).

Kirkham, Margaret, *Jane Austen, Feminism and Fiction* (London: Athlone Press, 1997).

Kowaleski-Wallace, Elizabeth, *Consuming Subjects: Women, Shopping, and Business in the Eighteenth-Century* (New York: Columbia University Press, 1997), pp. 37–51.

Labbe, Jacqueline M., *Charlotte Smith in British Romanticism* (London: Pickering and Chatto, 2008).

——, *Charlotte Smith: Romanticism, Poetry and the Culture of Gender* (Manchester: Manchester University Press, 2003).

——, 'Selling One's Sorrows: Charlotte Smith, Mary Robinson, and the Marketing of Poetry', *The Wordsworth Circle*, 35 (1994), 68–71.

——, 'Towards an Ungendered Romanticism: Blake, Robinson and Smith in 1793', in *Women Reading William Blake*, ed. Helen Bruder (Basingstoke: Palgrave Macmillan, 2007, pp. 118–26.

Landry, Donna, *Muses of Resistance: Laboring-Class Women's Poetry in Britain, 1739–1796* (Cambridge: Cambridge University Press, 1990).

——, 'Ruined Cottages: The Contradictory Legacy of the Picturesque for England's Green and Pleasant Land', in *Green and Pleasant Land: English Culture and the Romantic Countryside*, ed. Amanda Gilroy (Leuven: Peeters, 2004), pp. 1–17.

LeBlanc, Jacqueline, 'Politics and Commercial Sensibility in Helen Maria Williams's *Letters from France*', *Eighteenth Century Life*, 21 (1997), 26–44.

Lee, Debbie, *Slavery and the Romantic Imagination* (Philadelphia: University of Pennsylvania Press, 2002).

Looser, Devoney, *British Women Writers and the Writing of History, 1670–1820* (Baltimore: Johns Hopkins University Press, 2000).

Lovell, Terry, *Consuming Fiction* (New York: Verso, 1987).

Macheski, Cecilia and Mary Anne Schofield, eds, *Fetter'd or Free? British Women Novelists, 1670–1815* (Athens, OH: Ohio University Press, 1986).

Mack, Phyllis, 'In a Female Voice: Preaching and Politics in Eighteenth-Century British Quakerism', in *Women Preachers and Prophets through Two Millennia of Christianity*, ed. Beverly Mayne Kienzle and Pamela J. Walker (Berkeley and London: University of California Press, 1998), pp. 248–63.

Massé, Michelle, *In the Name of Love: Women, Masochism, and the Gothic* (Ithaca: Cornell University Press, 1992).

Mazzeo, Tilar, *Plagiarism and Literary Property in the Romantic Period* (Philadelphia: University of Pennsylvania Press, 2007).

McDowell, Paula, *The Women of Grub Street: Press, Politics and Gender in the London Literary Marketplace 1678–1730* (Oxford: Clarendon Press, 1998).

Mellor, Anne K., *Mothers of the Nation: Women's Political Writing in England, 1780–1830* (Bloomington: Indiana University Press, 2000).

——, 'A Novel of Their Own: Romantic Women's Fiction, 1790–1830', in *The Columbia History of the British Novel* (New York: Columbia University Press, 1994), pp. 327–51.

——, ed., *Romanticism and Feminism* (Bloomington: Indiana University Press, 1988).

——, *Romanticism and Gender* (New York: Routledge, 1993).

Midgley, Clare, *Women Against Slavery: The British Campaigns, 1780–1870* (London and New York: Routledge, 1992).

Moers, Ellen, *Literary Women: The Great Writers* (Garden City, NY: Anchor Books, 1977).

Myers, Sylvia Harcstarck, *The Bluestocking Circle: Women, Friendship, and the Life of the Mind in Eighteenth-Century England* (Oxford: Clarendon Press, 1990).

Nagle, Christopher C., *Sexuality and the Culture of Sensibility in the British Romantic Era* (New York: Palgrave, 2007).

Newlyn, Lucy, *Reading, Writing, and Romanticism: The Anxiety of Reception* (Oxford: Oxford University Press, 2000).

Nussbaum, Felicity, 'Effeminacy and Femininity: Domestic Prose Satire and *David Simple*', *Eighteenth-Century Fiction*, 11 (1999), 421–44.

——, *Torrid Zones: Maternity, Sexuality and Empire in Eighteenth-Century English Narratives* (Baltimore: Johns Hopkins University Press, 1995).

Nussbaum, Felicity and Laura Brown, eds, *The New Eighteenth Century: Theory, Politics, English Literature* (New York: Methuen, 1987).

Pascoe, Judith, *Romantic Theatricality: Gender, Poetry, and Spectatorship* (Ithaca: Cornell University Press, 1997).

Perry, Ruth, *Novel Relations: The Transformation of Kinship in English Literature and Culture, 1748–1818* (Cambridge: Cambridge University Press, 2004).

Pohl, Nicole and Betty Schellenberg, eds, *Reconsidering the Bluestockings* (San Marino: Huntington Library, 2003).

Poovey, Mary, *The Proper Lady and the Woman Writer: Ideology as Style in the Works of Mary Wollstonecraft, Mary Shelley, and Jane Austen* (Chicago: University of Chicago Press, 1984).

Prescott, Sarah, *Eighteenth-Century Writing from Wales: Bards and Britons* (Cardiff: University of Wales Press, 2008).

Richetti, John, ed., *The Cambridge Companion to the Eighteenth-Century Novel* (Cambridge: Cambridge University Press, 1996).

Roberts, Michael and Simone Clarke, eds, *Women and Gender in Early Modern Wales* (Cardiff: University of Wales Press, 2000).

Ross, Marlon, *The Contours of Masculine Desire: Romanticism and the Rise of Women's Poetry* (New York: Oxford University Press, 1989).

Schellenberg, Betty A., *The Conversational Circle: Rereading the English Novel, 1740–1775* (Lexington: University Press of Kentucky, 1996).

——, *The Professionalization of Women Writers in Eighteenth-Century Britain* (Cambridge: Cambridge University Press, 2005).

Schofield, Mary Anne, *Masking and Unmasking the Female Mind: Disguising Romances in Feminine Fiction, 1713–1799* (Newark: University of Delaware Press; London and Toronto: Associated University Press, 1990).

Sedgwick, Eve K., *Between Men: English Literature and Male Homosocial Desire.* (New York: Columbia University Press, 1985).

Shaw, Philip, ed., *Romantic War: Studies in Culture and Conflict, 1793–1820* (Aldershot: Ashgate, 2000).

Siegel, Kristi, *Gender, Genre and Identity in Women's Travel Writing* (New York: Peter Lang, 2004).

Siskin, Clifford, *The Work of Writing: Literature and Social Change in Britain, 1700–1830* (Baltimore: Johns Hopkins University Press, 1998).

Spacks, Patricia Meyer, *Desire and Truth: Functions of Plot in Eighteenth-Century English Novels* (Chicago and London: University of Chicago Press, 1990).

Spencer, Jane, *The Rise of the Woman Novelist: From Aphra Behn to Jane Austen* (Oxford: Basil Blackwell, 1986).

Spender, Dale, ed., *Mothers of the Novel* (London: Pandora, 1986).

Staves, Susan, *A Literary History of Women's Writing in Britain, 1660–1789* (Cambridge: Cambridge University Press, 2006).

Stevenson, Jane, *Women Writers in English Literature* (Harlow, Essex: Longman Group, 1992).

Stone, Lawrence, *The Family, Sex and Marriage in England 1500–1800* (New York: Harper and Row, 1977).

Stott, Anne, *Hannah More: The First Victorian* (Oxford: Oxford University Press, 2003).

Taylor, Barbara, *Mary Wollstonecraft and the Feminist Imagination* (Cambridge: Cambridge University Press, 2003).

Sweet, Nanora and Julie Melnyk, eds, *Felicia Hemans: Reimagining Poetry in the Nineteenth Century* (Basingstoke: Palgrave Macmillan, 2001).

Todd, Janet, *Mary Wollstonecraft: A Revolutionary Life* (London: Phoenix, 2000).

——, *The Sign of Angellica: Women, Writing and Fiction, 1660–1800* (London: Virago, 1989).

Tompkins, J.M.S., *The Popular Novel in England, 1770–1800* (London: Methuen and Co Ltd, 1932).

Turner, Cheryl, *Living by the Pen: Women Writers in the Eighteenth Century* (London and New York: Routledge, 1992).

Varma, Devendra, *The Gothic Flame, Being a History of the Gothic Novel in England: Its Origins, Its Efflorescence, Disintegration, and Residuary Influences* (London: Barker, 1957).

Vincent, Patrick, *The Romantic Poetess: European Culture, Politics and Gender 1820–1840* (Durham, NH: University of New Hampshire Press, 2004).

Wallace, Diana, *The Woman's Historical Novel: British Women Writers, 1900–2000* (New York: Palgrave Macmillan, 2005).

Waters, Mary A., *British Women Writers and the Profession of Literary Criticism, 1789–1832* (New York: Palgrave Macmillan, 2004).

Watt, Ian, *The Rise of the Novel* (London: Hogarth Press, 1957).

Williams, Anne, *Art of Darkness: A Poetics of Gothic* (Chicago: University of Chicago Press, 1995).

Wilson, Carol Shiner and Joel Haefner, eds, *Re-Visioning Romanticism: British Women Writers, 1776–1837* (Philadelphia: University of Pennsylvania Press, 1994).

Wilson, Kathleen, *The Island Race: Englishness, Empire and Gender in the Eighteenth Century* (London: Routledge, 2003).

Wolstenholme, Susan, *Gothic (Re)Visions: Writing Women as Readers* (Albany: State University of New York Press, 1993).

Wood, Marcus, *The Poetry of Slavery: An Anglo-American Anthology, 1764–1865* (Oxford: Oxford University Press, 2005).

Index

CPSIA information can be obtained at www.ICGtesting.com
Printed in the USA
LVOW102149070313

323266LV00015B/140/P